CHRISTIAN DISC

CHRISTIAN DISCOURSES

AND

THE LILIES OF THE FIELD AND THE BIRDS OF THE AIR

AND

THREE DISCOURSES AT THE COMMUNION ON FRIDAYS

by

SØREN KIERKEGAARD

TRANSLATED WITH AN INTRODUCTION

by

WALTER LOWRIE, D.D.

PRINCETON UNIVERSITY PRESS

PRINCETON, NEW JERSEY

ISBN 0-691-01973-8

First Princeton Paperback Printing, 1971

Second Printing, 1974

Originally published in 1940 by Oxford University Press

Printed in the United States of America
by Princeton University Press, Princeton, New Jersey

PREFACE

In the co-operative labour of making the works of Kierkegaard available to English readers, I have chosen as my part the task of translating the works written after the profound religious experience of Holy Week 1848, which for the first time made 'direct communication' possible to the author and finally issued in the directest speech that was ever uttered by a Christian against Christendom. I have not included in my task the tremendous attack upon established Christianity which S. K. waged openly in newspapers and pamphlets, and died in the doing of it; for though I admit my sympathy with this attack and believe that it is profitable for reproof, for correction, and for instruction in righteousness, I account that it would not be profitable to make it available in English until it has become clearly evident, through the publication of the decisively Christian writings of S. K.'s last years, that (unlike most attacks upon the Church) this was not from without but from *within*.

It was the last and the most trenchant of his *religious* writings I translated *first*, because they seem to me the most important, and because they are the most important to me. But with that I found myself in a dilemma. For not only had I forged ahead of my fellow-workers who might be expected to make S. K.'s earlier works available (especially the pseudonymous or 'aesthetic' works), but I had outstripped myself by translating *first* the works which ought to be published *last*—namely, *Training in Christianity*, *For Self-examination*, and *Judge for Yourselves*. Professor Swenson was troubled when he learned that I proposed to publish these works at once. Because I felt the force of his objection I have deferred them. For these last works insist so strongly upon the Christian ideal—which he declines to regard as a counsel of perfection which the average Christian might safely disregard—that they cannot but be terrible to a man who takes them seriously, and it may be that the reader who is unacquainted with the milder tone of the earlier discourses is more likely to be repelled by them than one who has been gradually educated by Kierkegaard. I can only regret that no one has translated the *Eighteen Edifying Discourses* which 'accompanied' by twos and threes Kierkegaard's pseudonymous works and ultimately were collected in one volume. But Professor Swenson has translated three of them, the *Three Edifying Discourses* which accompanied the *Philosophical Fragments* he lately translated. However, they are printed only privately. It is fortunate (it might seem fortuitous) that the most important of the *Three Edifying Discourses in Various Spirits* was translated at the same time in America by Professor Steere (*Purity of Heart*, Harpers, 1938) and in England by Messrs Aldworth and Ferrie (*Purify your Hearts!* Daniel, London, 1937). So of the distinctively religious works nothing remains entirely unaccounted for but *The Works of Love.*

Of the pseudonymous or 'aesthetic' works there are several which are due to appear before this volume. Mr. Payne's translations of *Fear and Trembling* and *Repetition* will be published, I understand, on the same day by the Oxford University Press, and Mr. Jensen tells me that he has found an American publisher for his translation of the first of these books. He has also translated the other. This is an evident proof that the interest in Kierkegaard which developed so recently, I might say, so suddenly, in England and America, is already widespread. In order to complete the publication of the more strictly biographical material initiated by my *Kierkegaard* and Mr. Dru's *Journals*, the Oxford University Press will bring out on the same day, and somewhat in advance of this volume, my translation of *The Point of View*, etc., and Mr. Dru's translation of *Two Minor Ethico-Religious Treatises*, etc. If his translation of *The Concept of Dread* and Mr. Payne's translation of *The Sickness unto Death* are not out before this volume, they will not be tardy in following it. As Mr. Dru is at work on the translation of *Either/Or*, there is no important pseudonymous work except the *Stages* which remains unaccounted for and that I have undertaken. This incredible accomplishment in so short a time is due chiefly to the wisdom and audacity of the Oxford University Press—more particularly to Mr. Charles Williams.

And now, to redress so far as I am able the embarrassing situation produced by getting the last works ready first, I have hastened to translate the three series of 'discourses' which are now presented in this volume. The others, though they were the first to be translated, must wait a few months longer before they see the light. The discourses contained in this volume, although they were published in 1848 and 1849 (that is to say, at the same time when the more trenchant works were written) are many of them in a tone as mild as Kierkegaard ever used, and since they are as 'poetical' as anything he ever wrote, they express the thought of God's immanence, which in the later writings is obscured by the solemn emphasis upon His transcendence.

In this instance I regret to say (and it is the first time I have to say it) that there is no one to whom I can express obligation for aid in the preparation of this book. If S. K. is here worthily translated, I cannot ascribe it to my proficiency in the Danish language; I would ascribe it to Providence or (to use S. K.'s word) to Governance, being conscious of a strange congeniality with S. K.'s way of thinking, so that I feel as if I knew before-hand what he wants to say, just as he himself was conscious of congeniality with Socrates, and as Hamann boasted of an almost mystical intimacy with Plato, asserting that he 'would have been able to transcribe the half of Plato without having read him.'

I may need to remark expressly that all the notes are mine—not S. K.'s. There can be no confusion here between 'mine and thine', for S. K. consistently treated his Discourses as delivered addresses, and hence added no footnotes, such as in his other works he used freely. But why add any notes (some one may ask superciliously), seeing that the German translations have none, and the Danish editions have none worth mentioning? To this I make no answer. Yet I hope that 'the individual' may be grateful for just these little helps which I felt the need of and sought in vain when I was first struggling to orient myself in this immense field of literature ('a literature within a literature') which one man produced. And it is my opinion that it would be profitable to add many more notes, with more precise data of reference, when the time comes that all of S. K.'s works shall have been published in English, and when a man comes who is competent to survey the whole. This would be a legitimate way of co-ordinating S. K.'s thoughts, whereas in the spirit of the polemical Dane I must oppose indignantly the insistence of several critics (all of them of course 'professors') that what the age demands is a compendious and systematic presentation of

S. K.'s thoughts on all subjects, so that in this pre-digested form (which resolves into 'direct communication' even the 'indirect communication' of the pseudonyms) the reader may be able to appropriate the 'results' of the author's thought without passing through the same laborious process of thinking. A far more profitable thing than these pretentious compendiums (which have been produced in abundance by men who, as S. K. complained, were 'eating' him), but a far more humble task, would be the production of a real index. Such a thing does not exist. The Danish editors, at the expense of the munificent Carlsberg Fund, have published an immense volume called an Index—which is of no use whatever because it deals only with *words*, without the least selection or discrimination. Even if it were well done, its value would be diminished by half for the fact that it does not include the Journal. S. K. has been shabbily treated in Denmark. The complete edition of his works (at the expense of the Carlsberg Fund) seems to be meant chiefly for public libraries, as if it were inconceivable that any individual might want to possess a few of the books; for the works are lumped in big volumes on a chronological principle, and not even the ordinary facilities for finding the book one wants are provided for the reader—not even the titles of the works appear on the outside of the volumes. But S. K.'s works were most of them small in compass (there being only four exceptions), and they were published separately in handy volumes which could be readily bought as well as easily carried about. Although some of these works are too small for the modern market, it is proposed by the English translators (following the criteria proposed by Mr. Dru) to make S. K.'s works easily available. In this volume, and in others for which I am responsible, several kindred works are published together in one volume; but this is done in part for the convenience of the reader, and only in part to facilitate the task of the publisher.

   With the thrift for which my race is notorious I have employed the empty pages which follow the titles, etc., of the *Christian Discourses* by printing there pertinent entries from the Journal, which otherwise would encumber the Introduction and might not be remembered in the right place.

WALTER LOWRIE.

PRINCETON, *May 5*, 1939.

CONTENTS

INTRODUCTION

KIERKEGAARD said of the year 1848, 'It was beyond all comparison the richest and most fruitful year I have experienced as an author.' That is saying a great deal, considering how much he had produced every year since 1841, when (according to his reckoning) he first became an author. But 1848 was also a critical year in S. K.'s life. Externally, it was a year of political change, for after a short war with Germany Denmark lost the provinces of Schleswig and Holstein, and by a bloodless revolution, which was tardily incited by the liberal political ideas of the French Revolution, the absolute power of its monarchy was abolished. Although these changes do not seem very momentous in retrospect, they seemed catastrophic to S. K. and his contemporaries. And internally, S. K. experienced a change which was one of the most momentous of his life. We may think of it as a conversion—it was the third and last which he experienced on the way to 'becoming a Christian'. He did not use this word, but he called it a 'metamorphosis'—which certainly does not indicate a less striking experience. In his Journal, on the date of April 19, 1848, which was Wednesday in Holy Week, he exclaimed, 'My whole nature is changed. I must speak'—meaning that for the first time in his life he *could* speak, i.e. employ 'direct communication'. But though in this entry he mentions only the *effect*, we learn that the deep cause of it was the instantaneous apprehension that God had *forgotten* his sins—as well as forgiven them.

The result of this metamorphosis is apparent in his writings, which from this time on are characterized by 'direct communication'. Although he still clung for a while to the use of a pseudonym, Anti-Climacus, this meant anything but a relapse into maieutic or 'indirect communication'. In 1847 he spent much labour upon a treatise (never completed) on 'The Dialectic of Ethico-Religious Communication', in which he elaborated and defended his favourite thesis that such communication must always be indirect. He never completely renounced his attachment to this thesis, but the 'change' in his whole nature is demonstrated by the fact he no longer acted in accordance with the theory, and expressly recognized that there comes a time sooner or later when Christian communication must be direct, must be personal 'witness'—'maieutic cannot be the last form'.

The most ostensible sign of his metamorphosis is the ease with which he wrote *The Point of View for my work as an Author*, which is an exquisitely personal revelation of himself. Only the year before (in 1847) he had attempted in vain to write his 'Apology', with the aim of explaining to his contemporaries the purpose and purport of his pseudonymous works, which he had enveloped in so much mystification that no one could be expected to divine their serious religious purpose. An 'apology', of course, was the last thing one could expect from S. K.; but, after all, he had the example of 'The Apology' of Socrates, and the need of an explanation was pressing. In the year 1847 he even proposed to deliver a course of lectures on 'The Organizing Tendency in My Writings'—but that naturally came to nothing. In 1848 *The Point of View* was written without difficulty in two months—but at the thought of publishing it, of baring himself before the eyes of his contemporaries, he drew back, and the manuscript was left to be published after his death as 'a report to history'. What had to be done in his lifetime to explain the works, he did more briefly and far less personally in the short work entitled *On My Work as an Author*, which he wrote in 1849 and published not long before August 7, 1851.

The Sickness unto Death, 'a Christian psychological exposition for edification and awakening,' which S. K. regarded as the greatest of his religious works, was produced in 1848 and published on June 30 of the following year.

In 1846 S. K. had become profoundly engrossed with the 'phenomenon' of Magister Adler, a priest in the Danish Church who was deposed for the claim he too lightly made and unmade that his books were written at the direct dictation of Jesus Christ. S. K. wrote and rewrote and rewrote again his 'big book on Adler'—and in the end felt that it could not be published because, dealing so personally with Adler, it would seem like striking a man when he was down. Perhaps also the multitude of thoughts which the case suggested to S. K. were so personal to him, and in another sense so peculiar, that he was diffident about making them public. And yet they were so important to him that he was continually occupied with them for two more years, and he felt that they ought to be made known. In 1848 he attempted to present a number of these thoughts in a work which was to have been entitled, 'A Cycle of Ethico-Religious Treatises.' That was never finished—not to say published— although he was working at it again in 1849. However something did come out of it: *Two Minor Ethico-Religious Treatises*, which Mr. Dru has lately published. The first of them is entitled 'Has a man a right to let himself be put to death for the truth?' The second, 'On the difference between a genius and an Apostle.' S. K. could not muster up courage to publish them till May 19, 1849.

To get a notion of the literary activity of this year one must take into account not only the productions which were not produced, but several which were merely planned. In January S. K. was planning a quarterly which was to be sold by sub-scription, with the title, 'Edifying Reading'. In July he was thinking of a book to be entitled, 'Fundamental Cure, or the Forgiveness and Atonement of Sin'. In November he considered publishing in one volume several of the works which he had already completed, and of giving it the title, 'The Collected Works of Completion.' By December he had written in a fair copy his appreciation of a celebrated actor who was his neighbour: 'Herr Pheister, in the role of Captain Scipio.' In giving an account of S. K.'s literary labours one must not omit to mention the Journal for this year, which as it is now printed occupies 390 large pages. No single book written during this period was so large as that.

It is reasonable enough to remark, as a way of accounting for the amazing mass of S. K.'s literary production, that he had absolutely nothing else to do, had no companionship at home to distract him, and no diversion abroad except his solitary carriage-rides in the country and his social promenades in the street. But it must be remembered that this year he had assumed responsibility for a disciple. In spite of his dictum that 'the greatest of all misfortunes is a disciple', he had admitted to this status Rasmus Nielsen, Professor of Philosophy in the

University. To this he was moved by the consideration that, were he to die during that year, as he thought likely, there would at least be one who understood the intent of his works. Thus the disciple was in a way a substitute for the 'Apology' which he did not feel free to publish. His assumption of Rasmus Nielsen as a disciple was a consequence of the metamorphosis, another instance of 'direct communication' prompted by the pressure of the feeling, 'I must speak.' But we can easily understand that this involved much time and trouble, and that for a solitary like S. K. it must occasionally have been vexatious.

In the course of this year there were other vexations. In January he had to find a new home, and on April 1, the conventional 'moving day', he had to move into it. And in this emergency he was deprived of his faithful servitor Anders, who had been called to the colours. Nor did this represent all he suffered on account of the disastrous war with Germany, for by the fall of securities he lost a great part of the sum he had received for the sale of his father's house, and this accounts in part for the economic anxieties which now began to trouble him. The reader will hardly need to be reminded that what he says in the *Christian Discourses* about the 'anxieties of the heathen' were addressed in the first place to himself, to comfort and sustain himself—and as a rebuke to himself. His contemporaries thought that he was indifferent to the political revolution in Denmark; but perhaps no one felt it more deeply than this essentially aristocratic and conservative man, who had presaged it, and who better than any one else was able to understand its significance. And yet perhaps the deepest distress he suffered during the course of this year was the dramatic failure of his attempt to approach Councillor Olsen, the father of his one-time fiancée—the Councillor ran away as fast as his legs would carry him.

A little book, *The Crisis and a Crisis in the Life of an Actress*, was published in the first instance as a *feuilleton* in a daily paper (July 24–7, 1848). It was the last 'aesthetic' work to be published, and S. K. was dubious about publishing it at a time when he had long been engaged exclusively with serious religious writing. As it was written in 1847 it does not belong strictly to the productions of the year we are here dealing with, though his agonizing debate whether or not he ought to publish it involved no inconsiderable activity of mind and spirit. The *Christian Discourses* with which this volume begins were published on April 26, 1848 (a week after the metamorphosis), but they were of course written before that event; in fact they had been sent to the printer on March 6, and the greater part had been finished in 1847.

An entry in the Journal contains 'instructions' for the second part of this work, 'Joyful Notes in the Strife of Suffering.' In this we have a hint which the contemporary readers did not have—unless they were able to perceive it in the introductory disquisition about the significance of the edifying. It shows how much mystification and 'craftiness' there was in S. K.'s writings before his nature was 'entirely changed'. 'These Discourses are constantly kept tangential to the consciousness of sin and the sufferings of sin. Sin is another matter, and these Discourses just reach that point. While consolation rises lyrically as high as possible above every earthly need and wretchedness, even such as are hardest to bear, the dreadfulness of sin is constantly indicated. Thus there is craftily concealed in these Discourses another theme: Sin is man's ruin.' The very title of these '*Christian* Discourses' implies an advance towards 'direct communication'—even before the liberating experience of 1848. For the earlier Discourses could be religiously 'edifying' without stressing the positions most distinctive of Christianity. Hence S. K. was scrupulous not to call them Christian. What is more, he was honest enough not to express in the earlier Discourses positions which he himself had not yet securely attained on his laborious path to 'becoming' a Christian. Moreover, in the title to the third part of the 'Christian Discourses' ('Thoughts which wound from behind . . . for edification') he contrived slyly to introduce the phrase, 'for edification', which hitherto (with a subtilty of distinction between this and the qualification 'edifying', which is not visible to most of us) he had doggedly maintained was 'not my category'. The reader of these 'Christian Discourses' will doubtless find occasion to observe that thoughts which stab from behind are not confined to Part Three, but emerge disconcertingly in other places.

Just before the entry recording the metamorphosis we find the first suggestion of the Part I. of *Training in Christianity*. The idea of the third and second parts (in this order) had come to him in the course of the previous year. This book—one of his greatest works—was written in 1848, but qualms about making it public retarded its publication until 1850. The moment of conversion was evidently richly productive, for three days later (on Easter Even) the Journal records the first idea of the 'Three Godly Discourses' about *The Lilies and the Birds*, which also was written in the course of this year, although it was not published until May 14, 1849. S. K.'s interest in birds may be inferred from the many discourses in which he treats them as an instructive parable. It is confirmed by the fact that, although in his youth he had thought of devoting himself to natural science, in his large library, when after his death it was catalogued for sale, there were found but two books which had any relation to this subject, and one of them was a book about 'The Birds of Denmark'. The idea of the three Discourses at the Communion on Fridays ('The High Priest' etc. etc.), which conclude this volume, was first recorded on September 1.

Until this year S. K. was fairly well content with his description of himself as 'a poet and thinker', which combines qualities which are not commonly found together—and besides, as he said, he was a very peculiar sort of thinker and a very passionate one. After the metamorphosis this no longer contented him—he recognized that the poetical must go, but he would give it a festal send off. The Discourses on the Lilies and the Birds were to be a poem to end poetry. He says in his Journal: 'The purpose of these discourses therefore will be to make evident the conflict between poetry and Christianity, how Christianity, in a certain sense, when compared with poetry (which is wishful, infatuating, benumbing, transforming life's reality into an oriental dream, as when a young girl could wish to lie all day on a sofa and let herself be enchanted)—how Christianity in comparison with this is prose—and yet is precisely the poetry of eternity. Consequently the lilies and the birds (i.e. the description of nature) shall on this occasion receive a more poetical colouring and splendour of hue, just to show that the poetical is to be given up. For when poetry really must fall (not before the rant of a glum and sullen parson) it must wear its festal dress.' The reader has an opportunity here to see how this programme was carried out.

One of S. K.'s preoccupations since the middle of the year

1847 was the popular demand for a second edition of *Either/Or*. It was distasteful to him to fix attention upon this popular 'aesthetic' book at a time when his whole effort was concentrated on the task of propounding 'directly' the most decisive categories of Christianity. Moreover, he was in conflict with the publisher, who offered him 500 Danish dollars, whereas S. K. held out for 700. It was not until 1849 he decided to republish it, and then he was tormented by the problem of selecting from among the many works already finished the one most fit to 'accompany' it. His choice happily fell upon *The Lilies and the Birds*, and both were published on the same day, May 14, 1849.

In reading the three works published in this volume, the first of which was written before the metamorphosis, and the others after, the reader may be at a loss to detect any great difference with respect to 'direct communication'. But that is not strange, for S. K. constantly affirmed that his 'Discourses, which always were published in his own name, were instances of "direct communication"'. That is quite true in a way—only he had hitherto been reticent about expressing *all* that he believed—because of the characteristic scruple 'whether a man has a right to let it be known how good he is'. 'Discourse' was the word he elected to use in order to avoid the implication that he claimed the authority which belongs to the 'sermon'. When he gave up 'indirect communication' he naturally clung to the form of the discourse, and everything he wrote from this time on—even the works ascribed to Anti-Climacus—were homoletical, based upon a passage of Scripture as a text which he faithfully commented upon. They are sermons which certainly have a tone of authority.

Nevertheless there is a difference observable even as between the works contained in this volume which were so closely related in time, and still more between the earlier Discourses on the one hand, and the trenchant attacks upon the corruptions of Christianity which are not obscurely veiled in *Training in Christianity*, *For Self-Examination*, and *Judge for Yourselves*, or even in the Discourses which accompanied these—all of which are to be published before long in two volumes. Comparing the works published in this present volume, the reader will easily perceive that in the Discourses on *The Lilies and the Birds* there is no theme 'craftily concealed', as, according to the hint quoted above, there was in the second part of the *Christian Discourses*. In the third part, 'Thoughts which wound from behind' (as though a friend were to approach smilingly to embrace you—and you felt his dagger in your loins), there is not much concealment—and for this reason S. K. was reluctant to publish it. But so far as the first part is concerned, S. K. hints plainly enough in the Introduction what a double-edged dagger the word 'heathen' is.

S. K. (God be praised!) remained subtle to the end, but from this period on he was not over-subtle and he resorted to no mystification. That is the reason why I was eager to translate *first* the last books, in which he makes as clear as day what he is aiming at, so that the reader can decide at once whether he wants to listen to anything more from this author. It is only for prudential ('economic') reasons that the first Discourses of 1848 are now presented first—and I expect that the later works will follow in a few months.

CHRISTIAN DISCOURSES

by

S. KIERKEGAARD

Copenhagen
1848
[April 26]

NOTES CULLED FROM THE JOURNAL

The *Christian Discourses* were published without a preface, but in the Journal we find the first draft of a preface which contains a sharp expression of S. K.'s bitter resentment against Copenhagen, 'the market town', which counts it 'a crime for a man to be more gifted and industrious than the average', and which 'prostrates its spirit in the idolatrous worship of undanish [viz. German] spirit, instead of favouring and encouraging its legitimate children'. Later this was abbreviated by the omission of the more violent protest, and though it still seemed to S. K. too personal to be made public, it is to be found among his Papers in the following form.

PREFACE

'I would beg the reader in plain terms, as I have never before done, not to lose patience. I myself perceive very clearly how difficult it must be for a contemporary to keep up with me without growing weary, since I grant no repose either to him or to myself. I perceive how difficult it must be to get the right impression. This I myself perceive full well, precisely because, better than any one else perhaps, I understand that only after I am dead and gone will the time come for my works, when they and my life will (as the artists say) be seen to advantage and show off well, because so long as I live it is part of my task to employ about two-thirds of my strength in confusing, in working against myself and weakening the impression—which is precisely what makes me difficult for the contemporaries.'

Nothing could show more plainly the difficulty—and misfortune—of 'indirect communication'. But this blunt statement also shows that in 1847 S. K. was on the point of emancipating himself. To the psychologist this is an interesting instance of the fact that what suddenly emerges in consciousness has been slowly elaborated below the threshold of consciousness. For it was not till Holy Week of the following year that S. K. became suddenly conscious of his liberation—that he 'must', and by implication *could*, speak out. And when on December 28, 1847, he conceived of the theme of Part III, 'Thoughts which wound from behind,' and early in 1848 embodied it in seven most trenchant discourses, he was already in full swing of 'direct communication'.

'Thoughts which attack from behind' was one of the first suggestions for the title, and 'A Christian Attack' for the sub-title. But before this 'assault of thoughts' (as he called it in one place) was published (although the manuscript had long been in the hands of the printer), Germany had assaulted Denmark, and the Danes were engaged in a very different sort of strife. This total change in the situation prompted in S. K. the misgivings which he expressed in the following entries in the Journal.

'Perhaps not a soul will read my Christian Discourses—perhaps there will be a tumult in the camp, and I the maltreated sacrifice. Perhaps. Oh, it is hard to support the thought of such a possibility.'

'What is it after all for one in a confused state of mind to let oneself be killed on the field of battle, arm-in-arm with a thousand others, carried along by public opinion, perhaps in the end without having a single thought, at the most an obscure feeling—what is that in comparison with this slow, consciously arranged advance, with the constant possibility of being able to prevent the decisive engagement!'

CONTENTS

PART I

PART II

PART III

PART IV

FROM THE JOURNAL

Again I have for a moment taken into consideration my responsibility for letting the Christian Discourses, especially Part III., appear at this time. It is plainly perilous for me to let that which was written in a totally different situation be read in this situation. But I can do no other. It is providence which has arranged the thing thus for me. It is not that I have cast myself into danger. My manuscript was delivered to the printer long before this last thing happened, which doubtless has altered men a great deal. Nothing is more certain than that every word in my Discourses is true; I have nothing to alter. So then, should I now take it back for fear of personal danger? No, that I dare not do. What I am, I am solely and only by believing and obeying God. The moment I catch myself in fleeing cowardly from any danger into which He would lead me, I have avoided sure enough the danger—but to my own destruction. Woe unto me, I collapse into nothing! But along with God I can endure everything—so I hope to God—without Him, nothing.

Perhaps there is also much hypochondria in this fear of mine; but that's neither here nor there. God knows how I suffer—but God also will help me and my cause.

So here I sit. Outside everything is in movement, nationalism surges high in all, everyone talks of sacrificing life and blood, is perhaps also ready to do it, but supported by the omnipotence of public opinion. And here I sit in a quiet room (doubtless I soon will be in bad repute for indifference to the national cause); I recognize only one danger: the religious danger. But about that no one cares—and no one has a presentiment of what is going on in me. Thus it is with my life, I cannot escape it. Always misunderstanding. Where I suffer I am not understood—and I am hated.

[*Marginal note.* On a week-day I opened the book and read my sermon by Mynster, as I am accustomed to do only on Sundays; and, behold, it was on Nicodemus. What a warning not to retreat!]

And now that existence entirely corresponds with all I have been expounding, now that providence has helped me by the fact that I had already delivered the manuscript to the printer, there is here no question of taking a step forward, but of taking a cowardly step backward; now that I entirely understood myself in being a solitary man, without relationship to anybody, with deep inward pains, with only one comfort, God who is love, only one friend whom I crave, the Lord Jesus Christ, with a yearning for a deceased father, being separated by worse than death from the only person now living whom I have loved in a decisive sense—now to retreat . . . no, no!

PART I

FROM THE JOURNAL

If one is to lift a whole generation, verily one must know it. Hence it is that these proclaimers of Christianity who begin straightway with orthodoxy have not much influence, and that only upon the few. For Christendom is very far behind. One must begin with paganism. So it was that I began with *Either/Or*. Thereby I got the generation to go with me; it did not even dream whither it was going, or where we now are. But people became aware of the problems. They cannot be quit of me, just because they went along with *Either/Or* so gladly, so gladly. They might now leave me alone, they might put me to death—it avails nothing, they have me for life. If a man begins at once with Christianity, they say, 'That isn't anything for us,' so at once they are on the defensive.

But, as the title of my last Discourses suggests, my whole work as an author is one great thought, and that is: to wound from behind.

THE ANXIETIES OF THE HEATHEN

CHRISTIAN DISCOURSES

by

S. KIERKEGAARD

Copenhagen
1848

FROM THE JOURNAL

The man whom in the first Discourse of 'The Anxieties of the Heathen' I have represented as talking so crudely about the seriousness of life is not, as one can promptly perceive, what we call a poor man. Ah, it never could occur to me to talk to such a man in such a way. No, it is a journalist of sorts, one of those who live by —and perhaps in luxury and abundance live by—writing on . . . pauperism.

CONTENTS

PRAYER

Father in heaven, when spring is come, everything in nature returns in new freshness and beauty, the lilies and the birds have lost nothing of their charm—oh, that we also might return to the instruction of these teachers! Ah, but if in the time that has elapsed we have lost our health, would that we might regain it by learning again from the lilies of the field and the birds of the air!

No man can serve two masters: for either he will hate the one and love the other; or else he will hold to the one and despise the other. Ye cannot serve God and mammon. Therefore I say unto you, Be not anxious for your life, what ye shall eat, or what ye shall drink; nor yet for your body, what ye shall put on. Is not the life more than food, and the body than raiment? Behold the birds of the heaven, that they sow not, neither do they reap, nor gather into barns; and your heavenly Father feedeth them. Are not ye of much more value than they? And which of you by being anxious can add one cubit unto his stature? And why are ye anxious concerning raiment? Consider the lilies of the field, how they grow; they toil not, neither do they spin: yet I say unto you, that even Solomon in all his glory was not arrayed like one of these. But if God doth so clothe the grass of the field, which today is, and tomorrow is cast into the oven, shall he not much more clothe you, O ye of little faith? Be not therefore anxious, saying, What shall we eat? or, What shall we drink? or, Wherewithal shall we be clothed? For after all these things do the heathen seek; for your heavenly Father knoweth that ye have need of all these things. But seek ye first his kingdom and his righteousness; and all these things shall be added unto you. Be not therefore anxious for the morrow: for the morrow shall be anxious for itself. Every day has enough in its own worries.

INTRODUCTORY

I<small>T</small> was on the summit of Sinai the Law was given, amidst the thunders of heaven; every beast that approached the holy mountain (alas, innocently and unawares) must be put to death—according to the Law. It is at the foot of the mountain the Sermon on the Mount is preached. Thus it is the Law is related to the Gospel, which is the heavenly come down to earth. It is at the foot of the mountain; so mild is the Gospel, so close is the heavenly which descends, and yet all the more heavenly for that. It is at the foot of the mountain; yea, what is more, the birds and the lilies are in the company—it sounds almost as if it were turning the thing into a jest that they come along . . . playfully. For although the seriousness becomes all the more sacred just for the reason that the birds and the lilies are in the company, yet the jest continues, and it remains nevertheless a jest that the lilies and the birds are in the company, they are in the company, and what is more they are there to teach; for it is true enough that the Gospel itself is the real teacher, that He is 'the Teacher'—and the Way and the Truth and the Life in the instruction, and yet the birds and the lilies come along as assistant teachers of a sort.

How is this possible? Well, really, the thing is not so difficult. For the fact is that neither the lilies nor the birds are *heathen*, but neither are the lilies and the birds *Christians*, and just for this reason they could be especially helpful by way of giving instruction in Christianity. Consider the lilies and the birds, and then thou dost discover how the heathen live, for it is precisely not like the lilies and the birds that they live; if thou dost live like the lilies and the birds, thou art a Christian—which the lilies and the birds neither are nor can become. Paganism stands in opposition to Christianity, but the lilies and the birds stand in no opposition to any of these contending parties; if one may say so, they play apart by themselves, keep shrewdly aloof from all oppositions. So then, the Gospel, in order not to condemn and denounce, uses the lilies and the birds to show what paganism is, but also at the same time to show what is required of Christians. In order to avoid a tone of condemnation the lilies and the birds are thrust in between; for the lilies and the birds condemn nobody—and as for thee, thou shalt not condemn the heathen, thou shalt learn from the lilies and the birds. Yes, it is a difficult task the lilies and the birds have, a difficult position they are in as instructors; there was nobody else could do it, every other teacher would so easily be tempted to accuse and condemn the heathen and praise the Christians (instead of imparting instruction), or mockingly to condemn the so-called Christians who do not live as they ought. But the lilies and the birds, which are engaged solely in teaching and are absorbed in it, do not express any opinions, look neither to the right hand nor to the left, neither commend nor reprove, as teachers generally are wont to do. Like Him, 'the Teacher', of whom it is said, that He 'careth not for any man' (Mark xii. 14), so they care not for any man, or rather they care for themselves. And yet, and yet it is almost an impossibility not to learn something from them, if one considers them. Ah, a man may do all he is capable of doing, and yet it sometimes may be doubtful whether the pupil learns anything from him; but the lilies and the birds do nothing whatever, and yet it is almost an impossibility not to learn something from them. Surely one can learn from them in the very first instance what it is to teach, what it is to teach in a Christian sense, can learn from them the great art of teaching, namely, to be careless about it, to care for oneself, and yet to do this in such an arousing way, so arrestingly, so ingratiatingly, and, so far as expense is concerned, so cheaply, and withal so persuasively, that it is impossible not to learn something from it. For doubtless when a human teacher has done everything and the pupil has learned nothing, he can say, 'It is not owing to me!' Oh, but when thou hast learnt so much from the lilies and the birds, is it not as though they said, 'It is not owing to us'? So benevolent are these teachers towards the pupil, so benevolent, so humane, so worthy of their divine commission. If thou hast forgotten something, they are willing at once to repeat it to thee, and to repeat and repeat, so that at last thou mightest learn it; if thou dost learn nothing from them, they do not reproach thee, but merely continue with rare zeal to go on with the instruction, concerned only with teaching; and if thou dost learn something from them, they attribute it all to thee, act as if they had no part in it, as if it were not to them thou owest it. They despair of no one, however indocile he may be, and they do not require slavish dependence upon them, even of him who has learnt the most. Ah, ye marvellous teachers, if one were to learn from you nothing else, if only he learned to teach, how much he would have learnt! It is already a great thing if a human teacher put into effect some part of his own teaching, since usually one makes much ado and does little—ah, but also this observation about others the lilies and the birds never made! But, you marvellous teachers—well in a certain sense you do not do what you say; you do it without saying anything. Yet this laconic silence of yours and this faithfulness towards yourselves, year in and year out, long as the day may be, whether you are appreciated or unappreciated, understood or misunderstood, seen or unseen, doing the same thing—oh, marvellous masters of the art of teaching!

So then, by the aid of the lilies and the birds, we learn to know the anxieties of the heathen, what they are, such, namely, as the lilies and the birds do not have, notwithstanding they have the corresponding needs. One might, however, learn to know these anxieties in another way: by journeying to a heathen land and seeing how men live there, what they are anxious about. And finally in a third way: by journeying—but what am I saying?—why 'journeying'? we are in fact living on the spot, in a Christian land where all are Christians, so that one might conclude that the anxieties which are not found among us, notwithstanding that the corresponding needs and pressure are present, must be the anxieties of the heathen. So one might conclude—if, alas, another consideration did not take away from us the power of drawing this conclusion by taking away the hypothesis, and we were compelled to conclude in another way: 'These anxieties are found amongst men in this land, *ergo* this Christian land is pagan.' The discourse about the anxieties of the heathen will then sound like sly mockery. Yet we dare not permit ourselves to take such a severe view of Christendom, or to employ this almost cruel mockery, a mockery, be it observed, which would finally fall upon the head of the speaker himself, who doubtless is not by any means such a perfect Christian. But let us not forget that the discourse might as it were have this mockery up its sleeve, that if an angel were to speak, he might thus make sport of us who call ourselves Christians, by giving this turn to his discourse, and instead of rebuking our mediocre Christianity, he might describe the heathen anxieties, adding immediately, 'but in this land which is Christian there are to be found of course no such anxieties, drawing his conclusion from the consideration that these anxieties are in fact the anxieties of the heathen; or, conversely, proceeding from the assumption that the land is indeed Christian, he might conclude that such anxieties were therefore not justly called heathen; or, by imagining a Christian land where there really were none but Christians, and assuming that this land is our land, he might conclude: 'Since these anxieties are not to be found there, they must be the anxieties of the heathen.' Let us not forget this, neither let us forget that the heathen who are to be found in Christendom are the most deeply sunken. Those in the heathen land have not yet been lifted up to Christianity, these have sunk beneath the level of paganism; those belong to the fallen race, these, after having been lifted up, have fallen again, and fallen still deeper.

Thus the edifying address combats in many ways to bring it about that the eternal may be victorious in men, but it does not forget at the right place to soften this combat to a smile. O thou combatant, let thyself be softened! One may forget how to laugh, but God preserve a man from ever forgetting how to smile! A man can forget much without detriment, and in old age one must put up with forgetting much one might wish to remember; but God forbid that up to his last blessed end a man should forget the lilies and the birds!

I

The anxiety of poverty

Be not therefore anxious, saying, what shall we eat? or, What shall we drink?—after all these things do the heathen seek.

THIS *anxiety the bird has not.* What does the bird live on—for about the lily we will say nothing, it can get along of course, for it lives on air—but what does the bird live on? The civil magistrate has, as every one knows, much to be anxious about; at one moment he has the anxiety that there are some people who have nothing to live on, but then again at other times he is not satisfied to know that a man has something to live on, he summons him and interrogates him about what he lives on. What then does the bird live on? Surely not on what it gathers into barns, for it does not gather into barns—and really a man never lives on what he has laid up in the barn. But what does the bird live on? The bird cannot give an account of itself; in case it were to be summoned, it would have to answer like the man born blind, who was interrogated about Him who had given him his sight, and said, 'I know not, but this I know, that I, the blind man, see.' So the bird must make answer, 'I know not, but this I know, that I live.' On what does it live? The bird lives on the *'daily bread'*, this heavenly food which cannot be too long kept,[1] this immense store of provision which is in such good custody that no one can steal it; for only that which is kept over the night can the thief steal, that which is used during the day no one can steal.

So then the daily bread is the bird's living. The daily bread is the most scantily measured supply, it is exactly enough, but not the least bit more, it is that little which poverty needs. But then, indeed, the bird is poor. Instead of answering we will ask, Is the bird poor? No, the bird is not poor. Behold, here it appears that the bird is a teacher: it is in such a situation that, to judge by its outward condition, one must call it poor, and yet

[1] The allusion here and hereafter is to the manna (Exodus xvi.).

it is not poor; it never could occur to any one to call it poor. And what does this mean? It means that its condition is that of poverty, but it has not the anxiety of poverty. If it were to be summoned—there is not the least doubt that the magistrate would find that in the strictest sense it belongs under Poor Relief; but if only one lets it fly away again, it is not poor. True enough, if the Poor Relief were allowed to have its way, the bird would still be poor; for one would torment it with so many questions about its way of gaining a living, that it would observe for itself that it was poor.

Be not therefore anxious, saying, What shall we eat? or, What shall we drink?—after all these things do the heathen seek; for *the Christian does not have this anxiety*. Is the Christian then rich? Well, perhaps it may well be that there is a Christian who is rich; but about that in fact we are not talking, we are talking about the Christian who is poor, about the poor Christian. He is poor, but he has not this anxiety, so he is poor and yet not poor. For when in poverty one is without the anxiety of poverty, one is poor and yet not poor, and then one is—if one is not a bird but a man, and yet like a bird . . . then one is a Christian.

What then does the poor Christian live on? On the *daily bread*. Therein he resembles the bird. But the bird, which true enough is not a heathen, is yet not a Christian either—for the Christian *prays* for the daily bread. But then is he not even poorer than the bird, for the fact that he must pray for it, whereas the bird gets it without praying? Yes, so the heathen thinks. The Christian prays for the daily bread, by praying for it he receives it, yet without having anything to keep over night; he prays for it, and by praying for it he keeps away the anxiety at night, while he sleeps soundly, to awaken the next day to the daily bread which he prays for. The Christian therefore does not live on the daily bread like the bird or like a character in a fairy-tale who takes it where he finds it; for the Christian finds it where he seeks it, and he seeks it by praying. But therefore he has also, however poor he may be, something more to live on than the daily bread, which to him has an added flavour, a value, a satisfying quality, which it does not have for the bird; for the Christian indeed prays for it, and so he knows that the daily bread is *from God*. And in another sphere, does not a trifling gift, a little insignificance, possess infinite value for the lover because he knows that it comes from the beloved? Therefore the Christian does not say merely that the daily bread is enough for him, in so far as it supplies his earthly want and need, but he speaks also of something else (and no bird and no heathen knows what it is he is talking about) when he says, 'For me it is enough, it is from Him', that is, from God. Like the simple wise man [1] who talked constantly about food and drink, yet talked profoundly of the highest things, so does the poor Christian, when he talks about food, talk with simplicity of the highest things; for when he says, 'the daily bread', he is not thinking so much about food as of the fact that he receives it from God's table. So also the bird does not live on the daily bread; it surely does not, like the heathen, live to eat, it eats to live—and yet does it really *live*?

The Christian lives on the daily bread; there is no question about that, but neither is there any question about what he shall eat or what he shall drink. He knows that in this respect he is understood by the heavenly Father, who knows that he has need of all these things; the poor Christian does not question about all such things as the heathen seek after. On the other hand, there is something else he seeks, and therefore he *lives* (for indeed it seemed doubtful in how far one can properly say that the bird 'lives')—he lives therefore, or it is for this he lives, and it is for this reason he can say that he lives. He believes that he has a Father in heaven who every day openeth His bountiful hand and filleth all things living (him included) with blessing; yet what he seeks is not the satisfaction of his appetite, it is the heavenly Father. He believes that man is not distinguished from the birds for the fact that he cannot live on so little, but for the fact that he cannot live 'on bread alone'; he believes that it is the blessing which satisfies; yet what he seeks is not to be satisfied, but the blessing. He believes (what no sparrow knows anything of—and what does it help a sparrow that it is so?) that no sparrow falls to the ground without the will of the heavenly Father. He believes that so long as he has to live here on earth he surely will receive the daily bread, and that then some day he shall live blessedly in the hereafter. Thus it is he explains the saying that 'the life is more than food'; for no doubt the temporal life is more than food, but an eternal life is surely beyond comparison with food and drink, wherein a *man's* life does no more consist

[1] Socrates.

than does the kingdom of God! He constantly bears in mind that a life of holiness was led here on earth in poverty, that 'He' was hungry in the desert and thirsted upon the cross; so that not only can one live in poverty, but in poverty one can *live*.— Hence he prays, it is true, for the daily bread, and gives thanks for it, but to pray and give thanks is to him more important than the food, and is indeed his meat, as it was Christ's 'meat to do the Father's will'.

But then indeed the poor Christian is rich? Yes, without doubt he is rich. For the bird which in poverty is without the anxiety of poverty, the poor bird, is to be sure no heathen, and therefore is not really poor; but neither is it a Christian, and hence it is poor nevertheless—the poor bird, ah, indescribably poor! How poor not to be able to pray, how poor not to be able to give thanks, how poor to have to receive everything as with ingratitude, how poor to be as it were non-existent for its Benefactor to whom it owes life! For to be able to pray and to give thanks is precisely to be existent for God, who certainly did not once for all give him earthly riches, ah, no, He every day gives him the daily bread. Every day! Yes, every day the poor Christian has occasion to be aware of his Benefactor, in prayer and thanksgiving. And his riches indeed increase with every time he prays and gives thanks, with every time it becomes clearer that he exists for God and God for him; whereas earthly riches become poorer and poorer with every time the rich man forgets to pray and to give thanks. Ah, how poor to have received thus once for all his provision for the whole of life; what riches on the other hand to receive his provision 'every day'! How dubious a blessing to have occasion almost every day to forget that man has received what he has; how blessed to be reminded of it every day, that is, to be reminded of his Benefactor, that is, of his God, his Creator, his Provider, his Father in heaven, and so of the love for which alone life is worth living, and which alone is worth living for!

But then indeed the poor Christian is rich? Yes, certainly he is rich, and thou shalt recognize him by the fact that he does not wish to talk about his earthly poverty, but rather of his heavenly riches. And hence his talk sometimes sounds so strange. For while everything about him recalls his poverty, he talks of his riches—and hence no one can understand him . . . except a

Christian. It is related of a hermit who for many, many years, dead to the world, had lived in the strict observance of the vows of poverty, that he had won the friendship and devotion of a rich man. Then the rich man died, and that hermit, who now for so long a time had lived on the daily bread, was constituted heir to his whole fortune. But when one came and reported this to the hermit, he replied, 'It must be a mistake. How can he make me his heir, seeing that I am dead long before him!' Ah, what a poor showing riches make by the side of . . . riches! Earthly riches always make a poor showing in relation to death. But the Christian who in poverty is without the anxiety of poverty is also dead to the world and from the world. Hence he *lives*. For the bird ceases to live by dying, but the Christian lives by dying. And therefore all the wealth of the world which suffices a man for a whole life makes so poor a showing in comparison with his . . . poverty, yea, or his riches. That a dead man needs no money, we all know; but the living man who really has no use for it must either be very rich—and then it well may be that he needs much of it—or he must be a poor Christian.

In so far then as the poor Christian is rich he does not resemble the bird. For the bird is poor and yet not poor; but the Christian is poor yet not poor, rich. The bird is not anxious for the lower things which it does not seek, but neither does it seek the higher things; the bird itself is without anxiety, but also, for it, its life is as though it were not the object of anxiety for any one else. The Christian shares as it were with God; he lets God take thought for meat and drink and all such things, while he seeks God's kingdom and His righteousness. The poor bird soars high aloft in the sky without being weighed down by the anxiety of poverty, but the Christian soars still higher; it is as though the bird were seeking God in its flight towards heaven, but the Christian finds Him; it is as though the bird were flying far, far away after God, but the Christian finds Him, and he finds Him (oh, heavenly bliss!), he finds Him upon earth; it is as though the bird were flying into heaven, yet heaven remains closed to it, only for the Christian does heaven open!

Be not therefore anxious, saying, What shall we eat? or, What shall we drink—after all these things do the heathen seek. *Yea, the heathen are anxious about such things.*

The bird is in poverty without the anxiety of poverty—it keeps silent; the Christian is in poverty without the anxiety of poverty, but he does not talk of his poverty, rather of his riches. The heathen has the anxiety of poverty. Instead of being in poverty without anxiety, he is (and the one thing corresponds exactly to the other) 'without God in the world' (Ephes. ii. 12). Behold, for this reason he has anxiety. He does not keep silent like the care-free bird, he does not talk like the Christian, who talks of his riches; he actually has and knows nothing to talk of except poverty and its anxiety. He asks, What shall I eat? and What shall I drink?—today, tomorrow, the day after, the coming winter, the following spring, when I am old, as for me and mine and the whole land, what shall we eat and drink? This question he does not ask only at a moment, alas, of pressing anxiety, then again to regret it however; alas, in a time of distress, then again praying God to forgive it however. No, he is without God in the world and he gives himself importance by asking the question which he calls the real vital question; he becomes self-important with the thought that he concerns himself exclusively with this vital question; he finds it inexcusable of the public authority (for with God he has nothing to do) if he lacks something, he who lives solely for this vital question. Every one who does not concern himself therewith, or it may be with supporting him, he regards as a dreamer; even the highest and the holiest thoughts, in com- parison with this deepest vital question, he regards as vain trumpery. He finds it foolish to refer a grown man to birds and lilies; for what might there be there to see, and what could one learn from them! When one is a man like him, a man who has learnt the seriousness of life, when one is a man, a citizen and a father, it is surely a rather insipid joke and a childish conceit to require one to pay attention to the lilies and the birds, as if one had nothing else to attend to. 'If it were not for a sense of pro- priety and a regard for my children, who after all must be given the customary instruction in religion, I would say quite openly that one finds mighty little in Holy Scripture in answer to the most important question, and on the whole very little that is of practical advantage, with the exception of one single splendid passage. One reads about Christ and the Apostles, but there is not the least contribution to the question which really is the most vital, namely, what they lived on, how they managed to pay every man his due and meet the rent and taxes. To solve the

problem of death by a miracle is a very fatuous answer to this
question—even if it is true, what does it prove? To have neg-
lected entirely beforehand to think of any expedient, and then
when the time-limit was reached and the payment of the tax was
demanded, then to have a disciple pull a fish out of the water
with a stater in its mouth with which one pays the tax—even if
it is true, what does it prove? In general I feel the lack of seriousness in the Holy Scriptures, of a serious reply to a serious question; a serious man does not wish to be taken for a fool, as if
one were engaging in a comedy. Let the parsons preachify about
such things to women and children; every serious and enlight-
ened man must in his secret heart agree with me, and where
serious people come together, as in public meetings, honour is
paid only to the shrewdness which has a sense for reality.'

So speaks the heathen. For paganism was without God in the
world, but Christianity makes it perfectly clear that paganism is
ungodliness. The ungodliness does not consist after all in being
anxious, though certainly it is not Christian to be so; the ungodliness consists in not being willing to know anything else, and
not being willing to know that this anxiety is sinful, and that
for this reason the Scripture says that in exactly the same sense
in which a man can 'overcharge' his heart with surfeiting and
drunkenness he can overcharge it with the cares of this life
(Luke xxi. 34). Everywhere in life there are cross-ways. Every
man stands once, in the beginning, at the cross-ways—this is his
perfection, not his merit. Where he stands at the conclusion (for
at the conclusion it is impossible to stand at the cross-ways) is
his choice and his responsibility. For him who is in poverty and
thus cannot veer from the path of poverty, the cross-ways is
either to turn away from anxiety in a Christian spirit by turning
to 'the Way', upward—or to abandon himself to anxiety in an
ungodly fashion by deviating into a by-way, downward; for in
the eternal understanding of the situation there are never two
ways, in spite of the name cross-ways, there is only one way,
the other way is a by-way. The deeper he then sinks in anxiety,
the farther he removes himself from God and from the Christian
position; he is most deeply sunken when he *will* not know anything higher, but on the contrary wills that this anxiety shall be,
not merely the heaviest (which in truth it is not, for the heaviest
is the pain of repentance), no, but that it shall be the highest.

But they that desire to be rich fall into manifold temptations and snares; and what is the anxiety of poverty if it is not that of desiring to be rich? Perhaps the anxiety does not at once require riches; compelled by hard necessity, and in the impossibility (of obtaining more), it is perhaps for the time being content with less. Yet this same anxiety, if it gets its present wish fulfilled, if there is opened a prospect of more, will continually covet more and more. It is a delusion to think that the anxiety of poverty, in case it has not been willing to accept godly healing (and in this case the healing may begin with a little less just as well as with a little more), would find any condition in life that contented it short of attaining riches—and with that it would not be content. Oh, what a long road lies before the anxiety of poverty, and the most dreadful part of it is that this road is everywhere intersected by temptations! For we all are in danger wheresoever we go, but he who desires to be rich is everywhere in danger, and it is inevitable that he shall fall into this temptation, into which God has not led him, but into which he has cast himself. He who is in poverty is for this very fact in a difficult position, but not in the least forsaken of God; the salvation is *commanded*, namely, to be without anxiety—for that the salvation proffered by God is the only true salvation is to be known precisely by the fact that it is 'commanded'. To be without anxiety, yea, that is a difficult gait to go, almost like walking upon the water; but if thou art able to believe, it can nevertheless be done. It is true of all danger that the principal thing is to get away from the thought of it. Thou canst not get away from poverty, but thou canst get away from the thought of it by thinking constantly of God. So it is the Christian goes *his* gait; he turns his eyes upward, he looks away from danger, in poverty he is without the anxiety of poverty. But he who desires to be rich—his thought is constantly upon the ground, with his anxiety about earthly things; he walks with bowed head, looking constantly before him, if perchance he might find riches. He looks constantly before him—ah, commonly this is the best means of avoiding temptation, but for him (alas, he know it not), for him this looking before him is precisely the way to walk into the pitfall, the way to discover temptations which are ever greater and greater, and to sink deeper and deeper in them. He already is in temptation's power, for anxiety is temptation's shrewdest servant; and temptation is down upon the earth, where are 'all such things as the heathen seek after'; and temptation is down upon the earth—and the more it gets a man to look down towards it, so much the more certain is his destruction. For what is *the* temptation, seeing that in itself temptation is the manifold? It is the temptation—not indeed like the glutton to live in order to eat, but (ah, what rebellion against the divine order!)—to live *in order* to slave; it is the temptation to lose oneself, to lose one's soul, to cease to be a man and to live like a man, instead of being freer than the bird, to slave, godforsaken, more wretched than the beast. Yes, to slave! Instead of *labouring* for the daily bread, as every man is commanded to do, to *slave* for it—because one has become the slave of man and of his own anxiety, and has forgotten that it is to God one should pray for it. Instead of being willing to be what one is, a poor man, but at the same time beloved of God, which also one is, never to be happy in oneself, never happy in God, to subject oneself and one's life to the curse of this slavery, in despondent grief day and night, in gloomy and brooding dejection, in spiritless activity, the heart oppressed with care about sustenance—infected with avarice although in poverty!

Think in conclusion of the bird, which has its place in the Gospel, and should have its place in the discourse. In comparison with the ungodly melancholy of the heathen, the bird, which in poverty is without the anxiety of poverty, is care-free; in comparison with the pious faith of the Christian, the care-freeness of the bird is light-mindedness. In comparison with the lightness of the bird, the heathen is as heavily weighted as a stone; in comparison with the freedom of the Christian, the bird too, however, is subjected to the law of gravity. In comparison with the bird, which is alive, the heathen is dead; in comparison with the Christian, however, one cannot properly say that the bird lives. In comparison with the bird, which keeps silent, the heathen is garrulous; in comparison with the Christian, however, the heathen is dumb, he neither prays nor gives thanks, and that in the deepest sense is human language, everything else, everything the heathen says, is related to this as a bird which has learnt to talk is related to a man. The bird is poor and yet not poor; the Christian is poor yet not poor, rich; the heathen is poor, and poor, and poor, and poorer than the poorest bird. *Who* is *that* poor man who is so poor that this is the only thing one can say about him, just as it is the only thing he himself can talk about? It is the heathen. According to the teaching of Christianity, no one else, no one is poor, neither the bird nor the Christian. It is a long road—in poverty to desire to be rich. The bird's short cut is the shortest, the Christian's way the most blessed.

II

The anxiety of abundance

Be not therefore anxious, saying, What shall we eat? or, What shall we drink?—after all such things do the heathen seek.

THIS *anxiety the bird has not*. But is abundance then an anxiety? Perhaps it is merely disingenuous sophistry to talk in like terms of things so different as poverty and abundance, to treat them as equivalent in the way the Gospel does, ah, rather almost as if abundance were simply abundance of anxiety. A person supposes, in fact, that riches and abundance should keep him free from anxieties—also from anxiety for riches I should like to know! For riches and abundance come hypocritically clad in sheep's clothing, pretending to be security against anxieties, and they become then the object of anxiety, of 'the anxiety'; they secure a man against anxieties just about as well as the wolf which is put to tending the sheep secures them . . . against the wolf.

The bird, however, has not this anxiety. Is the bird poor? No; this we have made clear in the foregoing discourse. Is then the bird rich? Yes, though if it is that, it must not know it, if it is that, it must be ignorant of it. Or where has the bird stored its provision? If every proprietor and every crofter were to stand by his barn and say, 'No, away from here! This is mine', where is the barn that belongs to the bird? So then, the bird has not the anxiety of possessing abundance, it has not the anxiety of abundance, the anxiety that others own more, nor, alas, that others own less or nothing at all.

How then does the bird live? Well, it is God who every day metes out to the bird the definite measure, i.e. enough; but it never occurs to the bird that it has or might wish to have more than enough. What God gives every day is . . . enough. But the bird does not desire to have either more or less than enough. The measure which God employs in meting out food to the bird is the same measure, if I may say so, which the bird has in its mouth: He gives the bird 'enough', then the bird measures it and says, 'It is enough.' If the little bird quenches its thirst on a dew-drop, which is exactly enough, or if it drinks from the largest lake, it takes just as little, it does not require to have all that it sees, not to have the whole lake because it drinks from it, not to take the lake with it so that it may be secured for its whole life; although at the season of harvest the bird has the richest provision, it does not know what abundance is, what it is for more abundant knowledge; although in the forest where the bird builds and dwells with its family there is the greatest possible abundance of everything he and his have need of, yet were it to live never so long, it does not know what abundance is, neither it nor its mate nor its young—but when a person even when he has abundance does not know what abundance is, it is then impossible that abundance should be an occasion for anxiety. When the bird has eaten and drunken it never occurs to it to ask, Where am I to get something the next time? Therefore the poor bird is not poor after all, but it never occurs to it to ask what it shall do with the remainder, with the whole lake, with the immense provision of corn which remains over when the bird has taken the three grains which were 'enough'—it has not, it does not possess, abundance, and has not the anxiety of it. And when the season comes and the longing to be off is aroused, it then leaves the house and home which is all that it possesses and has, the nest built with diligence and art, the favourable spot so happily chosen, the like of which perhaps it never will find again: it thinks, Sufficient unto the day is the evil—and so the bird flies away. For the bird is a traveller, even the bird which does not migrate is a traveller, hence it will have nothing to do with abundance, and nothing to do with its anxiety.

So it depends in fact upon the bird that it has not abundance and that it has not the anxiety of abundance. The first barrel of gold, says the capitalist, will be the most difficult to gain; when one has that, the rest comes of itself. But the first farthing, with the knowledge that one is beginning to lay up for abundance, is also earnest-money—the bird will have nothing, not a farthing, in the way of abundance, in order to avoid the rest (which follows of itself): anxiety. With the most punctilious precision it regularly takes each time exactly 'enough', not the least bit more, in order not to come into contact in the remotest way with the equivocal knowledge about what abundance is. In poverty the bird is without the anxiety of poverty; against the anxiety of abundance it has prudently secured itself.

How is it now that the bird is a teacher? where is the point of contact in the instruction it imparts? Why! naturally, it teaches us the surest way to avoid the anxiety of riches and abundance, namely, not to lay up riches and abundance—bearing in mind that one is a traveller; and in the second place, it teaches us (what is especially appropriate to this discourse), in abundance to be ignorant of the fact that one has abundance—bearing in mind that one is a traveller. For, like that simple wise man of ancient times, the bird imparts to us instruction in ignorance. Ah, it is difficult, when one is beautiful, not to know it (a thing, however, which both the bird and the lily can do), still more difficult, when one has abundance, not to know it! But in abundance the bird is as ignorant of the fact that it has abundance as if it did not have it.

The Christian has not this anxiety of abundance. Is then the Christian poor? Certainly there are Christians who are poor; but about that we are not talking here, we are talking about the rich Christian who has riches and abundance, and we are saying that nevertheless he has not anxiety. For when one in abundance is without the anxiety of it . . . through ignorance, he is either a bird, or (in case he is a man and yet like a bird) he is a Christian.

So the rich Christian *has* abundance but is ignorant of it, and that then is something he must *have become*. For it requires no art to be ignorant, but to *become* ignorant, and by becoming so, to be ignorant, that is the art. To this extent the Christian is different from the bird, for the bird *is* ignorant, but the Christian becomes ignorant; the bird begins with ignorance and ends with it, the Christian ends by being ignorant—and Christianly the question is never raised what a man was, but what he became, not about what sort of a man he was, but what sort he became, not about the beginning, but about the end. But to become ignorant in this wise may take a long time and is a difficult task, before a man succeeds little by little, and until he succeeds thoroughly, in being ignorant of what he knows, and in becoming ignorant in such wise, and continuing to be so, that he does not sink back again, captured in the snare of knowledge. The Christian when he has abundance is as one who has not abundance; and so he is ignorant, and so in fact he has not abundance, if he really is as one who has it not. But primarily the Christian is a man, and as such he is not like this; he becomes such as a Christian, and the more he becomes a Christian, the more he is as one who has not.

For what is it that is able to deprive a man of riches and abundance? That is something need and want is able to do, or the God who gave can also take away. When this occurs the . . . formerly rich man becomes actually poor. Of this however we are not talking, nor of the consideration that the rich man may give away all his riches and abundance, for then indeed he becomes a formerly rich man. But is there not something that is able so to take away from a man riches and abundance that he is deprived of it without becoming a . . . formerly rich man, that he is deprived of it and still is the rich man? Indeed there is such a thing. What power then is this? It is thought and the power of thought. Can thought then take abundance away from the rich man in any outward way? No, that is not in the power of thought. In connexion with abundance, thought can take from the rich man the thought of *possession*, the thought that he owns and possesses this wealth and abundance as *his*. And yet thought allows him to retain the whole of it in an outward sense; there is no other man who gets his riches and abundance, every one else must say that they belong to the rich man. Thus it is thought goes about it; if it succeeds, if the rich man consents to it, abandons himself and his abundance entirely to the power of thought, then is he who has as one who has not. And this the Christian does.

Yes, it is a cunning power, this power of thought! In such wise no thief can steal, no ruffian can rob, in such wise even God cannot take away from the rich man, even when he takes from him the power of thought and understanding; and yet no thief and no robber can so thoroughly take everything from the rich man as thought can when it is allowed to have its way. How then does this come about? When I do not know what I am to live on tomorrow, I evidently possess nothing. But when I reflect that I might die tonight, 'this very night', then I possess nothing, however rich I may be. To be rich I must possess something until the morrow, etc., must be secured *for* the morrow; but to be rich I must also be assured *of* the morrow. Take away riches, and then no longer can I be called rich; but take away the morrow, and then too, alas, I no longer can be called rich. For to be rich I must possess something, but to be rich I must also surely be in existence. And this the rich man does not know, he does not know whether he will be alive on the morrow, or he knows that he does not know it. At bottom every man knows it; but the Christian bears in mind, 'this very day' and every day, that he does not know it, does not know whether perchance he will die 'this very night'.—Moreover, when I possess nothing, and so can lose nothing, I am not rich; but when unfortunately I possess something which can be lost and which every instant can be lost, am I then rich? When I have nothing in my hand, then I hold on to nothing; but when I hold in the hand what runs through the fingers, what is liable to loss, what then do I hold on to? Riches are indeed a possession, but really and essentially to possess that the essential property of which is that it can be lost, liability to loss, is just as impossible as to sit and yet walk— thought at any rate cannot get it through its head that this might be anything but an illusion. But if it is true that liability to loss is an essential attribute of wealth, it is evident that no essential change has been wrought in it when it is lost; it is essentially the same thing; but then it is essentially the same while I possess it: it is lost. For it must be essentially the same every instant. When lost it is essentially the same; when possessed it is essentially the same, i.e. lost—which means that in a deeper sense it may not be possessed, the notion of possession is an illusion. From all unlawful goods the thought of retributive justice can, after its manner, take away the thought of possession . . . by harsh means; but from riches and abundance, even if they are lawfully possessed, the thought of eternity takes away the thought of possession . . . by fair means, without employing any other power than the power of thought, and just in the degree than a man will abandon himself to the power of thought, or wills his own good.

Yes, it is a cunning power, this power of thought; if man were not in so many ways secured, or had . . . secured himself, against this power, he would acknowledge that it is cunning, but at the same time he would sense that it is in the service of truth it is so cunning. The sharp-sighted eye of the falcon does not so promptly and so surely discover its prey as this saving thought discovers what it shall swoop down upon. It does not sight with false aim at the strife of words about who is to be called wealthy, who prosperous, who well-to-do, etc., it aims at the thought of possession. And the Christian does not seek to screen himself from being thus aimed at, he himself helps to make the healing wound as deep as possible.

Then thought directs its aim also in another way at the thought of possession. If I am to be rich, I must indeed possess something, and that which I possess is accordingly mine. But then when I possess something which is not mine! Behold, here is a contradiction; and this strife of contradiction can be fought out only in the relationship of man to man. In so far as it is not mine I do not properly possess it; and yet there is no other man who possesses it, humanly speaking it is mine; but if it is mine, then I do indeed possess it. But this is meaningless. There must therefore (for the sake of meaning and thought) be a third party which has to be taken into account whenever in these innumerable relationships between man and man there is a question of ' mine ', a third party who says, 'It is mine.' It is like the echo: every time a man says, 'Mine', it is heard repeating, 'Mine'. 'It is mine,' thou sayest; 'It is mine,' says He, He who is the third party. 'It is all mine,' says He, 'as everything is.' Really everybody knows well enough that no one has but what was given him—at bottom everybody knows this. But the rich Christian bears in mind that he knows it, and he takes account of his responsibility if he does not know it; this is all a part of his accounting for mine and thine. He bears in mind that he possesses nothing except what has been given him, not to the intent that he should retain it, but as a loan, as a trust. That in the last resort no man can retain the riches he has, that everybody knows substantially; but the rich Christian bears in mind that he has not received them in order to retain them but as a trust. So therefore he administers them in the best way, as accountable to the owner, shuddering at the mere thought that there might be a false entry in the account of mine and thine. But the owner is God. And God does not, as though He were a capitalist, want his fortune to be increased by sagacious investments, but on the contrary, to have it administered in an entirely different way, if He is to be well pleased. This the rich Christian who is a householder understands full well—and hence he cannot understand

why interpreters have encountered such great difficulty in explaining the parable of the unjust steward. For, says he, supposing it had been the lawful property of that steward, God has
no objection if thou wouldst sit down and write . . . false acquittances, writing acquittances on receipt of half as much as was
due, that is, God has no objection if thou wouldst remit thy
creditors half their debt; thou well mayest remit the whole of it,
and in that way acquire friends who could receive thee in the
hereafter. The unfaithfulness was that the steward dealt thus
with the property of another. Therefore it was shrewd, and hence
the children of this world, who have understanding of the affairs
of this world, extol his shrewdness. If he had not been the
steward but the master, and had dealt with his own property as
the steward did with his master's, that would have been noble,
highminded, Christian—and then the children of this world, not
only would not have found it shrewd, but would have found it
weak and foolish, and would have derided him. Properly the
parable would teach that in this world the noble is regarded as
stupidity, evil as shrewdness. For by remitting a debt—to steal
from one's own pocket, how stupid! But to steal deftly from
another man's pocket, how shrewd! The parable extols nevertheless the nobility of acting as the steward did—but, but with
one's own property. Yet what am I saying? 'One's own property', the rich Christian understands precisely that in the highest
sense riches are not his own property. Are we then back again
in the same position as the steward? Oh, no; the proprietor is
God, who wishes His property administered exactly in this way.
So far from calling the earthly riches 'mine', the rich Christian
realizes that they are God's, and that they are to be administered
as far as possible in accordance with the proprietor's wish, administered with the proprietor's indifference to money and money
value, administered by giving them away at the right time and
place.

However, when earthly goods are to be thus administered they
are best administered by a *traveller*—the steward also, so soon
as he had done the shrewdest thing, was considering the equally
shrewd expedient . . . of packing up. And we, though certainly
we should not resemble the steward, might learn from him. But
like the bird, every Christian is a traveller; so too the rich Christian. As a traveller he is a Christian, and as a Christian he is a

traveller who knows precisely what he shall take with him and what he shall not take with him, what is his and what is not his. One has perhaps occasionally something in the house which is not one's own property but is kept there for some use; the moment however one thinks of travelling one distinguishes scrupulously between what is one's own and what is another's. And the rich Christian, who every moment is a traveller, thinks and speaks thus every moment about his earthly riches; having quite different things to think about, he does not wish to be reminded precisely now . . . at the last moment, of what he is to take with him, and what is not his. Perhaps for thee it is rather difficult to understand him? Well, he understands that, and he understands himself; at one time perhaps it was difficult for him to understand it, but now he understands it.[1] Sometimes it is difficult perhaps for the wife and children of the rich man to understand him, they are so much inclined to obtrude upon him a knowledge of his riches, to make him believe that he has abundance; but then he says reprovingly, 'I don't want to have anything to say about such things, and I don't want to hear it from you, especially now, at this last moment.' And so there is no one except a Christian that can understand him, since he neither is sick, nor, so far as the passport office knows, is he about to start tomorrow on a journey. So ignorant is he of his earthly riches—as he became and becomes by becoming aware of something quite different (for by becoming aware of something else one *becomes* ignorant of what one previously knew),[2] aware, namely, that he might die this very night, that earthly riches cannot essentially be possessed, that they are a trust, that he himself is a traveller; so ignorant is the rich Christian of his earthly riches —even like an absent-minded person.

The rich Christian, being thus ignorant of the abundance he has, cannot possibly have the anxiety of abundance: he has no anxiety with regard to that which, according to a pretty saying, is commonly gathered with disquietude and abandoned with disquietude. He has no anxiety in gathering abundance, for he does

---

[1] This is evidently autobiographical, for at one time it was difficult for S. K. to understand it. Now when he understands it he is on the point of becoming . . . 'a formerly rich man'.

[2] There is a play on words which cannot be rendered: 'become aware' (*blive vidende*), 'become ignorant' (*vorder uvidende*).

not care to gather abundance; he has no anxiety in retaining, for it is easy enough to retain what one has not, and he is as one who has not; he has no anxiety about losing, for he indeed is as one who has not; he has no anxiety for the fact that others possess more, for he is as one who possesses nothing; he knows without anxiety that others possess less, for he is as one who possesses nothing; and he has no anxiety about what he shall leave to his heirs. Thus he has no anxiety because of his abundance, and on the other hand he has the surprise, every time he employs his means to do good therewith, he has such a surprise as when one finds something; for since he who has is as one who has not, he in fact finds what he has not.

But then indeed the rich Christian is essentially just as poor as the poor Christian, is he not? Yes, that he is. But he is rich as a Christian. As ignorant as the poor Christian is of his earthly poverty, just so ignorant is the rich Christian of his earthly riches; as the former does not talk of his earthly poverty, so he too does not talk of his earthly riches; they both talk of one and the same thing, of the heavenly riches, of being in existence for God as one who prays and gives thanks for the daily bread, as one who is God's steward.

And with this understanding, but only with this understanding, the rich Christian has joy in his earthly riches. But is it not very observable how much quicker it went when starting from poverty and attaining joy, and on the other hand how many difficulties are connected with starting from earthly riches and attaining joy? So then, as a Christian, the Christian has joy in his earthly riches. He believes as a Christian that he has a Father in heaven, and that it is this Father who gives him the earthly riches; yet for him the giver is infinitely more than the gift, he therefore does not seek the gift but the giver. He believes (what every Christian believes, but what for the rich Christian is so necessary) that the riches of a Christian are in heaven; hence his heart tends thither where his treasure is. He keeps constantly in mind that He who possessed all the riches of the world gave up all that He possessed and lived in poverty, that therefore the life of holiness is lived in poverty, and so again in ignorance of all the riches that are possessed. Hence the rich Christian is in a position to have joy in his earthly riches, finding joy whenever he is granted opportunity to do some good with his riches, that he can do another man a service, and by this same act can serve God. Oh, it is accounted a difficult thing to do two things at the same time; but it surely would be difficult to find a more blessed two-fold action to be done at the same time, than to do a service to another man and by the same act to do a service to God! It is accounted difficult to remember two things at once, difficult enough for many a man to remember the word, 'To do good and to communicate forget not', and yet the rich Christian remembers one more word, 'Forget not God when thou doest good and dost communicate.' Hence the rich Christian has a double joy in doing good, because he is at the same time led to think of God. The rich Christian believes (what seems most nearly to concern the receiver, but Christianly concerns quite as much the giver) that every good and perfect gift is from above, so that if the gift he gives is to be good and perfect, it must be God that gives it through him. Hence he has joy in his riches because it gives him occasion to learn to know God, who indeed is the real, the hidden, giver, the rich man being His confidant who is employed on these errands of blessing; and therefore the rich Christian has joy in his earthly riches for the fact that he helps others to thank and praise God, whereas in turn he also makes to himself friends, who indeed cannot make requital, but who nevertheless (ah, this is almost usury!) can in requital receive him in the hereafter.

Thus the rich Christian in abundance is without the anxiety of abundance, as ignorant as the bird, to that extent as poor as the poor Christian, and so has infinite joy in his earthly riches.

He has an advantage over the bird in being rich as a Christian, and, with this understanding, he has in turn the advantage of joy in his earthly riches; he is not merely without anxiety like the bird.

Therefore you are not to ask What shall we eat? or, What shall we drink?—after all such things do the heathen seek. *For the rich heathen has this anxiety.*

The rich heathen is as far as possible from being ignorant of his riches and abundance. For a man can *become* ignorant of his riches and abundance only by becoming aware of something else; but the rich heathen neither knows nor wishes to know of anything else. Yes, it is difficult for a man who has riches and abundance to be unaware of that which day in and day out, so many times and in so many ways, but always ensnaringly, obtrudes itself upon one. Nevertheless it is a thing that can be done by becoming aware of God. For this knowledge entirely employs the Christian's mind and thought, excludes everything else from his memory, captivates his heart for ever, so that he becomes entirely ignorant. The rich heathen, on the other hand, has also only one thought, that of riches; about that all his thoughts revolve—yet he is anything but a thinker. Not only is he without God in the world, but riches is his god, attracting his every thought. He has need of but one thing, the one thing needful—and so he does not need God. But where one's treasure is, there will one's heart be also, and the rich heathen's heart is with riches, it is on the earth—he is no traveller, he is bound as a serf to the soil. If the rich Christian who has riches is as one who has not, the rich heathen is as one who has nothing else— nothing else to think of, nothing else to put his trust in, nothing else to be glad of, nothing else to be anxious for, nothing else to talk of. He is in a position to be able to look away from everything else, from everything that is lofty and noble and holy and lovely, but to look away from his riches is not possible to him for an instant.

Yes, the rich heathen has indeed knowledge of his riches and abundance, and with the increase of knowledge the increase of anxiety; he is aware of that which causes anxiety, and as this is the only thing he is aware of, he has nothing but anxiety. Thou canst see it in him by looking upon him, upon him the sallow tight-wad who gathers and gathers . . . anxiety unto himself; him the famished gourmand who is hungry in abundance, who also says, What shall I eat? and, What shall I drink? How will it be possible tomorrow (for today is provided for) to discover a dish so delicate that it could please my palate? him the sleepless niggard whom money, more cruel than the cruellest executioner, keeps more sleepless than the most abominable criminal; him the squinting money-changer who never looks away from his money except to see with envy that another possesses more; him the withered miser who for money starves himself to death—a thing which no one else has ever been heard of doing for money. Behold them—and hear what they say; they all say, and this is the only thing they talk about, they all say substantially, What shall we eat? and, What shall we drink? For the more riches and abundance they get, the more knowledge they acquire also, and this knowledge is anxiety, it does not satisfy hunger, it does not quench thirst; no, it stimulates hunger, it incites thirst.

Verily, they that desire to be rich fall into many temptations and snares which corrupt a man—and what indeed is the temptation of riches but that of desiring to be rich—of desiring to be quite certain of remaining rich, of desiring to be richer? It is a delusion that the anxiety of riches, which is not healed in a godly way (and in such case this may just as well occur whether one possesses a little less or a little more), might find any condition in life wherewith it would be content; as there never has lived any bird which ever took more than 'enough', so there never has lived a rich heathen who had 'enough'. No, there is no hunger so insatiable as the unnatural hunger of abundance, no knowledge so dissatisfied as the defiling knowledge of riches and abundance.

And what then is *the temptation* which comprises the many temptations? It is, by doing away with God, to cease to be a man; instead of being purer than the innocent bird, to be godforsaken, worse than bestially defiled, to sink lower than the beast; poorer than the poorest slave of the heathen, to serve in the most miserable and senseless thraldom, in abundance to slave for meat and drink, in wealth to slave for money, a curse to oneself, to nature an abhorrence, to the race a defilement.

Let us now in conclusion consider the bird, which indeed has its place in the Gospel and should have a place in the discourse. The bird is—well, if it is rich, it is ignorant that it is rich; the rich Christian *became* ignorant of it, he is rich, poor, rich; the rich heathen is poor, poor, poor. The bird keeps silent, it can well do that, it keeps silent about what it does not know; the rich Christian does not talk at all of his earthly riches, but only of the riches; the rich heathen knows of nothing to talk about except his mammon. In comparison with the ignorant bird the rich Christian is a wise man in ignorance, but the rich heathen is a fool, exceedingly knowing in the knowledge which is foolishness. The ignorant bird is, in comparison with the Christian, like a little booby; in comparison with the heathen it is like a wise man. The ignorant bird is innocently aware of nothing, the rich heathen is guiltily aware, and only aware, of that which is defiling. The ignorant bird lives like a somnambulist in the power of slumber, it sees nothing; the rich Christian who became ignorant of his earthly riches can, as though in a game, see nothing—

because eternity blinds him he cannot see by the earthly light of day; the rich heathen sees dismally only in the dark—he cannot see by the light of eternity. The bird is the light and nimble traveller; the rich Christian who became ignorant travelled for ever farther afield; the rich heathen remained heavy, like a stone, upon the ground, all the heavier by reason of his defilement. When one is rich there is only one way of becoming rich: that of becoming ignorant of one's riches, of becoming poor. The bird's way is the shortest, that of the Christian the most blessed. According to the teaching of Christianity, there is only one rich man, namely, the Christian; every one else is poor, both the poor man and the rich. A man is most healthy when he does not notice at all or know that he has a body, and the rich man is in health when, as healthy as the bird, he knows nothing of his earthly riches; but when he knows of it, when it is the only thing he knows, then he is lost. When the rich Christian became entirely ignorant of his earthly riches he gained more than the bird, he gained heaven; when the rich heathen became entirely and solely conscious of his riches he lost what no bird loses when it falls to the ground, he lost heaven.

III

The anxiety of lowliness

Be not anxious what ye shall put on—after all such things do the heathen seek.

THE sparrows are divided into grey sparrows and yellow, or if you will, golden sparrows; but this distinction, this division, lowly/superior, does not exist for them, not for any one of them. The bird which flies at the head when they are flocking, or on the right hand, is followed indeed by the others, there is a distinction between the foremost and the hindmost, between right and left, but the distinction lowly/superior does not exist; in the active swing of their flight, as the flock describes free and graceful figures in the air, the positions of first and last, of right and left, are altered. And when the thousands of voices sing in chorus there likely is one which gives the note, this distinction there is, but lowly/superior is a distinction which does not exist, and joy is unrestrained in the interchange of voices. It delights 'the individual' bird indescribably to sing in chorus with the others, yet it does not sing to delight the others, it is delighted by its own song and by the song of the others, hence it breaks off quite arbitrarily, ceases for an instant, until again it feels like joining in . . . and hearing itself.

So the bird has not this anxiety. How then does this come about? It is due to the fact that the bird is what it is, is itself, content to be itself, delighted with itself; it hardly knows distinctly, or is in its own mind quite clear what it is, and still less what others are. But it is delighted with itself and with what it is . . . whatever that may be; for it has no time for reflection, or even for making a start at it, so delighted it is with being what it is. In order to be, in order to have joy in being, it does not have to take the long road of learning first to know something about the others in order thereby to learn to know what it is itself. No, it takes the most delightful short cut; it is what it is; for it there is no question about 'to be or not to be'; by the help of the short cut it easily avoids all those anxieties of difference. Whether a bird's a bird for a' that, whether it is 'just as good a bird' as the others of the same species; yes, even if it is like its mate—about all such matters it thinks not at all, so impatient is it in its joy at being; no young girl who is on tiptoe to go to a dance can be so impatient to be off as is the bird to get started at being what it is. For it has not an instant to waste if this might delay it fiom being; the shortest instant would be a distressingly long period, if in that time it might not be what it is; it would die of impatience at the very least objection to being allowed without more ado to . . . be. It is what it is, but it *is*; it lets five be an even number . . . and it is. Such surely is the case with the bird. If thou hast not beheld the proud soaring of the royal bird—if thou seest merely the little bird that sits and swings on a twig and amuses itself by singing—is there the least trace of the anxiety of lowliness? For thou wilt surely not raise the objection (which is precisely the instructive thought) that the bird is 'high upon a straw' [a proverbial expression for, 'in high station']. And if thou wilt—then take the straw upon which it sits. Although more vivacious than the lily in its joy at being, the bird is yet quite like the lily in its innocent self-contentment. If thou hast never beheld the splendid lily which in its beauty humbly holds its head so high—when thou seest merely the insignificant flower which stands in a ditch and jests with the wind as though it were its peer, if only thou wouldst see it after a storm has done its best to make the flower feel its insignificance, if thou wouldst consider it as it sticks its head out again to see if it might not be fair weather again—does it seem to thee that there is the least trace of the anxiety of lowliness? Or when it stands at the foot of the mighty tree and looks up at it with astonishment, does it seem to thee that there is the least trace of the anxiety of lowliness on the part of the astonished lily? Or dost thou believe that it would feel itself belittled if the tree were half as big again? Is it not rather as if it had the conceit to imagine that everything was for its sake?

So easy it is for the lily and the bird to be, they are so easy-going about this matter of living; the beginning, or making a start at it, strikes them as a thing so natural. For the lily and the bird are fortunately favoured by the fact that it is so easy for them to begin to exist that no sooner have they come into existence than they have at once begun, are at once in the full swing of being, they feel not the least need of anything that is to come

before the beginning, and they are not in the least tempted by
that trial which amongst men is so much talked about and is
described as a difficulty so fraught with peril, the difficulty of
beginning.

How then is the bird a teacher, and where is the point of
contact in the instruction it gives? Why surely in this, that it
makes the circuitous route to reach the beginning, this route
which can be so very long—that it makes it as short as possible,
in order as quickly as possible to come to itself, to be itself.

This anxiety the lowly Christian has not. Yet he is different
from the bird in this respect, that he must be tried in this difficulty of beginning; for he is aware of the distinction lowly/
superior. He knows, and he knows that the others know this
same thing of him, that he is a lowly man; and he knows what
this means. He knows also what is to be understood by the
advantages of worldly station, and that whereas ordinarily they
exist to express what the others are who possess these advantages,
in his case they serve only to indicate how lowly he is. For with
every new advantage the superior person attains, the more
superior he becomes, and with every advantage the lowly man
must admit he is denied, the more lowly, in one sense, he becomes; that which exists for the sake of indicating how much the
superior person is, seems from the other side to exist in order to
indicate how little there is to the lowly man.—Oh, how difficult
is the beginning of existence or of coming into existence: to exist,
thereupon to continue in existence, and only after all that to exist ;
ah, cunningly hidden snare which is not spread for any bird! For
it seems indeed as if, in order to be himself, a man must first be
expertly informed about what the others are, and thereby learn to
know what he himself is—in order then to be that. However, if
he walks into the snare of this optical illusion, he never reaches
the point of being himself. He goes then on and on like one who
follows a road which the passers-by tell him certainly leads to the
city, but neglect to tell him that if he would go to the city, he
must turn around; for he is following the road which leads to the
city, that he is following it . . . away from the city.

But the lowly Christian does not walk into this snare of optical
illusion, he sees with the eyes of faith, and with the swiftness of
the faith which seeks God he is at the beginning, he is himself
before God, content with being himself. He has learned to know

from the world or from the others that he is a lowly man, but he has not abandoned himself to this knowledge, he does not lose himself in it after a worldly fashion, he does not altogether realize it, by holding on to God with the tenacity of eternity he has become himself. He is like one who has two names, one of them being for all the rest, the other for his dearest ones; in the world, in intercourse with the others, he is the lowly man, he does not give himself out as anything else, and he is not taken for anything else, but before God he is himself. In the contacts of daily intercourse it seems as though he must constantly wait for the others in order to learn to know what he is now, at this moment. But he does not wait; he makes speed by being before God. He is the lowly man as a part of the multitude of men, and what he is as such depends upon his relationship to them; but in being himself he is not dependent upon the multitude, before God he is himself. For from 'the others', naturally, one properly only learns to know what the others are—it is in this way the world would beguile a man from being himself. 'The others', in turn do not know at all what they themselves are, but only what the others are. There is only One who knows what He Himself is, that is God; and He knows also what every man in himself is, for it is precisely by being before God that every man is. The man who is not before God is not himself, for this a man can be only by being before Him who is in and for himself.[1] If one is oneself by being in Him who is in and for Himself, one can be in others or before others, but one cannot by being merely before others be oneself.

The lowly Christian is himself *before God*. In this wise the bird is not itself; for the bird simply *is* what it is. By the aid of this mode of being it has every instant evaded the difficulty of the beginning, but in this wise it did not attain the glorious end of the difficult beginning, to be doubly itself. The bird is like a single cipher, a man who is himself is more than a decade. The bird luckily evades the difficulty of the beginning and therefore gets no conception how lowly it is; but thus it is incomparably more lowly than one who knows how lowly he is. The *conception* of

---

[1] What the 'self' is, 'the individual', what it means for a man to be 'before God' —these are the themes which most engrossed S. K. But fortunately he rarely uses in the Discourses the abstract vocabulary of German philosophy: *an sich*; *das an-und-für-sich-Seiende*.

lowliness is nonexistent for the bird; but the lowly Christian *is not essentially existent for this conception,* he will not be essentially existent for it, for essentially he is and wills to be himself before God. The bird therefore is properly the lowly one. The lowly Christian is, in opposition to his lowliness, himself—without for this cause wishing to cease to be the lowly man he is in relation to others; he is *in lowliness* himself. And thus the lowly Christian is in lowliness without the anxiety of lowliness. Wherein does this lowliness consist? In the relationship to 'the others'. But what is the ground of this anxiety? It lies in existing only before others, in not knowing anything else but the relationship to others. The bird is not aware of the relationship to others, and to that extent it is not lowly, and again to that extent it is without the anxiety of lowliness; but of course it is not aware that it has a higher relationship.

And what then is the lowly Christian who before God is himself? He is a *man.* In so far as he is a man he is in a certain sense like the bird, which is what it is. But upon this we will not here dwell further.

But at the same time he is a *Christian,* as is implied in the question which asks what the lowly *Christian* is. In so far as he is a Christian he is not like the bird, for the bird *is* what it is. But it is not thus one can be a Christian; if one is a Christian, he must *have become* such. So the lowly Christian too has become (amounted to) something in the world; alas, the bird cannot become (amount to) anything, it is what it is. In likeness to the bird, the lowly Christian was a man, but then he became a Christian, he became (amounted to) something in the world. And he can constantly become (amount to) more and more, for he can constantly become more and more a Christian. *As* a man he was not created in the image (pattern) of God, but as a Christian he has God for a pattern! This disquieting thought (a pattern) which incessantly challenges one, the bird does not know; the bird is what it is, nothing whatever disturbs it in that being it has; yes, it is true, nothing disturbs it—not even the blissful thought of having God for its pattern. A pattern is to be sure a challenge . . . but what bliss! Even in the case of the poet we speak of it as good fortune when we say there is something within him which challenges him to sing; but the pattern is a still stronger challenge, an even stronger stimulus, to every one before whose eyes it is shown, for whom it is existent. The pattern is a promise, no other is so sure, for the pattern is indeed the fulfilment.—For the bird there is no pattern; but for the lowly Christian the pattern is in existence, and he is in existence for his Pattern—he can constantly grow to resemble it more and more.[1]

The lowly Christian who is himself before God is as a Christian *in existence for his Pattern*. He believes that He has lived on earth, that He let Himself be born in poor and lowly circumstances, yes, in dishonour, and thereupon as a child lived with the simple man He called His father and with the despised maiden who was His mother. That thereupon He wandered about in the lowly form of a servant, not to be distinguished from other lowly men even by His extraordinary lowliness, until He ended in the utmost wretchedness, crucified as a criminal—and then, to be sure, left behind Him a Name; but the lowly Christian's request is merely to dare in life and in death to appropriate His Name, or to be named after Him. The lowly Christian believes that, as it is related, He chose for His disciples lowly men of the simplest condition, and sought out for His companions those whom the world repudiated and despised; that throughout the various vicissitudes of His life, when men would highly exalt Him, and when they would abase Him if possible even more than He had abased Himself, He remained faithful to the lowly people to whom He was bound by the closer ties, faithful to the lowly men whom He had bound to Himself, faithful to the despised men whom they had even expelled from the synagogue because He had helped them. The lowly Christian believes that this lowly man, or that His life in lowliness, has showed how much a lowly man matters, and, alas, humanly speaking, what it means to be a superior man, how infinitely much it may mean to be a lowly man, and how infinitely little to be a superior man, if one is nothing else. The lowly man believes that this Pattern exists expressly for him who in fact is a lowly man, struggling perhaps with poverty and narrow circumstances, or, more lowly still, being despised and rejected. He admits indeed that it was not he himself that chose this scorned and despised condition of lowliness, and that to this extent he does not resemble the Pattern; yet he consoles

[1] Christ as the Pattern is the persistent theme of S. K.'s last works: *Training in Christianity* and *Judge for Yourselves*.

himself with the thought that the Pattern exists for him, this Pattern which by means of lowliness presses itself as it were compassionately upon him, as though it would say to him, 'Lowly man, canst thou not perceive that the Pattern is for thee?' True, he has not himself, with his own eyes, seen the Pattern, but he believes that He existed. There was, in a certain sense, nothing at all to *see*—except lowliness (for glory is something that must be *believed*), and of lowliness he is well able to form a conception. He has not with his own eyes seen the Pattern, nor does he make any attempt to have the senses construct such a picture. Yet he often sees the Pattern. For as often as in faith's gladness at the glory of this Pattern he completely forgets his poverty, his lowliness, the contempt in which he is held, he sees the Pattern—and he himself approximately resembles it. For if in such a blissful moment, when he is lost to himself in the Pattern, another man beholds him, this other man sees before his eyes merely a lowly man—precisely so it was in the case of the Pattern, one saw merely a lowly man. He believes and hopes that he shall approach ever more and more to likeness with this Pattern, who only in the beyond will reveal Himself in glory, for here on earth the Pattern can only be in lowliness and can only be seen in lowliness. He believes that this Pattern, if he steadily strives to resemble it, brings him again into kinship with God, and into a still closer kinship, that he not only has God for his Creator, as all creatures have, but has God for his Brother.

But then after all the lowly Christian is something rather exalted? Yes, that he is, to be sure, something so exalted that one quite loses sight of the bird. Like the bird he is lowly without the anxiety of lowliness, though oppressed in a certain sense, as the bird is not, he is nevertheless highly exalted. He does not talk of his lowliness, at least not despondently; it only reminds him of the Pattern, and with that he thinks of His exaltation— and when he does so he is himself approximately a reminder of the Pattern.

The lowly heathen, on the other hand, has this anxiety. The lowly heathen is without God in the world, and moreover he is never essentially himself (which one only is by being before God), nor ever satisfied with being himself, which of course one cannot be if one is not oneself. He is not himself, not content with being himself, not content like the bird with being what it is; he is discontented with what he is, a burden to himself, he sighs and protests against his fate.

What is he then? He is the lowly man, nothing else; that is, he is what the others make of him, and what he makes of himself by only being for others. His anxiety is that he is nothing, yes, nothing whatever. So far is he from being like the bird, which is what it is. And hence again his anxiety is *to become something* in the world. To exist before God, that, as he thinks, is not to be anything—that makes no showing in the world in contrast or in comparison with others. To be a man, that, as he thinks, is not to be anything—that is in fact to be nothing, for in this there is no distinction from nor advantage over all other men. To be a Christian, as he thinks, is not to be anything—that indeed we all are. But to be Councillor of Justice—that would be something —and by all means he must become something in the world, it is enough to drive one to despair not to be anything at all.

'That is enough to drive one to despair'—he talks as if he were not already in despair; yet he is in despair, and despair is his anxiety.[1] It is assumed indeed that in every state the lowly man is ordinarily exempted from bearing the burdens which the more favoured classes have to bear; but the lowly man who is in despair, i.e. the heathen, even though he is lowly, is not exempted from bearing the heaviest of all burdens. They talk about the king bearing the weight of the crown, the man in high place bearing the weight of responsibility for government, him to whom much is given the weight of looking out for others, whereas it must also be taken into account that the king after all is the king, the man in high place is highly placed, the man to whom much is given is the man who has much; but the lowly man in despair, the heathen, worries himself to death under the weight of what he is not, he strains himself (yes, the situation is a crazy one) under the weight of a burden he doesn't bear. Whether it is a fact that it is the king who, like the foundation, sustains all the others, or that the others sustain the king as the topmost, we will not investigate here—but the lowly man in despair, the heathen, bears up all the others. This prodigious weight, 'all the others', weighs upon him, and that with the redoubled weight of despair, for it is not through the conception that he is something this weight weighs

---

[1] Despair is the theme of the two works expressly called psychological: *The Concept of Dread* and *The Sickness unto Death*.

upon him, no, it weighs upon him through the conception that he is nothing. Verily, so inhumanly has no state or society ever dealt with any man, that by reason of the circumstance that one is nothing one should bear the burden of all; so inhumanly does only the lowly man in despair, the heathen, deal with himself. Deeper and deeper he sinks in the anxiety of despair, but he finds no footing to support the weight—he is in fact nothing, as to his own anguish he becomes convinced of it through the conception of what the others are. More and more ridiculous—oh, no, more and more pitiable, or rather more and more ungodly, more and more inhuman he becomes in his foolish effort to become something after all, something, however little it might be, which according to his notion was worth being.

Thus the lowly man in despair, the heathen, sinks under the prodigious weight of comparison which he lays upon himself. The thing of being a lowly man, which for the lowly Christian is a part of being a Christian, just as the weak and scarcely audible breathing is a part of the audible letter (and thus it is the lowly Christian talks about his lowliness, he talks about it only as a way of expressing the fact that he is a Christian)—this for the heathen is his anxiety day and night, about this his every thought is employed. Without the prospect of eternity, never strengthened by the heavenly hope, never himself, godforsaken, he lives in despair, as if for a punishment he were condemned to live these seventy years, tortured by the thought of being nothing, tortured by the fruitlessness of his effort to be something. For him the bird suggests no thought of self-reliance, heaven has no comfort —and that is only natural, for neither has the earth any comfort for him. It cannot be said of him that he is bound in thraldom to the earth, overcome by the enchantments of earthly life which made him forgetful of heaven; no, it is rather as if the temporal did everything to repel him by bringing him to nothing. And yet he desires to belong to the temporal on the most miserable conditions, he will not let it go, he clings tighter to being nothing, tighter and tighter as he seeks in vain to be something in a worldly sense, he clings despairingly tighter and tighter . . . to that which to the point of despair he would not be; thus he lives, not upon the earth, but as if he were cast out into the underworld. Behold that king [1] whom the gods punished, he suffered the

[1] Tantalus.

dreadful punishment that whenever he was hungry the most delicious fruits appeared, but when he grasped at them they vanished; the lowly man in despair, the heathen, suffers a more anguishing punishment through self-contradiction. For while, tormented by being nothing, he seeks in vain to be something, he is not merely something but much; it is not fruits which withdraw themselves from him, it is he himself that withdraws even from being what he is. For he is not a man—and he cannot become a Christian.

Let us then in conclusion think of the bird; it has its place in the Gospel and should have its place in the discourse. The lowly bird is without the anxiety of lowliness; the lowly Christian is in lowly station without having the anxiety of lowliness, and so . . . is highly exalted above all earthly highness; the lowly heathen is in his anxiety far below himself, even if he were the lowest of the low. The bird does not look narrowly into what it is, the lowly Christian looks narrowly into what he is as a Christian; the lowly heathen gazes fixedly in desperation upon the fact that he is lowly. 'What! . . . lowly . . .' says the bird, 'let us never think of such things, one flies away from them!' 'What! . . . lowly,' says the Christian, 'I am a Christian!' 'Alas, lowly!' says the heathen. 'I am what I am,' says the bird; 'What I shall be is not yet revealed,' says the lowly Christian; 'I am nothing, and I come to nothing,' says the lowly heathen. 'I exist,' says the bird; 'In death life begins,' says the lowly Christian; 'I am nothing, and in death I become nothing,' says the lowly heathen. In comparison with the lowly Christian the bird is a child; in comparison with the lowly heathen it is a happy child. Like the free bird as it soars highest in the joy of existing, so does the lowly Christian rise even higher; like the captured bird when in discouragement and anguish it beats itself to death in the net, so does the lowly heathen deprive himself of life still more pitiably in captivity to nothingness. According to the teaching of Christianity there is only one exaltation, that of being a Christian, everything else is lowly, both lowliness and exaltation. When one is lowly there is only one way to exaltation, that of becoming a Christian; this way the bird does not know, it remains what it is; but then there is another way which the bird does not know, that is the way the heathen takes. The bird's way of being is enigmatical, it is not to be found; the Christian's way was found by Him who is the

Way; the heathen's way ends in darkness, no one has found his way back by that way. The bird avoids all danger by that by-way it has; the lowly Christian does not take the by-way and is saved blissfully in glory; the lowly heathen chooses the by-way and 'goes his own way' to perdition.

IV

The anxiety of highness

Be not anxious what ye shall put on—after all such things do the heathen seek.

THIS *anxiety the bird has not.* But is highness then an anxiety? One would think that the higher a man stood, the more he would be exempted from all anxieties, for he has all the more men about him who are anxious and employed about nothing else but to keep all anxieties away from him. Alas, there is no false sarcasm in talking, as the Gospel does, in perfectly equivalent terms of the anxiety of highness and the anxiety of lowliness. For highness and power and honour and prestige tender their . . . faithful services as myrmidons which are to stand about the man of high estate to protect him from every anxiety, as it were on bended knee they promise . . . faithful allegiance—oh, but it is just this body-guard with which the man of high estate has not the courage to break, it is just this body-guard, which for safety's sake is so close to his body, just this it is that costs him his night's sleep. A factual situation may serve as a symbol: an emperor who rules over the whole world, surrounded by his faithful body-guard which rules over the emperor; an emperor who makes the whole world tremble, surrounded by his brave body-guard behind which and before which the emperor trembles.

But the bird, notwithstanding it always is on high, has not the anxiety of highness—*neither* that anxiety which is not in question here, the anxiety which does honour to the man of high station, that of being careful for the welfare of those committed to him (for in this little work we talk only of the anxiety a man may be without, indeed should be without, not of the anxiety without which it is impossible to be a Christian); *nor* that anxiety which here is in question. It hardly occurs to the bird to be careful of itself, still less that it might be commissioned to take care of others; the bird says in all innocence about its relationship to others, 'Am I my brother's keeper?' It never occurs to any bird, not even to the bird that flies highest, that it might be so high that it should rule over others; but thus it has no anxiety whatever as to whether the others show it due deference or refuse to show it—or whether perhaps they even may be plotting to cast it down from its highness. No bird is so highly placed as that.

And yet every bird is in fact on high; but it is as though essentially every bird were placed equally high. This heavenly equality amongst the birds, or their equal highness under heaven, has something in common with the highness of eternal life—where likewise there is neither high nor low, and yet there is highness. Under the dome of heaven there is abundant room for the bird to soar as high as it will; but also the bird which walks on the ground is on high. The bird has no other way of understanding the thing. If one were to say to it, 'But then thou art not really exalted if thou art not *more* exalted than the others,' the bird would reply, 'Why, how is that? Am I not on high?'— and with that the bird flies high, or it remains on the ground, where it is none the less on high and conscious of its highness. Hence it is on high without the anxiety of highness, on high without being exalted over any one—under the dome of heaven there is too much room for that . . . or there is no room for narrow-mindedness.

Do but regard that solitary bird where it holds itself high aloft in the sky, so calm, so proud, without the least movement, not even the flap of a wing. And if thou perhaps hast attended to thy business and after the lapse of several hours dost return to the same place—look, it remains in the air unaltered, resting proudly upon the outstretched wings which it does not move, while it surveys the earth. It is difficult for the unpractised eye to estimate distance in the air or upon the water, but perhaps it has not altered its position by half a yard. It stands without footing, for it stands upon the air, so tranquil in highness—shall I say, so like a ruler of men? Or was there never a ruler so tranquil? It fears nothing, it beholds no danger, no abyss beneath it, its eye is never dizzy at that height, its sight never confused by the altitude, ah, and yet there never was a man so sharp-sighted, not even one who in lowliness envies highness. But what is it then which keeps it so tranquil on high? It is highness. For in highness in and for itself there is no danger, and beneath it there is no abyss. Only when beneath it there is highness which yet is more lowly than it is, and so on in turn—in short when there is somebody beneath it, then there is something beneath it, and then also there is the abyss beneath it. But for the bird there is no one lowlier, hence it is on high without having the abyss beneath it, and hence without anxiety, which comes with and from the abyss.

The bird is on high without being higher than anybody else, therefore without the anxiety of highness. Thus it is an apt teacher, and here is the point of contact in the instruction. To be on high in that fashion is possible without anxiety. If some one were to say, 'To be on high in that fashion is not to be on high at all, it is merely a play on words to talk of the bird as His Highness'—well, that only proves him an indocile pupil, a naughty boy who will not sit still during the lesson hour, but disturbs the instruction. For it is true enough that if he will not take pains to understand the bird, if instead of learning to reform his notions in conformity with the instruction the bird gives, he would take the bird to task and require it to accept his notions, thus rejecting it as a teacher, then indeed it is impossible to learn anything from the bird—and (be it said to the credit of the bird) this is literally the only way one cannot learn anything from the bird. But he who desires to learn will learn about highness that the only way one who is on high can truly be without anxiety is not to be higher than any one else.

The Christian of high position [1] *has not this anxiety.* What then is the Christian of high rank? Well, if thou dost ask in a worldly sense whether he be king or emperor, or his highness, or his grace, etc., it is impossible to give an answer which covers the case generally. But if thou dost ask in a Christian sense, the answer is easy. He is a Christian. And as a Christian he knows full well all about shutting the door when he is to talk with God —not lest any one might get to know that he was talking with God, but lest anything or anybody might disturb him; when he talks with God he lays aside all earthly and all spurious pomp and glory, but also all false illusions.

He believes that there is a God in heaven with whom there is no respect of persons, that the man (if such a thing can be

---

[1] *Fornemme*: it is the German *vornehm*—but how render it in English? A sympathetic reader will surely commiserate me when he detects the many turns I have had to give this word throughout the remainder of this discourse.

imagined) who might rule over the whole human race is not the least bit more important to God than the lowliest man—or than the sparrow which falls to the ground. He understands it therefore as an illusion that because he is so important to all men, or to such a countless number of them, and is plainly important to so many for their very life, that because he enjoys in his lifetime the heightened consciousness of being indispensable, and by anticipation the rich consciousness of being missed after his death, that therefore his life should also be more important to God; for to God he is not more important than the sparrow which falls to the ground—neither he, the mightiest of men, nor the wisest man that ever lived, nor any man whatsoever. He believes (instead of heeding the much talk about the many who could not live without him) that it is he who in order to live has need every instant, yea, every second, of this God, without whose will doubtless no sparrow falls to the ground, but without whom also no sparrow comes into existence and is. If the rest of us have another understanding, thinking that prayers are made for him because we need him, have need of his continuing in life, he for his part has a different understanding with God, recognizing that he, precisely for the fact that his task is incomparably the greatest, has more need than any other man that prayers be made for him. He believes that it is an unchangeable God [1] who dwells in heaven, who will have His way—although all were to rise up against Him, which to Him would signify nothing; an unchangeable God who requires obedience, as well in the greatest matters as in the least, in the least detail of the most comprehensive world-historical achievement as in the most every-day undertaking, as well of the mightiest man that has ever lived as of the lowliest, and of all nature as well, which does not presume to do anything whatever without His will. He understands therefore that it is an illusion if any one would make him believe that because a word of power from him is enough to set in motion thousands of men, yea, almost to transform the face of the earth, because thousands press upon him and court the smile of the mighty, that therefore God should treat him differently than He does every other man, that towards him the unchangeable God should not also be unchangeable, unchangeable as eternity, unchangeable as the rocks—but believes

[1] S. K.'s last Discourse was on *The Unchangeableness of God*.

that God might be almightily able to transform everything, more dreadfully than he, both the throne and the legions, both heaven and earth. He believes that before this God he is a sinner, and that this God is just as jealous of sin whoever the sinner may be. He understands therefore that it is an illusion if any one would make him believe that because there is hardly a man who is capable of taking account of his stewardship, of what he wrongly did and of what he left undone, because no man dares to condemn him, that therefore the righteous God (for whom it is not more important that the mightiest sins than that the lowliest does so—however different, humanly speaking, the magnitude of the consequences are—not more forgiveable that the mightiest sins than that the lowliest does so), being amazed at human power, might not be able, or might not dare, to judge him with all the severity of the law. He believes that every instant he needs the forgiveness of the gracious God. Therefore he believes that God walked upon earth in lowliness, and thus pronounced all earthly power and might to be nothing. He believes that as no one enters into the kingdom of heaven except by becoming again *as* a little child, so no one comes to Christ except *as* a lowly man, as one who by himself and with all that he is by himself is nothing. He believes that even if Christ had not chosen lowly men for His disciples, but men of high station, these must first have become lowly men in order to be His disciples. He believes that before Christ there is no respect of persons, because before Christ there is only lowliness; that as certainly as no hale man can be healed by Christ, just so certainly can no superior man be saved as such, but only as a lowly man. For no one can become or be a Christian except in the character of, or as, a lowly man.

'But then in fact the Christian of high rank is essentially just as lowly as the lowly Christian?' Yes, certainly, that he is. 'But then essentially the Christian of high rank really doesn't know how superior he is?' No, essentially he doesn't know that. 'But then really the discourse has deceived the reader by not talking of earthly highness, of titles, dignities, and of their anxiety!' Well, yes—and yet no, the discourse has not deceived, for the Christian of high rank has not this anxiety—and this is precisely what the discourse is about, that he has not this anxiety. And what discourse is it which most truly expresses this; is it one which protests and protests that he has not this anxiety, or is it one which, by talking of that which properly engages the mind of the Christian of rank, namely, *lowliness*, lets it tacitly be understood that he has not that anxiety of *highness*?

One can become or be a Christian only as, or in the character of, a lowly man. The thing of becoming (and so also of being) a Christian is surely a thought, but it is a duplex thought, which consequently has duplex vision. It is therefore one and the same thought which permits the lowly Christian to understand his highness and the Christian of high rank to understand his lowliness. The Christian of rank and position lets the conception (the Christian conception) take from him the power and highness (of the earthly sort), or, in other words, he abandons himself to the power of the conception; therewith he becomes the lowly man which one must be in order to become and to be a Christian. In case an actor were to go out in the street and be a king because he played the part of a king the night before, everybody would laugh at him. In case a child who in a game with children of his own age was 'the Emperor' were to approach his elders with the same presumption, we should all laugh at the child. And why? Because the play and the children's game are unreality. But the thing of being in reality of superior rank is not, Christianly understood, reality; the real is the eternal, the Christian. The true highness is the Christian highness; but in true Christian highness no one is higher than the others. So this thing of rank is unreality in comparison with the true highness. And so, Christianly, it is quite right that the superior Christian *himself* (for that others should do so has no place nor justification in Christianity, but only in the disgusting impudence of ungodly worldliness) should smile at his earthly highness, at his so-called real highness; for only the Christian highness is the real.

Yet if such is the case, has it not been more difficult for the man of high station to become a Christian (for here we are talking of the Christian of high station) than for the lowly man? To this question the Scripture answers, Yes. It is commonly thought, I know, that it must be equally easy and equally difficult for the lowly man and for the lofty to become a Christian, for it is said that the lowliness here in question is not the outward but the inward thing, a sense of one's own lowliness, which the man of high station can have just as well as the lowly man; Christianity is far too spiritual a thing to talk about outward lowliness. Well, that is true in a way. However, the Scripture does nevertheless (perhaps as a precaution and with knowledge of the human heart) talk also in another fashion, it talks of being literally a lowly man; and so also does the Pattern, witnessing more potently than any words or phrases, for 'He' lived in actual earthly lowliness; accordingly, in resolving to be the Pattern, he did not choose to be a man of rank and yet inwardly the lowly man. No, He was literally the lowly man, and that in a much more serious sense than when a king lays aside momentarily his dignity—and is recognized by the courtiers and then still more applauded . . . for his humility.

There is something in the spiritual life which corresponds to what spelling is in contrast to continuous reading. One spells, one advances slowly, distinguishing clearly and evidently between details, for fear of finally reducing the whole content of life to 'resolved moments' [1] and life itself to much ado about nothing. So it is with the possession of external superiority in connexion with becoming a Christian. Christianity has never taught that to be literally a lowly man is synonymous with being a Christian, nor that from the literal condition of lowliness there is direct transition as a matter of course to becoming a Christian; neither has it taught that if the man of worldly position were to give up all his power, he therefore would be a Christian. But from literal lowliness to the point of becoming a Christian there is however only one step. The position of being literally a lowly man is by no means an unfavourable preparation for becoming a Christian; the position of being in possession of the advantages of outward circumstance is a circuitous path, which for the more scrupulous makes necessary a double preparation. In mathematical science one speaks of a 'help-line' [2] and draws the help-line as it is called; the proof of the proposition can be inferred without the help-line, but one draws it—not for the sake of the proof, but to help oneself; it is not the proof which stands in

---

[1] The *ophaevende moment* is the Hegelian *aufgehobenes Moment*. The next phrase, *tom Ophaevelse* is a play on words which is lost when it must be translated 'much ado about nothing'.

[2] Such is the Danish (and German) description of this mathematical device, which we call, less picturesquely, an 'artificial line'.

need of the help-line, but we ourselves. So likewise one who has the advantages of outward circumstance helps himself by becoming literally poor, despised and lowly. If he does not do this he must with all the more inward concern watch over himself, wondering if he dare trust himself, and if he knows in his own heart that nothing of all this outward rank and highness has so blinded him that he could not easily endure to be the lowly man of the people.

In this way, undeniably, the thing can be done. Christianity has never required unconditionally of any one that he should literally give up the advantages of outward circumstance, it has proposed to men rather a little precautionary rule. If one thinks one does not need it, as they thought they did in those ages when they scrupulously spelled their way—oh, what a strenuous life, to stand there on high, surrounded by all this seduction, and to be sure of oneself that one could easily endure to be the simple labouring man, because to be a Christian is of such great importance to one that with the strictest self-examination one has convinced oneself naturally that there is nothing whatever in all this which infatuates him in the least degree! What prodigious precaution with fire and light one must take if one lives in a powder magazine; and what strenuous precautions if one would be a Christian in this environment! Oh, what a difficult life it is to live thus! Thou wilt have only a slight hint of the daily difficulty of this life if thou wilt consider how much easier it proved in the foregoing discourse to advance from lowliness and attain the Christian highness, than it is here from earthly highness, through lowliness, to attain the Christian highness. Yet the Christian of high position lives thus. He has power and honour and public esteem, is in possession of earthly advantages, but he is as one who has not; he sees all this around him, sees how as in an enchantment it only awaits his bidding, only the expression of his wish, but he is as one that sees it not, being under the spell of a still greater enchantment; he hears all this, with its almost constant flattery perhaps, but his ears are closed—for him all this is merely like being the king in a play, and like the child who in his game is 'the Emperor'—for he is a Christian.

And as a Christian he is in real highness. For, in the Christian understanding of it, in God's kingdom it is precisely as under the blue sky: there all are on high, but without being higher than anybody else. The bird is on high without being higher than anybody; the Christian of high station, although in earthly highness exalted above others, is on high without being higher than anybody else. Hence he is without the anxiety of highness; for, as has been said, in this way it is possible for one to be a Christian. And when in this way one is on high, if one is not a bird, or if one is a man and yet like a bird, then one is a Christian—it makes no difference if by the by he is in a worldly sense high or low.

The heathen in high place on the other hand has this anxiety. The heathen in high place is without God in the world; if the Christian of high station is in ignorance of his earthly highness, the heathen is ignorant of what true highness is. He knows no other highness than this earthly sort—and to learn to know truly what highness is, is impossible, since he is in himself untruth, vapour, vain imagination, from which no cognition of truth can issue, except that this is what it is. He knows from the bottom up all about high, higher, highest, *allerhöchste*, but he does not know that at the bottom of all this lies nothing, and that therefore all that he knows is nothing. In this nothingness he has his place. What this is he defines by means of definitions which belong within nothingness. One describes a nightmare as a 'ghost-ride'—the sleeper groans and pants, but he does not budge from the spot. So it is with the heathen man in high station. Now he mounts on high, now he sinks, he exults, he sighs, he pants, he groans, but he does not budge from the spot; now there is another who mounts above him, now one who plunges down from on high —yet nothing, nothing whatsoever, not even this last, can awaken him from sleep, disabuse him of his vain imagination, open his eyes to perceive that the whole thing is nothing. But might this really be nothing? Is there need of any better proof that it is not nothing than merely to look at him, how he struggles and fights and craves and aspires, and never grants himself an instant of repose, how many he holds venally in his service, with how many he keeps on good terms that they may be helpful to him in grasping what he aspires after? Might this nevertheless be nothing, might 'nothing' be able to set things thus in motion? Why, then that busy man [1] also must have been in the wrong

[1] A character in Holberg's play, *Den Stundenløse* (The Idler).

when he argues that he had a great deal of business from the fact that he keeps five clerks and himself has no time to eat or drink.

Thus it is the heathen of high estate lives in highness. That there are many beneath him he knows full well; but what he does not know is beneath him, that nevertheless is beneath him —the abyss. For, as has been remarked, when one in highness is above others, or is higher than others, one has also the abyss beneath one, and in earthly highness it is only thus one can be on high. And the heathen of high station, who knows nothing else and has nothing else to think about but his earthly highness, has therefore not present to him the knowledge of the true highness which might keep him suspended aloft in ignorance of the earthly highness. No, he has the abyss beneath him, and from this the anxiety arises, or he sinks into the anxiety.

And what is the anxiety? A longing to become more and more . . . nothing, for it all indeed is nothing; a longing to rise higher and higher in highness, that is, to sink deeper and deeper into the anxiety of the abyss—for what is the anxiety of earthly highness but anxiety of the abyss? And what is this anxiety? The anxiety is lest any one by guile, by might, by lies, or by the truth, might take this vain imagination from him. Hence he secures himself in every way, since he descries danger everywhere, plots everywhere, envy everywhere, ghosts everywhere—naturally enough, for not in the darkest night is there so much that can afright the imagination of even a nervous person, as there are terrors in a vain imagination.

In the end the anxiety devours its prey. As pithless stumps of rotten trees shine in the darkness, as the will-o'-the-wisp glimmers in dank mists, so is he existent for others in the glimmering light of this earthly highness of his. But his self is non-existent, his inmost being has become pithless and corroded in the service of nothingness; the thrall of vanity, having no command of himself, in the power of giddy worldliness, god-forsaken, he ceases to be a man, in his most inward being he is as dead, but his highness walks ghostlike among us—it lives. It is not with a man thou art talking when thou talkest with him; in his hankering after highness he had become the thing he aspired to—he is a title. Within there is mere emptiness and vanity, yea, there is nothing; but the appearance is there, the vain appearance which wears the distinctive insignia of worldly highness, which the passers-by point out with deference—whereas he bears all this business rather as at his burial the cushions bear the medals and decorations. Oh, it may be dreadful to see a man who is almost unrecognizable in his humbleness and wretchedness, to see such wretchedness that one can hardly distinguish a man ; but to see meaningless highness and to perceive that there is no man there, is horrible. It may be dreadful to see a man going about like a shadow of his former highness; but to see worldly highness and within it hardly the shadow of a man, is horrible. Him death does not have to bring to nothing; he does not need to be buried; while he lives one already can say, as is often said at the grave, 'Behold what earthly highness is!'

Let us then in conclusion think of the bird, which had its place in the Gospel and should have a place in the discourse. The bird is on high without the anxiety of highness; the Christian of high station, who in earthly highness is exalted above others, is on high without the anxiety of highness; the heathen of high station belongs with his anxiety to the abyss, he is not really on high but in the abyss. The bird is on high, the Christian of high station is on high, the heathen of high station is in the abyss. The bird's highness is a symbol of the Christian's highness, which in turn is a counterpart of the bird's highness, the one corresponding to the other with perfect understanding, though with endless difference; thou canst understand the bird's highness by understanding that of the Christian, and by understanding the bird's thou canst understand the Christian's; the highness of the heathen is nowhere at home, either in heaven or on earth. The highness of the bird is a shadow, that of the Christian reality, that of the heathen nothingness. The bird has air within it, hence it holds itself aloft; the heathen of high station has emptiness within him, hence his highness is imaginary; the Christian of high station has faith within him, hence he soars above the abyss of earthly highness. The Christian in his highness never forgets the bird, which to him is more than the nautical signal is to the mariner, it is the teacher, and yet, alas, it is in turn a teacher whom the disciple left far behind him as it called out, 'Remember me when thou comest into thy highness'; the heathen of high station never saw the bird. The bird is on high, and yet really is only on the way to highness, and if it could understand this, it must sink; the Christian understands this, and precisely by this understanding attains to highness. There is, however, according to the teaching of Christianity, only one highness, that of being a Christian; and one abyss, heathenism; to that height no bird ever attained, nor ever flew over this abyss. Over this abyss no bird can fly, it must perish on the way; that height no bird can attain, it is only on the way. Thus the bird is happy in its highness, ignorant of the abyss, but also ignorant of blessedness; the Christian is blessed in his highness; the proud heathen is haplessly lost in the abyss.

V

The anxiety of presumption

No one can add a cubit unto his stature—after all such things do the heathen seek.

T HIS *anxiety the lily and the bird have not*; for neither the lily nor the bird is presumptuous. It is not the same with presumptuousness as it was with poverty and abundance, with lowliness and highness. In the former case (to mention only a single instance) poverty was assumed, and the task was to be poor without the anxiety of poverty. But it is not so here, as though it were assumed that a person must be presumptuous, and the task were to be presumptuous without the anxiety of presumption. No, here no situation is posited, the task is, not to be presumptuous; and this is the only way to be without the anxiety of presumption. For poverty and abundance, lowliness and highness, are things in themselves indifferent, innocent things, not what one is entirely responsible for having or for being. Hence the discourse begins with the anxiety, it does not inveigh against poverty or abundance, against lowliness or highness, but against the anxiety. With presumption it is different; no one ever turned out to be presumptuous without being responsible for it, hence the address aims precisely at that, and not so much at the anxiety of presumption. Indeed, if it were possible to accomplish the impossible and remove the anxiety without removing the presumption, the discourse would by no means desire it; hence the anxiety is to be regarded precisely as a curse upon presumptuousness.

The lily and the bird, however, have not this anxiety. Though an individual lily with erect stem shoots up almost to a man's height—it does not crave to add either a cubit or an inch unto its stature, it does not crave anything more; neither is there any presumption in the height it reaches in comparison with other lilies which likewise do not crave this distinction—*that* indeed would be presumption. That the golden sparrow wears all its finery, whereas the grey sparrow is poorly clad, implies no presumption on the part of the golden sparrow; the grey sparrow does not crave it—*that* indeed would be presumption. And when the bird casts itself down from the dizzy height, there is in that no presumption, nor is it tempting God—there is One that bears it up more securely than if all angels were bearing it up lest· it dash its foot against a stone. And even though the bird sees so distinctly that it sees the grass grow, there is no presumption in that, it does not with its sharp sight pry into forbidden knowledge; nor when it sees clearly in the darkness of the night, for it employs no unlawful means. And though the bird is ignorant of God, there is no presumption in that; for it is innocently ignorant, not spiritlessly ignorant.

So then, neither the bird nor the lily is guilty of any presumption, and therefore self-evidently they are without the anxiety of presumption. How does this come about? It comes from the fact that the bird and the lily *constantly will as God wills and constantly do as God wills*. Because the bird constantly wills as God wills, therefore it enjoys without anxiety all its freedom. And so, when it is flying in the air at its best, and gets a notion that it would like to sit down, down it sits on a branch, and this (yes, here comes the strange part)—this is precisely what God would have it do. And then when one morning it wakes and makes up its mind, 'Today thou must travel,' it accordingly travels many, many hundreds of miles, and (yes, here comes the strange part)—this is precisely what God would have it do. Heavy as the stork is, it travels the long road thither and the long road back, it never takes it differently than precisely as it does now; it knows no other road than precisely this one on which it travels now; it takes no observations of the road for the sake of the next journey, no note of time for the sake of the next journey; it engages in no deliberation before, and in none afterwards. But then, when one morning it wakes, that same morning it journeys, and this then was precisely what God would have it do. A man usually needs long deliberation and preparation for a journey, and yet perhaps rarely has any one ever undertaken a journey with such assurance that it is God's will, as the bird when it journeys. Good luck to thee then, thou hasty traveller, if thou hast any need of our good wishes! Men have envied thee, they have envied thine easy conveyance through the air—if I were to envy thee, I should envy the sureness with which thou dost always do so precisely that which is God's will for thee! With regard to subsistence, it is true that thou hast it only from hand to mouth; ah, but then again thou hast a still shorter way from thought to execution, from resolution to the decisive act! Hence thine inexplicable sureness! Thou art happily hindered from being able to be presumptuous.—Because the lily constantly wills as God wills and constantly does as God wills, therefore it enjoys its happy existence without anxiety, being beautiful without the knowledge which desecrates beauty. And then when it thinks it has been standing long enough looking like a dunce, it one day throws off all its outer garments and stands forth in all its beauty, and this (yes, here comes the strange part)—this is precisely what God would have it do. It never occurs to the lily to wish to wear its finery at any other season or day than precisely when God wills.—And because it is thus with the lily and the bird, it is as if God, were He to speak about them, would say, 'After all, the lilies and the birds are the children in whom I have most joy, they are the easiest to bring up, they are thoroughly good natured and never naughty; they constantly will what I will and constantly do what I will; in them I have nothing but pleasure.' And He has no need to add, as parents commonly do, 'I hope it will continue thus.'

But how then are the lilies and the birds teachers? This surely is easy to perceive. It is perfectly certain that neither the lilies nor the birds permit themselves the least act of presumption—so be thou like the lilies and the birds. For in their relationship to God the lilies and the birds are like a child in its tender years when it still is practically one with the mother. But when the child has become bigger, although it is in the house of its parents, as close to them as can be, never out of their sight, there is nevertheless an endless distance between it and the parents, and in this distance lies the possibility of being able to be presumptuous. Though the mother grasps the child, though she folds it in her arms in order by her closeness to insure it completely against every danger, nevertheless, in the possibility of being able to be presumptuous, it is endlessly far away from her. It is an immense distance, an immense remoteness. For surely he too lives remote who lives in the old familiar place but remote from his only wish—so also the child, although in the home of its parents, is remote by reason of this possibility of being able to act presumptuously.

And so also the man, in the possibility of being able to act presumptuously, is endlessly remote from God, in whom nevertheless he lives and moves and has his being. But if again he comes, from this remoteness and in this remoteness, anything like so near as the bird and the lily, then he has become a Christian.

The Christian has not this anxiety. Yet what is presumptuousness?—for it is about this we are talking, about not being presumptuous. What presumptuousness is, that is to say, what the particular expressions of it are, we shall learn to recognize better when we are speaking about the heathen, who have in fact this anxiety. But here we have to know provisionally what presumptuousness is in order to see that the Christian is not presumptuous, or that precisely by never being presumptuous in the least degree he is a Christian. Presumption essentially has to do with a man's relationship to God, and hence it is indifferent whether a man is presumptuous in the smallest matter or in the greatest, for even the least presumption is the greatest, being against God. Presumption is essentially against God, and from this is derived the secondary but correct use of the word when we say that a child acts presumptuously towards the parents, a subject towards the king, a pupil towards the teacher. Between God and man there is the everlasting and essential difference of eternity; and when this distinction is in any way encroached upon, we have presumption. Presumption therefore is *either*, in a forbidden, in a rebellious, in an ungodly way, *to want to have God's help, or* in a forbidden, in a rebellious, in an ungodly way, *to want to dispense with God's help*.

Therefore, first and foremost, it is presumptuous to be spiritlessly ignorant of how much a man needs God's help every instant, and that without God he is nothing. So perhaps it is that many men are living, lost in worldliness and sensuality. They think they understand life and themselves, and yet they have left out God entirely; but they are only too self-assured, they are just like the others—they are in fact, if one may say so, false reprints; for every man as he comes from God's hand is an original edition. If then one were to reproach them for acting presumptuously towards God, they would surely reply, 'That really is a thing that never occurred to us.' But precisely this is the presumption, that it never occurred to them . . . to think of

God; or if once in their youth they had been required to think of the Creator, this then is the presumption, that they have subsequently forgotten Him entirely—worse than the beast, for the beast has nothing to forget.

But the Christian knows that a sense of the need of God is man's perfection. Thus the Christian is *once for all* aware of God and is saved from the presumption which might be called ungodly unawareness. The Christian is not aware of God once in a while during his life, on the occasion of great events and such like; no, with daily attentiveness he is aware that he cannot do without God for an instant. Thus the Christian is awake, as neither the innocent bird is, nor the man who is spiritlessly ignorant; he is awake, awakened to God. The Christian is awake, and he is incessantly awake to God's will, he craves only *to be satisfied with God's grace*; he does not ask that he may help himself, but prays for God's grace, nor does he ask that God should help him otherwise than as God wills, he prays only to be satisfied with God's grace. The Christian has no self-will, he surrenders unconditionally.[1] But again in relation to God's grace he has no self-will, he is satisfied with God's grace. He accepts everything by God's grace . . . even the grace itself; he understands that he cannot do without God's grace even in praying for His grace. So weakened is the Christian in respect to self-will that in relation to God's grace he is weaker than is the bird in relation to instinct which holds it entirely in its power, is weaker than the bird is strong in relation to instinct, which is its power.

But then at bottom the Christian is farther from presumption towards God than the bird is? Yes, that he is too, in spite of the fact that in the possibility of being able to act presumptuously he was infinitely nearer to it than the bird. But to this end the Christian must *learn* slowly, as the bird is under no necessity of doing, since it finds it easy enough only to will as God wills. The Christian must learn to be satisfied with God's grace, to which end sometimes an angel of Satan may be necessary to smite him upon the mouth lest he exalt himself. For first he must learn to be satisfied with God's grace; but when he is in the course of learning this there comes the last difficulty. Namely, the discovery that to be satisfied with God's grace, which at first sight appears so poor and humiliating a thing, is in reality the highest

---

[1] 'For grace or ungrace' is the Danish idiom.

and most blessed thing—is there in fact any higher good than God's grace? Hence he must learn not to exalt himself, not to be presumptuous . . . at being satisfied with God's grace.

So the Christian, being schooled thus from the ground up, is far more remote from presumption towards God than the bird is—how might it be possible to be presumptuous towards Him whose will is grace? But only the Christian knows that God's will is grace, the bird knows at the most that its will is His will. The Christian is far more remote from presumption, and precisely for this cause far nearer to God than the bird is. That there is a God in heaven without whose will no sparrow falls to the ground, concerns also the sparrow; but that there is a gracious God in heaven concerns only the Christian. The bird keeps close to God by willing as He wills; but the Christian keeps still closer to Him by keeping hold of His grace—just as the older but obedient child who desires to please his parents has in a more heartfelt sense the love of the parents and an existence for them than has the tender babe which is one with the mother. The bird with its need is as close as it can be, it can by no means do without Him; the Christian needs Him even more, he *knows* that he cannot do without Him; the Christian is still closer, he cannot do without . . . His grace. God encompasses the bird on every side, but holds Himself back; for the Christian He opens Himself, and His *grace* encompasses the Christian on every side who in nothing is presumptuous, who desires nothing but His grace and never desires anything but His grace. Thus God's grace encompasses the Christian blessedly and closely, and keeps far from him the least expression of presumption. 'His grace *prevents* the Christian' (Ps. lix. 10), so that he may will to be satisfied with God's grace, and *follows* him, so that he may not have willed in vain, and that in his bliss he may never regret that he was satisfied with God's grace.[1]

The heathen on the contrary has this anxiety; for in reality the heathen is presumptuous and rebellious against God.

First and foremost we mention the presumption of *spiritless-*

---

[1] This is the thought expressed in the Collect for the Seventeenth Sunday after Trinity: 'that God's grace may always prevent and follow us'. In other contexts S. K. insisted upon the importance of prevenient grace, 'grace in the first instance', as he called it, whereas 'grace in the second instance' might be abused as a dispensation.

ness [1] in being ignorant of God, a presumption which strictly speaking only occurs in Christendom. It is quite possible that such a heathen, lost in worldliness and sensuality, supposes that he is without anxieties, especially the many useless anxieties with which the God-fearing man plagues himself. But this is not true. It may well be true that he is without these anxieties with which the God-fearing man plagues himself, and that this is an advantage to him both in this life and in that which is to come; but it is not true that the heathen in his torpid security is without anxiety. On the contrary, he precisely is under the dominion of anguishing *dread*, [2] dreading to live—and dreading to die. Whenever some event or the expectation of it wrenches him out of his brute-transformation, dread which dwells deeply within him awakens and casts him into despair, in which essentially he was.

So presumption is dull ignorance of God. To such a heathen aptly applies what is related in the parable about the husband-men who appropriated the vineyard and behaved as if the owner were not in existence; and in so far as he is instructed in Christianity, that also applies to him where it is related that they said, 'Let us kill the son, and then the vineyard will be ours.' The life of every man is God's property, man is His bondservant. To kill God, however, is what man cannot do, what he can do is to kill the thought of Him, as they say, and the man who is dully unconscious of God has at one time been conscious of Him, and so, as one says with special emphasis, he has got rid of this thought, slain it. So when one has succeeded in killing the thought of God, suppressing every feeling and mood which as His messenger would remind man of Him, one lives on as if one were one's own master, were the artificer of his own fortune, whether he be one who actually has to provide for himself, or one to whom everything comes as his due—thus cheating God of His due. Is not this also a way of desiring to add a cubit unto one's stature—by getting the proprietor killed, or the thought of him, so as to become oneself the master instead of the bond-servant? In dull ignorance of God and in vain knowledge of

---

[1] Such is the literal meaning, which I must call attention to here where the word is emphasized. It may mean merely dullness, shallowness.

[2] *Angest* (*Angst*) had best be translated by 'dread'—but with the understanding that this is inadequate. It is the theme of *The Concept of Dread* and despair is the theme of *The Sickness unto Death*.

the world the heathen thus sinks below the beast. To murder God is the most horrible form of suicide, entirely to forget God is man's deepest fall, no beast ever fell so deep as that.

The other form of presumption is that which in a forbidden, a rebellious, and ungodly way, would do without God. This is *unbelief*. Unbelief is not dull ignorance, unbelief would positively deny God, so in a way it has to deal with God.

It may well be that such a heathen declares that he is without anxiety. But it is not so, as in general it is indeed impossible to be presumptuous without having the anxiety of presumption. However he may harden himself, he yet carries in his inmost heart the token that God is the strongest, the token that he *wills* to have God against him. If the God-fearing man 'halts upon his thigh' after having striven with God, truly the unbeliever is inwardly annihilated. And, precisely, his anxiety is to add a cubit unto his stature; for it would be adding an immense cubit unto his stature if a man face to face with God were able to deny God, or if it might even be so that perhaps it is God who stands in need of man (as the wisdom of this age has understood it—if such a thing can be understood) . . . in order to understand Himself. But it is certain that no blessing goes with stolen goods and that no prescriptive right can be acquired over them, and so the presumptuous man has the anxiety, and has it every instant, that God may take everything from him. And if it is easy to labour when one has God for a helper, verily the hardest labour one can impose upon oneself is the labour of doing without God.

Hence the heathen is really under the dominion of dread; for really he never rightly knows under whose dominion he is—is not this a dreadful anguish? Although an unbeliever, he scarcely knows whether he is under the sway of incredulity or of credulity —and verily it is exceedingly difficult for another man to know this Forsaken of God whom he would deny, overwhelmed by God whom he would dispense with, he is without resource either in God or in himself (for in oneself one has no resource without God's concourse), under the domination of the power of evil, the domination of incredulity and credulity. In such wise no bird is tossed about even in the most terrible tempest.

Finally, this too is a form of presumption: in a forbidden, a rebellious, and ungodly way, to desire to have God's aid. This is superstition.

In this way the presumptuous heathen would senselessly add a cubit unto his stature, would senselessly will what he denies, in blind confidence would risk a foolhardy act and cast himself down from the pinnacle of the Temple—and what is more presumptuous still, he expects God to help him in it; abandoning himself more and more to this hapless game, he would by illicit means penetrate forbidden places, discover hidden things, behold the future, perhaps, like that Simon of whom the Scripture tells, he would purchase the Holy Ghost with money, or would make money by means of the Holy Ghost, he would be importunate with God, would importune His aid and assistance, he the uncalled would make himself what only God's call can make a man. For the unbeliever would presumptuously dispense with God, is unwilling to let himself be helped by God, and would presumptuously let God know it; but the superstitious man would have God serve him. What else does it mean but that, even though the superstitious man says that it is God's help he would have—when he arbitrarily will have it, what else is this but to will that God shall serve him? Truly that would be adding a cubit to one's stature if a man were to reach the point of being so extraordinary as to have God for a servant. But God will not be mocked. Where therefore is anxiety and dread and pallid fear and the apprehensive shudder more at home than in the mumbling realm of superstition? This dread no bird has known, not even the bird that is startled anxiously in alarm.

So it is with the presumptuous heathen. He does not will as God wills (like the bird); still less is he willing to be satisfied with God's grace (like the Christian); 'on him abideth the wrath of God'. If the bird has not God's grace, which only the Christian has, neither has it, verily, God's wrath, which only the heathen has. However far the bird flies it never loses its relation to God; but how far should the heathen have to fly! and fly as far as he may, he would fly in vain to escape God's wrath—fly as far as he may, unless he were fleeing [1] to grace. And if there is to be retribution and anguish upon every soul of man that worketh evil, then first and foremost upon the presumptuous man. For as grace comes by God upon every man who approaches Him as a Christian, so anguish comes by itself upon every one who pre-

[1] In Danish *flyve* means to flee as well as to fly.

sumptuously departs from God or presumptuously approaches Him.

Let us in conclusion think of the bird, which had its place in the Gospel and should have a place in the discourse. Let there be joy upon earth over the lilies and the birds which will as God wills and do as God wills; in heaven there is joy over the Christian who is satisfied with God's grace; but there is anguish both here and hereafter upon the heathen who is presumptuous. The nearer the bird is to the Christian, so much farther than the bird is the heathen from God. The greatest distance, greater than that of the farthest star from the earth, greater than human art can depict, is the distance from God's grace to God's wrath, from the Christian to the heathen, from being saved in bliss by God's grace to 'eternal destruction from the face of the Lord', from looking to God . . . to seeing from the abyss that one has lost God. It would be a meaningless jest were one seriously to make use of the situation of the bird in order to depict that distance. Solely in comparison with the bird can the Christian use this situation as a landmark, but if the distance is Christian—heathen, the bird serves to determine nothing; for here it is not poverty and abundance that is in question, nor lowliness and highness, but presumption.

VI

The anxiety of self-torment

Be not therefore anxious for the morrow—after all such things do the heathen seek.

THIS anxiety the bird has not. From whatever height the bird surveyed the whole world, and whatever it saw, it never saw 'the next day'; whatever it saw on its long journeys, it never saw 'the next day'. And though we say of the lily, 'it today is, and tomorrow is cast into the oven'—oh, this noble and simple sage, the lily, is as one whom this does not concern, however much and however closely it concerns it; it is solely preoccupied with that which after all concerns it more closely, that it *is* today! However many days the bird saw dawn and come to a close, it never saw 'the next day'. For the bird sees no apparitions—but the next day is to be seen only 'in the spirit'; and the bird is not troubled by dreams—but the next day is a persistent dream which constantly returns; and the bird is never disquieted—but the next day is the disquietude of every day. And when the bird makes the long flight to the distant clime, it is the very bird which arrived that same day at its destination, the self-same day it departed from home. One travels so swiftly by railway that one arrives at a distant place the same day; but the bird is nimbler and swifter, it travels for many, many days and arrives the same day. By railway one cannot travel so quickly as that if one is to travel equally far. No, there is none can make time fly so swiftly as the bird, and none that in so short a time can get so far as the bird. There is no yesterday and no tomorrow for the bird, it lives but one day, and the lily blooms but one day.

Consequently the bird has no anxiety for the next day. But anxiety for the next day is precisely what self-torment is, and hence the bird is without the anxiety of self-torment. For what is self-torment? It is the worry which today (having enough worry of its own) does not have. And what is it to be a self-tormentor? It is to cause oneself this worry? For the bird also has worry the one day it lives, the day may have for it too enough worry of its own; but the worry of the next day the bird does not have—because it lives but one day, which we might express also in another way, by saying that it has no self. Worry and today are in correspondence with one another; self-torment and the next day are also a pair.

But how then is the bird a teacher? Quite simply. That the bird has no next day is sure enough—so then, be thou like the bird, get rid of the next day, and thus thou art without the anxiety of self-torment; and this must be practicable, precisely for the reason that the next day is derived from the self. On the other hand, if we let today disappear almost entirely in comparison with the next day's worry, we are deepest in self-torment. The whole difference is that of only one day—and yet what an immense difference! It is easy enough for the bird to *be* quit of the next—but to *become* quit of it! Oh, of all the enemies which assail a man by might or by cunning, none perhaps is so obstinately intrusive as this next day, which always is the same next day. It is said that to conquer one's spirit is greater than to take a city; but if one is to conquer his spirit, he must begin by *becoming* quit of the next day. The next day—it is like a goblin which is able to assume every form, it looks so exceedingly different, but for all that it is . . . the next day.

The Christian has not this anxiety. Anxiety for the next day is commonly associated with anxiety for subsistence. This is a very superficial view. All earthly and worldly anxiety is at bottom anxiety for the next day. Earthly and worldly anxiety is rendered possible by the fact that man, compounded of the temporal and the eternal, became a self; [1] but in becoming a self the next day became existent for him. And here it is fundamentally that the battle is fought. Ah, worldly and earthly anxiety!—at the mere mention of that word what an immense miscellany is suggested, what a motley crowd of passions, what a mixture of opposites! And yet it is all only one battle, the battle with the next day. And the next day—a little hamlet as it were, which yet became famous and remains so; for it was and is at this point that the greatest battle is fought and the most decisive, here the decision is made between time and eternity. The next day—it is the grappling-hook by which the prodigious hulk of anxiety gets a hold upon

[1] This theme is prominent in *The Sickness unto Death.*

'the individual's' light craft. If it succeeds, then he is under the domination of that power. The next day is the first link of the chain which fetters a man in a gang with thousands to that superfluous anxiety which is of the evil one. The next day—it is strange indeed, for ordinarily when one is sentenced for life the sentence reads, 'for life', but he who sentences himself to anxiety 'for the next day', sentences himself for life. Behold therefore if in heaven there might not be found salvation from the next day, for on earth it is not to be found; not even by dying the next day dost thou avoid it, for it was until that day thou didst live. But if for thee there is no next day, then all earthly anxiety is annihilated —and not only the anxiety about subsistence, for everything earthly and worldly is desirable only for the sake of the next day . . . and is uncertain by reason of the next day; the next day it loses its enchantment and its anxious uncertainty. And if for thee there is no next day, thou art either a dying man, or one who by dying to the temporal hast grasped the eternal, either one who really is dying or one who *really* lives.

The Gospel says that 'every day has enough worries of its own'. But is this a gospel? It seems rather as if it were from a book of lamentations, in fact it makes the whole of life sheer worry, or admits that it is such, if every day has worry enough. One would think indeed that the Gospel must proclaim that every day was free from worry, or that there were individual unlucky days. Nevertheless it is a gospel, and verily it does not strain out a gnat to swallow a camel; for it is levelled against the monster of self-torment, and it assumes that with the daily worries a man can manage to get along. It says therefore in effect, every day *shall* have its worries. It is true, this word does not stand in the Gospel; but this stands there: 'for the morrow *shall* be anxious for itself'; but if it shall be anxious for itself, thou shalt be without anxiety for it and let it take care of itself. So, as far as worry is concerned, thou *shalt* have enough in that which each day has, since thou *shalt* let the next day take care of itself. Is not this so? When the teacher says to the pupil, 'Thou shalt leave thy neighbour in peace. Let him take care of himself,' he says in effect, 'Thou hast enough to do to look after thyself, and this *shall* be enough for thee.' Every day shall have its worry, that is to say, take care to be free from the next day's worry, accept tranquilly and gratefully the worry of today, thou dost get off easily with that . . . by becoming free from the next day's worry. Be thou therefore content, have godliness with contentment; for every day has *enough* of its own worries. In this respect also God provides: He measures out the amount of worry which is *enough* for every day, so take no more than what is measured out, which is exactly enough; to be anxious for the next day is covetousness.

The most important thing in life is to be in the correct position, to assume the correct position. This the Christian assumes in relation to the next day; for to him it is non-existent.—It is well known that in front of the actor, blinded as he is by the footlights, there is the deepest darkness, the blackest night. One might think that this would discompose him, render him uneasy. But no, ask him, and thou shalt hear him admit that this is precisely what gives him support, makes him calm, keeps him in the enchantment of deception. On the other hand, it would discompose him if he could see any single individual, catch a glimpse of an auditor. So it is with the next day. One sometimes complains and finds it tragic that the future is so dark before one. Ah, the misfortune is just this, that it is not dark enough when fear and presentiment and expectation and earthly impatience glimpse the next day! One who rows a boat turns his back to the goal towards which he labours. So it is with the next day. When by the help of eternity a man lives absorbed in today, he turns his back to the next day. The more he is eternally absorbed in today, the more decisively does he turn his back upon the next day, so that he does not see it at all. If he turns around, eternity is confused before his eyes, it becomes the next day. But if for the sake of labouring more effectually towards the goal (eternity) he turns his back, he does not see the next day at all, whereas by the help of eternity he sees quite clearly today and its task. But if a man is to labour effectually today, he must be in this position. It always involves delay and distraction to want to look impatiently every instant towards the goal, to see if one is coming a little nearer, and now a little nearer. No, be eternally and seriously resolved, then thou dost turn completely to the labour . . . and turn the back to the goal. Such is one's position in rowing a boat, but such is also the position when one believes. One might think that the believer would be very far from the eternal when he turns his back to it and lives today, while the glimpser stands and looks towards it. And yet it is the believer who is nearest the eternal, while the apocalyptic visionary is farthest from the eternal. Faith turns its back to the eternal in order precisely to have this with him today. But if a man turns, especially with earthly passion, towards the future, then he is farthest from the eternal, and then the next day becomes a prodigious confused figure such as fairy-tales describe. Just as those demons of whom we read in the Book of Genesis begat children by earthly women, so is the future the monstrous demon which of men's womanish imagination begets the next day.

But the Christian believes, therefore he is quit of the next day. The Christian assumes exactly the opposite position to that of the self-tormentors; for these forget today entirely by reason of their anxiety and preoccupation with the next day. The believer is present, and at the same time is, as this word also denotes in Latin, mighty. The self-tormentor is an absentee, and an enfeebled person. The wish is often heard in the world to be contemporary with one or another great event or great man, with the notion that contemporaneousness might develop a man and make him something great. Perhaps! But might it not be worth more than a wish to be contemporary with oneself? For how rare it is for a man to be contemporary with himself. Most men, in feeling, in imagination, in purpose, in resolution, in wish, in longing, in apocalyptic vision, in theatrical make-believe, are a hundred thousand miles in advance of themselves, or several human generations in advance of themselves. But the believer (being present) is in the highest sense contemporary with himself. And to be by the help of eternity entirely contemporary with oneself is at the same time the thing that most educates and develops, it is the 'great gain' of eternity. Therefore the Christian extols a saying of Sirach (xxx. 23), as one of the severest of the Church Fathers does, not as a rule of shrewdness but as an expression of godliness: 'Love thy soul, and comfort thy heart, and drive care far from thee.' Who indeed is so cruel as the self-tormentor is towards himself! But all his pangs, all these cruelly invented and cruelly employed instruments of agonizing torture are comprised in this one word: the next day. And now for the cure of it! It is related that in a library in Spain there was found a book bearing this inscription on the cover: 'The Best

Cure for Heretics'. One opened it, or rather tried to; and, lo, it was not a book, it was a case containing a scourge. If one were to write a book entitled 'The Best Cure for Self-Torment', it could be written briefly: 'Let every day have enough in its own worries.' Hence when the Christian works, or when he prays, he talks only of today: he prays for the daily bread 'today', for a blessing upon his work 'today', that he may avoid the snares of the evil one 'today', that he may come nearer to God's kingdom 'today'. For if a man who had become acquainted with this terror were to pray thus in the passion of his soul, 'Save me, O God, from myself and from the next day', he would not be praying Christianly, and the next day would already have acquired too much power over him. For the Christian prays, 'Save me today from the evil.' This is the surest salvation from the next day, with the understanding that one will pray thus every day; if for one day this is forgotten, the next day comes at once into view. But the Christian does not forget to pray every day, hence he saves himself throughout his life, faith saves his courage, his joy, his hope. The dreadful enemy is on hand the next day, but the Christian does not paint the devil on the wall, does not conjure up evil and temptation, he does not talk at all of the next day, but only of today, and of this he talks with God.

To live thus, to cram today with eternity and not with the next day, the Christian has learnt and continues to learn (for the Christian is always learning) from the Pattern. How did He manage to live without anxiety for the next day—He who from the first instant of His public life when He stepped forward as a teacher knew how His life would end, that the next day was His crucifixion, knew this while the people exultantly hailed Him as King (ah, bitter knowledge to have at precisely that moment!), knew when they were crying, 'Hosanna!', at His entry into Jerusalem that they would cry, 'Crucify him!', and that it was to this end He made His entry; He who bore every day the prodigious weight of this superhuman knowledge—how did He manage to live without anxiety for the next day? He who did not suffer as the man suffers upon whom hardships and adversity suddenly fall but who has before him every instant the possibility that everything nevertheless might be redressed—for He knew that it was inevitable; He who knew that with every new sacrifice He made in behalf of the truth He was hastening His persecution and destruction, so that He had control of His fate, could ensure for Himself the splendour of royal power and the devout admiration of the race if He would let go of the truth, but knew also with even greater certainty that He would ensure His destruction, if (oh, eternally certain way to destruction!) He were in any respect to desert the truth—how did He manage to live without anxiety for the next day?—He who was not unacquainted with the suffering attendant upon this anxiety any more than with every other human suffering, He who in an access of pain uttered the sigh, that His hour was not yet come. In military language they talk of 'covering' the commander of an army, of covering him so that no one may fall upon him in the rear—how did He manage to cover Himself, while He was living today, from the enemy which would fall upon Him in the rear, namely, the next day? For just because, in quite a different way from any man, He had eternity with Him in the day that is called today, just for this reason He turned His back on the next day. How did He manage it? Far be it from us to endeavour to win human admiration by fathoming what is not to be fathomed; we do not believe that He came to this earth to propose to us themes for a learned investigation. But He came to this earth to prescribe the task, to leave behind Him a foot-print, so that we might learn from Him. We have therefore let the answer transpire in the question, have recalled how it was He managed to do what we should learn to do: He had Eternity with Him in the day that is called today, hence the next day had no power over Him, it had no existence for Him. It had no power over Him before it came, and when it came and was the day that is called today it had no other power over Him than that which was the Father's will, to which He had consented with eternal freedom, and to which He obediently bowed.

The heathen, on the other hand, has this anxiety; for heathenism is precisely self-torment. Instead of casting all his care upon God, the heathen has all the worries; he is without God, and hence he is the worried man, the self-tormentor. For since he is without God, it cannot in any sense be God that imposes worry upon him. The situation is not this: without God—no worry, with God—with worry; but it is this: with God—no worry, without God—with worry.

'Let us eat and drink, for tomorrow we die.' But then indeed the heathen is without anxiety for the next day, in fact he says himself that there is no next day! No—verily he does not deceive Christianity, neither does he succeed in deceiving himself. For just this sort of talk is vibrant with the dread of the next day, the day of annihilation, an anguishing dread which, although it is a shriek from the abyss, is madly meant to indicate joy. He is so much in dread of the next day that he casts himself into wild befuddlement in order to forget it . . . and to forget how much in dread he is. Is this what it means to be without anxiety for the next day? If there is anything this is 'without', it is without understanding, it means to be insane. And 'tomorrow' is thus the refrain of the day's joy, the verse regularly ends with, 'for tomorrow'. One speaks, it is true, of a *joie de vivre* which, because it has no next day, lives, so it is said, entirely for today. But this is a delusion, for this precisely is the way a man is rendered unable to live in the day that is called today, not to speak of living in it *entirely*. A man has the eternal within him, and therefore he cannot possibly be entirely in the purely momentary. The more effort he makes to do without the eternal, so much the farther he is from living in the day that is called today. Whether the heathen is to die tomorrow, we may leave undetermined, certain it is that he does not *live* today.

'But tomorrow!' For as the Christian constantly talks of today, so the heathen talks only of tomorrow. In reality it is of no consequence to him what today is; whether it be joyful or sorrowful, lucky or unlucky, he cannot reach the point of either enjoying it or employing it, for he cannot get away from the invisible writing on the wall: Tomorrow. Tomorrow I shall perhaps hunger, even if I did not today; tomorrow a thief will perhaps steal my riches, or a slanderer my honour, corruption my beauty, the envy of fate my good fortune—tomorrow, tomorrow! Today I stand upon the pinnacle of fortune—ah, recount to me while it is still today a misfortune—quickly, quickly!—else tomorrow everything will be lost irrevocably. What is dread? It is the next day. And why was the heathen most in dread when he was most fortunate? Because adversity and misfortune might have served in a way to quench the fire of his earthly anxiety. For earthly anxiety, as the begetter, brings forth dread, which in turn, as the nourisher, brings forth anxieties. For to bring embers to a flame a draught is necessary. But desire (the earthly) and uncertainty (the earthly)

—these two currents—constitute precisely the draught which inflames the fire of passion in which dread lurks.

With whom is it then the heathen strives in dread? With himself, with an imagination; for the next day is an impotent nothing if thou dost not thyself give it thy strength. And in case thou dost give it all thy strength, then, like the heathen, thou dost get to know in a terrible way how strong thou art—for what a prodigious power this next day is! The next day, which the heathen with terror in his heart advances to meet, resisting like one who is dragged to the place of execution, vainly striving like one who from a wreck stretches out his arms in desperation to the land, inconsolable like one who from the land sees his whole fortune sink into the sea!

Thus it is the heathen consumes himself, or the next day consumes him. Alas, there a human soul *went out*, he lost his self. No one knows how it happened; there was no neediness, nor misfortune, nor adversity, no one beheld the terrible power which consumed the man, but he was consumed. Like a hapless spirit which found no repose in the grave, so he lives as a ghost, that is to say, he does not live. As one speaks of intemperately turning night into day, so he in despair would turn today into the next day. 'He will not live till the next day', we say of the sick man whom the physician has given up; but at least the sick man lives today. The self-tormentor, on the other hand, in a still more precise sense will not live till the next day, he is given up, since he gave up God, he does not even live today, in spite of being alive, and still less until tomorrow, for in order to live till tomorrow one must surely be alive today. Like the bird which flies to a painted landscape on the wall in order to perch upon one of the trees, and exhausts itself, perhaps kills itself by wanting to perch upon one of these trees—so the self-tormentor renders himself inanimate by wanting today to live the next day. Like the bird which grew weary on its way over the great ocean and sinks with a feeble flap of its wings to the sea, and now can neither live nor die—so it is with the self-tormentor, who grows weary on his way across the distance between today and the next day. To live is to be in existence today; when one is dead there is no longer a today. But the self-tormentor lives—only not today, he lives not till tomorrow, yet he lives day after day. Upon him the good Lord cannot shed light, for all remains equally dark about him and equally hopeless, whether he be living or dead, who neither lives nor dies, and yet lives . . . as in a hell.

Let us in conclusion think of the bird, which had its place in the Gospel and should have a place in the discourse. The bird arrives the same day at its far-off destination; the Christian is the same day, 'this very day', in heaven where his life is; the heathen never budges from the spot. The bird is an egoist in a good sense, reasonably loving itself, hence it is no self-tormentor; the Christian loves God, hence he is no self-tormentor; the heathen (which God forbid and does indeed forbid) hates himself, he is a self-tormentor. The bird lives only one day, so the next day does not exist for it; the Christian lives eternally, so the next day does not exist for him; the heathen never lives, is always by the next day prevented from living. The bird is exempt from all dread; benediction upon the Christian saves him from all dread; the anxiety of the heathen is his punishment: self-torment—no sin so punishes itself as self-torment.

VII

THE ANXIETY OF IRRESOLUTION, FICKLENESS
AND DISCONSOLATENESS

No man can serve two masters [1]—after all such things do the heathen seek.

THAT anxiety the bird has not. If the angels are God's messengers who obey His every behest, if He makes use of the winds as His angels—the bird and the lily are just as obedient, although God does not employ them as His messengers and it is as if He had no use for them. The lily and the bird have no occasion to become self-important in view of the use that is made of them, they feel humiliated, as though they were superfluous. Yet they are not less dear to God on this account, nor is it the lowliest fortune to be superfluous. In man's busy life it is no rare occurrence that precisely the unusually talented person is more or less superfluous because he is not apt to fit into any of all the situations to which the bustle of business would assign him, with which it would occupy him and employ him—and yet precisely his superfluousness does more to magnify the Creator's honour than does all the self-importance of bustle; just as Mary did Christ more honour by sitting at His feet than did the activity of busy Martha—thus the lilies and the birds are a superfluity of beauty and joy which God has lavished upon creation. But just because they are thus superfluous there is required of them also the most perfect obedience. True, all that is is of grace; but he who owes everything to grace in such a degree that he understands he is superfluous must be all the more obedient.[2] True, all that exists is nothing in the hands of the Almighty who created it out of nothing; but that which by coming into existence attains

---

[1] The second of the 'Godly Discourses' about *The Lilies and the Birds* in this volume shows how diversely S. K. was capable of writing about the same theme. A more pungent exposition is to be found in the Second Part of *Judge for Yourselves*, which will be published before long.

[2] Such comfort in the consciousness of being superfluous S. K. had reason to apply to himself, seeing that in this busy world he was a superfluity, or was so regarded.

nothing more than to be superfluous must understand most profoundly that it is nothing. When parents give an entertainment for their own children they expect joyful obedience, or the joy which is obedience; but when they give an entertainment for poor children, doing everything for them just as if they were their own children, they expect still more decisively the joy whose secret is unconditional obedience.

But precisely thus are the lilies and the birds situated, serving only one Master, without a thought of any other, and without a single thought which is not directed to Him, more obedient in His hand than the pliable plant in the hands of the gardener, more obedient to His every behest than the tamed dove to its master. Everything that is called bird and lily belongs to one Master, but every bird and every lily serves only this one Master.

Hence the bird is never *irresolute*. It is not a sign of irresolution that the bird flies hither and thither; exactly the opposite is the case, for it is perfectly certain that it is for joy; it is not the uncertain flight of irresoluteness, it is the light soaring flight of complete obedience. True, the bird is soon weary of its place of residence and flies far away, but this is not *fickleness*, it is exactly the opposite, it is the fixed and firm resolution of perfect obedience; rarely perhaps was any man's resolution so fixed and stood so firm. True, one sometimes sees the bird sitting dejectedly,[1] it must have care and sorrow, but this is not *disconsolateness*: never is the obedient bird without consolation, and essentially its life is care-free, just because it serves only one master, and this is what is of most service both to bird and man, it serves to free them from sorrowing disconsolately.

How is it then that the birds and the lilies are teachers? Quite simply. The birds and the lilies serve only one Master, and, what is the same thing, they serve Him wholly—so be thou like the lilies and the birds, serve thou also only one Master, serve Him with all thy heart and with all thy soul and with all thy strength, and so thou too art without anxiety. More noble than the birds and the lilies, thou art akin to that Master (the lilies and the birds are like the poor children), but none the less thou dost obediently serve the same Master, if like the lilies and the birds thou dost serve Him wholly.

The Christian has not this anxiety. 'No man can serve two

---

[1] Literally, 'down at the beak', an idiomatic expression for dejection in man.

masters,' or there is only one master whom a man can serve *wholly*. For in the choice between two masters it is not true that if only a man chooses one of the two and then serves him, no matter which, he is thus serving only one master. No, there is only One who in such wise is Master, is the Lord,[1] that in serving Him one serves one master; and so it is clear enough that, if 'there is one Lord' only, one does not serve one master if one does not serve Him! It is not true therefore that one who has chosen to serve mammon wholly, serves only one master; against his will he is none the less in the service of the other master, in the Lord's service. If a man chooses another master than God, he must hate God, for 'either he will love the one and hate the other', that is, if he loves the one he must hate the other; but however much he may hate God, he nevertheless does not escape His service, and so he is not serving one master after all. A man's relationship to God in service is not the relationship of a man and his manservant who can run away from his service, and so far away that his former master cannot catch him, or may even take refuge in a relationship so altered that the former master must relinquish his claim upon him. No, a man who has chosen to serve another master than 'the Master', however desperate and determined his will may be, remains nevertheless in the service of two masters. And just this self-contradiction is his punishment, the contradiction of willing the impossible—for it is impossible to serve two masters. But only then is it possible to serve one master when one has chosen *wholly* to serve 'the Master' (the Lord). It looks almost like trying to impose upon one, it is almost as if the Gospel were disposed to behave with human high-handedness when it says: 'One of the two thou must choose.' Oh, but just here is the terrible seriousness of eternity in sticking to its position; for only the one canst thou choose in such a way that in serving Him thou dost serve only one master. Hence it is not true that he who comes to an agreement with himself to doubt serves only one master, doubt; for to doubt, as the origin of the word signifies, is to be in disagreement with oneself, to be divided between two. Neither is it true that one who (abhorrent as this may be) came to an agreement with himself to wish to be a villain serves only one master; for as there is no agreement in a den of

---

[1] If the reader will remember that in Danish *Herre* means 'lord' as well as 'master', he will understand this passage better—and sympathize with the translator.

robbers, so there is as little in the heart which is a den of robbers. But how might it be possible in *disagreement* to serve only *one master*?

The Christian serves only one Master; and he not merely serves Him but loves Him, he loves the Lord his God with all his heart and with all his strength. Just for this reason he serves Him wholly; for only love unites wholly, unites the most diverse parties in love, and in this instance unites man to God who is love. Love is the firmest of all bonds, for it makes the lover one with the beloved; more firmly no bond can bind, or so firmly can no bond bind. And the love which loves God is the bond of perfectness, which in perfect obedience makes man one with the God he loves. And the love which loves God is the most beneficial bond, which by keeping a man wholly in God's service saves him from anxieties. This love unifies a man, it makes him eternally in agreement with himself and with the Master who is one; and it unifies a man in likeness to God. Ah, blissful service, thus to serve God alone! Hence it sounds so solemn when we express it in one word, for this service is indeed 'divine service', the life of the Christian is nothing but divine service. The bird never attained such a height that one could call its life divine service, never did the bird become so *perfect* in obedience, although it was just as obedient.

But then in fact the Christian is even more obedient than the bird? Yes, that he is too. For the bird has no other will than God's will, but the Christian has another will which he constantly sacrifices in obedience to God—so much more obedient is he. A hard sacrifice, but well-pleasing to God, and hence so blissful! Ah, one speaks of so many *various* things which a man may love most dearly: a woman, his child, his father, his mother, his fatherland, his art, his science; but what *every* individual loves most, more than his only child, the child of promise, more than his only beloved on earth and in heaven—is his own will. Not for this shalt thou lay thy hand upon this child of thine—God is not cruel; nor forsake thy beloved—God is not hardhearted. There is something else, something far deeper within thee, for thine own salvation it is taken from thee, and yet to thine own hurt there is nothing thou holdest to so tightly, and nothing that holds so tightly to thee (for the child would more readily submit to being sacrificed, and the maiden to being sacrificed)—it is thine own will. See how promptly the bird is at hand to do God's will; but a long way off, in a certain sense, comes the Christian, who yet is more obedient than the bird! Which is the greater promptitude, his who stands at thy side and that very instant responds, or his who from afar off is yet that very instant on the spot? The bird comes as promptly as it can when God calls—all honour to it, this is a joy to behold; but the Christian comes with infinitely greater promptitude, for he comes just as promptly from . . . giving up his own will.

Hence the Christian also is free from anxiety, never *irresolute* —he is believing; never *fickle*—he is eternally resolved; never *disconsolate*—he is always joyful, always giving thanks. That obedience is the way to this end he has learnt and learns from Him who is the Way, from Him who Himself learned obedience and was obedient, obedient in all things, obedient in giving up all (the glory He had before the foundations of the earth were laid), obedience in doing without all (even that upon which He might lay His head), obedient in taking all upon Himself (the sin of the race), obedient in submitting to everything in life, obedient unto death.

Thus it is the Christian serves with perfect obedience only one Master. As the bird sings without ceasing to the glory of the Creator, such also is the Christian's life, or at least he understands and admits that it should be such; and already this understanding, this admission, ascribes honour to God. So the life of the Christian is a hymn in honour of the Lord, because this life obeys God more willingly and with more blissful accord than do the spheres. This life is a hymn of praise; for only by obedience can a man praise God, and best of all by perfect obedience. But the tone of this hymn is so lofty and so profoundly touching because humble and joyful obedience does not praise what a man understands but what he does not understand. And the instrument which accompanies this hymn is not that toy-trumpet of the human understanding, but it is the heavenly trombone of faith. The Christian's song of praise celebrates one thing, and celebrates that by obedience: that God does all, and that all God does is sheer grace and wisdom. And properly considered it is a kind of pertness and self-will, such as the Christian never could permit himself to display, when one thanks God somehow as a matter of course because that comes about which a man thinks he is able to understand as profitable or joyful. If such things are experienced by a Christian, he does to be sure give thanks, since he is always giving thanks; but precisely in this case he is doubtful, and dubious of himself, he beseeches God for forgiveness if he might be giving thanks too impetuously—too impetuously because, according to his childish notion, that which happened seemed to him profitable or joyful. For this properly is the hymn of praise, the paean, the song of songs: by joyful and unconditional obedience to praise God when one cannot understand Him. To praise Him upon the day when all goes against thee, when it becomes dark before thine eyes, when others perhaps could easily prove to thee that no God exists—then instead of assuming an air of importance by *proving* that there is a God, humbly to prove that thou dost believe that God exists, to prove it by joyful and unconditional obedience—that is the hymn of praise. The hymn is not something higher than obedience, but obedience is the only true hymn of praise; in obedience the hymn consists, and if the hymn is truth, it is obedience. With respect to a man, it is possible for thee to injure thyself by conforming to his will, though the injury is never great, seeing that there is a benediction upon sacrificing oneself for the sake of another. But might it also be possible that by obeying God's will I could in any wise injure myself—when His will is my only true good? But if this is not so, should not obedience always be joyful, might it hesitate a single instant to be joyful? It is in sooth solely and only my own good that is required of me.

All creatures praise God by obeying His behest; the life of the Christian praises Him by a still more perfect obedience, even when the Christian understands that he does not understand God. Why should the door be left open and the postern gate unguarded, by which irresolution or fickleness, not to speak of disconsolateness, might be able to sneak into the Christian soul? No, there is no fortress so secure as that of faith. Every other fortress—even if the enemy were to find no door open, no path built up the mountain, and no possibility of making it, nevertheless, by cutting it off entirely from all connexion with the surrounding world, from all supplies, he will be able at last to reduce it to starvation and compel it to surrender. But the more thou dost cut off faith from all supplies from the surrounding world (the supplies of irresolution, of fickleness, of disconsolateness—

there is nothing else indeed corresponding to the supplies a fortress needs from the surrounding world), all the safer is the fortress; thou art at fault in thinking that in this way thou art attacking it, thou art fortifying it. It is only a splendid untruth to call a fortress a world in itself. But the fortress of faith is a world in itself; and it has power over life; and what it least needs —yea, alas, what is most injurious to it—is supplies of any sort from the surrounding world. Cut off faith from all connexion with the surrounding world, starve it out—just so much the more impregnable it becomes, just so much the richer is its life. And along with faith in the fortress dwells obedience.

The heathen, on the contrary, has this anxiety. For heathenism, precisely understood, is doubleness, the two wills, masterlessness, or, what is the same thing, thraldom. Heathenism is a kingdom which is divided against itself, a kingdom in constant rebellion, where the one tyrant succeeds the other, but where for all that there is never any master. Heathenism is a mind in rebellion; by the devil's help the devil of the moment is driven out, and there enter in seven others that are worse. Heathenism, in whatever various ways it may express itself, is in the last resort disobedience, the impotent, self-contradictory attempt to wish to serve two masters. But hence the punishment pronounced upon it: 'Woe unto the sinner that goeth two ways!' [1] One can see this in a congregation where for many years there has been 'no priest', in spite of the fact that there have been many priests. So also it can be seen in the heathen, that there are many lords, or that there have been many lords, but no Lord ruled over this mind. There is one respect in which all heathen resemble one another, namely, disobedience to 'the Lord'; and there is one thing no heathen does, he does not serve one master. In all other ways he tries perhaps to serve one master, who yet is not master, or would wish to be without a master, or would wish to serve many masters —and the more he makes trial of all this, the more his last end becomes worse than his first.

His first is *irresolution.* So long as he is irresolute it appears as if there were no blame attached to it, as if the possibility of choosing the one master were still open to him, as if he were without anxiety and his irresoluteness were serious deliberation. Perhaps it is thought that the longer a man continues to deliber-

[1] Sirach 2: 12.

ate, the more serious his resolution is. Perhaps . . . if it ever comes to that! And above all do not forget that there are certainly some cases where no deliberation is necessary. So it is in relation to a trifling decision; in that case a long deliberation would surely be a very suspicious sign. There are many such trifling decisions in life; but there still remains a something with regard to which it is a very suspicious sign to need long deliberation—that is God, or the choice of God. The trifle stands in no proportion to long deliberation; but God's sublimity is also in no proportion to long deliberation and hesitation. Long deliberation is in this case so far from being seriousness that it proves precisely the lack of seriousness, and proves this by showing itself to be irresolution. For it is very far from being true that the longer a man deliberates and deliberates, the nearer he comes to God; on the contrary, the truth is that the longer the deliberation becomes while the choice is postponed, the farther he removes himself from God. To choose God is certainly the most decisive and the highest choice; but 'alas' for him who needs long deliberation, and 'woe' unto him the longer he needs it. For it is precisely faith's impatient quickness of judgement, the infinite sense of need which will hear of nothing else, that is not merely nearest to the choice but best prepared to choose. He who was guilty of the ungodliness of wanting to propose quite calmly whether he shall now choose God or another master is certainly irresolute, and presumably to such a degree that he never gets out of it. What a strange thing—in the case of a poor family one speaks of their being ashamed of making both ends meet; [1] but he who in irresolution became rich in deliberation has still greater difficulty in getting out of it. For God is not something one buys in the shop, nor like a property which one has shrewdly and cautiously examined for a long time, and after measuring and appraising it has finally convinced himself that it is worth buying. The ungodly calmness with which the irresolute man would begin in the case of God (for he would begin with doubt), precisely this is insubordination; for thereby God is deposed from the throne, from being the Lord. And when one has done this, one really has already chosen another master, wilfulness, and thus becomes the thrall of irresoluteness.

[1] Such is the meaning of the Danish idiom *komme ud af det,* which literally means 'get out of it' and has this sense in the neighbouring phrases.

Then when irresoluteness has ruled long enough, *fickleness* (Luke xii. 29) assumes the government. For a long while it seemed perhaps as if irresoluteness concealed in itself the elasticity of choice, or its possibility. That is now consumed, if ever it was there, the soul of the heathen is unstrung, it becomes evident what irresoluteness really conceals in itself. In irresoluteness there still is a power of holding out against thoughts, irresolution still makes an effort to be master in the house and to put thoughts in their place. But now masterlessness over the thoughts, or the whim of the moment, has assumed the government, whim rules—even with respect to the question whether to choose God. As a momentary whim it appears then to the heathen that it would be a good thing to choose God, and then again something else as second, and after that a third. But these movements, which signify nothing, have no significance, leave behind no trace, except the increased sluggishness and enervation. As in the sluggishness of stagnant water a bubble slowly rises up and bursts emptily, so does fickleness bubble in the whim, and bubbles yet again.

And then when fickleness has ruled long enough, and of course like all ungodly rulers has sucked the blood and enfeebled the body, *disconsolateness* assumes the government. First the heathen desired to be entirely rid of the thought of God; he desires now to sink down in the inanity of worldliness, there to seek forgetfulness, forgetfulness of the most dangerous thought, because it is the most uplifting of all thoughts, the thought of being remembered by God, the thought of existing before God. For what indeed is more dangerous, if one *will* sink, than everything that would uplift one! Yet he has overcome, as he thinks, his pain, has dispelled all illusions, learned to console himself. Ah! Really! —yes, pretty much as when one deeply sunken, as a way of consoling himself (oh, dreadful disconsolateness!), says to a man by the sight of whom he is reminded of something higher, 'Let me count for what I am.' [1] Then the light of the spirit goes out, a drowsy mist hangs before his eyes, he cares for nothing, but yet he wishes not to die, he is alive after a sort. Oh, what a horrible dissolution, worse than that of death, to rot while he is alive, without strength for even so much as to despair of himself and of

[1] S. K. did actually witness the spirit of an acquaintance 'go out' with these words —and the horror of it he could never forget.

his situation! But the light of the spirit has gone out, and the disconsolate man becomes crazily busy about all sorts of things, lest anything might remind him of God; he slaves from morning till night, makes money, lays by, engages in financial transactions —yea, if thou wert to talk with him, thou wouldst hear him constantly talk of the seriousness of life. Ah, horrible seriousness, it would have been better to lose one's senses!

What is disconsolateness? The wildest shriek of pain or the presumption of despair—this is not precisely disconsolateness. But this agreement with oneself arrived at in the stillness of extinction, that everything higher is lost, whereas nevertheless one is able to go on living if only nothing reminds him of this— this is disconsolateness. Not even sorrowing disconsolately, but completely ceasing to sorrow, being able to lose God in such a way that one became therewith entirely indifferent and did not even find life unsupportable—this is disconsolateness, and at the same time it is the most dreadful sort of disobedience, more dreadful than any defiance. To hate God and to curse Him is not so dreadful as to lose Him in this way, or, what comes to the same thing, to lose oneself. To lose a trifle in such a way that one has no mind to pick it up—well, perhaps that is natural; but to lose one's own self (to lose God) in such a way that one has not even an inclination to stoop and pick it up, or in such a way that the loss is not noticed—oh, what a dreadful loss! For not only is there an infinite difference between what one loses and what one loses, but also between *how* one loses. To lose God in such a way that repentance hastens at once in contrition to recover what was lost; to lose God in such a way that one is offended in Him, rebels against Him, or sighs against Him; to lose God in such a way that one despairs at it—but to lose God as if He were nothing, and as if the loss were nothing!

Let us in conclusion think of the birds, which had their place in the Gospel and should have their place in the discourse. The bird so obeys God that this is the same thing as being wilful; the Christian so denies himself that this is the same thing as obeying God; the heathen is so wilful that it is eternally apparent that he does not obey God. The bird has no self-will to give up; the Christian gives up his own will; the heathen gives up God. The bird neither won nor lost God; the Christian won God and accounted it as everything; the heathen lost God and accounted it as nothing. The bird serves only one Master whom it does not know; the Christian serves only one Master whom he loves; the heathen serves the master who is the enemy of God. The bird obeys promptly when God calls, the Christian even more promptly; God cannot even call to the heathen, for it is as if there were no one to call upon. The obedience of the bird serves to the honour of God, the Christian's more perfect obedience still more so; the disobedience of the heathen refuses to honour God, he serves for nothing but to be cast out as salt which has lost its savour.

PART II

Before this book was finished S. K. had it in mind to publish another, with the title, 'Some Joyful Thoughts', containing four Discourses:

No. 1.   Tribulation worketh Patience.
No. 2.   Patience worketh Probation.
No. 3.   Probation Hope.
No. 4.   Hope maketh not Ashamed.

In a marginal note he reflected that the subject of hope might better be included in 'The Gospel of Sufferings', which was the title he first proposed to apply to Part III of the *Christian Discourses*.

In another place in the Journal he notes that three of the themes he had in mind for this part were eventually discarded for the sake of keeping the number down to seven. The discarded themes were: No. 1.   How joyful—that if in temptation the believer is not able to hold the anchor, the anchor is able to hold the believer; No. 2.   [about tribulation, patience, hope]; No. 3.   How joyful—that it is for joy one cannot venture to trust the most blessed news. So in Acts xii. 14, the maid Rhoda, who ought to have opened for Peter, on hearing Peter's voice, 'she opened not the gate for joy'—for joy she let him stand outside.

Thou believest it not—but only take courage, for really the reason only is that it is too joyful, take courage, for it is joy that prevents thee—is not this joyful? It is said of the disciples (Luke xxiv. 41) that 'for joy they disbelieved'.

It appears that S. K. had at his disposal a superabundance of joyful thoughts, of the thoughts which cheer and comfort—a far greater abundance of them than of the thoughts which wound and dismay.

He provided no preface for 'Notes in the Strife of Suffering', but he says in the Journal that if any had been used, it would have been to the following effect:

'The bravest nation of antiquity (the Lacedemonians) prepared themselves for warfare by music: so these are notes (*Stemninger*) of triumphant joy which tune [*stemme*] to warfare, and so far from dejecting [*forstemme*] one, will make one well disposed [*velstemt*] for the contest.'

It is just as well this preface was not used, for it contains little but a play on words, yet it helps us to understand how the title is to be understood and translated.

JOYFUL NOTES
IN THE STRIFE OF SUFFERING
CHRISTIAN DISCOURSES

by

S. KIERKEGAARD

'I will incline mine ear to the parable, and propound
my dark sayings upon the harp' (Psalm 49. 4).

Copenhagen
1848

CONTENTS

I

H E who wills the end must will the means. But this involves, does it not, the assumption or admission that a
man knows what he wills. This being assumed, we bring
him to a halt by the 'means', by saying, '*Then* thou must also will
the means'. Sometimes, however, it may be necessary to go back
a step farther and say, 'He who wills something must first of all
know what it is he wills, must have an understanding of what he
wills'. The impatient person who would attain his end at once
finds that even this thing about the means retards him terribly—
oh, but how awfully tiresome the slowness of having to begin
so far back: 'he who wills something must also know what he
wills, must have an understanding of what he wills'.

So it is now with regard to what is indeed the aim of the
edifying discourse, namely, to edify, or rather the aim of edifying.
Perhaps there was a man who would be edified, is desirous of
being edified, one who, if he were to take time to understand what
he wants, or take time to have it explained to him, would be
more than eager to wish himself exempted from being edified.
Such misunderstanding occurs often in life. A man may
vehemently, passionately, yea, persistently, desire something the
exact nature of which he has no idea of—and, alas, the exact
nature of which is perhaps the exact opposite of that which the
wisher supposed it to be. So it is with the edifying, which verily
is the Good in-and-for-itself, and precisely for this reason must
require that the individual who would be edified has understood
himself, lest light-mindedly, in a worldly spirit, thoughtlessly
wishful, he take the edifying in vain, and then will say, I beg to
be excused, when he gets to know more exactly what it is.

For what is the edifying? The first answer to this tells what
the edifying first is: it is the *dismaying*. The edifying is not for
the healthy-minded but for the sick; to the supposedly healthy
and strong it must therefore in the first instance appear as the
dismaying. The sick person understands as a matter of course

that he is subjected to the treatment of the physician; but for a
person in sound health it would be dismaying to discover that
he had fallen into the hands of a physician who without more ado
was treating him as a sick man. So it is with the edifying, which
first is the dismaying—for the non-contrite it is a means to contrition. Where there is nothing at all dismaying and no dismay,
there is nothing at all edifying and no edification. There is forgiveness for sin, that is edifying, the dismaying thing is that
there is sin; and the degree of the dismay in the inwardness of
sin-consciousness corresponds to the degree of edification. There
is healing for all pain, victory in all conflict, salvation from all
danger—that is edifying; the dismaying thing is that there is
pain, conflict, danger; and the degree of the dismaying and of the
dismay corresponds to the edifying and to the edification.

So deep lies the edifying. Finding the edifying is like boring
an artesian well, where one must sink the shaft many, many
fathoms—and all the better, for then the jet is higher. First one
must look well to find the dismaying. For the dismaying is
related to the edifying as the dowsing-rod is to the spring—
when the rod bends down, there in the depths is a spring; and
where the dismaying is, there in the vicinity, at the bottom, is the
edifying. Thereupon, after one has looked well to find the dismaying, and then looks well again, he finds the edifying.

So sure of itself is the edifying, so reliable in itself. One should
not be terrified by the dismay, as though it might stand in the
way of edification, nor keep it timorously at a distance, in the
hope of making the edification acceptable; for with the fear of
dismay the edification vanishes. But on the other hand it is
precisely in dismay that edification lies. So triumphant is the
edifying that the very thing which at the first glance might
seem to be its enemy is turned into a presupposition, into a
servant, into a friend. If the art of the physician triumphantly
overcomes the difficulty of transforming poison into a medicine,
still more gloriously is dismay transformed into the edifying,
for edification.

So it is now with the subject of this discourse. We suffer but
once. This is said so glibly that it sounds almost frivolous, just as
in the world one often hears the frivolous saying, 'Enjoy life, we
live but once.' But to find the edifying one must first find the
dismaying, and so in this case one must take time to understand

that in this saying is implied the gloomiest conception of life. We live but once—that is as if it were to be said of a man that he was sick only once in his life, only once unhappy—that is, all his life long. Now it is that the edification is about to begin. But earthly shrewdness and impatience, and worldly anxiety, which in a worldly way are in search of healing, must not expect the impossible, that one might be able to speak to them for edification, if one is to speak Christianly. For the Christian experience properly begins just there, or the proper Christian experience begins just there, where human impatience will find whatever actual sufferings it has to complain of endlessly increased . . . by the consolation, yea, by the consolation which drives to despair; for in a worldly sense Christian consolation is more apt to drive to despair than are the heaviest earthly sufferings and the greatest temporal misfortunes. *There* edification begins, the Christian edification which is named after Him, our Lord and Saviour, for He too suffered only once . . . but His whole life was suffering.

So let us speak about

THE JOY OF IT—THAT WE SUFFER ONLY ONCE, BUT TRIUMPH ETERNALLY.

We suffer only *once*, but we triumph eternally. So far as that goes, we triumph also only *once*. Quite true. But the difference is infinite: that *the once of suffering is the instant, that of triumph, eternity; the 'once' of suffering, therefore, when it is past, is no time, the 'once' of triumph is, in another sense, no time, for it is never past; the once of suffering is a transition, or a thing we pass through, that of triumph, an eternally enduring triumph.*

The once of suffering is the instant, or we suffer only once. Though suffering lasts seventy years, that is only once; though the 'once' is the seventy times ten of the seventy years, that is only once, it is still only one time. For time itself in its totality is the instant; eternally understood, the temporal is the instant, and the instant eternally understood is only 'once'. In vain would the temporal assume an air of importance, count the instants, and add them all together—— if eternity has any say in the matter, the temporal never gets farther than, never comes to more than, the 'once'. For eternity is the opposite; it is not the opposite to a single instant (this is meaningless), it is the opposite to the temporal as a whole, and it opposes itself with the power of eternity against the temporal amounting to more than that.[1] As God said to the waters, 'Hitherto, and no farther', so says eternity to time, 'Hitherto, and no farther; however long thou mayest last, thou art the instant, neither more nor less; this I vouch for, I that am Eternity, or this I bring about by compulsion, I that am Eternity.' No more than does a parasitical plant, however long it may continue to grow, and however widely it may spread upon the ground,[2] ever grow in height, no more does the temporal, however long it may last, ever become more than the instant and the 'once'—if eternity has anything to say. Therefore the youth who stands at the beginning of life says with the same justification as does the old man who stands at the end of it and looks back over the distance travelled: 'We live only once.' With the same justification, that is to say, by virtue of eternity, but not with the same truth, although the saying is equally true. For the young man *says what is true*, but the old man has verified it, has *made that true* which yet is eternally true. The only difference here is that which in these times has been overlooked, when with all this proving and proving it has been forgotten that the highest thing a man is capable of is to make an eternal truth true, to make it true, to make it true that it is true . . . by doing it, by being himself the proof, by a life which also perhaps will be able to convince others.[3] Did Christ ever undertake to prove some truth or another, or to prove the truth? No, but He made the truth true, or He made it true that He is the Truth.

We suffer only once. But just as that parasitical plant which slinks along the ground betrays every instant, if thou wilt observe it, an inclination to grow to a height, and in case it encounters in its path anything upon which it can twine itself, it sneaks up to a height, or arrogates to itself loftiness—so also the temporal, when in its sneaking gate it finds something to which it can cling, would sneak up in order to come to some importance—by foreign

[1] S. K. vehemently opposes here as elsewhere the notion that eternity is merely the infinite prolongation of time (which Hegel called *die schlechte Ewigkeit*), in favour of the Platonic eternity—and the Christian.

[2] What a pity that S. K. was not so well instructed about the habits of plants as about birds!

[3] This is a characteristic instance of S. K.'s 'existential' thinking—as well as an instance of his characteristic denunciation of the futile attempt to furnish an intellectual *proof* of the existence of God or of the truth of Christianity.

assistance. Yes, by foreign assistance—and yet no, not by foreign assistance, for if this comes about, if the temporal comes to some importance, it comes about by the assistance of that man to whose misfortune it comes about. If man does not derive his strength from the eternal and in solidarity with the eternal obtain strength to hold down the temporal, it steals his strength from him and thus becomes something prodigious, it becomes the man's impatience, his despair, perhaps his ruin. Pride slays its own master; but the temporal is just as ungrateful, it comes to something by stealing the strength of eternity from a man, and by way of requital it then remains with him and makes him its slave. Alas, in this way man gets to know a great deal about the instant; bigger and bigger become the figures he calculates with—ah, and this calculation amounts only to 'one times one', if eternity has any say in the matter. Now one day of suffering is long, one month awfully long, one year terribly long, unendurably long, enough to drive one to despair; now one can recall that time, and that time, and that time, and at last so many times that no one knows the beginning or the end of the many times of suffering. But was not the lord of the vineyard in the right when according to the agreement he let the labourers be paid an equally big wage although they were called to the work at different hours, *eternally* understood was he not in the right, inasmuch as, eternally understood, they had only laboured 'once'? The labourers who complained as though an injustice were done them must have learned to know something about the temporal which is not eternally true, and it is precisely this that accounts for their mistake, and it was they who were in the wrong, not the lord of the vineyard. The lord of the vineyard is eternity, for whom diversity of time does not exist, for whom the temporal is only 'once'; and again the equal reward is eternity. Therefore they had no ground for complaint; for with respect to eternity only one agreement is possible, that which is equal for all men; and with respect to receiving the reward of eternity, the one has not laboured longer because he was called at the third hour than the other who was called at the eleventh.

O thou sufferer, every evening indeed thou dost hear the cry of the night-watchman, 'Be cautious with candles and fire!' Thou dost sometimes hear also perhaps the cry, 'Make use of time! Employ the hour!' I would rather cry out to thee and to myself, 'Take care above all things to deal cautiously with time, more cautiously than with candles and fire, so that it never may become to thee more than the 'once'! Never begin the dreadful calculation which no one who ever began got through with, to want to count instants and times! Take care above all to cancel the fractions continually by the aid of eternity, in which all instants are equated, and in such a way that they only come to 'once'! By this defend thyself from ever in thy life getting to the point of suffering more than 'once'! For if it be 'for once', oh, well, that is something a man can bear after all; but if he has to suffer twice—then impatience is aroused. Was it not in fact impatience which taught him that it was the second time? By the aid of eternity a man suffers but once. Therefore when evening comes let the day's sufferings be forgotten, so that when the same sufferings begin the next day thou dost still suffer only once! And then when the year is at an end let this year's sufferings be forgotten, so that when the same sufferings begin next year thou dost still suffer only once! And then when thy last hour is come let this life's sufferings be forgotten—yea, it is true, is it not, they are then forgotten, thou dost suffer only once! O thou sufferer, whosoever thou art, however thou dost feel thyself imprisoned in the life-long confinement of suffering, alas, like a captive beast in its cage—see how the captive goes around and around its cage, how it measures the length of its chain to give itself exercise—so do thou measure the length of the chain by going as far as the thought of death and eternity, thus thou wilt get exercise in order to be able to hold out, and thou wilt get the zest of living! Suffer patiently! But everything that can be said about suffering patiently is essentially and substantially comprehended in this one word: Let eternity help thee to be able to suffer but once.

The 'one time' of suffering is no time. As the proverb says, 'Once is no habit' (literally, one time is no time).[1] Whether this is true in the situation to which the proverb applies, I leave undecided; it is quite possible that the proverb is not true, and yet what the proverb says is true—a proverb in fact is anything but an eternal truth, it talks only of the temporal. But when the contrast is that between time and eternity, it is eternally certain that one

---

[1] *Ene Gang—ingen Gang*—it is enough to drive one to despair! The translation of this paragraph is perhaps more impossible than difficult.

time is no time, and in no other case is its truth so clearly and decisively evident. What indeed is seventy years compared with eternity! And in eternity it will be made evident that all this suffering, this 'one time', is no time. One will not be able to observe in the blessed ones that they have suffered, how they have suffered, will not be able to observe it by the slightest signs; every tear shall be wiped away from the eyes which now glisten with radiant joy, every want shall be appeased in the heart which now blissfully possesses all things, and possesses them *there* (oh, blessed security of ownership!) where nothing can take away the joy of it, there where the hallowed ones say blissfully, 'Once is no time.'

Sin alone is man's destruction, sin alone has the power to set such a mark upon a man that it is not obliterated at once, or entirely, or perhaps never to all eternity. Of all temporal sufferings it is true that once is no time.

The 'once' of suffering is a transition, a passage-way. Thou must go through it, and though it were to last as long as life, and though it were as hard as a sword which transfixes thy heart, it is yet only a passage-way. It is not true that it is the suffering which goes through thee, it is thou that goest through it—in the eternal understanding of the case, entirely unharmed. In time and in the sense of the temporal it seems so dreadful, as though suffering went piercingly through thee, so that thou perished in it. That is an illusion. It is as when one of the actors in the play kills another; it seems exactly as if he pierced him through, but we all know that in fact he did not hurt a hair of his head. But not more unharmed does the murdered actor go again to his home, and not more unharmed did Daniel go from the lions' den, and not more unharmed did the Three Children go into the fiery furnace—than the soul of a believer goes into eternity, unharmed by all the sufferings of the temporal, unharmed by death. For all the sufferings of the temporal are illusion, and death itself, eternally understood, is a comedian! As little as moth and rust can consume the treasure of eternity (and what indeed is more impossible!), as little as a thievish hand can steal it, so little is all temporal suffering, however long it may last, capable in the remotest degree of injuring the soul. This neither sickness can do, nor want, nor distress, nor heat and cold—much as they can consume; this neither slander can do, nor scorn, nor indignity, nor persecution—whatever they may steal and plunder; this not death itself can do.

The 'once' of suffering is passage-way which leaves no trace at all upon the soul, or, still more gloriously, it is a passage-way which purifies the soul by sanctifying it, so that purity remains as the trace left by the passage-way. For as gold is purified in the fire, so is the soul in suffering. But of what does the fire bereave the gold? Yea, it is a strange mode of speech to call it 'bereaving', it bereaves the gold of all the base constituents. What then does gold lose in the fire? Yea, it is a strange mode of speech to call it 'losing', gold loses in the fire all the base elements, that is, gold gains in the fire. So it is with all temporal suffering; in itself impotent, it is not able to take anything; and, if the sufferer allows eternity to have a say, it takes away the impure elements, that is, it gives purity.

Sin is man's destruction. Only the rust of sin can consume the soul—or eternally *destroy* it. For here indeed is the remarkable thing from which already that simple wise man of olden time [1] derived a proof of the immortality of the soul, that the sickness of the soul (sin) is not like bodily sickness which kills the body. Sin is not a passage-way which a man has to pass through once, for from it one shall flee; sin is not (like suffering) the instant, but an eternal fall from the eternal, hence it is not 'once', and it cannot possibly be that its 'once' is no time. No, just as between that rich man in hell and Lazarus in Abraham's bosom there was a yawning gulf fixed, so is there also a yawning distinction between suffering and sin. Let us not confuse it, lest talk about suffering might become less frank-hearted, because it had also sin in mind, and this less frank-hearted talk might be boldly impudent inasmuch as it was talking in this way about sin. This precisely is the Christian position, that there is this infinite distinction between evil and evil, as they are confusingly named; this precisely is the Christian characteristic, to talk of temporal sufferings ever more and more frank-heartedly, more triumphantly, more joyfully, because, Christianly regarded, sin, and sin only, is destruction.

We suffer only once, but triumph eternally. Let me make this distinction vivid to thee. In a church somewhere here in the country there is a painting behind the altar which depicts two

---

[1] This is S. K.'s stereotype formula for indicating Socrates.

angels holding out to Christ the cup of suffering. When thou dost contemplate the picture, it makes upon thee at once the impression the artist aimed to produce; thou art absorbed in this impression, for such indeed was the situation, the cup of suffering was held out to Him! But in case thou wert to remain a whole day sitting before the altar and looking at this picture, or in case thou wert to contemplate it every Sunday, year in and year out—ah, it surely is true that, however piously thou wert ever mindful of His suffering, praying Him, moreover, to remind thee constantly of it, surely it is true that there will come an instant when everything is for thee infinitely changed, when the picture will blessedly turn itself around,[1] when thou wilt say to thyself, 'No, after all, it did not last so long, the angels did not keep on holding out to Him the cup; in fact He took it willingly from the hands of the angels, obediently from the hand of God—He has drained it, this cup of suffering, for what He suffered, He suffered once, but He triumphs eternally!'—On the other hand, consider Him in His triumph; yea, if any artist were able to depict this, is it possible—however long thou wert to remain sitting, or though every Sunday thou wert to contemplate this picture—is it possible that the moment would ever come when thou wouldest say to thyself, 'But this lasts too long; why, it never comes to an end!' No, God be praised, it never comes to an end! And yet this triumph also is only *once*; but the 'once' of triumph is eternity, the 'once' of suffering was the instant. It may, no doubt, be impatience which cannot endure to look at the picture where the cup is held out to Him; but it may also be faith, which consequently does not turn away impatiently, but believingly substitutes the picture of triumph for that of suffering.

O thou sufferer, whosoever thou art; as thou dost begin every day with God, praying Him to give thee patience to suffer that day, so pray Him also every day to remind thee that a man only suffers once! In 'Our Father' the Christian prays for the daily bread today. With this one is likely to think more especially of the poor, whose task is to get along with the daily bread of poverty. But thou who with respect to sufferings hast been, perhaps from the very beginning of thy life and for thy whole life,

---

[1] In the well-known story of Agnes and the Merman, the pictures of the saints turn their faces to the wall when the guilty Agnes enters the church. S. K. often alludes to this.

so richly endowed with sufferings in abundance, for thee also this prayer was invented, for thee the task is the opposite and yet the same: to get along with the daily supply of suffering, so that at thy life's end, as the poor man says, 'I made a go of it all the same, and got the daily wherewithal', so thou then mightest be able to say, 'I made a go of it all the same, and got the daily wherewithal.' The poor man makes a go of it, defends himself against poverty, finds the daily wherewithal. It is perhaps more difficult with the abundance of suffering to make a go of it, but that is the task. Lay this also which follows well to heart. Reflect that though a man were to have lived his whole life in the undisturbed enjoyment of all earthly goods, reflect that at the instant of death he has nothing at all to remember, nothing at all with which to go forth to encounter the boundless future of remembrance. For *enjoyment* is agreeable in the instant, but like the vacuous instant it is not material for remembrance, and for an eternal remembrance it simply does not exist. On the other hand, there is no remembrance more blessed, and nothing more blessed to remember, than suffering overcome in solidarity with God; this is the mystery of suffering. So then: either seventy years passed in every possible enjoyment, and nothing, nothing for an eternity (most appalling of all deficiencies, as it is indeed the most long-lasting!); or seventy years past in suffering, and then an eternity for blessed remembrance. Blessed remembrance of sufferings overcome in alliance with God! Most blessed surely the remembrance of undeserved sufferings in a good cause, as indeed the Lord says, 'When men shall reproach you and say all manner of evil against you falsely, blessed are ye!' Yea, blessed it is to suffer thus, the most blessed remembrance! But this applies as well to every suffering which is endured in alliance with God, it is blessed to remember it in eternity. We suffer only once, but we triumph eternally. Strange how the situation is inverted! For long protracted duration, which seems to belong to the temporal, the seventy years, is—if the temporal is held down in subjection —no more than 'once'; but then it comes again in eternity, where at length it becomes perpetually blessed to remember this 'once'.

II

WHAT a strange business proposition—-to acquire hope in a way like that! Is it not as strange as though a merchant were to become rich by having nobody enter his shop, or that a traveller reached his destination because somebody showed him the wrong way? Ah, people often complain that life is so unimportant, so meaningless, so totally lacking in entertainment—it seems to me that in this one thought there is entertainment enough for an eternity! People often complain that life is so empty, so monotonous, leaves one so unstrung—it seems to me that in this one thought there is tension enough for an eternity! Poets often depict in their tales a character enigmatically masked who at the decisive moment turns out to be something quite different from what he appeared—to me it seems that the inventions of the poets in this line, all of them taken together, are mere child's-play in comparison with this disguise invented by eternity, that it is affliction which undertakes to create hope for a man! Or is there in any fairy-tale, in any poem, a character passing for evil (but yet at bottom good) which looks so terrifying as affliction? And to think that it should be affliction which recruits hope! Can any robber be more sure of the result of his thrust when it is aimed directly at the heart than the aim of affliction seems to be surely directed at the life of hope? And yet it is affliction which recruits hope! Marvellous! It does not give hope, it recruits hope. So it is not at one decisive moment it throws aside its disguise and says, 'I only wanted to terrify thee, here is the hope.' So all the while it stood there, this is what it was labouring for, labouring slowly for this one and only end, to provide the sufferer with hope.

Yes, let us *wonder* at it right heartily! If there is anything people in these times have forgotten, it is this thing of wondering—therefore also the thing of believing and hoping and loving. The very highest thing is proclaimed, the most marvellous, but no one wonders. It is proclaimed that there is forgiveness of sins, but no one says, 'It is impossible.' Hardly does any one turn away offended and say, 'It is impossible'; still less does any one say it in wonder, or as he says it who is so fain to wish that it might be true but dare not believe it, will not let go of the saying but is as an unhappy lover and cannot believe; still less is it said by him, precisely by him who believes in it, he whose repentance was softened into a quiet sorrow which never was transformed into a blessed joy, he therefore who in expressing to God his inexpressible thanks refreshes his soul by repeating, 'It is impossible!' Oh, blessed refreshment, that he who was brought so close to despair because it was impossible now believes it, blissfully believes it, but in the wonderment of his soul continues to say, 'It is impossible!' We all know well what is related of a man who had heard a story at which all laughed, but which nobody laughed at when he told it . . . because, as we know, he had forgotten the point.[1] But think of an Apostle in these times, an Apostle who of course knew well how to tell the story of the marvellous, think of his grief, or of the grief of the Holy Spirit within him, when he had to say, 'There is no one that wonders; they listen to it as indifferently as though it were of the utmost indifference, as though there were nobody whom it concerns, nobody to whom it is of importance, of immense importance, whether it is possible or not possible, whether it is so or not so, whether it is true or a lie!'

So as an introduction let us wonder at the fact that affliction recruits hope, let the soul be tuned to wonder, let us shout as the Psalmist shouts to his soul, 'Awake psaltery and harp!' And so let us talk about

THE JOY OF IT—THAT AFFLICTION DOES NOT BEREAVE OF HOPE, BUT RECRUITS HOPE

If with one word we were to indicate what is characteristic of child-life and youth-life, one must surely say that it is a dream-life. And so indeed we do speak. How often (to mention only this example) this sad phrase is repeated by an older person: 'They vanished, these dreams of childhood and youth.' They vanished—presumably because the dreamer vanished, was lost; for how should there be dreams when there is no dreamer! But what right have we to call it a dream-life, when by that we char-

---

[1] This story is told of an eccentric character in Copenhagen by the name of Loria.

acterize the child and the youth as sleepers, as sleep-walkers? In another sense the child is awake, in a degree that none of its elders are, its senses are open to every impression, the child being sheer life and movement, alert attention all the day long; and the youth is awake as seldom an older person is, his mind is without rest early and late, he is so stirred by passion that often he hardly can sleep. And yet child-life and youth-life is dream-life, for the innermost thing, that which in the deepest sense is man, slumbers. The child is completely turned outward, its inwardness is extra-version,[1] and to that extent the child is wide awake. But for a man, to be awake means to be eternally turned inward in inward-ness, and so the child is dreaming, it dreams itself sensuously at one with everything, almost to the extent of confounding itself with the sense-impression. In comparison with the child, the youth is more turned inward, but in imagination; he dreams, or it is as though everything about him were dreaming. On the other hand, he who in the sense of eternity is turned inward perceives only what is of the spirit, and for the rest he is like a sleeper, an absentee, a dead man, with respect to the perceptions of flesh and blood, of the temporal, of the imaginative—in him the spirit is awake, the lower functions sleep; hence he is awake. Dream-life is so denominated with a view to the nobler part—in the waking man the spirit wakes, whereas there is doubtless some-thing which sleeps, namely, the lower part. In the child and in the youth it is the spirit that sleeps, the lower part is awake; nevertheless, as it is the determining characteristic of spirit to be awake, this life is called a dream-life.

But he who dreams must be awakened, and the deeper the man is who slumbers, or the deeper he slumbers, the more important it is that he be awakened, and the more powerfully must he be awakened. In case there is nothing that awakens the youth, this dream-life is continued in manhood. The man doubtless thinks that he is dreaming no more, and in a sense he is not; perhaps he scorns and despises the dreams of youth, but precisely this shows that his life is a failure. In a sense he is awake, yet he is not in an eternal sense and in the deepest sense awake. And so his life is something far less significant than that of the youth, and it is his

[1] I cannot help using this word of Jung's, which is the only literal translation we have for S. K.'s *Udadvendthed*; but by this I do not pretend to decide if and how far S. K. anticipated the 'deep psychology'.

life rather which deserves to be despised; for he has become an unfruitful tree, or like a tree which has died, whereas the life of youth verily is not to be despised. The dream-life of childhood and youth is the time of blossoming. But in the case of a tree which is to bear fruit, the time of blossoming is a time of immaturity. It may indeed seem like retrogression when the tree which once stood naked and then burst into bloom, now casts off its blossoms; but it also may be progress. Fair is the time of blossoms, and fair is the blossoming hope in the child and in the youth; and yet it is immaturity.

Then comes *affliction* to awaken the dreamer, affliction which like a storm tears off the blossoms, affliction *which nevertheless does not bereave of hope, but recruits hope.*

Where then is hope? Is hope in the rushing wind of the storm? Oh, no, not more than God's voice was in the rushing wind, but in the gentle breeze, like a whisper in man's inmost parts, all too easily ignored. But what is it then that affliction would accomplish? It would have that whisper heard in the inmost parts. But does not then affliction counteract itself, must not its tempestuous wind drown out this voice? No, affliction is able to drown out every earthly voice, that is precisely what it has to do, but the voice of eternity within a man it cannot drown. Or conversely: it is the voice of eternity within which demands to be heard, and to make a hearing for itself it makes use of the loud voice of affliction. Then when by the aid of affliction all irrelevant voices are brought to silence, it can be heard, this voice within.

O thou sufferer, whosoever thou art, if only thou wilt listen! People generally think that it is the world, the environment, external relationships, which stand in one's way, in the way of one's good fortune and peace and joy. And at bottom it is always man himself that stands in his own way, man himself, who is too closely attached to the world, to the environment, to circumstances, to external relationships, so that he is not able to come to himself, come to rest, to have hope, he is constantly too much turned outward, instead of being turned inward, hence everything he says is true only as an illusion of the senses. Man himself maintains communication with the enemy, and the medium of communication is . . . *the hope of youth.*

But affliction *bereaves* of hope. Yea, that thou hast thyself experienced to the full, even if thou hast not as yet abandoned the league with this ambiguous experience. Thou didst hope that if thou wert not successful the first time, well then another time, and if not then, at least another time; thou didst hope that as compensation for thy many failures a little redress might be due thee the next time; thou didst hope that it still might be possible for an unexpected help to come, as it came to him who for thirty and eight years had lain paralysed, with salvation so near that it was always just one other that stepped down into the pool before him; after having relinquished all other friends thou didst at last set thy hopes upon that Friend—but the affliction endured.

For affliction recruits hope. It does not *bestow* hope, but it *recruits* it. It is man himself who acquires it, this hope of eternity which is deposited in him, hidden in his inner man; but affliction recruits it. For affliction prevents him mercilessly (yes, in the child's view of it, mercilessly) from obtaining any other help or relief whatsoever; affliction compels him mercilessly (yes, in the youth's view of it, mercilessly) to let go of everything else; affliction schools him mercilessly (yes, in immaturity's view of it, mercilessly), schools him thoroughly, that he may learn to grasp the eternal and to hold on to the eternal. Affliction does not help *directly*, it is not affliction that acquires or purchases hope and makes a present of it to a man; it helps *repellantly*, and can do no otherwise, because hope is in man himself. Affliction preaches awakening. For, alas, men are unfortunately only too hardy, so that there is little to be accomplished by the terror of mighty thoughts—affliction knows better how to make itself understood, its eloquence is striking, not only *once* like a witticism, but as one says of a stick, 'There are blows in that; striking is a permanent attribute it possesses.' Man would prefer to have the direct form of communication, by way of assurance and assurance; but this is so comfortable that it avails nothing. Affliction, on the other hand, does not jest. When affliction begins this work of recruiting hope, it seems for an instant as crazy as if one were to assault a beggar, hold a pistol to his heart, and say, 'Your money!' For, ah, the sufferer is just about to despair of hope (the hope of youth that is), which he is more than fain to hold fast, as he says—and then affliction assaults him and demands . . . his hope (the hope of eternity, that is). Affliction is no congratulatory caller who comes bearing hope in his hand as a present. Affliction is the villain who cruelly (yes, in the child's view, cruelly) says to the sufferer, 'I shall recruit hope for thee all right.' But as it always is in life, that he who has to play the villain is never appreciated, that nobody takes the time to put himself in the villain's place and to recognize how admirably he plays his part and conforms to his role, how admirably, without letting himself be moved by any sighs or tears or ingratiating prayers—so it is also with affliction, it always has to hear itself spoken ill of. But just as little as it troubles the physician that the sick man in his pain scolds and clamours, or even kicks at him, just so little is affliction put out at this; God be praised, it is not put out—it recruits hope. Just as Christianity, precisely by all that unappreciation and persecution and injustice which the truth must suffer, proves that righteousness must exist (oh, marvellous inference!), so there is in the extremity of affliction, when it presses hardest, this inference, this *ergo*: *Ergo* there is an eternity to set one's hope upon.

Imagine hidden in a simpler exterior a secret receptacle wherein the most precious treasure is deposited—there is a spring which has to be pressed, but the spring is hidden, and the pressure must have a certain strength, so that an accidental pressure would not be sufficient—so likewise is the hope of eternity hidden in man's inmost parts, and affliction is the pressure. When it presses the hidden spring, and strongly enough, then the contents appear in all their glory.

Imagine a grain of corn deposited in the earth—if it is to grow, what does it need? First of all room, it must have room, and then pressure, there must in addition be pressure—to germinate is precisely to make room through an opposing substance. So likewise is the hope of eternity deposited in man's inward parts. But affliction makes room by making away with all else, all the provisional and temporal which it reduces to despair, so that the pressure of affliction is what elicits the treasure.

Imagine an animal which (as actually is the case) has a weapon for its protection which it uses only in mortal danger—such is the hope of eternity in man's bosom, affliction is the mortal danger!

Imagine a creeping creature which nevertheless has wings which it can use when it is reduced to extremities, but for daily use thinks it not worth while to employ them—such likewise is the hope of eternity in man's bosom; he has wings, but he must be reduced to extremities before he discovers them, or before he obtains them, or before he employs them!

Imagine a hardened criminal whom justice can neither by craft nor by fair means induce to confess, but out of whom it forces an admission by means of the rack—so likewise is the hope of eternity in man's bosom. The natural man goes reluctantly, oh, so reluctantly, to confession. In the sense of childhood and youth, he is ready enough to hope. But to hope, in the sense of eternity, is contingent upon a prodigiously painful effort to which the natural man will never be brought by fair means to subject himself; for with pain man is born, but he is reborn to the eternal with perhaps even greater pain—the cry, however, signifies equally little in either case, since it is auxilliary to the act. So affliction must supervene to compel the admission, the admission of hope. Or imagine a stiff-necked witness who will not give testimony (and every man is to be a witness for the eternal and to present evidence for it)—affliction does not let him go because he refuses to give testimony; day after day it imposes upon him heavier and heavier fines for contempt of court, until he gives testimony. Or imagine, as one reads in the poets, an evil woman who knows the word of good counsel but out of malice constantly counsels wrong—when she is brought to the stake the word comes out. Such is the hope of eternity in the natural man's bosom. But he does not will his own good, therefore he will not come out with the right word, will hardly listen to it when it is said by another, let alone by himself, until affliction saves him by constraining him to it.

Thus it is that affliction recruits hope.—But is affliction then to cease, is the whole thing a painful operation which is then over with? No, it does not have to be over. When once affliction has attained what eternity wants of it, the situation adjusts itself properly; for, though the pressure remains, it constantly makes itself known conversely as hope, converts itself into hope. This is contained in the thought itself: a pressure may press down, but it may also signify to lift. Thou seest the jet of water, how it rises high in the air, thou dost not see the pressure, or that this is pressure and by pressure. There is a pressure which depresses, but there is also the pressure which uplifts. Him only can affliction depress who will not be helped eternally; him who wills this, affliction presses upward. Him only can affliction bereave of hope who will not have the hope of eternity; for him who will have this hope affliction recruits it.

Thus it is with affliction. In life there is only one danger which decisively brings with it destruction, that is sin; for sin is man's ruin. Affliction—yea, though it were more terrible than any man ever has experienced—affliction recruits hope.

III

THE JOY OF IT—THAT THE POORER THOU DOST BECOME, THE
RICHER THOU CANST MAKE OTHERS

THERE are many roads to riches. And whether a man succeeds in becoming rich by following one of these roads, or whether he does not succeed, there is always a great deal of talk in the world and ample knowledge about these many roads. But this road to riches—and yet it is verily the highest attainment of riches to be able to make others rich—this road to riches by becoming poor oneself, this road which nevertheless is 'the way' one rarely hears talked about, rarely sees trodden, is rarely recommended; alas, in the world it is almost as if it did not exist, in the world they have no conception at all that riches is precisely this, not to become or to be rich oneself, but to be able to make others rich.

And yet this marvellous road to riches does actually exist. But it is understandable when one reads in the tales of the poets how the man who has ventured into the hiding-place of robbers must be fearful of every step he takes lest there should be concealed a secret trap-door through which he may plunge into the abyss; it is understandable when incredulity and apprehensiveness preach their doctrine about the insecurity of life—for people are only too prone to believe in the possibility of ruin. But that life, that existence, is blessedly secured by the help of eternity, that precisely in danger there is concealed a trap-door . . . to restitution—this is what they do not believe. Precisely when a man is nearest to despair, there he has a place on which to tread (and in despair he is brought as near as possible to treading upon it), and therewith everything is infinitely changed. He follows then the same road, but in the opposite direction. Instead of sighing anxiously at having to walk in the path of poverty, of lowliness, of unappreciation, of persecution, he walks in that same path joyfully; for he believes, and as a believer he understands that the poorer he becomes, the richer he can make others.

So if no one else will talk about this road to riches, then we will talk about it, about

THE JOY OF IT—THAT THE POORER THOU DOST BECOME, THE
RICHER THOU CANST MAKE OTHERS

The difference is the inward one which changes everything infinitely, depending upon whether the sufferer will anxiously keep his gaze fixed upon how poor he has become, how insignificant, how unappreciated, or whether one who is bereaved of all earthly things will look away from this and then see his situation on its beautiful, its blessed side. Oh, if even for the artist it is a matter of course that when he has to paint a one-eyed man he depicts the side where he has an eye, should not then a man in bitter suffering look away from the bitterness in order to see the blessedness? In an outward sense there is to be sure no change; the sufferer remains where he was, in the same condition, and yet there is a change, a marvellous change, the miracle of faith. Viewed from the one side it is the poor man who becomes poorer and poorer; viewed from the other side it is the poor man who, the poorer he becomes, the richer he makes others—yet in an outward sense the same man.

Let us now proceed with the discourse as follows: let us first make clear to ourselves the difference between riches and riches— earthly/spiritual—and what consequences this has for the possessor, so as to understand that one must actually be poor in order to make others rich, and that the poorer one becomes, the richer one can make others.

All earthly and worldly goods are in themselves selfish, invidious, the possession of them, being invidious or envious, must of necessity make others poorer: what I have, another cannot have; the more I have, the less another has. The unrighteous mammon (and this term might well be applied to all earthly goods, including worldly honour, power, etc.) is itself unrighteous, does injustice (irrespective of whether it is unlawfully acquired or possessed), cannot in and for itself be acquired or possessed equally, for if one is to have much, there must necessarily be another who gets only a little, and what the one has, the other cannot possibly have; moreover, all the time and diligence, all the care and anxiety, expended for the acquisition or possession of earthly goods is selfish, invidious, or, the man who is so employed is selfish, in every such instant he has no thought for others, in every such instant he labours selfishly for himself or for some few others, but not equally for himself and for every other. Even though a man may be willing to communicate [1] in his earthly goods—yet every instant when he is employed in acquiring them or is dwelling upon the possession of them he is selfish, as that thing is which he possesses or acquires.

It is otherwise with the goods of the spirit. The goods of the spirit are, according to the very concept, communication, the possession of them is merciful, in and for itself it is communication. If a man has *faith*, truly he has not thereby deprived others of anything (without even taking into account what he does directly to communicate it to others), he has laboured for all others. The entire race, indeed, and every individual in the race is a sharer in the fact that he has faith. By having faith he expresses the purely human, or that which is the essential possibility of every man. His possession of faith truly does not envy others anything, the rich man's possession of money being a kind of envy which has taken this money from the poor, who perhaps in their turn envy the rich for it; for there is envy in both situations, because earthly riches is itself envy. No, the believer has taken nothing from anybody, in faith he possesses nothing invidious; and no one will envy him that, rather should every one rejoice with him because of it. For the believer possesses only what every man can possess; and just in proportion as his faith is the greater it is possible to see all the more clearly the gloriousness and blessedness of this possession which in the possibility is common to all men.—If a man has *love* —shall I add, yea, even if he had it beyond all measure? No, it would be amiss to talk so extravagantly. It might seem that in the same high degree in which he has this possession of love, the more obvious must it be that he had deprived others of something; yet exactly the contrary is the case: the higher the degree in which he has love, just so much the farther he is from having deprived others of anything. So then, if a man has love beyond all measure, he has not therefore deprived others of anything, on the contrary, he has thereby been labouring for all—without considering for a moment what he actually has done for others out of love. All the time he was labouring for his own sake to

---

[1] I do not hesitate to use this word in the Scriptural sense, as S. K. does; for we need to be reminded of the Scriptural meaning of κοινωνέω etc. (communicate, communion, etc.), seeing that in the English versions it is sometimes unfeelingly rendered by 'distribute' and 'distribution'.

acquire love, he has been labouring for all others. Although for an instant we very scrupulously exclude consideration of the use he makes of love, he has it not merely as a possession for himself, but the whole race and every individual in the race is a sharer in the fact that he has love.—If a man has *hope*, the hope of eternity, beyond all measure, he has not thereby in the very least deprived any one of anything, on the contrary, he has thereby laboured for all. For that one man has hope, or that there is one man who has hope, is for all other men far more joyful news, just because it is far more reassuring, than it is for all the other sailors who are steering for the same goal to learn that another has reached it. For in the case of the sailors, accidental circumstances may decide success for each one, and 'the other' sailors are not by an essential possibility sharers in the good luck of the one sailor. But that there is *one* man that has hope, or whenever there is one man that has hope, the thing is decisive for all, that they could have it. Here the rule is: one is all, and all one.

Thus the goods of the spirit are in and for themselves essentially communication, the possession of them is in and for itself a benefaction to all. He who strives after or possesses these goods does not therefore do good to himself merely, but bestows a benefaction upon all, labours for all, his effort to acquire these goods does in and for itself enrich others immediately; in him the others behold themselves, just as the spectators at the play behold themselves in the hero of the piece. This is the humanity of spiritual goods, in contrast to the inhumanity of earthly goods. For what is humanity? Human likeness or equality. Even at the moment when it most seems as if in acquiring these goods one is labouring for oneself alone, one is communicating; it is inherent in the goods themselves, in their very nature, that the possession of them is communication. In acquiring hope thou dost not acquire it merely for thyself but in acquiring it (oh, blessed acquisition!) thou art a communicator, for even in an immediate way the hope of eternity is a communication. Thou dost not merely possess hope, but even in the fact that thou dost possess it (oh, blessed possession!) thou art a communicator, thou art bestowing a benefaction upon others.

And how richly does heaven's blessing accompany these goods of the spirit—for 'to repeat the same thing, to me is not grievous', and it seems to me that the thought is so blessed that it cannot be repeated often enough; it would not even then be too often if a man's life were every day a repetition of this thought. Whereas the earthly goods are in themselves invidious, and therefore (oh, what great scope for fortuitous possibilities, what insecurity!) it must depend upon whether at a given instant they are possessed by one who will do good with them, and, alas, whereas they too often tempt the possessor to be just as invidious as are the goods themselves—the goods of the spirit are to such a degree a blessing that the mere possession of them (without talking now in any way of the use the possessor makes of them) is a blessing to others, is communication. As it is impossible to prevent the air from entering in through even the thickest walls, just so impossible it is to possess these goods in a selfish sense. This is inherent —and precisely here is the eternally reassuring fact—it is inherent, if I may so say, not in the possessor even, it is inherent in the goods themselves, which are communication, although it follows of itself that, if the possessor does not correspond to them, he does not possess at all the goods of the spirit. As the precious perfume diffuses a sweet odour not only when it is poured out, but to such a degree contains odour in itself, is essentially odour, that it penetrates the vessel in which it is contained, and even . . . in *concealment* diffuses sweet odour—so are the goods of the spirit to such a degree communication that possession is communication, that even to acquire them is to enrich others.

Hence it follows that all the time thou dost employ in acquiring these goods, every instant thou dost rejoice in the possession of them, thou art so far from being selfishly employed with thyself that thou art communicating directly.

Thus it is in truth with the true goods of the spirit, which at the same time have the reassuring quality, the hall-mark of the truth, that they can be possessed only in truth. If any man would possess them selfishly, possess them as his own in a selfish sense, he does not possess them at all. However, in contrast with the merely earthly goods, there are also spiritual goods of a less perfect sort. For example, insight, knowledge, talent, aptitudes, etc., are spiritual goods. But it holds true nevertheless of the less perfect spiritual goods that the decisive thing is the possessor, or what sort of a man the possessor is, whether he is benevolent and communicative, or whether he is selfish; for these goods in themselves are not yet communication. If then he who possesses these less perfect spiritual goods is selfish, it results that with him the goods themselves also become invidious and make others poorer. The possessor then confines himself with these goods of his, all the while he is labouring to acquire them or to possess them he is selfishly confined, has neither time nor opportunity to trouble himself about others, nor has thought for others. So the shrewd man becomes shrewder and shrewder, but in an invidious sense, in such a sense that for his own advantage he would like to have the others become simpler and simpler in comparison with his increasing shrewdness, would like to have these more simple others . . . inhumanly in his power. The learned man becomes more and more learned, but in an invidious sense, and at last so learned that no one can understand him, so learned that he cannot communicate himself. In this way, by being possessed in untruth, these less perfect spiritual goods are transformed into worldly and earthly goods, the characteristic of which is that in one way or another the possession of them makes others poorer. But so far as the true goods of the spirit are concerned, it is true that they can only be possessed in truth, that one who does not possess them in truth really does not possess them.

So these then are the facts about riches and riches, and these thoughts must lie at the base of and determine the thought of enriching others. On the one hand are the earthly goods (or the less perfect spiritual goods), the possession of which in itself is envy, the acquisition of which in itself is envy, and hence every hour, every thought which is employed in possessing or acquiring them is invidious; on the other hand are the true goods of the spirit, the acquisition of which is itself communication, and hence every hour, every thought which is employed in possessing or acquiring them is enriching to others.

How then can the one man make the other rich? Well, he who has the earthly goods can communicate them. All right, let us assume that he does so, and let us not forget for an instant that the earthly goods are after all not the true riches. So he communicates and does good with what he has of earthly goods. That can be done very expeditiously, he may do it once a month or one hour every day, and he may be giving away a good deal. But observe that in all the hours and days when he is employed in acquiring, in amassing, in preserving the earthly goods, he is selfish.[1] Yea, even were he to amass in order to communicate, yet so long as his thought is employed with the earthly goods he is selfish. In a sense this selfishness does not inhere in him, it inheres in the essential nature of the earthly goods. So this is seen to be only a very imperfect way of making others rich, even if we assume that he who possesses earthly goods is not ruined by them but is willing to give and to communicate, and even if for an instant we forget that the earthly goods are not the true riches.

No, the way, the perfect way of making others rich is to communicate the goods of the spirit, being oneself, moreover, solely employed in acquiring and possessing these goods. In such a case a man does truly make others rich, and this is the only thing he does, his sole business, and yet the business of his whole life. These goods are the true riches. At the time he himself is acquiring them he is communicating and directly making others rich. At the time he possesses them he is communicating and directly making others rich. And since he is solely employed with and concerned about these riches, he will surely strive to increase them. But with regard to the true riches, the nature of which is communication, increase is neither more nor less than direct communication and the increase of it; for here it is not as it is meanly in the case of false riches, which verily are not increased by being given away. Then by instruction, by reproof, by encouragement, by comfort, he communicates these goods, directly making others rich.

Let us now reflect upon our theme: how joyful it is that the poorer a man becomes, the richer he can make others. O thou sufferer, whosoever thou art, when life has deprived thee of thy riches, when from competence perhaps thou art reduced to poverty, all right then, if thou wilt let thyself be helped and wilt understand it as kindly meant in thy regard, all right then, thou art thus exempted from wasting thy time and thy day and thy thought upon that with which one can only be selfishly employed;

[1] This statement is perhaps not psychologically sound, and previous *dicta* to the effect that every increment of personal wealth makes others poorer may not be economically sound. Perhaps some such exaggeration is permissible for the sake of giving comfort to the poor. Incidentally, however, the whole discourse may be regarded as an exaltation of the monastic ideal, which made a strong appeal to S. K. A little later he made a little private attempt to practise asceticism—'to see how much I can bear', as he put it.

and thou art all the more prompted to employ thyself solely in acquiring and possessing the goods of the spirit—and, oh, in every such instant thou art making others rich! Or in case life has deprived thee of thy worldly prestige and influence, all right then, if thou wilt let thyself be helped and wilt understand it as kindly meant in thy regard, all right then, thou art thus exempted also from expending time and thought in drawing income and enjoying it, which one can only selfishly be employed about; and thou art all the more prompted to employ thyself solely in acquiring and possessing the goods of the spirit—and, oh, in every such instant thou art making others rich! Or in case thou wast expelled from human society, in case no one seeks thy company, no invitation incommodes thee, all right then, if thou wilt let thyself be helped and wilt understand it as kindly meant in thy regard, all right then, thou art thus exempted also from wasting thy time and thy thought in idle chatter, from being emptily employed in killing time to escape boredom, or in wasting it in foolish pastimes; and thou art all the more prompted to employ thyself solely in acquiring and possessing the goods of the spirit—and, oh, in every such instant thou art making others rich!

Perhaps it seems hard to thee to *become* poor, to become poorer and poorer; for in an outward sense it is a *fait accompli*. Perhaps thy soul still clings to the earthly things, selfishly preoccupied with the loss of them, as he who possesses them is preoccupied with the possession of them? Do not let thyself be pitiably deceived. It seems like such an easy thing to give some moneys to the poor when one is rich oneself, to help another on when one is mighty oneself—do not let thyself be deceived: the man who is employed in acquiring faith, hope and love, precisely he it is that makes others rich.

So become poorer still; for perhaps thou art maintaining with the lost possession a deceitful relationship of wish, perhaps thou dost cherish a hope traitorous to thyself of regaining it; become poorer still, let go entirely of the lost possession, and strive then solely for the goods of the spirit, that thou mayest make others rich. Rich in blessing be every such hour, every such instant; thou dost not only do good to thyself, but thou dost make others rich, thou art bestowing a benefaction upon others.

And when thou hast become thoroughly poor, thou hast more and more made the goods of the spirit thine own. Then thou shalt also be in a position to make others rich by communicating the goods of the spirit, by communicating what in thyself is communication. The poorer thou dost become, the rarer will be the moments in thy life when thou art selfishly employed with thyself or with what in thyself is selfish, with the earthly which so attracts to it a man's thought that for the time being he does not exist for others. But the rarer such moments become, the more constantly will the hours of thy day be filled with acquiring and possessing the goods of the spirit (ah, forget not, ah, forget not this, that when thou art doing thus thou art making others rich!) or with directly communicating the goods of the spirit, and thereby making others rich.

Think of our Pattern, the Lord Jesus Christ! He was poor, but yet He surely made others rich! And indeed His life never expresses anything accidental, as though accidentally He was poor. No His life is essential truth, and therefore it shows that to make others rich one must himself be poor. This is the thought of the Deity, very dissimilar from the thought which entered into the heart of man—the thought of the rich man who makes others rich. For not only are the earthly goods not true riches, but the rich man, however free-handed he may be in giving of his abundance, cannot avoid having times when he is employed with his riches, and so far forth he is not employed in making others rich. But He was poor so long as He lived here on earth, therefore His business so long as He lived was, every day, every hour, every instant, to make others rich—Himself poor, the only labour He was engaged in was to make others rich, and just by being Himself poor He was employed in it wholly. He did not descend from heaven to become *poor*, but He descended to make *others rich*. But to make others rich He had to be poor. He *became* poor, not as though this befell Him once in His life, perhaps after being for a time rich. Yet He *became* poor, for this was His own free resolution, His choice. He became poor, and *became* such in every sense and in every way. He lived as expelled from human society, He (oh, what light-mindedness to jest with His reputation, oh, what inexcusable indifference to the judgement of others, oh, what insolence, which indeed must deservedly abase Him deeply, deeply in the eyes of all!), He consorted only with publicans and sinners. Thus He became poor to make others rich. It was not His purpose to become poor, but His purpose was to make others rich, *hence* He became poor.—Think of the Apostle Paul, who himself utters this saying: As poor we make others rich. The Apostle put up tranquilly with being poor, living in poverty, expelled from human society, without even having a wife to whom he belonged or who belonged to him—he put up with it tranquilly, and for what reason unless because he *therein* found *the way* to make others rich?

So then this is the joyful thing, that the poorer thou dost become, the richer thou canst make others. Oh, the fact that the world bereaves thee of everything, or that thou dost lose the whole world, is really of no importance, yea, it even is for the best, if only thou thyself dost count it for the best! Precisely at the moment of despair, when the need is greatest, help is nearest, the change which infinitely alters everything: that thou the poor man art the rich man—for after all the true riches is surely to make others rich. Thus in this instance also the joy is concealed. For (and it is with this we wish to end every one of these discourses, that it may be thoroughly clear not only what we are talking about, but clear that one must talk in an entirely different way about a thing which is eternally different) sin only is man's ruin.

IV

IMAGINE a group of people who have come together for social intercourse; the conversation is in full swing, lively, almost violent, one man can hardly wait to have his say till the other is through with his, and everybody in the company takes part more or less actively in the debate—then in comes a stranger, who thus arrives in the midst of it all. Judging by the behaviour of the company and the loudness of the talk, he infers that the topic of conversation is one of great concern to them, and he courteously infers that it also must be a matter of considerable importance—and so with perfect calmness, since he has not been in the heat of it, he enquires what might be substantially the subject of their conversation. Imagine then that this, as often enough happens, was a mere trifle. The stranger is not in the least to blame for the effect he produces, he has courteously assumed that this was something of importance. But what a surprising effect, to become suddenly aware in this fashion that what for more than an hour perhaps had absorbed the attention of the whole company almost passionately is so unimportant that it hardly can be put in words, that it turns out to be a mere nothing—when a stranger calmly asks what the talk is about.

But a still stranger effect is often produced by godly talk when it is heard incidentally in the midst of the world's talk. Thus in the world there is plenty of talk about strife and strife and strife. There is talk about this man and that living in strife with one another, about that man and that woman, although they are united by the holy ties of matrimony, living in strife with one another, about the learned strife which has now begun between this man and that, about this one challenging another to a mortal duel, about there being a riot in the city, about the thousands of hostile troops which now are advancing against the country, about a European war which is impending, about the conflict of the elements which rages fearfully. Behold, it is this that is talked of in the world, day in and day out, by thousands and thousands; if in this sense thou hast anything to recount of a strife, thou wilt readily find hearers, and if thou shouldest wish to hear something, thou wilt readily find talkers. But imagine then that one of these talkers about strife took occasion to talk about the strife which every man has to strive . . . with God—what an astounding effect! Would it not rather appear to most people that it was he who was talking about nothing, whereas all the others were talking about something, or even about something very important? For, travel the world around, form acquaintance with the most various tribes, go about amongst men, enter into conversation with them, visit them in their houses, follow them to their meetings—and listen attentively to what they talk about; take part in the many, many conversations about the many, many countless ways in which a man may get into strife here in the world, take part in these conversations, but constantly in such a way that thou thyself are not the one to bring the subject up—and then tell me if thou hast ever heard anything said about this strife. And yet this strife is the affair of every man; there is no other strife of which it is true in the same degree that it is absolutely the affair of every man. For the strife between man and man—well, after all, there are many who live their lives peaceably without strife with anybody. And the strife between married people—well, after all, there are many happy marriages which this strife therefore does not concern. And after all it is a rare occurrence for a man to be challenged to a mortal duel, so this strife concerns very few. And even during a European war there are many, after all, yea, even if it was the most terrible war, there are still many—if not elsewhere, at least in America—who live on in peace. But this strife with God is absolutely the affair of every man.

This strife, however, is perhaps regarded as so sacred and solemn that for this reason it is never talked about. As God is not directly present so as to be noticed in the world, where on the other hand the immense multitude of the manifold attracts attention to itself, it is as if God did not exist at all—so this strife is perhaps a secret which every man has, but which is never talked about, whereas all the other things which are talked about attract attention to themselves, as if this strife did not exist. Perhaps it is so, perhaps.

But certain it is that every sufferer has occasion in one way or another to become aware of this strife. And it is to sufferers this discourse addresses itself. So let us talk about this strife, about

THE JOY OF IT—THAT THE WEAKER THOU DOST BECOME, THE STRONGER DOES GOD BECOME IN THEE.

For is it not true, thou sufferer, whosoever thou art, that this is indeed joyful? Still, here, as in all these discourses, everything depends upon how the situation is viewed. If the sufferer, despondent, low-spirited, perhaps in despair, would stare fixedly upon how weak he has become—no, there would be nothing joyful in that. But if he would look away from that, to perceive what it signified that he has become weak, who it is that becomes strong, that this is God—then that is indeed joyful. One sometimes hears a vanquished man say, 'I was vanquished, I was the weaker one (this is the painful part), but what comforts, yea, delights me, is that after all it was he that conquered.' Who is 'he'? Well, it may be one whom the vanquished man loves, esteems very highly. The joy is certainly not complete, he would rather have been the victor; but he compels defeat to yield a joyful aspect, he congratulates the victor upon his victory. But then when He who triumphs is God—and here again it is merely an error of vision on the part of the sufferer if, fixing his gaze *outwardly*, he concludes that these are his enemies, his jealous rivals who become stronger; for it well may be that they become stronger, and that it is precisely their strength which makes him weak, but with this the sufferer has nothing whatever to do. He becomes weak; *outwardly* understood this means simply and solely that God becomes strong. So then, when He who conquers is God! To congratulate God upon His victory, to comfort oneself that it is 'He' who has conquered, oh, essentially that is to congratulate oneself upon victory! For in relation to God a man can truly conquer only in that God conquers.

First, however, let us endeavour to make it evident that the fact of a man's being weak signifies inwardly *that God becomes strong in him.* And this is what we first of all must beg of the sufferer, what we must require of him in order to be able to talk to him, that as promptly as possible he take his eye off the outward aspect, and turns his glance *inward*, lest his glance, and he himself along with it, become riveted upon an outward view of the relation of his sufferings to his surroundings. Then when this first thing has been done, when it has been made evident that God becomes strong in him—*then surely it follows of itself that this is joyful.*

A man who but rarely, and then only cursorily, concerns himself with his relationship to God, hardly thinks or dreams that he has so closely to do with God, or that God is so close to him, that there exists a reciprocal relationship between him and God: the stronger a man is, the weaker God is, the weaker a man is, the stronger God is in him. Every one who assumes that a God exists naturally thinks of Him as the strongest, as He eternally is, being the Almighty who creates out of nothing, and for whom all the creation is as nothing; but such a man hardly thinks of the possibility of a reciprocal relationship.

And yet for God, the infinitely strongest, there is an obstacle; He has posited it Himself, yea, He has lovingly, with incomprehensible love, posited it Himself; for He posited it and posits it every time a man comes into existence, whom He in His love makes to be something, directly in apposition to Himself. Oh, marvellous omnipotence of love! A man cannot bear that his 'creations' should be something directly in apposition to himself, and so he speaks of them in a tone of disparagement as his 'creations'. But God who creates out of nothing, who almightily takes from nothing and says, 'Be', lovingly adjoins, 'Be something even in apposition to me.' Marvellous love, even His omnipotence is under the sway of love!

Hence the reciprocal relationship. If God were only the Almighty, there would be no reciprocal relationship, inasmuch as for the Almighty the creation is nothing. But for love it is something. Incomprehensible omnipotence of love! For in comparison with this omnipotence it seems as though one could comprehend better the omnipotence which creates out of nothing (which nevertheless one cannot comprehend); but this omnipotence, more marvellous than the genesis of all creation, which constrains itself and lovingly makes of the creature something in apposition to itself—oh, marvellous omnipotence of love! If thou wouldst but strain thy thought a little bit; it is not so very difficult, and it is so blissful. The omnipotence which creates out of nothing is not as incomprehensible as the almighty love which out of this which for omnipotence is nothing is able to make something which exists independently for love.

But just for this reason love requires also something of man. It never occurs to omnipotence that a man is more than nothing—he is nothing for omnipotence. People are inclined to think that it is the almighty God that requires something of men, and so perhaps that it is the loving God that abates the requirement a little. Oh, sorry misunderstanding, which forgets that God's love must already exist in order that a man may in such wise be existent for God that there can be any question of requiring anything of him. If the Almighty were to require anything of thee, in that very instant thou art nothing. But the loving God who in incomprehensible love made thee to be something for Him, lovingly requires something of thee. In human relationships it is the might of the mighty which requires something of thee, it is his love which remits. But it is not thus with the relationship to God. There is no earthly mighty man for whom thou art nothing, therefore it is his might which makes demands; but for God thou art nothing, therefore it is His love which, as it made thee to be something, requires something of thee. They speak of the omnipotence of God crushing a man. But it is not so; no man is so considerable that God would need omnipotence to crush him, since for omnipotence he is nothing. It is God's love which manifests itself as love even at the last instant by letting him be something for it. Woe unto him if omnipotence turns against him.

So then, love, which made a man to be something (for omnipotence let him come into existence, but love let him come into existence *for* [1] God) lovingly requires something of him. Here we have the reciprocal relationship. If a man would selfishly keep for himself this something which love made him to be, and would selfishly be something, then, in a worldly sense, he is strong—but God is weak. And it is almost as if the poor loving God were duped: with incomprehensible love God has gone ahead and made man something—and thereupon man dupes Him and holds on to this as if it were his own. The worldly man confirms himself in the notion that he is strong, he is perhaps

---

[1] In Danish '*for*' means both 'for' *and* 'before'. S. K.'s constant thought is, or rather his most profound religious feeling is, that a man exists *before* God, 'directly in the face of God', and though this is not the thought he stresses in this discourse, he hardly could use this word '*for*' without some subordinate reference to the other meaning.

confirmed in it by other people's worldly judgement to the same effect, perhaps by his presumed might he transforms the face of the world—but God is weak. On the other hand, if man himself relinquishes this something, the independence, the freedom to act for himself, which love bestowed upon him; if this perfection of his which consists in existing for God he does not abuse by taking it in vain; if God perhaps helps him in this respect by bitter sufferings, by taking from him his dearest one, by wounding him in the tenderest spot, by denying him his only wish, by depriving him of his last hope—then he is weak. That indeed everybody will say to him, and say of him, he will so be regarded by all, no one will make common cause with him; for it looks in fact as though he had become merely a burden which their compassion must bear. He is weak—but God is strong. He, the weak man, has relinquished entirely this something which love made him to be, he has whole-heartedly consented to it that God took from him everything there was to be taken. God only waits for him to give lovingly and humbly his glad consent, and therewith to relinquish it completely, then he is entirely weak—and then God is strongest.[1] There is only one who can prevent God from being the strongest, who nevertheless is eternally the strongest; this one is man himself. That God is the strongest is evidenced by one sign, that man is entirely weak. For God there is but one obstacle, man's selfishness, which steps in between God and man like the shadow of the earth when it produces the eclipse of the moon. If there is this selfishness, then man is strong, but his strength is God's weakness; if the selfishness is absent, then man is weak, and God strong; the weaker man becomes, the stronger God becomes.

However, if this is so, then in another sense, in the true sense, the relation is inverted; and with this we come to the joyfulness.

For he who is strong without God, precisely he it is who is weak. The strength by which a man stands alone may be strength in comparison with that of a child. But the strength by which a man stands alone without God is weakness. God is in such a degree the strong one that He is all strength, is strength itself. So to be without God is to be without strength. So to be strong

---

[1] The perfect sincerity of these discourses appears when one observes that in such a passage as this S. K. describes the path he trod in 'becoming a Christian'. It is evident that he was able to comfort sufferers because he was a sufferer.

without God is to be strong . . . without strength; it is like being loving without loving God, and so to be loving without love, for God is *love*.

But in him who became entirely weak God became strong. He who worshipping and praising and loving became weaker and weaker, himself of less importance to God than a sparrow, as himself nothing, in him God is stronger and stronger. *And the fact that God is stronger and stronger in him signifies that he is stronger and stronger.*—If thou couldst become entirely weak in perfect obedience, so that loving God thou didst understand that thou art able to do nothing at all, then would all the mighty ones of the earth, if they were to unite against thee, be unable to hurt a hair of thy head—what prodigious strength! But in fact this is not true, and let us not say anything untrue. Indeed they certainly would be able to do this, they would be able even to put thee to death, and the great conjunction of all the mighty ones of the earth is by no means requisite to this end, a far, far inferior power can easily enough do it. But yet if thou wert entirely weak in perfect obedience, then all the mighty ones of the earth in conjunction are not able to hurt a hair of thy head *otherwise* than as God wills. And when it is hurt *thus*, when thou art reviled *thus*, when thou art put to death *thus*—if thou wert entirely weak in perfect obedience—thou wouldst lovingly understand that it does thee no harm, not the very least, that it is for thy true welfare—what prodigious strength!

And even if it were not so that he in whose weakness God is strong is the strongest man—this nevertheless is the joyful thing, that God becomes stronger and stronger, that it is God who becomes stronger and stronger. Let us talk of a relationship between man and man which has, though very imperfectly, something in common with that which in the relationship between man and God is the essence of worship, let us talk about admiration. Admiration is in itself duplex, it can be viewed from two sides. Its first phase is a feeling of weakness, for the admirerer stands in relationship to superiority. But admiration is a happy relationship to superiority, and so it is a blissful feeling, perhaps it is more blissful to admire in complete unanimity with oneself than to be the object of admiration. That the first phase of admiration is a feeling of pain is evidenced by the fact that if one senses superiority and admits it unwillingly, not joyfully, he is very far from being happy; on the contrary he is very unhappy, is in the sharpest pain. On the other hand, so soon as he yields to the superiority (which yet at bottom he admires, but unhappily) and surrenders himself in admiration, the joyfulness of it triumphs in him. The more devoted he is, the more unanimous with himself in admiring, the nearer he comes to being almost superior to superiority; in his admiration he is happily and indescribably liberated from all the oppressive pressure of superiority, he is not overcome by superiority but triumphs in admiration.

Let us forget now the imperfection of the comparison of admiration as exhibited in the relationship of man to man, and worship in the relationship of man to God. God is infinitely the strongest; this every man believes, and, whether he will or no, he feels accordingly God's infinite superiority and his own nothingness, but so long as he only believes that God is the strongest, and (to make mention of the dreadful case) believes it as the devils also believe . . . and tremble; so long as he only believes it thus, and is loath to make the admission; so long as he only believes it in such wise that he is not glad of it—just so long is the relationship painful, unhappy, his feeling of weakness an agonizing perception. For *defiance* [1] is in relation to worship what envy is in relation to admiration. Defiance is weakness and impotence which makes itself unhappy by not willing to be weakness and impotence, it is the unhappy relationship of weakness and impotence to superiority, just as envy tortures itself because it will not be, what at bottom it is, admiration. What is required of man is already hinted at in relation to admiration (for the admirer loses himself in admiration of the one who is so far greater); it is required that he shall lose himself in God. If he does this with his whole heart, with all his strength, and with his whole mind, then he is in a happy relationship to God as the strong one, then he is a worshipper—never, never did any lover become so happy, never, never did the parched earth sighing at the drought sense so deliciously the refreshing rain, as the worshipper blissfully senses God's strength. Now these twain, God and the worshipper, are adapted to one another, happily, blissfully, as never were lovers adapted to one another. It is now the only wish of the worshipper to become weaker and weaker, for

---

[1] It is especially in *The Sickness unto Death* we learn what part—what a prodigious part—S. K. ascribes to defiance.

with that the more worship; the only need worship feels is that God may become stronger and stronger. The worshipper has lost himself, and in such wise that this is the only thing he wishes to be rid of, the only thing he flees from; he has gained God—and so indeed it is directly in his own interest that God becomes stronger and stronger.

The worshipper is the weak man; so he must appear to all the others, and this is the humiliating part. He is entirely weak; he is not able like others to make resolutions for a long life, no, he is entirely weak; he is scarcely able to make a resolution for the morrow without adding, 'If God will'. He is not able to rely defiantly upon his own strength, his talents, his gifts, his influence, he is not able to utter proud words about all he is able to do—for he is able to do nothing at all.[1] This is the humiliating part. But *inwardly* what bliss! For this weakness of his is a love-secret with God, it is worship. The weaker he becomes, the more genuinely he can pray; and the more genuinely he prays, the weaker he becomes—and the more blissful.

Is not this then joyful, that the weaker thou dost become, all the stronger does God become in thee, or, is it not joyful that thou dost become weak? Is there at bottom anything to complain of because a hard lot fell to thee, that perhaps which thou didst most dread and which made thee entirely impotent and weak? The weaker thou dost become, so much the stronger does God become in thee. And that this is joyful thou thyself wilt surely admit! Consider how poor a man would be if he could pass his whole life, proud and self-satisfied, without ever having admired any one; but how horrible a thing if he could pass his whole life without ever having marvelled at God, without ever having lost himself in worship through marvelling at God! But one can worship only by becoming oneself weak, thy weakness is essentially worship; woe to the presumptuous man who in his presumptive strength would be audacious enough as a strong man to worship God! The true God can be worshipped only in spirit and in truth—but precisely this is the truth, that thou art entirely weak.

---

[1] Upon the Lutheran dogma of human impotence ('that man can do nothing at all') S. K. often reflected, and often critically—yet in his own peculiar way he adhered to it . . . without basing upon it the doctrine of predestination or impugning the freedom of the will.

So then there is nothing in the world to fear, nothing to fear in that which can bereave thee of all thine own power and make thee entirely weak, which can break all thy confidence in thyself and make thee entirely weak, which can completely sap thy earthly courage and make thee entirely weak—f.. the weaker thou dost become, all the stronger does God become in thee.

No, so understood, there is nothing in the world to fear—for sin alone is man's ruin.

V

That this is gain one can readily perceive, and so exorbitant a gain that never did any merchant who made the most profitable bargain ever make one so profitable as this. The difficulty lies in another place, in the place, namely, where the bargain, if I may so call it, has to be closed, in the fact that this place is temporal existence. If one were in eternity, one without doubt would be well able to understand it. But in temporal existence, and at the very instant of the loss, that is, when the temporal makes itself most keenly felt, it may easily seem perhaps that eternity is so infinitely far off, that the prospects are so remote for this indubitably extraordinary gain—and what then is the good of the great profit when there are difficulties like this? A bird in the hand is worth two in the bush; a little smaller profit seems preferable to the immense . . . uncertain gain. Yes, so it seems in temporal existence, which sees everything topsy-turvy. And there is hardly anything more topsy-turvy than the notion that the eternal is the uncertain, and hardly any shrewdness more topsy-turvy than that which lets go of the eternal because it is uncertain, and grasps the temporal . . . because it is the certain. For if one does not at once get an opportunity to discover that after all eternity was the certain thing—that the temporal is the uncertain one can promptly get an opportunity to perceive. Therefore hardly any talk is more ludicrous than when a man holds the temporal in his hand and says, 'I hold to the certain.' But, as has been said, the difficulty lies in the place where the bargain has to be closed. When death has already cleared things up for one, to make the exchange of time and eternity is easy; but in temporal existence to get the view-point of eternity for bartering time for eternity, the view-point of eternity for reckoning that what is lost temporally is gained eternally, that indeed is difficult.

The sufferer, however, has by another process become sensible of the difficulty of life, how difficult it is to bear his loss, with all

the sorrow of it and the pain—so then, though the joyfulness . . .
of loss which is proposed to him presents difficulties in its turn,
this is nevertheless decidedly to be preferred. The difficulty is
to get eternity brought a little nearer; when eternity is quite
near the joy is quite complete. But this thing of getting eternity
brought a little nearer is of decisive importance for every sufferer
if he is to be comforted and if his comfort is to become joy. If
medical science recognizes a miraculous cure-all, one for all ill-
nesses, I do not know; but spiritually there is one, only one,
exceedingly simple cure—eternity. The difficulty merely is to
get it quite near. Observe that a child also can perhaps draw
after a fashion, and one who is not an artist can also perhaps draw
after a fashion, but all that they draw they draw straight up and
down on the paper. Ask an artist what the difficulty is, and thou
wilt hear him reply: 'The distance of perspective in the drawing'.
In relation to eternity the difficulty is the reverse of this: eternity
seems so far, the task is to get it as near as possible. For from the
view-point of temporal existence it seems to the impatience of the
unwise man (and the more temporal existence has to say about
it, the less wisdom there is and the more impatience) as if instead
of getting the lost thing again eternally he would have to wait an
eternity to get it again. But if eternity is quite near to thee, it is
true thou dost not yet get the lost object, for that comes about
first in eternity, but it is *eternally certain* to thee that thou wilt
eternally get it again. If such be the case, eternity is quite near
to thee. How near it is may perhaps be elucidated for thee by
another situation. A wise man has said, 'Every one who has
deserved punishment fears punishment, but every one who fears
punishment suffers punishment.' In a sense the guilty man has
not yet suffered his punishment, in another sense it impends
over him so near that he suffers it.

So let me try if possible to compel the sufferer for his own good
to become joyful, compel him to get eternity as near as possible,
while I talk about

THE JOY OF IT—THAT WHAT THOU DOST LOSE TEMPORALLY THOU
DOST GAIN ETERNALLY.

For in fact only the temporal can be lost temporally; anything else
but the temporal it is impossible for temporal existence to take
from thee; when thou knowest that it is temporal existence as

such which has taken something from thee, by that same token thou knowest that it must be something temporal it took. In case the dreadful thing occurs that a man in *temporal existence* loses the *eternal*, this is no longer a loss, it is perdition.[1] 'Loss' relates to the temporal. It is assumed, when anything is to be said about loss, about the pain and suffering of loss—if one is to speak for comfort, encouragement and joy, it is assumed that the sufferer himself is not guilty (as mere loss does not imply) of 'forfeiting his soul'. If such a dreadful loss is occasioned by losing the eternal in time, one must talk very differently. So this discourse presupposes that the sufferer to whom it is addressed, however great the pain of his loss may be, has maintained relationship with the eternal, by means of which he is to be comforted. If the loss has acquired such power over the sufferer that 'his heart has sinned in its sorrow',[2] that in desperation he would go to perdition, then one must talk quite differently. In the case of sin one must talk first and foremost with an aim to conversion, even when talking with an aim to comfort and joy; in the case of suffering one can at once talk of comfort and joy, even if the comforting speech is, as it is indeed if it is Christian, 'a hard saying'. And above all let us not forget that not only theft and murder and drunkenness and the like are sins, but that properly sin is: *in time to lose eternity*. One too often forgets this, yea, even the officially appointed pastors in the cure of souls are sometimes (and hence their failure) too much inclined to want to give comfort at once, without first, as becomes a physician, diagnosing the sufferer's condition. For as severity in the wrong place may be ruinous, so also leniency in the wrong place, leniency where the sufferer feels at bottom that one ought to speak severely, and therefore is disgusted not only with the comfort but with the comforter who shows that he does not recognize the ailment. Figure to thyself a woman, the most lovable of all women—thus we could imagine her. Along with her purity it would be abhorrent to think of what we call the grosser sins—oh, but vanity also, and pride, and envy, and arrogance are strangers to her lovable soul. She has lost her lover. In case she has said in despair, 'Now I care nothing either for God or for eternity', then certainly comfort, in the direct sense, would be the most ruinous thing of

---

[1] In Danish it is *Tab* (loss) and *Fortabelse* (perdition).
[2] A line quoted inexactly from a familiar Danish hymn.

all. And though thou thyself wert never so deeply touched and moved at the sight of her pain, yea, if thou wert so full of sympathy that thou wouldst willingly give all, thy very life, in order to comfort her if possible—in case thou wert a pastor in the cure of souls, how terrible if thou hadst not the courage to employ severity! Or what judgement wouldst thou pass upon a physician who, because he himself had a horror for the fevered man's thirst, did not dare to forbid him to drink (yea, utter it only and hear the contradiction)—out of sympathy prescribed for him cold water, that is, out of sympathy slew him! [1]

So then, when the sufferer, whatever he may have lost, is not himself guilty of disturbing dreadfully the divine order of things, only the temporal can be lost temporally. Because man has in him something eternal, therefore he can lose the eternal, but this is not to lose, it is to be lost; if there were nothing eternal in man, he could not be lost.

On the one hand this: only the temporal is lost temporally. On the other hand: *only the eternal can be gained eternally.* In case a man could be so presumptuous as to wish to gain the eternal temporally, this again is perdition. In case one were to grasp the eternal to have *earthly* profit from it, he is lost; in case one would buy the Holy Ghost with money, he is lost. And why is he lost? Because he *temporally lost the eternal*; for he lost the eternal precisely by wishing to abase it to the temporal. The purpose or the aim is always more important than the means. So if one would gain the eternal for the sake of earthly profit, the earthly profit is then more important to one than the eternal; but if this is so, one has lost the eternal; and when a man has lost the eternal he is lost. The eternal refuses to amalgamate with this talk of loss and loss; so soon as it is the eternal that is lost, everything is altered, even the language, and so this is (not a *pert* but) perdition.

Now let us draw these thoughts together (like a net) to catch joy, or to catch the sufferer for joy. If only the temporal can be lost temporally, and only the eternal can be gained eternally, the gain is indeed evident; in losing the temporal I gain eternity. O thou sufferer, whatsoever thou hast lost, thou hast lost only something temporal, it is impossible to *lose* anything else; and whatsoever thou hast lost, there is something to be gained, the eternal,

---

[1] Evidently the medical treatment of fever has changed in the course of a century —'*nous avons changé tout cela*'.

which thou dost gain eternally. If thou dost not will to be lost (and if this is to be, thou must thyself *will* it), if in the depths of thy soul thou dost shudder at this thought, then both the stern seriousness of this thought and the shudder unite in guaranteeing that thou wilt not shun comfort by willing to be lost—then, however heavy thy loss, it will be made manifest that nevertheless the joyful thing is that what thou dost lose temporally thou dost gain eternally.

But perhaps thou wouldst say, 'Will eternity give back to me the thing lost just as it was when my soul clung to it?' Oh, no, certainly not, for then the discourse would not be, as it is, about gain—thou dost get it again eternally. However, there is perhaps a little cunning hidden in this question of thine. For in losing the object, it was in fact taken from thee, it was no act of thine; and from this it cannot be deduced that thou hast thoroughly willed to let it go. Perhaps (oh, be on thy guard!) thou art not far from willing to have eternity as a means of getting again in eternity the temporal possession just as it was in temporal existence, thine eyes' delight and thy heart's desire [1]—this also is perdition. For, if such be the case, what thou wilt is not to gain the eternal eternally, but thou wouldst gain the eternal in order that it in eternity might give thee the lost temporal possession, that is, thou wouldst lose the eternal in order eternally to gain the temporal, and this means, temporally to lose the eternal, which is perdition. In case it was not earthly goods thou didst lose, in case it was that which smarts more painfully, in case e.g. it was honour thou didst lose, which slander stole from thee; in case thy whole soul clung to it with insatiable passion, so that it was thine only wish, thine only pleasure, to enjoy this satisfaction of vanity and pride, to be held in honour—this indeed eternity cannot give thee again. In case it was thy lover thou didst lose, of whom death bereaved thee, thy lover to whom thou wast attached with the intensity of all earthly passion, with the love of the one and only wish—thy lover whom thou (reflect how cruel it is!) wouldst prevent, if it depended upon thee, from becoming transfigured—no, in this wise eternity cannot give him back to thee! In eternity there is no pomp and splendour of worldly honour, and in eternity they neither marry nor are given in marriage.

[1] This phrase S. K. often used with reference to Regina, his lost love.

But why dost thou ask about some individual thing in time which thou wouldst have again—unless it be because thy soul clings to it temporally? This discourse ventures to go much farther, makes the loss much greater, talks of temporal existence as a whole, of everything temporal—but also about *letting go of* the lost temporal possession. Why dost thou talk of an individual temporal thing—and so passionately? Ah, be on thy guard; it is as though thou wert at the point of willing to lose something temporal in an eternal manner, to fix a temporal loss eternally fast in thy soul, to remember eternally a temporal loss; this also is perdition. If anything temporal is lost in this manner, it cannot be due to the temporal, for the temporal can only be lost temporally. So it must be due to the loser—that he *wills* to lose eternally something temporal, that is, to lose temporally the eternal, that is, to be lost.

What thou dost lose temporally thou dost gain eternally. Thou dost not get it back in the temporal sense, that is impossible, and it would not be any gain; but thou dost get it back in the sense of eternity—if thou dost lose it temporally, that is, if thou thyself wilt not (ah, by *willing* to be lost!) transform the temporal into something other than it is. If something temporal concerns thee as if it were not the temporal but the eternal, the fault is not in the temporal thing (which according to its concept can only be lost temporally), but in thee. If the loss of the temporal concerns thee so much that in despair thou dost not even care to gain the eternal, this is not due to the temporal thing (which according to its concept can only be lost temporally), but to thee. That is to say, if thou dost not *will* to be lost (and in such case the talk about 'loss' is senseless), it stands fast eternally that what thou hast lost temporally (be it what it may, be it regarded also by all others as the heaviest loss, or only so regarded by thee in thy pain), that thou dost gain eternally.

This stands fast eternally; even though all devils and all hair-splitters were to contest with us, they would not be able to disprove this. If therefore thou dost lose an earthly friend, perhaps thine only one, or the best—in case thou dost not lose him otherwise than as temporal existence bereaves thee of him, that is, in case thou dost lose him temporally (in no other way can *temporal existence* bereave thee of him, unless thou thyself *wilt* be to blame for it, since temporal existence verily is not to blame), then thou

dost gain him eternally. Thou losest thus an earthly friend—
thou gainest a transfigured friend. For eternity does not give
back to thee the lost temporal object in the temporal sense; no,
precisely this is the gain of eternity, which gives back the lost
object in the sense of eternity and eternally—unless (ah, consider
what a wrong against the loved one!) by being lost thou wilt
prevent thyself from receiving him back! In case it was earthly
riches thou didst lose—in case thou didst lose them temporally
(oh, remember that in no other way is it possible for the temporal
to bereave thee of them); in case thou wert not thyself guilty of
the dreadful thing of losing them in an entirely different way than
the temporal can bereave thee of them, namely, by losing thyself;
in case thou wast willing to let go of the temporal because thou
didst understand the truth, that it was lost temporally—then
thou didst gain the eternal. Thou didst lose the riches of the
temporal—thou didst gain the riches of eternity. In case thou
didst see thy dearest plan come to wreck in the world, the cause
defeated for which thou hadst sacrificed thyself—in case thou
didst lose only temporally (and remember that in no other way
is it possible for the temporal to bring to naught any plan or any
cause); in case thou thyself wast not guilty of the dreadful thing
of suffering defeat in an entirely different way than the temporal
is able to inflict it upon thee, namely, by losing thyself); in case
thou wast willing to let go of the lost temporal thing because thou
didst understand the truth, that it was lost temporally—then thou
didst gain the eternal. Thou didst suffer defeat of the temporal—
thou didst gain the victory of eternity. Dost thou not gain eternally what thou losest temporally? Would a man will to conquer
here in time—well, then, the temporal defeat means to him that
all is lost. But this is not due to time, it is due to him, on the
other hand, if he triumphs over his mind, the loss then becomes
what it is, a temporal loss, and he gains eternally.

Perhaps, however, some sufferer will say, 'Well, but what I
gain is not the same as what I lost.' No, certainly not; this discourse in fact has to do with gain. And moreover, in case it was
the same temporal possession thou didst get again, thou didst
not lose it temporally. In so far as that which thou didst lose
was compounded of the temporal and the eternal, the temporal
took its part, and that thou didst lose; but the eternal it did not
take away from that which thou didst lose, and that thou shalt

get again in eternity. So then, thou dost get back the lost. Or did thy deceased friend lose anything by the fact that death took from him the temporal, when it was obliged nevertheless to let him keep the eternal? Does a proprietor lose by the fact that his property gains in value?—On the other hand, in so far as that which thou didst lose was something purely temporal, the temporal took it from thee, and thou didst lose the temporal; but in the loss thou didst gain the corresponding eternal good, which thou dost get again in eternity. Thus after all thou dost get *that*, precisely *that*, *eternally* which thou didst lose *temporally*.

Is not this then joyful, that wherever in temporal existence there is loss and the pain of loss, eternity is then at hand to offer the sufferer more than compensation? The sufferer himself is in fact compounded of the temporal and the eternal. So when temporal existence inflicts upon him the greatest loss it is able to inflict, the question is whether, by an act of treason against himself and against eternity, he will bestow upon the loss of the temporal the power to become something other than it is, a temporal loss, whether he wills to lose the eternal; or whether, true to himself and to the eternal, he does not permit the loss of the temporal to become something other than it is, a temporal loss. If he does this, then the eternal in him has conquered. *To let go of the temporal in such a way that it is lost temporally*, to lose only temporally the lost temporal possession, is *a precise indication of the presence of the eternal in the loser*, is the token that the eternal in him has conquered.

This triumphant joy is entirely non-existent for the sensual man; it entirely escapes his notice that all a man's conflicts here in this life are really waged about something entirely different than is apparent at the first glance. For, understood in a godly sense, it is always perfectly indifferent whether a man strives to make both ends meet in life, or whether he is marching at the head of thousands and thousands accompanied by the cannon's thunder, what the strife is waged for is always to save his own soul—whether he *wills* to lose the eternal temporally, that is, to be lost, or by losing the temporal temporally to gain the eternal. That this is what is to be looked at entirely escapes the notice of the worldly man. Therefore when in temporal existence he suffers a decisive loss of the temporal, he despairs, that is to say, it then becomes evident that he was in despair.[1] But he who in truth would save his soul looks at that which should be looked at, and precisely by looking at that he discovers at the same time the joy of it that what one loses temporally one gains eternally. Ah, and as the severity of the teacher is sometimes necessary, not to punish inattention, but to punish attention, to compel the pupil to look at that which should be looked at, instead of sitting abstractedly and being lured to look at all sorts of things—so must the fear of perdition help the sufferer to look at that which should be looked at, and thereby help him to discover the joy.

Only by the aid of the eternal is a man able to let go of the lost temporal possession in such a way that he merely loses it temporally. If the eternal does not lend its aid, he loses much more than the temporal. But if temporally to lose the temporal is an indication of the eternal in the loser, then eternity is indeed very close to him. At the outset the only ground for fear we saw was that the prospects of the compensation of eternity are so remote, this being all there was to prevent one from finding the joy in the fact that what one loses temporally one gains eternally. In the eternal certainty that this is so, eternity is as close to a man as is possible, and as close as is necessary. But when eternity itself lends its aid, if the loser loses only the lost temporal possession, eternity is indeed quite close. And if eternity is so close, so is this joy that what one loses temporally one gains eternally. Thou wilt not have to wait half a century in uncertainty to get back what was lost. Oh, no, that is only the way it appears in temporal existence, if thou hast not the will to let go temporally of the temporal loss. If thou hast the will to do that, then the eternal in thee has conquered, or the eternal has conquered in thee, then the eternal has visited thee, then to thee it is eternally certain that thou dost get it again, and then thou canst easily wait. Therefore never thrust the blame upon the length of time; for an eternal certitude shortens the time to one day, even though it were a century of waiting. Neither thrust the blame upon the temporal; for it took only the temporal from thee, nothing else and no otherwise can it take away. Above all, do not hasten impatiently to thine own

---

[1] If you admit this proposition upon which S. K. very frequently insists (that the 'aesthetic' life has the seeds of despair in it), you must assent to the general argument implied in his 'aesthetic works', and you cannot gainsay the conclusion he reaches in *The Sickness unto Death*.

destruction, alas, 'as a bird hasteth to the snare'. Seek the fault in thyself; consider seriously and severely how near perdition lies; consider that, as understood in the purely eternal sense, every temporal loss is an instant—if thou dost require a very long time to understand this, it is because the eternal within thee has not yet acquired strength enough. Let then the eternal come quite close to thee, then thou art helped, and then it is joyful to thee.

So then there is really no loss in the world, but sheer gain. For every 'loss' is temporal; but what thou dost lose temporally thou dost gain eternally, the loss of the temporal is the gain of eternity. Only sin is man's ruin. But precisely this is sin: to lose the eternal temporally, or to lose the lost temporal possession otherwise than temporally, which is perdition.

VI

THE JOY OF IT—THAT WHEN I 'GAIN ALL' I LOSE NOTHING AT ALL

'To gain all'—more than this nobody can demand; and if he gains all, it is clearer than day that he loses nothing at all. And it is surely easy enough to perceive that this is joyful, every child can understand it *instantly*, yea, even the youth who most is agitated and rendered impatient by the hot aspiration of wishes, even he can *at once* understand it. If only he does not misunderstand it, and thereby misunderstand the whole discourse. For these discourses are not for the young, at least not for immediate use; only when life has furnished the youth with a text can he perhaps find use for them and better understand the theme.

But is it not strange that he who burns most hotly with the aspiration of youthful wishes, and he who in self-denial gave up the most, that these two unite in saying the same thing: 'To gain all', whereas between them there is nevertheless a world-wide difference, and they are as far as possible from talking of one and the same thing? In fact, God's Word by its promises encourages the believer 'to gain all'; and no youth, not even he who is most spoiled by having all his wishes fulfilled, has desired more than 'to gain all'. How strange! Just as in life there is a reversion when a man becomes again as a child, so in the language of thought there is a reversion through which the most different thoughts result, as it seems, in the same expression—and yet it is precisely then that the difference is greatest. There is absolutely no one so different from a child—not the little older, not the somewhat older, not the elderly man, not the aged man (all of this being direct comparison, where *likeness* is the point of departure for estimating the difference)—there is no one so different from the child as the aged man who becomes again a child; for this is inverse comparison, where everything is inverted, where the *difference* is the point of departure for estimating the likeness. And there is no one so different from a wisher, a hankerer, a desirerer who would gain all—not him who gave up little, not him who gave up somewhat, not him who gave up much (all this being direct comparison, so that he who gave up little, somewhat, much may quite well be a desirer who desires much, somewhat, little)—no, none is so different from a desirerer who would gain all, as he who gave up all—yet of that he does not talk, he talks, strangely enough, about gaining all, and therefore there is none so different from a desirerer who would gain all, as precisely the man who says the same thing.

But it is none the less certain that it is joyful to gain all, and that when I gain all I lose nothing at all. So let us talk of

THE JOY OF IT—THAT WHEN I 'GAIN ALL' I LOSE NOTHING AT ALL.

For if the 'all' which I gain is truly all, then that which in another sense is called all, the all which I lose, must be the false all; but when I lose the false all I in fact lose nothing; and when I gain the true all, I lose in fact the false all—so I lose nothing.

Thou knowest perhaps that for an instant it looks as if one might fight this joyful thought through to victory in two ways. One might strive to make it perfectly clear to oneself that the all which one loses is the false all, is nothing. Or one takes another path, aspiring after the full conviction of spiritual certitude that the all which one gains is truly all. The latter procedure is the best, the only way. For in order to acquire the power to understand that the false all is nothing, one must have the aid of the true all, otherwise the false all takes away one's power. Verily it is not by the aid of nothing one can succeed in seeing that the false all is nothing. There is a pretended wisdom whose secret is nothing, and which yet thinks it can see that all is nothing. But this is impossible; it is just as impossible as to see in the dark with a light which is not lit. There is much said in the world about there being two paths to the truth: that of faith, and that of doubt. But this is quite as strange as if one were to say: there are two paths to heaven, one of which leads to hell. So 'the way' is to aspire after the full conviction of spiritual certitude that thou dost gain all. And what is it to aspire thus? It is to believe. Believe that thou gainest all, then thou dost lose nothing. Wish to gain all, desire to gain all, expect to gain all—and perhaps thou wilt lose all. But believe that thou gainest all, then thou dost lose nothing. For the all to which faith is related is the true all, so then thou dost lose nothing at all.

But as for believing! Oh, this is such a peculiar thing about Christianity: in a certain sense it is so unspeakably easy to understand, and on the other hand it becomes really difficult just at the moment when it has to be believed. I know well enough that a profound topsy-turvy worldly wisdom has inverted the relationship, affirming that it is so easy to believe, so difficult to understand. But only put this to a test. Take what we are here talking about. What is easier to understand than the proposition: When I gain all I lose nothing? And only when it has to be believed the real difficulty emerges. What is easier to understand than that the whole world must appear to a man as Christianity says it is, must appear thus . . . when he is dead, dead in self-denial. But to *become* dead to the world! This thing of '*when* one is dead to the world'!

Believe that thou gainest all, therewith thou diest unto the world; and when thou art dead thou dost lose nothing by losing that which in the understanding of the living man is all. Lose gold and goods, lose might and power, lose glory and prestige, lose health and strength, lose thy best friend, lose thy well beloved, lose more than did that king who yet spoke of losing all when he said, 'All is lost save honour'—believe that thou gainest all, and then thou dost lose nothing! That when thou gainest all, it is impossible to lose even the least thing—oh, nothing is more certain, only believe then that thou gainest all! This is—I have to admit it—an unequal division of labour: that the discourse has only the task of saying the same thing over and over again (it is in fact to say the same thing when one says, 'He who gains all loses nothing,' for to gain all and to lose nothing is one and the same thing), whereas thou hast the task of grasping faith, and by believing to hold fast to it that thou dost gain all—oh, but then the discourse does not possess thy joy! Poor discourse! In a sense it does not budge from the spot, it says only one and the same thing;[1] in another sense it hovers helplessly between heaven and earth, for if it is not a certainty that there is one man who believes, then the discourse is empty. Therefore it is not the believer that needs the discourse, but rather it is the believer that pityingly comes to the relief of the discourse. For every time a man believes that he gains all, the discourse becomes true, then the empty and meaningless discourse, which is so all too easily

[1] So said Socrates of himself.

understood, becomes so full, so rich, in a favourable sense so difficult—but so true.

Believe that thou gainest all, then thou dost become a dead man. Just as ghosts flee before the dawn, and apparitions collapse when their name is uttered, and enchantment ceases when the magic word is spoken—so to thee does the world and what the world calls 'all' become nothing. Then lose the world and every pleasure it possesses, lose its friendship, let it become thine enemy which chases thee out of every refuge, thine enemy which hates thee: believe that thou dost gain all—and thou dost lose nothing! The world must hate a deceased man; there is nothing contemporaries more hardly endure in a contemporary than that he lives like a departed spirit. In a room it is disturbing when a blind man walks about and cannot see what he bumps against; but a believer is likewise a blind man, his eyes are blinded by the splendour of the all which he gains, he cannot see anything of the all wherein the world has its life and its pleasure, he can see nothing of this all because he has seen that it is nothing. Oh, mad inconsiderateness of faith, which out of consideration for the true all has become blind to all considerations! In a company it is disturbing when a deaf man is present who cannot hear what the others say and nevertheless takes part in the conversation, inasmuch as he is to be heard transforming the talk of the others into nonsense; but a believer is likewise a deaf man, his ears echo with the glory of the all which he gains, he can hear nothing of the all wherein the world has its life and its pleasure. Oh, mad inconsiderateness of faith, which out of consideration for the true all has become deaf to all considerations! But believe that thou dost gain all, and thou dost lose nothing.

Yes, believe that thou gainest all. Behold that expert scientist, he had all his calculations completed, he had perhaps spent many years getting all this studied out and put together, it was all in order—he was waiting only for a point outside the earth, and he would be man enough to hoist the whole earth by means of . . . the calculations?—yes, or by means of the point. So long as he has not the point, all his calculations, the fruit of many years of diligence, are an impotent nothing—and the discourse about the truth that when one gains all one loses nothing, yea, even though the speaker were a man who had pondered his whole life long only over this thought, or over this only thought, and though of all eloquent speakers he were the most eloquent, and though he had the whole structure of his eloquence complete—it is an impotent nothing, if there is no one who believes that he gains all. And if there is this believer who believes that he gains all—he loses nothing, nothing at all, even if he never chances to hear a word of all this eloquence.

Oh, victorious joy of faith! But can the discourse accomplish nothing because it cannot give thee faith, because in comparison with faith it is not the higher (as a wisdom which is higher only than . . . madness would make us believe) but is the lower thing? Yes indeed, it can tell thee how blessed it is to believe. For when one believes, he gains all; to gain all is precisely to believe, to believe that one gains all; and when one gains all one loses nothing. In relation to divers losses in life there is perhaps a special insurance company which provides compensation; but what security against all losses, that with them all one loses nothing! It is indeed like being secured against death by being deceased. If the desirous youth were to gain all, what security has he that he may not lose it? But oh, what security in gaining all, that one gained it by losing all—and yet lost nothing!

And he who lost the true 'all', only he truly lost all. But this is perdition; only sin is man's ruin.

VII

THE JOY OF IT—THAT MISFORTUNE IS GOOD FORTUNE

Misfortune is good fortune.[1] 'But this', I hear some one
say, 'is merely a jest, and easy enough to understand, for
if only one will look at everything in an inverted way,
there is some sense in it: directly understood, misfortune is misfortune; inversely, misfortune is good fortune. Such a thing is
only jesting, like propounding riddles, or as when a mountebank
says, "Nothing can be easier to do if only a man is accustomed to
walk on his head instead of on his legs." ' Well, yes, but for all
that is it then so easy to do? And because to the thought which
is untried by the reality of life and experiences no weight, it seems
so easy to swing up and down and down and up, both to the right
and to the left—is it then so easy when misfortune weighs upon
the thought which is to make the swing, is it so easy when the
thought has to have power enough to turn him about who is
suffering when misfortune persists in maintaining him in the
contrary position? That is to say, for the idle and masterless
thought, some sort of thought in general, the homeless thought
which is no thought, the thought which buffets the air with
indeterminate determinants and undefined definitions, 'here—
there,' 'right—left,' 'direct—inverse'—for the vagrant thought
it is easy enough to perform the trick. But when there is a con-
crete thought, when it is my thought, or when it is *thy* thought,
and . . . when thou art a sufferer, so that it becomes a serious
matter for the thought which easily enough can turn itself to
acquire power over thee so as to turn thee about in spite of the
much which in manifold ways resists its efforts—is this then so
easy? And because it is a jest to be able to walk on one's head
instead of on one's legs, is it therefore also a jest to look at every-

---

[1] *Modgang er Medgang*—it is enough to make a translator tear his hair. One time,
Professor Geismar read to me several beautiful passages from S. K.'s works to show
that many of them could not be translated. This might have been one of them. A
Danish reviewer, Professor Hal Koch, while praising, perhaps more than they
deserved, the translations I incorporated in my book on *Kierkegaard* remarked that
'something of the music of the language has been lost'. Oh, how heartily I agree
with him! and how grateful I am to him for adding, 'how could it be otherwise'!

thing inversely? Oh, far from it, or better, exactly the inverse is true, precisely this is seriousness, the seriousness of eternity. That which is a jest, a meaningless jest, so long as it is merely some sort of thought in general—when it becomes serious owing to the fact that it is thy thought, the thought which has to turn thee about, that then is precisely the seriousness of eternity. Eternity, which after all is surely the task and the surety of seriousness, says, 'This is the task, for this precisely is my view of life, eternity's view of life, to see everything inversely; and, thou sufferer, whoever thou art, if seriously thou wilt be comforted, comforted in such wise that even gladness triumphs, then thou must let me, eternity, come to thine aid—but then thou must also look at everything inversely!' This is eternity's comfort for the sufferer, the law which eternity prescribes, the conditon which eternity makes, to which all the promises are attached. For eternity knows of but one method: to look at everything inversely. So let us then look at the situation inversely, and thereby find

The Joy of it—that misfortune is good fortune.

But let us proceed in such a fashion that we strive first to get the sufferer in the right attitude, so that he may get an eye for this inverted prospect, and that he may be willing to abandon himself to this view and permit it to exercise power over him— then surely the joy follows of itself.

What is good fortune? Good fortune is what helps me to attain my goal, what leads to the goal; and misfortune is what would prevent me from attaining my goal.

But what then is the goal? Hypothetically we have made the one thought fast by defining what good fortune and misfortune are; but when we come to define the other thought (that of the goal) it is easily seen that in case this goal is different, is the opposite, the notion of good fortune and of misfortune must be altered in accordance with it.

We stand here at the beginning. But in another sense we are not standing at the beginning. The discourse addresses itself to a sufferer. But the sufferer is not beginning his life now; on the contrary, he is in the midst of it, alas, not merely in the midst of life, but in the midst of life's suffering. Such being the case, he must surely know what misfortune is, being himself sufficiently tried by it. Perhaps. But we are agreed that the question whether and how far he knows what misfortune is depends upon whether he knows what the goal is. Only he who has the true notion of what is the goal set before men, only he knows what misfortune is and what is good fortune. He who has the false notion of the goal has also a false notion of good fortune and misfortune, he calls that good fortune which leads him to . . . the false goal and so prevents him from attaining *the* goal (the true goal). But that which prevents one from attaining the goal is in fact misfortune.

Now there are divers things that can be striven after by men, but essentially there are only two goals: one goal which a man wishes, desires to attain; and another which he ought to attain. The one goal is that of temporal existence, the other is that of eternity; these are contrary the one to the other, but good fortune and misfortune must also be inverted in correspondence with them. If this discourse were addressed to a young man, it would strive to make the distinction of the two goals thoroughly clear to him, so that he might begin his life by choosing the right goal, begin by heading in the right direction. And yet perhaps the discourse might not be successful; for the soul of the youth will be on terms of suspicious intimacy with the temporal goal and with the false notion of good fortune and misfortune. And now for the sufferer, who does not stand at the beginning but is far advanced on the way and knows, alas, only too well what misfortune is; but, as has been said, the question is whether he also knows well what is the goal. The more vehemently he talks of his suffering and of how everything is against him, the clearer it becomes that he has the false notion of the goal. And if he has the false notion of the goal, he cannot talk truly about good fortune and misfortune.

So if he is to be helped, he must be required to reflect what is the goal set before men, lest, deceived by the vain notion that he knows well what the goal is, he continue to complain. For doubtless thou dost suffer misfortune, thou art unable to attain the goal thou didst so ardently wish to attain—but suppose then that this goal is the false one!

What then is required? It is required of the sufferer that he call a halt to his erring thought, that he reflect what the goal is, that is to say, it is required of him that he *turn himself about*. For in relation to sin conversion is required; in relation to the comfort of eternity the same is required, yet in the milder form, that one turn oneself about: for the severity of the law says to the sinner, 'Be converted'; to the sufferer eternity says, 'Oh, do but turn about.' So it is required that he turn about. Here already eternity shows itself to be the converse of temporal existence. For eternity presupposes that the natural man does not in the least know what the goal is, that on the contrary it is the untrue notion which is presupposed by temporal existence, that every man knows with ease what the goal is, so that the only difference that remains between man and man is whether they succeed or not in attaining it. On the contrary eternity assumes that the difference between man and man is that the one knows what the goal is and steers for it, the other does not know, and steers accordingly, that is, steers amiss. Thou sufferer, whoever thou art, thou findest it only too easy to make people understand thee when thou complainest of thy suffering—even if they have no comfort to give thee, they understand thee none the less—but eternity will not understand thee thus; and yet it is by eternity thou art to be helped.

So turn about! Oh, permit it to be said to thee—good Lord, it is in fact so evident that if a man is to attain the goal, he must know which the goal is and be rightly headed for it; it is so evident that if a man is to be gladdened by the magnificent view, he must turn towards the side where it is to be seen, not to the opposite side. Be not impatient, say not, 'I know perfectly what misfortune is,' make no attempt to terrify us too by the description of thy suffering, so that we too might turn to the wrong side and miss the view. For if thy suffering is so terrible, why then wilt thou fix thy gaze upon it? Or is this precisely the terrible thing, that thou canst not help gazing upon it? Yet it is not impossible. Say not, 'When one suffers as I suffer, one knows what misfortune is; and only he who suffers as I suffer knows what misfortune is.' No, say not this; oh, but listen well. In order not to wound thee we do not deny that thou knowest what misfortune is, what we are saying is that thou dost not yet know what the goal is.

And then when thou hast turned about and got an eye for the goal (that of eternity), let the goal become to thee so important, as indeed it is and ought to be, that there is no question about what sort of a path it is, but only whether it leads to the goal, so that thou mayest have courage to understand that whatever the path is, be it the worst of all, the most painful of all, in case it leads thee to the goal, it is good fortune. It is true, is it not, that if there is a place where it is of the utmost importance for thee to arrive because thou art so unspeakably eager to be there, thou wouldst say, 'Whether I run backwards or forwards, whether I ride, or walk, or crawl—that is perfectly indifferent, if only I can get there.' First and foremost this is what eternity would have, it would make the goal so important to thee that it acquires complete control over thee, and thou over thyself, to the effect of getting thy thought, thy mind, thine eye diverted from the hardship, the difficulty, from the *how* of getting there, because the only important thing for thee is to get *there*.

So then, in deference for the goal it has now become *indifferent* to thee whether what brings thee to the goal is what ordinarily is called misfortune or what ordinarily is called good fortune: what brings thee to the goal is good fortune. What an alteration! Dost thou think that the sensual man could be indifferent to this difference? What comfort would it be to him that misfortune led him to *the* goal, when he is only concerned about the goal to which good fortune leads?

But perhaps thou canst not yet forbear to glance back at the distinction ordinarily made between misfortune and good fortune. Thou hast acquired the right attitude but hast not yet come to repose in it. Well, eternity will help thee on farther. For if it is precisely what people ordinarily call misfortune which alone or principally leads to *the* goal, is there then any reason for glancing back? If it were the case, as we may assume, that it was only or most effectively by running backwards thou couldst get to the place where thou art so eager to be, would it then be the correct thing to say, 'Whether I run backwards or forwards is a matter of indifference to me'? Would it not be more correct to say, 'So it is well that I had to run backwards'? And so, too, in case it were possible that what is ordinarily called good fortune might more easily lead thee to *the* goal, there would be room for a wish. But now, thou sufferer, there is nothing to tempt thee, for misfortune is leading precisely to *the* goal. And thou surely wilt be true to thy word, that whatever leads to the goal is good fortune. So misfortune is good fortune.

Let us now make it quite clear to ourselves that what they ordinarily call good fortune and misfortune do not equally well lead to *the* goal, but that what ordinarily is called misfortune does alone or at least principally lead to *the* goal. What is it that may prevent a man from attaining *the* goal? Why precisely the temporal. And how does it most seriously prevent him? When good fortune so called leads him to the attainment of the goal of temporal existence. For when by means of good fortune a man attains the goal of temporal existence, he is farthest from attaining *the* goal. Man is to strive for the goal of eternity, but by means of good fortune temporal existence has delayed him. By the fact that good fortune accompanies him he is not led to the eternal, and so not to *the* goal. If there is anything that does this, it must be exactly the reverse, namely, that the temporal goes against him. But the opposition of the temporal is what one is accustomed to call misfortune.—When it is said, 'Seek ye *first* the kingdom of God,' the goal of eternity is thereby posited as that for which man shall strive. If this is to be done, and done according to the letter (and, ah, eternity will not be mocked, nor be deceived!), it is required above all that man seek not *first* something else. But what is this 'something else' he seeks? It is the temporal. If then he is to seek first God's kingdom, he must freely renounce every temporal goal. Oh, what a difficult task! when opportunity perhaps is proffered in abundance, when everything beckons him on, when what they call good fortune is ready promptly to bring him into possession of all the pleasant goods of temporal existence—and then to renounce all this! On the other hand, the sufferer has misfortune, hence he is called a sufferer. And what they call misfortune hinders the sufferer from attaining the temporal goal; misfortune makes it difficult, perhaps impossible. Oh, how hard a thing it is to see difficulties pile up before the wish, how hard that the fulfilment of the wish is thus rendered impossible! Is it not true? That indeed is a question I need not put to thee. But is it not true (ah, would to God it were so) that it is rather thou who wouldst now put to me the question, whether I myself have not now forgotten what the discourse is about. So then do tell us (it was only this I was wishing for), only tell us what the discourse is about, while I listen with joy and hear thee say, 'If what they call good fortune is what delays, what prevents one from attaining *the* goal, then indeed it is well that what they call misfortune makes it difficult or impossible . . . to be delayed, then it is misfortune precisely which brings one to *the* goal.'

O thou sufferer, whosoever thou art, break away from the sufferings and from the thoughts which would obtrude upon thee, try to think of life quite impartially. Imagine then a man who is in possession of all the good things of fortune, favoured in every way—but imagine that this man moreover was serious enough to have fixed his mind upon the goal of eternity. So he understands that all this that has been bestowed upon him he is to renounce. He is also willing to do it; but, behold, there awakens in his soul a despondent concern, an anxious concern about himself, as to whether after all he may be deceiving himself, whether his renunciation is only imaginary, inasmuch as he remains in possession of all these goods. He dare not throw away what has been bestowed upon him, for he understands that this might be an exaggeration of presumption which easily might be his ruin, instead of being for his good; and he has sadly conceived an anxious suspicion of himself, whether he might possibly be deceiving God, and all his renunciation be a sham. Then he might well wish that they were taken away from him altogether, so that it might become a serious affair, this thing of giving up the temporal to grasp the eternal. And if this does not come to pass, there perhaps develops in his inward man a mental disease, an incurable melancholy, which has its ground in the fact that in a profounder sense he became perplexed about himself.[1]

Hast thou thought of this? Yet for thee especially it would be an appropriate point of view, putting thee at the farthest distance from thine own. Contemplate thy situation from this point of view! Thou hast had indeed and hast misfortune in plenty—so thou hast merely the task *of renouncing what is denied thee*, whereas this man has the task *of renouncing what has been bestowed upon him*. In the next place, thou art exempted from anxiety as to whether thou hast given it up in an outward sense; for since thou dost not possess it, the job is easy enough. And in how many other ways thou art helped! That is denied thee which would prevent thee from attaining *the* goal, thou hast not thyself thrown it away and therewith incurred the responsibility which perhaps at a decisive moment would make thy life so very difficult because thou didst find thyself powerless in the face of a task thou hadst voluntarily undertaken. No, in thy case providence has assumed all the responsibility, that is to say, the providence which denied

[1] Is this to be taken as S. K.'s account of his own melancholy?

thee this. Thou hast only to come to the help of providence, of this providence which has helped thee. For misfortune is good fortune, and thou indeed hast misfortune.

So then, misfortune is good fortune. This is perfectly certain, not all the shrewdness of Satan shall be able to put it in doubt. And also thou canst well understand it. On the other hand, thou dost not perhaps believe thoroughly that it is so. But dost thou believe then (for the sake of providing a somewhat weaker diet, in case what the Scripture says about seeking first God's kingdom is too strong), dost thou believe then that the poet whose songs delight mankind, dost thou believe that he could have composed these songs if misfortune and bitter suffering had not been at hand to tune the soul?[1] For it is precisely in misfortune,

> When the heart of man is saddest,
> The harp's tense strings are gladdest.[2]

Or dost thou believe that he who knows how to comfort others would have been able to do it if misfortune had not been for him the requisite good fortune which helped him to proficiency in this fine art? Perhaps at the beginning he also felt it hard enough, almost cruel, that his soul should be tortured in order that it might become inventive in finding out comfort for others. But at last he learned to understand that without misfortune he could not have become and could not be the man he was; he learned to believe that misfortune is good fortune.

So believe thou too that misfortune is good fortune. To understand it is easy enough—but to believe it is difficult. Be not deceived by the vain wisdom which would make thee imagine that it is easy to believe but difficult to understand. But believe it. So long as thou dost not believe it, just so long does misfortune remain misfortune. It is no help to thee that it is eternally certain that misfortune is good fortune; so long as thou dost not believe it, it is not true for thee. Think of an older person in relation to a child. The older person knows the expedient for dealing with a nettle: only grasp it firmly, and then it will not sting thee. To

---

[1] This thought is powerfully expressed in the first Diapsalm in *Either/Or*. This was S. K.'s experience. He often averred that the loss of Regina made him a poet. And there is no doubt that it was his suffering which made him proficient in comforting others.

[2] Lines from a Christmas hymn by Brorson.

the child this must seem the most absurd thing; for, thinks the child, if one is stung merely by touching it, how much more when one grasps it tight. One tells this to the child. But when the child is about to grasp it his courage fails—he grasps it nevertheless, but not firmly enough, and it stings him. So it is with the saying that misfortune is good fortune: if thou art not resolute in faith, thou dost get nothing out of it but misfortune.

Believe then that misfortune is good fortune. This is certain, it is only waiting for thee to believe it. Be not disturbed in thy faith by others, 'the faith which thou hast, have thou to thyself before God' (Rom. xiv. 22). When the seaman is assured that the wind which now blows is carrying him to the goal—even if all others were to call it a contrary wind—what does he care, he calls it a fair wind. For a fair wind is the wind which carries one to the goal; and good fortune is everything which carries one to the goal; and misfortune carries one to *the* goal—so misfortune is good fortune.

It is not necessary to demonstrate that this is joyful. He who believes that misfortune is good fortune has truly no need of the discourse to explain to him that this is joyful. And for him who does not thoroughly believe, it is of more importance not to waste an instant but to lay hold on faith. So we need not talk about it, or say more than one word. Imagine then a chase, as it were, extending over the whole world, which has driven and collected together all the grounds of comfort which, as I believe, happy people have invented to be rid of the unhappy; and then in comparison think of the comfort of eternity, this concise word of comfort which distress has discovered, as it also has discovered that it takes a person in distress, a sufferer, not a happy person, to comfort others—this concise word of comfort: misfortune is good fortune! It is true, is it not, that thou wilt regard it as quite just, and in a certain sense well advised, that the human grounds of comfort do not pretend to make the sorrowful joyful, but merely undertake to comfort them after a fashion, which they do badly enough. Eternity, on the contrary, when it comforts, makes a man joyful, its comfort is really joy, is the real joy. In the case of human grounds of comfort it is as when the sick man who already has had many physicians gets a new one who perhaps hits upon something new which for a moment produces a slight change, whereas soon it is the same old thing again. No, when eternity is called in to look after the sick man it not only heals him completely but makes him sounder than all the sound people. In the case of human grounds of comfort it is as when the physician finds a new and perhaps slightly more convenient crutch for him who walks with crutches: to give him sound feet to walk with, and strength in his knees, surpasses the power of the physician. But when eternity is called in, the crutches are thrown away, the man cannot merely walk, oh, no, in another sense it may be said that he no longer walks—so lightly does he go. For eternity gives him feet to walk with. When in misfortune it seems impossible to budge from the spot, when in the impotence of suffering it is as if one could not move a foot—then eternity makes of misfortune good fortune.

In all misfortune there is but one danger: when the sufferer will not believe that misfortune is good fortune. This is perdition; only sin is man's ruin.

PART III

The first idea of the following Discourses.

There should be written several Discourses (about Dec. 28, '47).

Thoughts which wound/attack from behind—to edification.

'Keep thy foot when thou goest to the house of the Lord' (Ecclesiastes).

[A note in the margin refers to an earlier entry, of about Aug. 16, which reads]: Ecclesiastes v. 1, 'Keep thy foot, etc.', could very well be used for a sermon in contrast to the lax way of preaching which is busy only with getting people to come to church. Beware of going thither. It is a grave responsibility if subsequently thou dost not do according to what is preached, and if the sermon is rightly preached, thou mightest perhaps receive an impression which thou canst not later overcome, an impression of what God requires of thee: self-denial, etc. Hence beware!

This shall be the introduction.

Then in the succeeding Discourses the text shall be so chosen that it looks like a gospel, and also is such, but then comes the sting.

No. 1. 'What shall we have who have forsaken all?'

The satirical point for us in this question—for us who have not yet forsaken anything.

No. 2. All things work together for our good—*if* we love God. (Irony.)

No. 3. The resurrection of the dead is at hand, both of the just and of the unjust.

Rejoice, thou hast no need to ask for the 'three proofs'—it is certain enough that thou art immortal—it is perfectly certain—for thou shalt be brought before the Judgment. This is a new argument for immortality.

No. 4. It is blessed—to be mocked for a good cause. (Rejoice when men speak all manner of evil against you.)

So then, rejoice—but perhaps there is no one present to whom this Discourse applies. Thou, my hearer, dost rejoice perhaps at being highly honoured and esteemed and respected. Well then, for thee it is a meal like that of the stork with the raven.

The satirical

'Woe unto you if all men shall speak well of you.' Here the 'falsely' is not added, for if all men speak well of thee, it must be a lie.

No. 5. 'Now is our salvation nearer than when we first became believers.' But art thou sure that thou hast become a believer?

No. 6. He (Christ) was believed on in the world (1 Tim. iii. 16).

But this perhaps is only a bit of historical information.

Marginal note: An assault of thoughts.

THOUGHTS WHICH WOUND FROM BEHIND
—FOR EDIFICATION
CHRISTIAN ADDRESSES

by

S. KIERKEGAARD

Copenhagen
1848

The Christian cause is in need of no *defense*, it is not served by any *defense*—it is *aggressive*; to defend it is of all misrepresentations the most inexcusable—it is *unconscious crafty treachery*. Christianity is aggressive; in Christendom, as a matter of course, it attacks from behind.

CONTENTS

I

How quiet everything is in the house of God, what a sense of security. He who enters it feels as if by a single step he had arrived at a remote place, endlessly far away from all noise and outcry and vociferation, from the horrors of existence, from the storms of life, from the spectacle of dreadful events or from the sickly expectation of them. And here within, wherever thy glance is turned, everything gives thee a sense of security and peace. The lofty walls of the venerable edifice stand so fast, are such a reliable defence around this secure place of refuge, under whose mighty vault thou art free from every sense of pressing weight. And the beauty of the environment, its grandeur, is calculated to make upon thee a friendly impression, it is so inviting that it is as if the holy place would ingratiate itself with thee, by recalling also the good and quiet ages which presumably must have favoured these enterprises of peace. Behold, the man who carved these pictures in stone needed a long time for it, and during all this time his life must have been protected and secure, so that no one conflicted with him and nothing happened to him which in any way could render his hand or his thought uncertain. As an artist he needed the profoundest repose of peace—what he produced is therefore a reminder of that repose. Behold, he who wove the velvet with which the pulpit is adorned must have had repose to sit quietly at his work, which flourishes in times of peace and is not needed in time of war. And the woman who sewed the gold upon it must have been allowed to sit undisturbed and diligent at her work, solely employed with it and with sewing every stitch with equal care.

How comforting, how inviting—ah, and how much danger in this security! Wherefore it is verily true that really it is only God in heaven who in the actuality of life can preach to men with effect; for He has circumstances, has fates, has consternation in His power. And circumstances—and when 'thou' art in them, when they enclose 'thee' as the party properly concerned—yea, their eloquence is piercing and awakening. That thou hast experienced too. In case thou wast the sick man who at the hour of midnight lay sleepless upon the sick-bed, or in case thou wast merely the one that sat at the midnight hour beside the sick man's couch of pain and with alarming distinctness counted every tick of the clock and every sigh of the sick man, but without finding relief in the uniformity or in the mechanical exercise of counting—if then thou didst hear that pious song, 'It was upon the midnight hour our Saviour he was born:' [1] dost thou believe that all orators put together would be able to produce this effect? And why not? Because the sick-bed and the hour preach more mightily than all orators, and understand this secret of speaking to thee in such a fashion that thou dost get an apprehension that it is thou, precisely 'thou', not him that sits beside thee, not him out there, but precisely 'thou' that art spoken to, thou who dost feel thyself alone, alone in the whole world, alone at the midnight hour beside the sick-bed. Or in case a man lies *in extremis*, and fairly and honestly they have not concealed from him that which people desire to conceal from the dying man, the thing most important for him to know, that it is all over—dost thou not believe that the simple comforting word of the most commonplace man will produce an entirely different effect than is produced by all the most famous orators upon him who, sound and healthy, in his own thoughts also spiritually hale, sits secure in the gorgeous temple and hears . . . and perhaps criticizes the address. And why will that simple word produce an entirely different effect? Because death knows how to make itself understood by the man to whom it applies, knows how to make thee understand that it is 'thou', that thou art the individual in question, that it is not anybody else, not thy neighbour or thine opposite neighbour, or another man here in the town, but it is thou who art to die.

So it is in the actuality of life when it is God that preaches by means of circumstances to awaken. But in the house of God, in the splendid house of God, when the parson preaches . . . to tranquillize! Especially if he would satisfy human requirements, or what it is the fashion to call the requirements of the times. For whereas men in these times are becoming more and more apprehensive, more and more afraid for their own part of experiencing the dreadfulness of reality when they are delivered over into the power of circumstances, on the other hand, they are becoming

[1] An ancient chant of the night-watchman.

more and more fastidious in their desire for the trumpery of eloquence. They will not seriously listen to the dreadful happenings, they would rather read about this afterwards, very much as when in times of peace the warriors, or rather the non-warriors, play at war; they would artistically require everything that has to do with the beauty of the environment, and artistically require everything of the speaker, but for themselves, with a worldly and ungodly mind they would sit perfectly secure in the house of God, because they well know that no orator has the power which providence has to lay hold of a man, to cast him off into the power of circumstance, to let the desperation and trials and alarms of it preach seriously to him for awakening.

Oh, in the customary course of life there is so much to lull a man to sleep, to teach him to say, 'Peace and no danger.' It is for this cause we go into the house of God, to be awakened out of sleep and to be riven away from enchantments. But then again when there is so much in the house of God to lull us! Even that which in itself is arousing, such as thoughts, reflections, ideas, can by custom and monotony lose all their significance, just as a spring can lose the resilience which makes it what it is. So then (to approach nearer to the subject of this discourse), it is right, reasonable, and a plain duty, to invite men, over and over again, to come to the house of the Lord, to summon them to it. But one may become so accustomed to hearing this invitation that one loses all sense of its significance, so that at last one stays away and it ends with the invitation preaching the church empty. Or one may become so accustomed to hearing this invitation that it develops false ideas in those that come, makes us self-important in our own thoughts, that we are not as they who remain away, makes us self-satisfied, secure, because it envelops us in a delusion, as though, since we are so urgently invited, God were in need of us, as though it were not we who in fear and trembling should reflect what He may require of us, as though it were not we who should sincerely thank God that He will have dealings with us, that He will suffer and permit us to approach Him, suffer that we presume to believe that He cares for us, that without being ashamed He will be known as one who is called our God and our Father.

So concerning this matter let us for once talk differently, in talking of these words of the preacher: [1]

[1] Eccl. iv. 17.

KEEP THY FOOT WHEN THOU GOEST TO THE HOUSE OF THE LORD.

Keep thy foot[1] *when thou goest to the house of the Lord,* for thou dost assume an immense responsibility. Remember that here is One who is in heaven—and thou art upon earth. But do not imagine that in His exaltation He is far away: herein lies the seriousness and responsibility of the situation, that He, the infinitely exalted, is quite close to thee, closer than the men who are about thee daily, closer than thy most trusted friend before whom thou dost feel free to show thyself for what thou art. Exaltation and distance seem to correspond one with another, so that he who is exalted is remote from thee; equality and nearness seem to correspond one with another, so that he who is near thee is also thine equal; but when exaltation is quite close to thee, then thou art in a difficult position. It is precisely God, however, the infinitely exalted, who in the house of the Lord is quite close to thee in His exaltation; for it is not with God as with a man, who essentially becomes less exalted when he comes close to thee, the lowly person, has dealings with thee; no, God can come quite close to the lowliest and is none the less highly exalted. Oh, the seriousness of eternity! Oh, how difficult the position! For it is true doubtless that when it is merely a stranger that is present, thou art somewhat changed, and when the mightiest and most exalted in the land is present, thou art much changed, because he is so exalted, and because he is so rarely seen. But God in heaven is exalted in an entirely different degree, and yet when thou goest up to the house of the Lord, God in His infinite exaltation is quite close to thee, nearer than thou art to thyself, for He understands

[1] I can barely resist the temptation to translate by 'Watch thy step!' This would not be to mistranslate the Preacher, and it would express only more pungently the point S. K. presses—at least to Americans whose ears are accustomed to the reiterated warnings which the humble hired preachers of this mechanical age are taught to repeat monotonously to heedless travellers, in railway stations, in subways, in lifts: 'Watch your step!—Watch your step!—Watch your step!' Long before I knew this discourse of S. K.'s I preached on this text with a like purpose, and an experience of my own furnished an illustration S. K. might well have been envious of. Reconnoitring in a strange town, I observed with amazement that many people, all of them men, were on a week-day pouring into a pseudo-Gothic church, on the portal of which was carved the uninviting Virgilian line, *Procul, o procul estote profani.* I learned subsequently that this church had been 'preached empty' by the inviting formula: All are welcome and the seats are free . . . and ultimately had been bought by the Freemasons.

and discovers even the thought of thine which thou thyself dost not understand. Oh, what an immense weight of responsibility, that He, the infinitely exalted One, before whom thou wouldst prefer to show thyself at thy best, that He, in spite of His exaltation, is quite close to thee, sees thee—and in spite of His exaltation sees thee closely, as not even he sees thee who every day is in thy company! Even if thou, in consideration that thou art presenting thyself before the Most High, wouldst try to show thyself different from what thou art, thou canst not—He is too infinitely exalted for that, and (here it is again) He is too close to thee for that. If a man can lose his self-possession and forget what he was about to say when he is brought face to face with his Royal Majesty—ah, how dreadful to be brought face to face with God! For his Royal Majesty is neither so exalted, nor can he come so close to thee.

Therefore beware when thou goest to the house of the Lord. What wouldst thou do there? Thou wouldst invoke the Lord thy God, extol Him and praise His holy name. But is that then really and in all seriousness thine intention? Language, as thou knowest, has no expression more solemn which can be used to exact sincerity than this which one man employs in addressing another: 'Before God is this thy conviction or opinion?' And in the house of the Lord thou art indeed *before God*. Is then this invocation of thine, which invokes God, sincere in its intention? And what is sincerity before God? It is that thy life expresses that which thou sayest. We men may be content with less, with the fact that the one solemnly protests to the other that this or that is his sincere intention. But God in heaven, He who is infinitely exalted, or (yes, here we have it again) He who is the searcher of hearts, He who is quite close to thee—God is willing to understand only one sort of sincerity, namely, that a man's life expresses what he says. All other sincerity, all other solemnity, all mere protesting that a man means what he says, is before God an illusion, a falsehood; such an invocation is presumption towards Him. Beware lest thine invocation, instead of being well-pleasing to God, is presumption towards Him. Beware lest, self-deceived, because thou dost not understand thyself, thou dost presume to deceive God, as if in thy heart thou didst have the pious feelings which yet have not the power over thee to change thy life, to make thy life the expression of these feelings. Oh, we men often complain of the lack of words and expressions for our feelings, that language will not come to our aid, that we have to search for words, and generally in vain—before God such considerations need not give thee concern; if only thy life expresses that thou hast these feelings, then thou art indeed sincere before God, and that chatty sincerity is entirely superfluous.

Or perhaps thou goest up to the house of the Lord to pray God for help and assistance. Beware what thou doest. Hast thou rightly and before God comprehended to whom thou art appealing for help, what it means to invoke God's aid, what obligations it puts thee under? Is it perhaps with regard to childish concerns, insignificant things, thou wouldst invoke His aid—not that He might help thee to forget them, but with the will to be employed about them—with regard to insignificant things which perhaps tomorrow thou hast forgotten, and with this perhaps hast forgotten the by no means insignificant fact that thou hast invoked the aid of the Most High—then thou hast mocked God . . . and He forgets not that thou didst invoke His aid. If a physician becomes impatient, and with good reason, when childish parents summon him for every insignificant complaint, so that the whole thing is over when he arrives, and it is almost forgotten for what cause he was summoned—should God Almighty wish to be treated thus? Or darest thou understand thyself to mean that it is God that should serve thee, that He, the Most High, should be punctually at hand to hear thy prayers and fulfil thy wishes? Ah, if thou wouldst have to do with Him, it is thou that art thereby put absolutely under obligation to obey and to serve Him. And if thou dost not understand this, it is presumptuous to have dealings with Him, it is presumptuous to invoke His aid. Yes, certainly He is the Almighty and can do everything He would; it looks almost temptingly as if thou hadst nothing to do but wish. But beware. No rash word so surely involves its own punishment as a rash prayer, and no word involves such obligation as the prayer which cries to God for help; for this puts thee under the obligation to let thyself be helped as He will. Thou canst pray a man to help thee, and have forgotten it when he arrives with the help; thou canst pray a man to help thee, and when he is unwilling to help thee in the way thou wouldst be helped, thou canst say, 'This is not what I prayed for'—but if thou hast prayed to God for help, thou are under obligation, under obligation to accept the help He thinks best. Ah, there is so often heard this cry for help, and this cry that there is no help —verily there is always help enough. But the human heart is so cunning and so untrue to its word; when the help proves to be what one has most shuddered at, one says, 'But this is no help.' And yet if this help is from God, and if thou hast prayed to Him for help, thou art under obligation to accept the help, and with faith and gratitude to call it help.

Or perhaps thou goest up to the house of the Lord to pay thy vows unto God and to pledge thyself to a purpose, a resolution, for the future—beware what thou doest. Hast thou thoroughly comprehended what it means to promise God something, and considered whether what thou dost promise God is something a man can and dare promise God, that it is not something we men might jokingly promise one another, that it is something God will permit thee to promise Him—otherwise it is presumption. And hast thou comprehended how a promise to God binds thee? 'A promise is a snare,' they say—but a promise to God, yea, if it is what it ought to be, and results as it ought to result, it is so far from being a snare that it is rather a leading-string to salvation. But if not! If thou dost not comprehend what thou dost promise God, if thou hast not a true notion of what one can and dare promise God, then thou dost lose God, thou dost pamper thy soul to the point of taking God lightly and in vain. And if thou dost not keep thy promise to God, thou dost lose thine own self. Ah, and there is certainly one whom a man cannot escape: himself— and then one more . . . God in heaven!

Beware therefore when thou goest to the house of the Lord, consider the words of the Preacher: [1] 'Be not rash with thy mouth, and let not thy heart be hasty to utter anything before God; for God is in heaven, and thou upon earth: therefore let thy words be few. When thou vowest a vow unto God, defer not to pay it; for He hath no pleasure in fools: pay that which thou vowest. Better it is that thou shouldst not vow, than that thou shouldst vow and not pay.'

Keep thy foot when thou goest to the house of the Lord. For perhaps thou mightest learn to know much more than thou dost really wish to know, and perhaps thou wilt there get an impres-

[1] Eccl. v. 1–5.

sion which later thou wouldst fain seek to be rid of. Beware of the fire: it burns.[1]

It is heard again and again, and it is regarded in the world as a positive fact, that men would gladly know the truth if only they had the talents and the time for it, and if one could make it thoroughly clear to them. Oh, superfluous reason for concern! Oh, cunning evasion! Truly every man has enough talent to know the truth—could God in heaven be so inhuman as to have put any one at such a disadvantage? And every man, even one who is most deeply engaged in affairs, truly has time enough to learn to know the truth, nothing is more certain, for he *shall* have time. That the busy man has just as little time as the idler is no refutation of this! And since every one has talent and time enough, it cannot be so difficult a thing to make it clear, in case man himself *will* have it made clear. But just here lies the difficulty: it is so easy to put the blame upon lack of talent, upon lack of time, and upon the obscurity of the truth, and then on the other hand it makes so fine an impression and is so comfortable to protest that one would so gladly know the truth.

Verily, verily it is not so. He who has but some acquaintance with himself knows well out of his own experience that it is rather true that at the bottom of his heart a man has a secret dread and mistrust of the truth, a fear of getting to know too much. Or dost thou really believe that it is every man's sincere wish to get to know effectually what self-denial is, to get it made so clear that every excuse, every evasion, every palliation, every appeal to the false but favourable opinion of others is cut off from him? Indeed, I do not need to wait for thy reply; for if such were the case, every man would possess self-denial, for this (the understanding of it) is its first form. Oh, but even a man of the better sort, one who has overcome the first shudder at the truth and is not worldly enough to be altogether loath to get to know it—even he, he who also admits sincerely that he knows well from his own experience that one is not so eager to learn to know the truth—even he, or rather he especially, will indubitably admit that over and over again he has had reason to suspect himself of hiding from the truth, as Adam hid among the trees, that he quietly steals away

---

[1] Twelve years earlier, and before he had submitted to the definite impression of Christianity, S. K. uttered in his Journal this same warning to himself, 'not to come like moths too near the flame'.

from something and steals to something, that he sometimes would slip away into obscurity where there is only twilight, rather than that the truth should make things too luminous round about him.

Beware therefore when thou goest up to the house of the Lord; for there thou wilt hear the truth . . . for edification, yes, that is true, but beware of the edifying, there is nothing so gentle as the edifying, but there is nothing so imperious; the edifying is least of all loose talk, there is nothing so binding. And in the house of God thou dost get to know the truth—not from the parson, whose influence thou canst, and in a certain sense shalt evade, but from God or before God. Precisely this is the seriousness of the truth, in fact is the truth, that it is before God thou dost get to know it; what is of pre-eminent importance is this: 'before God.' In God's house there is One along with thee who knows that thou hast come to know the truth. Beware of this complicity in knowledge; from this thou shalt never again slip back into ignorance, that is to say, thou dost not slip back guiltlessly, nor dost thou slip out of the consciousness that thou art guilty.

Beware therefore of learning to know too much, lest with this thou shouldst learn that the asseveration which, while thy life went on pleasantly in the strength of it, made thee pleasing in thine own eyes and agreeable in the eyes of others, that the asseveration that thou art so fain to learn the truth, that this is a mere fancy, or, even worse, that it is a falsehood. Beware lest in the house of God thou dost get to know—but this indeed thou knowest, thou dost even perhaps exalt thyself for thy much knowledge above the simple orator who would talk about such old-fashioned things which every child knows—but beware lest in the house of God thou dost get to know it in such wise that thou must understand it: that it may be required of thee that in self-denial thou shalt give up all that in which the natural man has his life, his pleasure, his diversion. Hast thou considered what it is to be weary of life? Weariness with life results when a man is deprived of all the finite while yet he is allowed to hold on to life, when everything around him becomes waste and empty and cheerless, and time so unspeakably long, just as if he were dead —why yes! that is what self-denial calls dying, dying to the world; and the truth teaches that a man has to die to the finite (to its pleasures, its occupations, its pursuits, its diversions), has to pass through this death to life, has to taste (thus they speak of 'tasting' death) and apprehend how empty is that with which business fills up life, how unimportant is that which is the eyes' delight and the fleshly heart's desire—ah, the natural man understands it in exactly the opposite way, he thinks that the eternal is the empty. There is surely no instinct so strong in a man as that by which he clings to life—when death comes we all beg that we may live: but the dying of self-denial is as bitter as death. And in the house of the Lord thou dost learn to know the truth that thou must die to the world; and if (as is unavoidable) God has come to know that thou hast come to know this, then to all eternity no evasion shall avail thee. Therefore beware when thou goest to the house of the Lord.

Keep thy foot when thou goest to the house of the Lord. For even if thou hast come from the most dreadful experience that ever befell a man, fleeing from the horror without into God's house—yet thou dost come to a still more dreadful place. Here in the house of God the subject talked about is a danger the world does not know, a danger in comparison with which all that the world calls danger is child's-play: the danger of sin. Oh, here in God's house what essentially is talked about is a horror which never was encountered before nor will be later, in comparison with which the most terrible thing that can befall the most unhappy of all men is an insignificance: the horror that the race crucified God.

What wilt thou then in God's house? Is it poverty that brings thee, or illness, or another adversity, in short, any sort of earthly need and misery—about that nothing is said in God's house, at least not first. What first is talked of, and should first be talked of, is sin, of the fact that thou art a sinner, that before God thou art a sinner, and that thou in fear and trembling at this thought shalt forget thy earthly need. Truly, a singular way of comforting! Instead of enquiring sympathetically about thy welfare, instead of giving thee counsel and advice—if for this reason thou hast sought refuge there, thou hast made a mistake, thou hast come in fact to what is even more dreadful. For instead of finding sympathy with thy earthly misery and people busy to relieve it, there is laid upon thee a still heavier weight, thou art made to be a sinner. So this is what is talked about—and truly to edification—that there is salvation for sinners, comfort for the penitent. But perhaps all this does not apply to thee, to thee who in fleeing hither art solely concerned about thy earthly suffering. And yet it does apply to thee, in vain wilt thou say that it does not apply to thee, though thou wouldst go hence, it is in vain: it was said to thee, God knows along with thee that it was said, and that thou didst hear it!

What wilt thou in God's house? Perhaps thou didst suffer injustice, possibly thou art the innocent, the lovable man, and yet perhaps men deceived thee perfidiously; possibly thou art the noble, the good man, possibly thou shalt one day be reckoned among the benefactors of the race, and yet as a reward for this perhaps men thrust thee out of their society, maltreated thee, insulted thee, perhaps sought thy life—and thou didst flee hither to God's house in search of comfort. Whoever thou art, thou art making a mistake—thou hast come here to what is more dreadful! Here in God's house it is not a question, at least not first, of what we men may suffer in this world by way of a little bit of injustice, which in some other way at least we have richly deserved. No, here in God's house it is first and foremost a question of the horror the like of which was never seen and shall not again be seen in the confusion of the world, about the injustice which cries to heaven, such as never before was committed and never shall be again, more dreadful than the sea at its wildest, an occasion when the human race did not as usual rebel impotently against God, but triumphantly as it were laid hold of Him and crucified Him. So he is after all making a mistake who from the horror without flees into this place—to something still more dreadful! Yet the talk first and foremost must be about this. The figure of Him, our Lord and Saviour Jesus Christ, must be recalled—not as when the artist finds and takes plenty of time to represent it, not in such wise that it is removed from the environment of horror and set apart as an object for tranquil contemplation. No, He is to be remembered as at the moment of danger and horror, when the tranquil contemplator would prefer to remain at home, when to have looked upon Him in adoration or merely lovingly would make one an object of suspicion, when there was nothing to behold except this contemptuous, 'Behold, what a man!' when there was not even time to behold Him, because the horror took away one's eyes from one and riveted them staringly upon itself. And Christ's suffering is not to be remembered as a past event—oh, waste not thy sympathy! No, when this horror is represented it is a present fact, and thou art present, and I, with a present One—and as accomplices.

But thus thou didst go amiss in going to the house of the Lord. Instead of hearing comfort which might console thee for the injustice thou dost suffer, instead of being justified as against the men who do thee injustice, instead of this thou art put in the wrong, thou, precisely thou who art innocently persecuted, insulted, wronged! What thou dost get is guilt, an atrocious guilt laid upon thy conscience, that thou art an accomplice to His innocent suffering and death. Oh, hard words of comfort! Who can bear them? Oh, stern way of diverting thy sad and gloomy thoughts—that of giving thee something still more dreadful to weep over! [1]

Keep thy foot when thou goest to the house of the Lord—and why? Just because in the house of the Lord there is offered thee the only, the most blissful saving comfort, the very highest is offered thee, God's friendship, His grace in Christ Jesus. Hence we should not cease to invite men to come at least into the house of the Lord, we should always be ready to pray, in behalf of others as well as for ourselves, that our visit to the house of God may be blessed; but just for this reason, for this very reason, we should not hesitate to cry out to men, 'For God's sake, beware! Above all, take care to use worthily what is there offered thee—just because there is everything to gain, there is everything to lose. Use it believingly.' There is no assurance so heartfelt, so strong, so blissful, as that of faith. But the assurance of faith is not something one is born with, the youthful trustfulness of a joyous mind; still less is faith something one grasps out of the air. Faith is the assurance, the blissful assurance, which is found in fear and trembling. When faith is seen from the one side, the heavenly side, one sees in it only the bright reflection of blessedness; but seen from the other side, the merely human side, one sees sheer fear and trembling. But thus the talk is untrue which never will talk otherwise of the visit to God's house than invitingly, enticingly, winningly; for as seen from the other side it is dreadful. And hence also the talk is untrue which ends at last with scaring men completely away from coming to the house of the Lord, for

[1] The reader who knows that S. K. from his childhood was absorbed in the thought of the sufferings of Christ will not be tempted to suspect here that this prodigious emphasis upon the crucifixion is unreal or oratorical.

seen from the other side it is blissful, one day in God's house is better than a thousand elsewhere. Oh, and for this reason it is a difficult thing to steer aright, and hence a man seldom succeeds, and always only in weakness. For it is easy to win men enticingly; it is also easy to scare them away repellantly—but if possible with a heartiness which no one could resist to invite them to come, and at the same time, with a fearfulness which would teach even the boldest to shudder, to cry, 'Beware!'—yea, that is difficult. And the same thing applies to the speaker, the very same rule which he applies to the hearers. For it may be said to the speaker, 'Employ all the talents bestowed upon thee, being ready for every personal sacrifice and compliance in self-abnegation, employ them to win men—but woe unto thee if thou dost so win them as to leave out the dread; employ therefore all the talents bestowed upon thee, being ready for every sacrifice in self-abnegation, employ them to terrify men—but woe unto thee if essentially thou dost not employ them to win men for the truth.

II

BEHOLD, WE HAVE FORSAKEN ALL AND FOLLOWED THEE; WHAT
SHALL WE HAVE THEREFORE? (Matt. xix. 27)—AND WHAT
SHALL WE HAVE?

THE words here quoted are those of the Apostle Peter,
uttered in view of Christ's assertion how hard it is to enter
into the kingdom of God. And the conclusion of the question concerns us all: what shall we have, what does Christianity
promise us? But then as for the beginning of the question, 'we
have forsaken all and followed thee,' does that also concern us?
Most assuredly. But does it then fit our case? Perhaps. It is
possible that various expressions may be fitting to various people.
Blessed is he whom these words fit perfectly, that is, blessed is he
who can dare to say: I have forsaken all to follow Christ. Yet in
another way also these words might fit perfectly—as a mockery
of those who think and say that they are Christians, and yet cling
with their whole soul to the worldly interests. One might seek to
show by a more ample presentation of the subject that such
Christianity is a vain imagination, is a deceit; but one can state
the case more briefly, and yet in a way which would be less likely to
fail of its effect, by merely adducing these words of Peter, 'Behold
we have forsaken all and followed thee'—they fit perfectly!

People often talk of how glorious it is to be a Christian, of the
great advantage of being a Christian, of what he who is a Christian possesses and one day shall receive in fuller measure, of what
good things are promised a man in Christ Jesus; and these good
things are then extolled in the loftiest and strongest terms. And
this is also a matter of course, it is right and reasonable, it is a
plain duty to do so. But one can say the same thing, the very
same thing, in another and perhaps a more arousing way. Oh,
and which of the two speakers really speaks most truly of this
good: he who describes it in the most glorious terms; or he who
says, 'Behold, I have forsaken all for the sake of this good'? Thus
he does not say anything about how glorious the good is, to this
end he does not employ or waste a single word, he thinks that
this speaks more effectively: 'Behold, I have forsaken all, look,
examine my life, its outward condition, my soul's inward state,

its wishes and longings and desires, and thou wilt perceive that I have forsaken all.' Or is this not also a very suspicious self-contradiction, that a man should be perfectly convinced of the glory of that good which yet did not have so much power over him that for its sake he forsook the least of all that which is in strife with or cannot be possessed together with this good? Is not this a capital way of proving how glorious this good is to one, that one shows how much one has forsaken for the sake of it? In case there was a lover who with the most beautiful and glowing expressions extolled his lady's perfection and superiority, and there was another lover who said not a single word about this, but only, 'Behold, for her sake I have forsaken all'—which of these two spoke most gloriously in her praise? For nothing runs so fast as the tongue, and nothing is easier than to let the tongue run, and only this is equally easy: by the help of the tongue to run away from oneself, in what one says to be many, many thousand miles ahead of oneself. If therefore thou wouldst extol Christianity—oh, do not wish for thyself the tongues of angels, nor the art of all the poets, nor the eloquence of all orators: in the same degree that thy life shows how much thou hast forsaken for the sake of it, in that same degree dost thou extol Christianity. And if we would give proof of our Christian conviction, supposing that we are really assured and convinced of the glory of this good which Christianity promises, let us not seek in one or another orator a happy presentation which we are entirely in agreement with and make our own, nor, if we are orators, attempt for ourselves to extol in word and speech the glory of this good. But let us turn our glance within, and while we sincerely test our life, listen to these words of Peter as said of us, 'Behold, we have forsaken all'—and thereupon utter for ourselves the last words: What shall we have?

'*Behold, we have forsaken all and followed thee.*' In these words the Apostle does not represent himself as a man who has had a great loss in the world, a man from whom perhaps God has taken away everything—he is not a Job who says, 'The Lord hath taken away.' [1] No, the Apostle uses a different expression; he says, we have 'forsaken' all. This Job did not do, Job had not forsaken

---

[1] One of the most profound and persistent impressions of S. K.'s youth was his father's sincere utterance of these words of Job on the occasion of the death of several of his children.

the least thing; on the other hand, the Lord took from him everything, even unto the least. Job's piety appears in this, that when
the Lord had taken all, he said, 'Blessed be the name of the Lord,'
that therefore humbly and in faith he thankfully consented to put
up with the loss, or to regard it as for his good. Otherwise with
the Apostle, he has forsaken all, and so he has voluntarily given
up all; no might was employed against him to take away from
him even the least thing, no, but he voluntarily gave it all up.
This is Christianity. For that a man puts up with the unavoidable loss is also to be seen in paganism. That a man puts up with
an unavoidable loss in such a way that he not merely does not lose
faith in God but believingly adores and extols His glory, that is
Jewish piety. But *voluntarily* to give up all is Christianity.

Oh, there often is heard false talk which would make men
believe that to give up voluntarily the earthly goods would be to
tempt God, that to venture voluntarily to encounter a danger
which one could avoid would be to tempt God. They think that
this is tempting God, and so they say in condemnation of one
who thus gets into danger, 'He is himself to blame for it.' Yes,
quite certainly—he is himself to blame for it, and this precisely
is a eulogy upon him. If he had shrewdly held back, and for fear
of tempting God had allowed himself to make a fool of God, he
would presumably have remained out of danger, in the secure
possession of all he possessed. But the Apostle says, 'Behold, we
have forsaken all,' and so far from thinking of reproaching himself for this, he evidently accounts it to his credit, as something
that must please God. But that goes without saying when he adds,
'and followed thee' (Christ); it is a matter of course that if one
gives up all and forsakes everything to follow his own nose, he is
tempting God.

On the other hand, it is actually true that Christianity requires
the Christian to give up and forsake all things. This was not
required in Old Testament times, God did not require Job to give
up anything, and of Abraham he required expressly, as a test,
only that he give up Isaac. But in fact Christianity is also the
religion of freedom, it is precisely the voluntary which is the
Christian. Voluntarily to give up all is to be convinced of the
glory of the good which Christianity promises. In a cowardly
and apprehensive spirit not to dare to venture this for fear of
tempting God implies a spirit of slavery; cunningly to pretend

that it is because one is afraid of tempting God is to make a fool
of God. There is one thing God cannot take away from a man,
namely, the voluntary [1]—and it is precisely this which Chris-

[1] There is nothing S. K. more frequently insisted upon, or more hotly, than man's
freedom—the fact that God had made man free to choose. This is the key to his
'anthropology', and hence to his theology.

The most carefully considered statement of this position is found in the Journal,
and hence it will not be available to English readers unless I translate it here, as I
do in the following paragraph:

'The whole question of God's omnipotence and the relation of goodness to evil
may perhaps (instead of resorting to the distinction that God brings about the good
and merely permits the evil) be resolved quite simply in this way. The highest that
conceivably can be done for a being, higher than any elevation it might be made to
attain, is to make it free. It requires omnipotence for this. It may seem strange,
since omnipotence would seem to require dependence. But if one will think omnipotence, he will perceive that precisely therein must be involved the distinctive characteristic of being able in the expression of omnipotence to withdraw itself again, and
that precisely for this cause what came into existence by omnipotence can be independent. Hence it is that the one man cannot quite make the other free, since he
who has the power is captive to the possession of it, and therefore gets a wrong
relationship to him he would make free. In addition to this, there is in every finite
power (talents etc.) a finite selfishness. Only omnipotence is able to withdraw (take
itself back) in giving out, and it is this relationship precisely which constitutes the
independence of the recipient. Hence God's omnipotence is His goodness. For
goodness means to give out completely, but in such wise that by withdrawing it
makes the recipient free. All finite power makes dependent, only omnipotence can
make independent, can bring forth from nothing that which has continuance in
itself by reason of the fact that omnipotence withdraws. Omnipotence does not
succumb to something else, for there is nothing else comparable to it; no, it is able
to give without at the same time giving up the least of its power, i.e. it can make
independent. This is the inconceivable thing, that omnipotence is not merely able
to produce the most imposing phenomenon, the totality of the visible universe, but
also the very frailest thing of all: a being which in the very face of omnipotence is
independent. So that omnipotence which can make its mighty hand so heavy upon
the world, can make it so light that the being which comes into existence acquires
independence.—It is but a worthless and worldly conception of the dialectic of
power that it is greater and greater in proportion as it can compel and make dependent. No, Socrates understood it better, that the art of power is precisely to make
free. But in the relationship between man and man this cannot be done; although
it may need to be emphasized again and again that this is the highest thing, yet it is
only omnipotence that can truly do it. In case, therefore, a man had outwardly (in a
material respect) the least self-substantial existence over against God, He could
not make him free. Creation out of nothing is thus an expression for being able to
make independent. He to whom I absolutely owe all, whereas He with like absolute-
ness has retained all, precisely He it is that has made me independent. In case for the
sake of creating man God Himself lost a little of His power, He could not make man
independent.'

tianity requires of man. God is able to take away from a man everything; but He has left it to man to give up everything voluntarily, and precisely this is what Christianity requires. In a human sense it can be said of all the glorious ones who gave up all to follow Christ, that it was their own fault that they got into all these troubles and adversities, were exposed to all sorts of scoffing and persecution, it was their own fault that they suffered death. Once (yes, this is to be said in the ears of the world in disparagement of them, in God's ears to their honour) it was in their power to hold back, to avoid all these dangers; but voluntarily they forsook all. This is Christianity—and hence it is an offence. For at the most the world can comprehend that one may be able to hit upon some small comfort for them that suffer the unavoidable loss. But that one should voluntarily expose onself to loss and danger, in the eyes of the world that is madness—and precisely that is Christianity.

This thing of voluntarily forsaking all to follow Christ, which the world neither can nor will hear without being offended, is also the thing which so-called Christendom would rather have suppressed, or if it is uttered would so much prefer to ignore, in any case would hear in such wise as to get something different out of it. Hence it is not impossible that even a discourse which had the intent of terrifying might have a lulling effect. Thus one could represent it as so terrible, as indeed it is, when in those remote ages of Christendom, the ages of persecution, a man perhaps ventured out [1] and would be a martyr, and then, possibly after having suffered in manifold ways and for a long while, at last, at the moment of mortal danger, in sight of the painful death, he lost courage, gave up—he abjures Christianity. So this ought to be terrifying, as indeed it is. But where then is the possibility of the lulling effect? The lulling effect is or would be produced by the wrong application, if it were added, or if it were tacitly left to the hearer to add for himself: We have not thus denied Christ —we, we who perhaps with cowardly shrewdness know well how to keep out of every danger in which our Christianity might be tested. Ah, and which sort of denial is the worst? Surely it is precisely this latter sort, the cowardly, shrewd and calculating

---

[1] 'To venture out', or 'to venture far out', are expressions which S. K. frequently used of himself at this time, wondering whether he might acquire the courage to be a martyr.

denial, continued from year to year, protracted throughout a
whole life, steadily, daily (oh, how terrible to comply thus with
Christ's requirement of daily self-denial!), the daily denial of
Christ. Well, of course, this denial is not conspicuous (at least
not in a theatrical sense—to the searcher of hearts, the ever-
present, it is surely just as conspicuous) as when such a luckless
wight at the decisive instant of the painful death denies Christ.
But there can be no doubt which is the worst. There still is, and
always will be, salvation and hope for every man whose sin
became notorious, salvation is all the nearer, the more terrible the
form in which his sin must be visible to him. But for this cunning
game of shrewdness there is no salvation: its secret consists
precisely in maintaining that one has not denied Christ. That
there is some distinction between sin and sin, everybody knows;
but there is a distinction which people do not always seem to be
sufficiently aware of, that namely between the sin of the instant,
or sin at the instant, and the continuous daily sin, of a life which
consciously and with a full view of the situation has adjusted itself
to sin, providing itself moreover with the hypocrisy requisite for
preserving the appearance of goodness. The proverb says, 'To sin
is human, but to continue in sin is devilish,' and yet this about
which we are speaking is even more terrible, this thing of consciously adjusting oneself shrewdly to sin, or if not with complete
consciousness of it, at least with the consciousness that one con-
serves in the soul an obscurity about that which for good reasons
one does not want clarity.—That there is some distinction between sin and sin, everybody knows; but there is a distinction
which people do not always seem sufficiently aware of: between
the sin which the world regards as abhorrent, and that which the
world regards as the Good, or for which at least it has mitigating
and extenuating names. The latter sin is obviously the worst; for
it is impossible that the sin which the world regards as sin can be
the worst—in that case the world itself must be good. All sin is
of the evil, but the sin for which the world has in readiness the
mitigating name is even in a stricter sense from the evil, is sin in
the second potency, having support and countenance in the evil
which is the sin of the world. There is therefore no sin so heinous
in God's eyes as the sin of shrewdness, precisely because it has
the countenance of the world. Or, to stick to the example which
was adduced, what is it, if the world were to be sincere, what is it

the world condemns in such a luckless wight who at the decisive moment denies the faith, what is it really but just this, that he was so lacking in shrewdness as to venture so far out that his denial could in such a decisive way become notorious? So it is his first act, the beginning, that is condemned; but it is precisely the beginning that was good; he who does not begin thus never reaches the glorious end of proving himself true to his conviction by a painful death. It is the sin of shrewdness to sin in such a way that one knows cunningly how to avoid punishment, yea, knows cunningly how to give this the appearance of the Good; the sin of shrewdness is cunning enough to avoid every decisive act, and thereby to win the distinction of never having denied—this the world regards as something far above the ordinary. For verily the world does not hate the evil, on the contrary it abhors and hates the man who lacks shrewdness, that is to say, it loves the evil.—'Behold, we have forsaken all and followed thee'—and we, what shall we have?

'*Behold we have forsaken all and followed thee.*' The Apostle Peter is no stripling who somehow at the beginning of his life talks in an enthusiastic fashion about this thing of forsaking all things. He himself knew perfectly well what he understood by it, and we know how true it was at the time he said it, and how true it remained in his subsequent life, how true it is that the Apostle had forsaken all.

He forsook his customary occupation, the quiet, homely life which, content with a modest competence, was passed in security; he forsook the tranquillizing reliance upon the probable, within which a man for the most part passes his life, untried in anything but in that which for the most part turns out all right in the end —*he forsook the certain and chose the uncertain.* For Christ, on whose account and in order to follow Him he forsook all, was no man of means who could give His disciple something certain as a yearly stipend, or could secure for him an assured position and a living—He, the poorest of all, He who so far as his own life was concerned was sure of only one thing: that He would be sacrificed! But as soon as Christ called him, he forsook all this, as we read in Matt. iv. 20. This was a magnanimous resolution, and we must not think of Peter, a man like us, as one for whom there was never an instant when the lower nature was ready to suggest misgivings and anxieties; for the truly great man is not thus, he is not without anxieties and misgivings, but he is what he is precisely by overcoming them. Nevertheless, he formed this magnanimous resolution to forsake all things. But the difficulty for the magnanimous man is always a double one: first, to triumph within himself over the lower and earthly; then, when this is done, there comes the next difficulty, that in every age the contemporaries find the magnanimous act so silly and foolish. For that a man chooses a life whereby he gains many advantages (a thing by no means magnanimous) the world admires; but that a man gives up all advantages, even that of being honoured by the world (which precisely is magnanimity), the world finds ludicrous.—Peter forsook all the certain things and chose the uncertain, to be a disciple of Christ, a disciple of Him who Himself had not whereon to lay His head. Peter chose the uncertain— and yet, no, he did not choose the uncertain. He to whom he attached himself was no adventurer who kept the possibilities equally open: the possibility of becoming something great in the world, and the possibility of losing everything. Christ did not leave the disciples in uncertainty about what awaited them and Him—certain destruction. So then Peter chose certain destruction.

He forsook family and friends and comrades, even the very conceptions and ideas in which they had their life, he became to them more of a stranger than one who speaks a strange tongue. For there is a still higher and more endless difference between two persons, one of whom thinks and speaks only of the heavenly, of the kingdom of God and of His righteousness, the other only of sustenance and livelihood and wife and children, and what news there is in the town, and about coming to something in the world. He forsook all this, notwithstanding that at the beginning his family and friends found it in their language queer and eccentric of him, therefore transformed themselves into enemies who mocked him, and later, when they saw how perilous his life was, they went about busily saying, 'It was his own fault.'

He forsook his father's faith, so that he had to hate father and mother. For this indeed is the meaning of Christ's saying, that he who for His sake does not hate father and mother is not worthy of Him—and Peter was worthy of Him. When there is a difference of religion, and thus an eternal difference of eternity between father and son, and the son sincerely believes with all his heart and with all his strength and with all his soul that only in this religion is there blessedness—then he hates the father, that is, he loves something else so highly that his love for his father is like hate. When one has a legitimate, a sacred claim, has the prior claim upon thy love, then to love another, even if this means only to become indifferent to that first object, is as if thou didst hate him, just because he has a claim upon thy love. But to love something so highly that one believes that therein alone salvation is to be found and blessedness, and apart from that only perdition— when the father then to whom thou art attached by the most heartfelt ties does not believe the same thing, when consequently the believer, the more sincerely he holds fast to the one thing in which there is salvation, is compelled (oh, horror, as though it were laying violent hands upon his father!), is compelled to conclude, and must (oh, horror, as though it were denying his father the necessities of life!), must compel his heart to conclude that his father is lost—this indeed is to hate the father. Is not this to hate another, to believe that he is lost? And is it any the less so because it seems unspeakably hard to one? So then, this is to hate the father, or more correctly, it is to hate him and yet to love him! Oh, abomination without equal, to hate the loved one, so that one's love is turned to hate; ah, of all soul-sufferings the bitterest, the most agonizing, to hate the loved one and yet love him! To want to do everything for him, to wish to offer one's life for him —but to be bound, bound, yea, or nailed, or crucified upon the stipulation over which one has no control, the stipulation which attaches blessedness to one condition, so that apart from this there is no blessedness, so that the choice is, either to give up one's own blessedness in order to live hapless with the loved one; or to believe for oneself unto salvation—ah, and thus with hate to let go of the loved one!

He forsook the faith of the fathers, and therewith the nation and people he belonged to, and the fatherland, the love of which binds with the strongest bonds. For he belonged no more to any nation or people, he belonged only to the Lord Jesus Christ. As a believer he had to understand that this elect people of God to which he belonged by birth was cast off, that there no longer existed an elect people; as a believer he had to understand that what doubtless had once been his proudest thought, to belong to God's elect people, that this thought from now on was obduracy and perdition for every man who continued to hold to this thought.

Thus it was the Apostle forsook all, broke with everything which binds a man to the earth, and with everything which holds one a prisoner to the earth. He forsook out of love for Christ, or out of hatred for the world, he forsook all things, his position in life, livelihood, family, friends, the human language, love to father and mother, love for the fatherland, the faith of the fathers, he forsook the God he had hitherto worshipped. He forsook this *otherwise* than does he who by the ocean is separated from the land of his birth; *more inwardly* than he who leaves father and mother to cling to his wife, *more heartily* than a woman who leaves the paternal home—he did not even turn to look back, nor demand time to bury the dead. He forsook it all, yes, and in the most decisive way; for he remained on the spot, surrounded by all that he forsook: the daily difficulties of his life were the formal attestation that he forsook this. He remained amongst those whom he forsook: that they hated and persecuted him was the expression of the fact that he had forsaken all. He did not in fact journey away from it all, no, he remained to bear witness that he had forsaken it, exposing himself to all the consequences thereof, which in turn were the evidence that he had forsaken all.

'*Behold, we have forsaken all and followed thee; what shall we have therefore?* The Apostle had forsaken all—and, as has been shown, it is to be taken seriously in the strictest sense that he forsook all things; it was not as with us who, without altering anything in outward respects, protest that we are willing to forsake all things, if it is required of us.[1] Then the Apostle asks, 'What shall we have?'—and I ask, or better, thou, my hearer, dost ask of thyself (for this is both more meet and more profitable), thou dost ask, What shall we have?

Oh, there is nothing so deceitful and cunning as the human heart, so inventive in seeking evasions and in finding excuses; nothing is so difficult and so rare as true sincerity before God. Verily we should beware of delivering ranting sermons of censure, and especially of being the one to exact of others as it were the

---

[1] There is a passage in the Journal prompted by a sermon of Bishop Mynster's in which he solemnly protested that he was ready to give up everything . . . 'if it should be required'. S. K.'s indignant comment was the query if ever there was a time which so clearly called for self-sacrifice and even martyrdom.

payment of outstanding debts to God. For it is true enough that God can demand sincerity of every man, and so also of 'me'; but this by no means implies that I am commissioned on behalf of God to exact it of others. If I were to give myself out as having such a commission, I myself would be guilty of insincerity towards God. No, we would not appal men in such a way. But the appalling thing of being insincere towards God has another side. There is only one help for a man in heaven or on earth, whether all other help is at his disposition, or it is all shattered, there is only this help, that God helps him. Perhaps a man often thinks that God is slow in helping, or that by reason of the infinitely many complications in the government of the world, help becomes so slowly available. Far from it! God is a present help, swifter than thought, and for God there is no complication. But man is insincere towards God in desiring His help, or in any case very slow in becoming sincere.

When a man protests that he is willing to forsake all things for Christ's sake, if it is required of him—well, how could I dare to say that this is insincere? But in those ages when they were actually serious about forsaking all things, were there then to be found so many who were willing, and the few who were to be found, were they not found among the poor and the lowly? But now, now that it is not so easy to take seriously the obligation of forsaking all things, now we are all willing . . . if it is required of us. Let us not deceive ourselves, nor deceive God. It does not do to have so high an opinion of oneself: to remain in possession of all, and be such a hero too. If God does not require us to forsake all, He does nevertheless require of us sincerity. Instead of impatiently and hot-headedly urging another to try his hand impatiently and hot-headedly at forsaking all things, which God perhaps does not require, or does not require of him, we on the contrary would extol sincerity, which God requires of every one; but surely it is preposterous to treat this as a mere phrase, or as a mere form of speech to ascribe to us all that which at a time when it was really taken seriously was fully carried out by one among thousands and thousands.—Perhaps God does not require it of him, that is to say, it is required of every one but not *unconditionally* required of every one, i.e. it is left to freedom. He who does this believingly, and therefore humbly, acts Christianly; but he who humbly has an understanding with himself in not doing it, who has a lowly opinion of himself, also acts Christianly. Perhaps God does not require it, that is, God does not require it in the same way of us who live in Christendom. And the voluntary act, the voluntary forsaking of all things, is only then Christian when, as was shown, it is for the sake of following Christ, and is thus in correspondence with God's requirement; and the voluntary act is in Christendom only then deserving of praise when before God it has an understanding of the essential distinction that the Apostles and the early Christians did what they did when they were surrounded by Jews and pagans, that is, by non-Christians. For him who lives in Christendom—one thing there is in any case he is not to forsake, as the Apostles did, the faith of the fathers; and after all there is and remains the difficulty of being persecuted, being executed, not by Jews, not by pagans, but by Christians . . . in the name of Christianity.

There was a time in Christendom when people thought they could do penance by actually forsaking all things, by fleeing to the solitude of the desert, or seeking to be persecuted in the swarming city. There is another way of doing penance, that of being thoroughly sincere towards God. I do not know—and in case I knew differently, I trust to God that I would make bold to talk differently—I do not know that anywhere it is unconditionally required of a man in Christendom that to be a Christian and to become blessed he must in a literal sense forsake everything, or even sacrifice his life, be executed, for the sake of Christianity. But this I know, that with an insincere man God can have nothing to do. It is therefore, according to my conception, a theme for a penitential sermon, this which we have chosen, these words of Peter, 'Behold, we have left all and followed thee, what shall we have therefore?'—that is to say, when thou art prompted by this question to ask thyself, What shall we have? No man, however, can become blessed except by grace, the Apostles also were accepted only by grace. But there is one sin which makes grace impossible, that is, insincerity; and there is one thing which God must unconditionally require, that is, sincerity. If on the contrary a man holds God at arm's length by insincerity, such a man can *neither* learn to understand whether God would require him in the strictest sense to forsake all things, *nor* learn to understand himself in the humble admission that he had not indeed forsaken all things, but nevertheless confides in God's grace.

Oh, different as these situations are in the human understanding of it, when the Apostle says, 'Behold we have left all and followed thee, what shall we have?'—and when a man, humbly confessing that he was not put to such a test, sincerely admitting before God that he could not in any way venture to believe that he was capable of it, says, 'What shall we have?'—by God's grace they both of them get one and the same thing.[1]

[1] Perhaps, as S. K. feared, hardly 'a single soul' read his *Christian Discourses*. If many souls had taken to heart this passage, S. K. would hardly have felt the need of saying the same thing more harshly in his *Training in Christianity*, nor would he have needed to proclaim again this indulgence in the Moral of that book and in its thrice repeated Preface—nor would he have needed to assert again, as he did in 'The Midnight Cry', that the one thing he demanded was honesty. It here appears clearly that the 'indulgence', in spite of the fact that it was 'withdrawn' in the heat of his last conflict, was really an essential constituent, an integral part, of S. K.'s thought.

III

IF a man were to protest in the most solemn and emphatic
terms that he loved God, that God, and God alone, was the
object of his love, the first and only love—and this man, if he
were asked the reason why, were to respond, 'Because God is the
highest, the holiest, the most perfect being'; and if this man,
when some one asked him whether he had never loved God for
any other reason, were to reply, 'No'—then one m:ght well
suspect him of being a fanatic, might well warn him in all seriousness to have a care lest this fanatic mood might end in presumption. The simple and humble thing is to love God because one
needs Him. It may seem so natural that in order to love God
one must raise oneself to heaven where God dwells: the best and
surest way, however, to love God is to remain on the earth. It
may seem so lofty a thing to love God because He is so perfect,
it may seem so selfish to love Him because one needs Him: yet
the latter way is the only way in which a man can in truth love
God. Woe to the presumptuous man who would make bold to
love God without needing Him! In the relationship between
man and man there may perhaps be the possibility of such an
enthusiastic love which loves a man merely for his perfection,
but the prime condition at the basis of a man's love for God is to
understand effectually that one needs God, to love Him simply
because one needs Him. The man who most deeply recognizes
his need of God loves Him most truly. Thou shalt not presume
to love God for God's sake; thou shalt eternally understand that
thy life's welfare eternally depends upon this, and for this reason
thou shalt love Him.

So let every one ask himself, for the sake of his own welfare,
whether he loves God. This in the deepest sense is the enquiry
about one's welfare: Do I love God? If the answer is, Yes, then
thy welfare is assured also eternally, for 'all things must work
together for good to them that love God'. Oh, how often this
text has been quoted, repeated and repeated again, explained,

interpreted for edification, for comfort, for consolation. They have shown how experience has confirmed the truth of it, how all things have actually worked together for good to them that love God. They have combated all doubts, have made it so clear that this is so—that however different things may appear in a time or times of suffering, of trial, of temptation, all things must in the end work together for good to them that love God, that there is no repose for thought, that there is no doubt that can resist this assurance, but in the end it must acknowledge its defeat and submit.

But what of that? Because it is eternally certain that all things work together for good to them that love God, does it follow that 'I' love God? And this precisely is the decisive question. The more one combats impersonally all the objections of doubt, and then, after having refuted all these objections, assumes that the whole matter is decided, all the more is attention diverted from the question which is really decisive. Yes, men are often strangely busy in the wrong place. They contend and contend, ponder and ponder, to prove the truth of Christianity—then they are tranquillized, then they think that everything is all right. This is to betake oneself to rest at the beginning, as one should not do till the end—which is strange especially in these times when people are so busy about going farther![1] Oh, the man who has but a little understanding of the matter easily perceives that everything else is only preliminary work, an introduction to the main matter: Is it thus WITH ME? But they have turned the whole thing around, and therefore have on their hands a job which Christianity never dreamt of. Christianity was proclaimed with divine authority; its thought was that not a single instant ought to be wasted in proving it true, but that each man severally should turn to himself and say, 'What relation hast thou to Christianity?' This personal concern, this fear and trembling, as to whether a man is himself a believer, is the best remedy against all doubt about the truth of the doctrine; for in his personal concern a man sets to work with all the powers of his soul at a totally different place. But because they have entirely done away with this personal concern, they have also got on their hands a kind of doubt which Satan himself could not contend against—though he might well

---

[1] S. K. frequently complained that not only Hegel but the Hegelian theologians, like Martensen, were proud of 'going farther' than Christianity.

invent it—a kind of doubt against which it is impossible to contend because it actually is required that to contend against it one must pass over to its side, and so to vanquish it must betray Christianity. Christianly understood, the only weapon against doubt is, 'Keep still!' or in Luther's phrase, 'Keep your mouth shut!' Doubt, on the other hand, says, 'Be so kind as to fight with my own weapons.' How unreasonable, and how impossible! If a liar were to say, 'Be so kind as to fight with my own weapons', could truth be served by that proposal, or by winning such a victory? [1]

So then, because such is the situation, and because it is so general, it is doubtless advantageous to turn the thing around again, to put back again the main-spring of personal concern which they have managed to take out of Christianity. So in this discourse, instead of proving the truth of the proposition that all things work together for good to them that love God, we would, as is meet and right, assume this quite simply as eternally certain, as the most certain thing in the world, and on the other hand talk about the statement that

ALL THINGS WORK TOGETHER FOR OUR GOOD—*IF* WE LOVE GOD.

So the Discourse really revolves about the word '*if*'. It is a little word, but it has immense significance; it is a little word, about which nevertheless a world revolves, the world of personality. Thou knowest that people which was notorious for its brief, laconic expressions, and presumably thou knowest that laconic answer, 'If'. [2] This was proudly said by the superior power, talking about what his countless hosts would do if they conquered all; and it was a brief answer: 'If'. And the case is somewhat similar with all this proving and proving and refuting which talks with proud words of what it is able to accomplish— seeing that it is not able to accomplish the least thing, *if* it does not itself believe, seeing that it has not itself the least profit from this proving, *if* it does not itself believe, seeing that it does not

[1] S. K.'s first philosophical work (after *The Concept of Irony*), which he began and did not complete, was entitled *De omnibus dubitandum est* in which he derided the use made of this maxim by the *followers* of Descartes—not by the master.

[2] The reply of the Spartans to King Philip of Macedonia when he threatened to depopulate the land, if he should enter Laconia. It needs to be noted that the Danish word *naar* means either 'when' or 'if'. In this passage the translator has to stick to one of them.

profit thee in the least, *if* thou dost not believe, cannot in the very least help thee to believe, and on the other hand it may be a thing totally indifferent to thee, *if* thou dost believe. Yea, it is a little word, this *if*! If God is love, then it follows as a matter of course that all things must work together for good to them that love God; but from the fact that God is love it by no means follows that thou dost believe that God is love, or that thou dost love Him. If on the other hand 'thou' dost believe, it follows as a matter of course that all things work together for good to 'thee', for this is implied in what thou believest of God. In the one case man puts himself as it were inside God and proves something about Him, proves that He is love and what follows from this; in the other case man understands humbly that the question is whether *he* believes that God is love, for if he believes this, then all the rest follows as a matter of course, without proof—from the proof nothing ensues *for me*, from faith everything ensues *for me*.[1]

So the discourse is about this *if*, and therewith about faith, which of all goods is the highest and the only true good. For of all other goods it may be said that there is always a 'but' attached to them, that they have a side from which it seems doubtful whether this good is a good, whether it might not have been better that a man did not get this good. But faith is the good which is of such a nature that if thou believest, in case thou believest, when thou believest, inasmuch as thou believest—even though there were to befall thee that which thou most hast feared—thou wilt believingly understand that for thee it must be for the best, and therefore a good. Whereas doubt has power over everything we commonly call goods, power to make them doubtful, faith too has power over all the good and all the evil that can befall thee, power to put beyond all doubt that it is a good.

All things must work together for our good—IF *we love God.*

Imagine a man in possession of all the goods of fortune, untouched by affliction and adversity, unacquainted with any suffering or danger, envied by the narrow-hearted, counted fortunate

---

[1] Even in his pseudonymous works S. K. constantly insists upon 'subjectivity' in religion. From first to last it is one of his most important themes: 'truth is that which is true for me'.

by the young—dare he count himself fortunate? Yes—*if* he
believes that God is love; for then all these things work together
for his good. 'If'—it is a naughty little word, this 'if'! Yea, woe
to the man who ventures to cast doubt of God into another man's
heart, for all this doubt is sinful, and to awaken this doubt in
another is seduction. But honour be to the man, praise and
thanksgiving to him who is so serious that he does not fear to
awaken in another the doubt which teaches a man to doubt
himself, the doubt which is the origin of personal concern. So
then, we say 'if'. This 'if' is a revivalist, a penitential preacher.
Thou perhaps art inclined to suppose that the penitential preacher
is like a great strong wind which produces physical terror. No,
the true preacher is heard, as God's voice was heard, in the gentle
breeze—yet for that reason not lenient but stern, stern as the
seriousness of eternity. The true preacher aims only at one
thing, to come to such close quarters with thee or with me, with
the individual, to wound one in such a way that he thereupon
becomes his own penitential preacher. Beware of this 'if'—in
another sense, take care to love this 'if'—in case it has scored a
hit upon thee, it may take thee a year and a day to be done with
it, or rather, in case it has stabbed thee deeply, thou wilt never
be done with this 'if'—that thou wilt not. This 'if' remains like
an arrow in thy heart; it will remain there till the last.[1] Be not
therefore afraid of the penitential preacher, who perhaps has
terror in his appearance and wrath in his voice, who chides and
rebukes and thunders. A thing like that is only play and produces only a sort of shuddering pleasure. No, in the inmost
depths of every man's heart there dwells his penitential preacher.
When he has a chance to speak, he does not preach to others, he
does not make a penitential preacher of thee, he preaches before
thee alone; he does not preach in any church before an assembled
multitude, he preaches in the secret chamber of the heart—and
before thee, whether thou wilt hear him or not; he has nothing
else whatever to attend to but to attend to thee, and he takes good
care to be heard when all about thee is still, when the stillness
makes thee lonely.

Thou fortunate man whom so many envy and so many count
fortunate—in case thou art wounded by this 'if' or hast wounded

---

[1] This 'if' is the reason why 'till the last' S. K. would not speak of himself as
being a Christian, but of *becoming* a Christian.

thyself, thou wilt not seek to find comfort in the assurance of any other man that thou art fortunate, yea, though all men were united in assuring thee of this, it will not give thee the least certitude. It is with thyself thou hast now to deal, with the preacher in thine inward man. He does not employ many words, he is too well informed for that, he says merely, 'If'. And whether thou wouldst deliver to him a long discourse, or propose to him a brief question, he says merely, 'If'. In consideration of thy wealth, with the thought that it is placed in thy power to make thy life as comfortable as possible, as rich in pleasure, or with the thought which is still more glorious, that it is placed in thy power to do good to so many, if in consideration of this thou wouldst count thyself fortunate—then says the preacher, 'Yes—if thou dost believe that God is love, if thou dost love God, for then all these things work together for thy good.' This reply is a bit disturbing, it is in a sense so cold, so calm in its ambiguity, it is neither yea nor nay. If thou wouldst ask him, 'Do I then love God?', he replies, 'Of that I know nothing, I declare merely how the case stands: if thou dost love God, then . . .' Wouldst thou beg and conjure him to answer finally *yes*, thou dost move him no whit more, thou canst not win him with flattery nor with prayers, thou canst not put him to death except in a very figurative sense, and in any case he does not fear death. But so long as he lives, so long as thou dost still hear his voice, he repeats this 'if'. In case thou wouldst say to him, 'I give half of my wealth to the poor, if only I may thus attain the certitude that the remainder truly redounds to my good', and he made thee no answer, because he cannot make answer to such a speech, or he replied, 'Yes—if' —in case thou, being then brought to extremities by sensing what power there is in this 'if' as uttered by him to thee, wouldst say, 'I give the whole of my wealth to the poor, if only I may thus attain the certitude that poverty truly redounds to my good'; then he makes answer, 'Yes—if thou dost love God.'

If thou lovest God, or if thou believest that God is love—for if thou believest that God is love, thou dost love Him also—then all things work together for thy good. But make no mistake, do not rush ahead and love God with an exuberant sense of thy good fortune, as though thou wert not really in need of Him because thou art fortunate enough. No, thou must learn to need God, to love Him because thou hast need of Him, thou, the most fortunate of men. Thy welfare is by no means, oh, by no means decided by thy good fortune, it is only then decided, but then also it is eternally decided, when [1] thou dost believe that God is love. O thou fortunate man—*if* thou believest it. Hail to thy good fortune! Then all these things work together for thy good: thy riches, thy good health, thy splendid intellectual gifts, thy joy at the side of thy beloved, thy honour, thy prestige among men, the blissful diversion of thy children: these things work together for thy good—if thou dost love God; and then thou art really fortunate. We say of a man that, however fortunate he may be, he lacks one thing if he has not the consciousness of his good fortune. But the true consciousness of his good fortune (without which, as has been said, the good fortune is not good fortune) is contained in, framed in, the consciousness that God is love. Knowledge about God being love is not yet the consciousness of it. For to have consciousness, a personal consciousness, it is requisite that in my knowing I have at the same time knowledge of myself and of my relationship to my knowing. This is to believe that God is love, it is to love Him.

Surely thou hast often heard people talk about the power of words, of what the man is capable of who has words thoroughly at his command—and yet this little word 'if' has infinitely more power when it is the preacher in one's inward parts who utters it to 'this man'. The power of words has cast down thrones, changed the face of the world, but this little 'if' has a still greater power, it is a still greater change when a man is eternally changed by this 'if'. It is an eternal change, more remarkable than the most remarkable occurrence in the world, when a man comes to love God. Whether that happens, when that happens, no one can tell the man. The preacher in his inmost parts can help him to become attentive, help him to seek with personal concern the certitude of the Spirit, when God's Spirit witnesseth with this man's spirit that *he* loves God. But God alone can give him this certitude. What the penitential preacher can do is to keep him awake in uncertainty: he says, 'All things work together for thy good—*if* thou dost love God.' With this word he challenges the youth in the morning of life, with this word he calls out to the man, at sundry times and in divers manners, in the busy days of life, with this word he prevents the aged man from becoming

[1] *Naar* is the word S. K. uses for the disquieting 'if'—but it also means 'when'.

torpid and drowsy. He adds not one syllable more, he takes not one syllable away, he alters not his voice, nor does he vary the emphasis upon the word; unchangeable as a dead man, calm as eternity, he reiterates, 'If.'

All things must work together for our good—IF *we love God.*

Imagine a man, the most miserable of all—human sympathy has already long ago given him up and forsaken him, for its own sake alas, dare not come near him, wishes—for its own sake, alas —that it might remain unaware of his misery, if only thereby it could be unaware that such misery can befall a man—might this miserable man say, 'Nothing but evil befalls me, and out of that comes constantly more evil'? By no means—but, yes, if he does not love God, he might be right in that; only the question then is something quite different from what he was talking about. For, in the divine understanding of it, not to love God is man's decided and conclusive misery, whether in other respects he be fortunate or unfortunate. That which human speech, on the other hand, calls need, adversity, suffering, sheer misery—that still can work together for a man's good . . . if he loves God.

Why what a strangely compounded double nature this 'if' has! Yes, and that's as it should be; for it is true, is it not, that the penitential preacher, if he is the true one, is also always the com-forter, who knows how to give comfort and to hold out long after human help has proved vain and has given up the sufferer. Therefore he is loved just as much as he is feared. In the dark night of despair, when every light is extinguished for the sufferer, there is still one place where the light is still lit, namely, upon the path the desperate man has to take, the short-cut: 'if' thou dost love God. At the moment of terrible despondency, when no longer there is any question or thought of any illative clause, but humanly speaking the meaning has petered out—there still is one clause left, a courageous clause of comfort which dauntlessly makes its way into the most dreadful situations and creates new meaning: 'if' thou dost love God. In the terrible moment of decision, when humanly speaking no turning is any longer possible, when there is only misery on all sides, wherever thou dost turn, and however thou dost turn—there is yet one turn possible which shall marvellously turn for thee everything into good: 'if' thou dost love God.

'But where is it then?' says a man, 'where is this?' Ah, in the deepest depths of every man there dwells a comfort which also is found in the depths where the penitential preacher dwells. Thou art helped but little if another man would preach to thee penitence; he cannot do it, it remains an empty play, the utmost he can do is to help thee to become thine own penitential preacher. And thou art helped but little if another man would comfort thee. In case thou art tried in difficult decisions, the comfort of another man will not understand thee and therefore cannot help thee; and in case thou hast become thoroughly miserable, thou canst not reasonably demand that another man's sympathy should venture to put itself in thy situation. But most deeply within thee, where the penitential preacher dwells, comfort also dwells, this 'if'. And just as this word cannot be corrupted by the flatteries and prayers of the fortunate man and mocks at his menaces, so, God be praised, it is also undismayed in the day of need. In case thou art inclined to suppose that the most diseased and the most troubled imagination is capable of inventing a horror which would bring this word to silence, thou art in error. Relate to this comforter what thou wilt, confide to him what is on the point of gaining the mastery over thee, that however thou dost shudder at it thou hast this upon thy tongue, that in spite of the opposition of thy heart thou art about to conclude that God is not love—he is not affrighted, he merely repeats, '*if* thou dost love God, then shall all these things work together for thy good'.

Oh, final comfort, oh, blessed comfort; oh, comfort beyond all measure! For, as was said, when human sympathy gives up, when the one man does not dare to go in to the other—most deeply within a man there is a comfort. The Scripture says, 'Have salt in yourselves', and it is true also that deepest within every man there is comfort. But this comforter has by no means disavowed his role as penitential preacher. For if by all thy misery, by thy cry of pain in suffering, or thy cry of dread in anticipation of the suffering thou fearest, thou wouldst seek to move him to give thee a certitude that thou dost love God—he would reply, '*if* thou dost love God'. Do not fancy that it is out of sympathy for all thy misery he utters and repeats this word of comfort. No, it is because the fears that in desperation thou mightest cast thyself into that which in the divine understanding of it is man's misery, into the misery of not loving God. He is not employed in wanting to do away with thy misery, nor does he give thee what he is unable to give, certitude that thou dost love God. But while misery preaches penitence to thee, he preaches comfort, not human but divine comfort; and in divine comfort penitence is always included and required.

O thou sufferer, *if* thou dost believe that God is love, or (what is the same thing) *if* thou dost love God (for if thou believest that God is love, then thou dost love Him also)—then all this works together for thy good. Say not that thou canst not understand how all this misery should work together for thy good, yield not to the error of doubt, so as to begin with the question whether God is love—be fearful of thyself, but find also comfort within thyself, attend to this word which rings in thine inmost parts: *if* thou dost love God. The certitude that thou dost love God, this word cannot give thee, that only God can give thee when His Spirit beareth witness with thy spirit that thou lovest Him, when thou dost know with Him that thou believest that He is love. But that word can help thee to seek this certitude. When despair would close around thee, this word still provides a prospect of salvation; when thou art about to collapse in weariness and to give up, that word still holds open a possibility of help, *if* thou dost love God.

All things must work together for good—IF *we love God.*

Imagine a man equipped if possible in more than an extraordinary measure with intellectual gifts, with a profundity in pondering, a keenness in comprehending, a clarity in presentation, a thinker the like of whom was never seen and never shall be seen; he has pondered upon the nature of God, upon the fact that God is love, upon what follows from this as a consequence, that the world also must be the best, and all things must work together for good. And what he has fathomed he has elucidated in a book which is regarded as the possession of the whole race and the object of its pride; it is translated into all languages, referred to on all occasions of scientific discussion, and from this book the parsons fetch their proofs. This thinker has lived hitherto unacquainted with the world, protected by favourable conditions, which indeed are required for scientific research. Then it befalls him to come to grief in consequence of an important decision; he must act in a difficult situation and at a critical moment. And this action entails a consequence which he had not in the least anticipated, a consequence which plunges him and many others into misery. This is a consequence of his act—and yet he is convinced that he could not have acted otherwise than he did act after the most honest reflection. So here it is not a question of misfortune merely, but of blame which attaches to him, however blameless he knows himself to be. Now he is wounded; there awakens in his soul a doubt whether this also can work together for his good. And in him, the thinker, this doubt at once takes the direction of thought: whether after all God is love—for in the believer doubt takes another direction, that of concern about himself. Over this man the objective concern acquires more and more power, so that at last he hardly knows where he is. In this situation he has recourse to a parson who is not personally acquainted with him. He opens his mind to him and seeks comfort. The clergyman, who is abreast of the times and is a thinker of sorts, would now prove to him that this also must be for the best and work for his good, since God is love; but he soon ascertains that he is not the man to maintain his side in a conflict of thought with this unknown individual. After several vain attempts, the clergyman says: 'Well I have only one counsel left to give you; there is a book about the love of God by so and so, read it, study it, if that does not help you, no man can help you.' The unknown man replies, 'I myself am the author of this book.'

Observe now that what the author had set down in that book was excellent—how could I venture to doubt it! What the thinker had understood about God was also doubtless true and profound. But this thinker had not understood himself, he had hitherto been living under the delusion that when it is proved that God is love, it must follow somehow as a matter of course that we—thou and I—believe it. He has perhaps as a thinker thought very meanly of faith, until . . . as a man he learned to think more meanly than before of thought, especially of the 'pure' [1] sort. The course of his thought became inverted, his thought-process became different. He did not say: God is love, *ergo* all things work together for a man's good; but he said: '*If* I believe that God is love, then all things work together for *my* good.' Now the thinker is matured for life as a man; for hitherto

---

[1] The reference is to Hegel, not to Kant.

there had been something rather inhuman about him. What it means for a little child to get the name by which it will be known its whole life long, is substantially what it means once in a man's life, decisively, eternally, to wound himself with this 'if' and thereby come to love God, although subsequently this 'if' is always at hand to preserve this love with which one loves God, is eternally young, as God is eternal, eternally young in the first tension of passion, but ever more and more heartfelt.

All things work together for our good—IF *we love God.*

Now, whether this is so, whether it is true as a matter of fact, whether I can prove it? Oh, if thou dost believe it, in case thou dost believe it, thou wilt blissfully ascertain that not only, as sometimes occurs, is that which thou seekest here, so that there is no need to go out to seek it, but thou hast found it, thou hast it. In case thou dost believe it, thou wilt easily understand that all proving leads thee away from what thou hast, whereas this proving deceitfully assumes the appearance of leading thee to it.

Let us understand one another. Thou art surely acquainted (as who is not?) with that happy expression, that heartfelt word of a noble poet who lets the unfortunate girl speak to this effect: 'I desire nothing more, I have lived and I have loved,' or what to her thinking would have been precisely the same thing: I have loved—and lived. And why the same thing? Because she humanly regards love for man as the highest good, hence to her thinking these two ideas are completely synonymous: to live and to love. If she is bereaved of her lover, life is over—but she has loved. We will not contend with this lovable girl—and besides she is in fact the stronger. She is stronger than our understanding—for she *believes* in love. She is stronger than all earthly power, in a sense she has overcome death, does not fear it, for already she is bereaved of life, life indeed was her love—and, alas, she *has* loved.

But now for this thing of loving God! This after all is surely the highest good; to this therefore we can apply with the truth of eternity what the girl, vainly deceived by her heart, applied to earthly love: to love God is to live. 'To live'! When one uses this word thus with special emphasis, one signifies thereby the full, rich life which is in possession of all the requisites for living, one signifies thereby a life which is truly worth living, a life which expands as it were with the blissful feeling of vitality. Only when one possesses the highest good does one live thus; but the highest good is to love God. But accordingly he possesses the highest good who, whatever may befall him, loves God; for to love God is the highest good. Ah, surely this is true! For the sake of a God-fearing jest, to make sport for once of this conceit of proving things, permit me to adjoin: *quod est demonstrandum!*

And the same thing applies when we talk of loss. In speaking of loss, or of what a man can lose in the world, one is prone to forget that the highest good is to love God. Though a man were to lose everything in the world—if he does not lose faith in God's love, he does not in fact lose the highest good. Or imagine two men, both of whom have lost everything, but one of whom has at the same time lost faith in God's love: what is the difference between these two? Should we make the miserable reply that after all the one was somewhat better off than the other? No, let us tell the truth. The difference is that one actually lost everything, the other really lost nothing, since he retained the highest good.

I F *we love God!* O my hearer, thou who perhaps art accustomed to require everything of the speaker, here thou canst see that it all lies in the hearer. Wilt thou deny that the speaker speaks truly who says, 'All things work together for thy good— *if* thou dost love God'? That thou surely wilt not deny. Very well, but then thou wouldst require of him the impossible, if thou wert to require that he produce a definite effect: either to tranquillize, or to terrify. For what effect this true discourse will produce depends solely upon who the hearer is. There may perhaps have been one in whom this discourse inspires such a dread as he never before has known ; but this is not the fault of the discourse, it lies in the hearer. There was perhaps one who in entire agreement said yea and amen to it, listened to it with the most blissful tranquillity; but this is not the merit of the discourse, it lies in the hearer. It is not the discourse which has terrified the one, and it is not the discourse which has tranquillized the other; it is the one and the other who in this discourse have understood themselves.

IV

THE RESURRECTION OF THE DEAD IS AT HAND . . . OF THE JUST
AND OF THE UNJUST

My hearer, thou thyself perhaps hast been in the following situation, or at least thou art aware that such is the situation of many. At various seasons in his life a person has wished that some one might prove to him the immortality of the soul. He does not require that the proofs should make all effort on his part superfluous. He is willing to co-operate by thinking the thing out on his own account. He has procured one or another of the works which deal with this subject, and he has read it tranquilly, or he has heard and followed an oral lecture which undertook to prove the immortality of the soul. What is this man's whole situation? How might I describe it? In civil life we talk about the security there is in the city: public security is assured, one goes home tranquilly even late at night without fearing any danger; theft is seldom heard of, and that only in a small way just to keep in practice; as for assault, it never occurs. Hence one is safe, lives in safety. So it is with safety in a spiritual sense: thoughts come and go, even the most decisively important thoughts merely graze the soul, in dealing with the most terrifying thoughts one thinks a little about them, then a little more, but inwardly there is safety, it is assured that one is safe, or, as it would be preferable to say in this instance, one is secure.

On the other hand, this discourse on immortality has plainly the intent of committing a breach of public safety, or here it is more properly a question of private safety, it has the intent of disturbing security—it is like an assault, as bold as an assault in full daylight, as terrifying as an assault by night. Before it proves anything—but no, let us not keep the mind in vain expectancy, it will not *prove* anything whatsoever. It makes a classification of men as the just and the unjust, and therewith it asks thee whether thou dost reckon thyself among the just or the unjust. It brings this question into the closest relationship with immortality; in fact it is not about immortality it speaks but rather about this difference. Is not this like an assault? Certainly it has never occurred to any of the provers to make this classification or to put this question—that would be the rudeness of treading too close on a man's heels, and one is afraid of presuming to come too close to the hearer or the reader, it would be unscientific and uncultured. How very odd. One is afraid of treading up too close to the hearer or reader—whereas one is engaged in proving to him the very thing which concerns him most closely—indeed there is nothing that more closely concerns a man than his immortality. However, one might prove this to the hearer without approaching him too closely, and presumably the hearer himself on the strength of this proof will espouse in a way *his* immortality without *himself* approaching it too rudely or too closely. In that way the proving of immortality becomes a sort of game. And when this game is long continued and becomes very popular, it is like an assault when a discourse, assuming immortality as a thing most certain, comes as close as possible to one, when instead of proving it (for that is to put it at a distance from one and hold it there), it comes out bluntly with the consequences which follow from it. Instead of beseeching thee to lend it thine attention and to listen tranquilly while it proves immortality, it assaults thee somewhat in this fashion: 'Nothing is more certain than immortality; thou shalt not be concerned about it, not waste thy time upon it, nor seek evasions by wanting to prove it, or wishing it proved—fear it, it is all-too-certain, do not doubt whether thou art immortal, but tremble, for thou art immortal.'

The words of the text are uttered by Paul,[1] and presumably both Pharisees and Sadducees were equally wroth with him. The Scripture relates expressly that the Sadducees, who did not accept immortality,[2] were enraged when Paul talked of immortality. But may it not have been due to the way he talked about immortality that the Pharisees were equally exasperated? This would have been the most favourable opportunity for Paul, yea the situation was like a challenge to him, it was as if this was what the age demanded of him—to propound some proofs of the immortality of the soul. If he had done that, being invited to a meeting where he proposed to give some proofs of the immortality of the soul—well, in that case not even the Sadducees would have made any objection. As men of scientific culture they were presumably free-minded enough to think thus: 'Notwithstanding we deny

[1] Acts xxiv. 15.　　　　[2] Acts xxiii. 7 f.

the immortality of the soul, this man may be able to say some-thing for the other side, we may as well listen to him.' But for a man to attack one, to pounce upon him with this question about just and unjust, to forsake the scientific attitude and become personal—who indeed can wonder that people were enraged at such behaviour? People come together as men of culture, a group of serious persons who would hear something about immortality, whether there is an immortality, whether there really is an immor-tality, a personal immortality, whether people will really recognize one another again, about what ways there may be of passing one's time in eternity, whether yonder in the high-vaulted halls one will find oneself again in his self-same person, embroidered in the tapestry of remembrance at his happiest moments, the day of one's marriage, the day when one enchanted everybody in the festive circle—instead of all this, instead of passing an agree-able hour and like serious persons being able to say later, 'After all it is a very serious question, this of immortality'—instead of this, to have the thing so thoroughly decided that one becomes anxious and alarmed!

Well, yes—he who never had his immortality so thoroughly decided that he became anxious and alarmed has never believed in his immortality. This is what people have entirely forgotten in these times which, quite consistently, are so busy about proving immortality, in these times when they are about ready to leave it impudently to every one's good pleasure whether he will or will not, whether he pretty much, pretty nearly, just about, up to a certain point, or in a sort of a way, wants to believe in immor-tality. For immortality is by way of becoming a sort of luxury, a matter of taste. And for this reason, for this reason precisely, so many books are written to *prove* after a sort the immortality of the soul—and precisely for this reason it is needful to give the thing a different turn. So we will speak on these words:

The resurrection of the dead is at hand, of the just . . . and of the unjust, or about the proof of the immortality of the soul which runs thus: it is only too certain—fear it!

For immortality is the Judgement. Immortality is not a life indefinitely prolonged, nor even a life somehow prolonged into eternity, but immortality is the eternal separation between the just and the unjust. Immortality is not a continuation which follows as a matter of course, but it is a separation which follows as a consequence of the past.

What has given occasion to all this error about immortality is the fact that people have completely confused the statement of the case, have made a question out of immortality, out of a task have made a question, out of a task for action, a question for thought. Would not that be the most depraved age which completely transformed its 'duties' into problems for thought? For what is duty? Duty is what one *must do*. There must be no question about duty, but the question must be whether I do my duty. There must be no question about immortality, as to whether it is; but the question must be whether I live as my immortality requires me to live. There must be no talk about immortality, as to whether it is, but about what my immortality requires of me, about my immense responsibility in being immortal.

That is to say, immortality and the Judgement are one and the same thing. We can speak rightly about immortality only when we speak of the Judgement; and naturally when we speak of the Judgement we speak of immortality. Hence Felix was afraid when he heard Paul's discourse about immortality; for Paul would not speak of it except in speaking of the Judgement, of the separation between the just and the unjust. If Paul had been willing to speak differently, to follow the new fashion of separating the Judgement and immortality from one another, if he had talked (or twaddled) about immortality without interjecting a word about the Judgement, talked about immortality and let it be assumed that there is no Judgement—then doubtless Felix would not have been afraid, he surely would have listened with attention to a cultured man and remarked afterwards, 'It is quite entertaining to hear the man, but it is kind of fanaticism which is capable, all the same, of delighting a person as long as he listens to it; it has something in common with a display of fireworks.'

Immortality is the Judgement. There is not a word more to be said about immortality. He who says one word more, or a word which has another slant, let him beware of the Judgement. People have transformed immortality into something entirely different and hence have sapped it. They have abstracted from it all its power, have tricked it out of its authority—by wanting to *prove* it, and so have left it to be accepted by anybody who will, whereas in fact it is exactly the contrary of this: either thou wilt or thou wilt not, about this there is no question raised, thou art immortal—only beware! In case an officer with authority commands that something be done—and then several persons, wishing presumably to assist him by proving that he is a very clever man etc., would persuade the subordinates to yield obedience to this officer—what then? Why, then these eloquent men have cheated him out of his authority; for he ought not to be obeyed because he is clever, ought not to be obeyed for this reason and that, but simply because he has authority. When duty, instead of being the commanding instance, is relegated to the position of a problem—then, even if men were to do *what* duty bids, they would not be doing *their duty*; for duty desires to be done because it *must* be done. So also in case a man by the aid of all sorts of proofs were to reach the point of assuming the notion of his immortality, he does not for all this *believe* in his immortality. For thou art under no obligation to carry the thing to the point of making it appear more than plausible that thou art immortal. No, God has entirely exempted thee from this bother; thou art immortal, and thou shalt give account to God of how thou hast lived, O thou immortal! Precisely because thou art immortal thou shalt not be able to slip out of God's hand, hide thyself in a grave and pretend that it doesn't matter; and the scale according to which thou shalt be judged is that thou art immortal.

Immortality is the Judgement or the separation between the just and the unjust. Thus it is Paul conjoins these two things. He does not waste a word in talking about immortality, as to whether it actually *is*; he states what it is, that it is the separation between the just and the unjust. The imperfection of this early life, its earthliness, consists precisely in the fact that it cannot make manifest this difference between the just and the unjust. Here in this earthly life there is the confusion that the unjust can assume the appearance of being the just, that the just must suffer as if he were the unjust, that there lies an impenetrable darkness over the question who is the just and who the unjust, that justice seems to be man's own invention, so that the right thing is that which the majority regards as such, so that righteousness seems to have the same quality as everything else that is earthly, of being right only up to a certain point, that just as it is required for beauty that one be neither too big nor too little, so righteousness is a kind of *via media*, it must not be pursued immoderately, therefore it is a righteous dispensation when (as a consequence of man's mediocrity) suffering and human opposition are the lot of one who wills righteousness only, who loves righteousness more dearly than his life. But the truth and perfection of eternal life is to exhibit eternally the difference between right and wrong with the severity appropriate to eternity, precise as only eternity is, with a sublimity which to the earthly-minded might seem petty and odd. In eternity therefore it will be easy enough to distinguish between right and wrong; but the point is that it is not in eternity thou art for the first time to make this distinction, in eternity thou shalt be judged as to whether in the earthly life thou hast made it as eternity would have it made. For what is eternity? It is the distinction between right and wrong. Everything else is transitory: heaven and earth shall pass away; every other distinction is evanescent, all distinction between man and man belongs to the interlude of human life and therefore is to cease. But the difference between right and wrong remains eternally, as does He, the Eternal, who fixed this difference *from eternity* (not like the difference which *in the beginning* He fixed between heaven and earth), and it remains *unto eternity*, as He, the Eternal, remains, He who rolls up the heavens like a garment, changes everything, but never Himself —and hence never this difference which belongs to eternity. Eternity is the distinction between right and wrong, hence immortality is the separation between the just and the unjust. Immortality is not a continuation, it is not so related to the present life that this is continued, but it is separation, so that life indeed is continued, but in separation. It is an idle, indolent, effeminate thought to wish for a life after death in the sense of a long life. Eternity's thought is that in this earthly life men differ, in eternity occurs the separation.

But how can eternity be a distinction? To be a distinction—is not that far too imperfect a mode of being to be the eternal? Well, is isn't that eternity is the distinction, eternity is righteousness. But the nature of righteousness possesses this perfection, that it has within itself a duplication; this duplication which it has within itself is the distinction between right and wrong. A being which has no distinction within itself is a very imperfect being, it may be an imaginary being, such as the being of a mathematical point. A being which has the difference outside itself is an evanescent being; such is the case with the distinctions of this early life, which therefore vanish. Eternity, righteousness, has the distinction within itself, the distinction between right and wrong. But if instead of habituating oneself to believe that there is an eternal distinction between right and wrong, instead of exercising oneself in it so that one might have one's life in it (which costs much time and effort, whereto all this earthly life is devised)—if instead one turns away from it, habituates oneself to think that there is surely some sort of distinction between right and wrong, but that after all one must not be pedantic, that it is well enough to make the distinction once in a while, but it would spoil all to do it for daily use—in that case it seems difficult to conceive, although in the very conception it is implied, that in eternity there should be an eternal distinction between right and wrong. For there is an eternal distinction between right and wrong (which ought to be seen already in this life; but, alas, it is not seen)— and how then might it not be in eternity! Take any earthly distinction to illustrate the fact that a distinction is naturally best seen where it has its stronghold. Take the distinction between noble and bourgeois. When the nobleman lives in a town where he is the only nobleman and all the others bourgeois, he cannot maintain his distinction, the bourgeois overpower him, but when he comes to his own sort and is fortified by being conjoined with them, you perceive the distinction. So it is with the eternal distinction between right and wrong. Hence in the earthly life it is overwhelmed as it were, it cannot well maintain itself, it is abased; but when it comes home in eternity it is then in its full strength. Whether men believe or no that there is this distinction in eternity, in eternity it is. But the situation in eternity is not, as it often is with the strong man, the sagacious man, the thinker, the teacher, that *at last*, overwhelmed by the crowd, he has to yield. Precisely the contrary! In temporal existence it rather looks as if eternity had already yielded; but it does not yield *at last*, no, *at last* comes the dreadful thing. It puts men to the proof here in the earthly life, it sometimes lets itself be mocked here in the earthly life, but at last, at last it judges; for immortality is the Judgement.

Immortality is the Judgement; and this applies to 'ME'; *in* 'MY' *thoughts it applies to* 'ME' *most of all, just as in* 'THY' *thoughts it applies to* 'THEE' *most of all.* In no other way have I been able to understand this matter. But that perhaps is due to my narrow capacity. For (inconceivable as it is in my thought) there are men who present the matter to themselves quite differently. They are confident enough in regard to what will happen to them in that discrimination of eternity, confident enough so far as concerns their own blessedness, that they are righteous, or confident enough that they are believers—and now they raise the query whether others can become blessed. To me this matter has never presented itself thus, nothing else has ever occurred to me but that every other man surely will become blessed, only about 'me' was it doubtful in 'my' thoughts. Yea, if I had caught myself doubting about the blessedness of any other single man, it would have been enough for me to despair of mine.

But the matter must be presented in one of two ways; one cannot be in two places at once, nor work with his thoughts in two places at once. *Either* one works unceasingly with every effort of his soul in fear and trembling upon the thought of self-concern, 'whether one shall himself become blessed'; and then verily one has no time or thought to doubt about others, nor is he in the least disposed to do so. *Or* one has become quite confident on his own account—and so he has time to think about others, time to strike attitudes and make gestures indicative of grief, time to practise the art of seeming to shudder, whereas he shudders on another person's account.

He, however, who has become so perfectly sure, so sure of hand that he presumes to handle this eternally decisive question (a boldness more to be wondered at than the sureness of the surgeon in using the knife, for in this instance it is impossible to cut another without cutting oneself), this man, however, has not always been so sure. Hence in the course of time he has changed. And that is natural, a person does indeed change in the course of time. It is evident that when a person becomes older there occurs a change in respect to his body: the smooth velvet of the skin becomes wrinkled, the soft connexions of the joints become stiff, the sinews harden, the bones petrify—is this change, this consolidation, a change for the better? The young girl who blushed if merely she heard 'his' name mentioned, blushed when in private she uttered it aloud; the young girl whose heart beat audibly every time the clock struck the hour when 'he' should come; the young girl who once shuddered at having displeased him by the very least insignificant act, or by the mere thought of it; the young girl who once became cold as death for fear that for an instant he had been less loving to her than usual—this young girl has now been married to him many years. Now she has become sure, sure that she is certainly good enough to him; she is aware of none of those virginal feelings, she is quite sure for her part; she is well-pleasing unto herself—even if she be not pleasing to . . . I was about to say 'the loved one', but of that there is no more any question, she has no loved one, though she has him for a husband; she is merely occupied with judging other women; she is quite well pleased with herself, even in her changed condition, she is not even like that old man who walked with his back bent low and his beard almost touching his knees, who when he was asked why he was so downcast, replied, lifting up his hands, 'I have lost my youth on the ground, and now I am seeking it everywhere'—she seeks nothing, she who once sought, ah, with all the sincerity of love sought to please, she is well-pleasing unto herself, she is quite sure. Is this assurance a change for the better?

No, away from me, dreadful assurance; save me, O God, from ever becoming quite sure, preserve me until the last in insecurity, so that then, if I attain blessedness, I might be quite sure that I receive it of grace! For this is a hollow sham, to protest that one believes it to be of grace—and yet to be quite sure. The true, the essential expression of the fact that it is grace is precisely the fear and trembling of insecurity. There it is faith lies, just as far, exactly as far from despair as from security. He who fools away his life without thinking of immortality can perhaps not be said to despise the highest good; but he who became quite sure is the one who despises it. He who flirted away his life can well be said to have forfeited his life; but he who became quite sure forfeited it in a more horrible way. Eternal God, keep therefore my deepest concern silent in my most inward parts, understood only by Thee, that I may never talk of it directly to any man. For otherwise I should get to the point of becoming just as sure as various others, more sure than several others—and quite sure. Preserve me from men, and preserve me from deceiving any other man; for this deceit lies all too near when one treats the relationship with God as if it were a direct relationship to other men, so that one falls into the way of comparison and human assurance. If there were a person accounted by many a man of rare nobility and uprightness, and he continues nevertheless to labour for his salvation, the others would be angry with him. For they would like to have his assurance as a specious pretext for their sense of security, and they would that their security should be his assurance. But, O my God and Father, the question of my blessedness concerns no one else but me and Thee.

Should there not then remain insecurity in fear and trembling until the last, I being what I am and Thou what Thou art, I upon earth, Thou in heaven—ah, a difference infinitely great!—I a sinner, Thou the Holy One! Should there not then, ought there not, must there not remain fear and trembling until the last? Or was not this the fault of the foolish virgins, that they became sure and went to sleep, whereas on the contrary the wise virgins kept awake? But what is it to keep awake? It is uncertainty in fear and trembling. And what indeed is faith but an empty imagination, if it is not awake? And when faith is not awake, what else is it but this dreadful security.

So this concerns *me* in *my* thoughts most of all, and I can understand that in *thy* thoughts likewise it concerns *thee* most of all. In no other way can I understand thee, in no other way am I willing to understand thee, and in no other way would I be understood by thee. I know nothing with regard to my blessedness; for what I know, I know only with God in fear and trembling, so that I cannot talk. When in the Council of State something indeed has been talked about but nothing as yet determined, would it not be a crime to divulge it in the city? And my blessedness is not yet determined. And I know nothing with regard to thy blessedness; thou only canst know of that with God. But this I believe, that the resurrection of the dead is at hand, of the just and of . . . the unjust.

My hearer, is not this discourse reassuring after all? One cannot well talk more reassuringly than as in this instance, when to one who so eagerly desired to believe in immortality, so eagerly desired to see it proved, the discourse says: 'As for that matter, be quite assured, thou art immortal, whether thou wilt or no.' More reassuringly one cannot talk—unless it is precisely this affirmation which disquiets a man. But if it is disquieting, there must have been deceit in the mouth or in the heart of him who desired so eagerly, oh, so eagerly desired, etc. And if he is deceitful, his disquietude is not my fault, who, if what he said was true, might have talked to him reassuringly. If there was deceit in him, he was accordingly just the contrary of what he said he was, he was afraid of immortality—hence he so eagerly desired to have it *proved*, because he obscurely understood that immortality, by becoming an object of proof, is cast down from the throne, deposed, a poor impotent figure which men can jeer at, as the Philistines jeered at Samson their prisoner. There is in the human race, in our race, a cunning which is slyer than the cunningest of shrewd politicians. And it is precisely this cunning of the race which has got the question of immortality inverted. The individuals do not by any means always understand how sly the whole thing is, and hence what they say is almost in the air they breathe, since it is in the race. It is the race that has willed to rebel against God, it is the race that has willed to do away with immortality and has attained the end of having it treated as a problem. For given immortality (and with that the immortality of the individual which is implied), then God is Lord and Sovereign, and the 'individual' stands in relationship to Him. But when immortality becomes a problem, God is done away with, and the race is God. The individuals perhaps do not notice how they are in the power of the race, how through them it is the race that speaks. They think therefore that he who calls upon them and calls them '*individuals*' is a *rebel*—and that he is too, in God's name he rebels against making the race God and immortality a problem. In God's name he rebels, and he appeals to God's Word, that the resurrection of the dead is at hand, of the just . . . and of the unjust!

V

Now are we nearer our salvation ... than when
WE BECAME BELIEVERS

'Great God, where are we!' So the navigator cries when in
the dark night the ship will not obey the helm, and no star
is visible, when all is darkness and gloom, while storms
rave, and when it is not possible to observe the position—'Great
God, where are we!' But he too in these days who has to preach
Christianity, must he not say, 'Where are we?' We are in Christendom—yes, that is true. *There* so and so many Christians are
born every year, so many are baptized, so many confirmed, we
are so and so many Christians, just about as many as there are
inhabitants in the land. But what does that signify? Does that
determine our position? Or is he who preaches Christianity to
keep the whole thing at a distance from reality, so as not to come
embarrassingly near? Is he to talk about Christianity but leave it
undetermined whom he is talking to? Is he to talk about our
salvation being nearer than when we believed, but leave it entirely
vague who these 'we' are, whether it is they who lived a hundred
or several hundred years ago—is he to talk thus and therefore
punch the air, so that the preaching of Christianity is no more
than punching the air? Where are we? He who has to talk about
Christianity in Christendom, is he a missionary who has to spread
Christianity, so that all this notion of Christendom is a vain
conceit, or is he to assume that we are all Christians, or shall he
make a distinction, and, if so, how is he to make a distinction—
where are we?

In these times people seem to be less observant of this difficulty. They regard Christianity as a sum of doctrinal statements,
they lecture upon them, just as they do upon ancient philosophy,
the Hebrew language, or any other scientific discipline, treating
the relation to them of the hearers or learners as entirely indifferent. Substantially this is paganism. The Christian position
clearly is that the personal relationship to Christianity is the
decisive thing. One may be thoroughly informed about Christianity as a whole, may know how to explain it, to present it and

to expound it—but if with all this he thinks that his own relationship to Christianity is a matter of indifference, he is a pagan. However, as men have cast down all régimes, so also they have deposed Christianity from its sovereignty. Instead of allowing it to rule over men, to change their lives (not only on Sunday but every day), and to intervene decisively in every relationship of life, they keep it at a scientific distance as a mere doctrine, they point out the correspondence between various doctrinal statements—but the correspondence or non-correspondence of my life or thine with this teaching is a matter of indifference.

Hence we have chosen these words to talk about. For if this discourse is not to be entirely meaningless, we must in one way or another come closer to men, or rather prompt them to come closer to themselves. And this is what we would do. Our aim is not in the least to condemn Christendom or any single person in Christendom; we do our best to come as close to ourselves as possible, which is the best way of preventing us from coming condemningly too close to others. But it is indeed our aim to prompt the hearer to test his life, his Christianity, to be observant of where he is. And to talk on these words, 'Now is our salvation etc.', without defining who 'we' are would be as inane as to travel from Copenhagen to Jerusalem on the map. To talk on these words without defining this 'now' and this 'when' is just as fatuous as to travel in imagination from one planet to another.

NOW IS OUR SALVATION NEARER . . . THAN WHEN WE BECAME BELIEVERS.

Two points are required for every determination of place. To say of a city that it is situated 'there', of a road that it leads 'there', of a man that he dwells 'there', is to make a fool of him with whom we talk, or to make a fool of oneself, if one had not the purpose of jeering at the other but meant to talk seriously. If there is to be any sense and seriousness in this discourse, and if he to whom it is addressed is to derive profit therefrom, he must be given one point the position of which he knows, in relation to which he can determine the 'there'. The reason why a stranger goes astray in the desert, and the reason why a person becomes dizzy at sea, is that he has no 'there' in relation to which he can determine where he is, or because he has no point of reference for determining the 'there'.

The same thing is true of the determination of time. If I am to determine where I am 'now', I must have another point in time well determined in relation to which I define this 'now'. Hence the words chosen as the subject of this discourse contain quite properly another determination by means of which the speaker defines this 'now': 'now' we are nearer salvation than 'when' we became believers. This makes excellent sense. When a man says, 'I am now farther along with this or that work than when I began it,' there is sense in this determination of the time. In the fact that he began he has one fixed point of time, and he measures the distance from the beginning in order to see where he is now. But in case this man had never begun this work—why, then his talk is senseless: it is senseless to say, one is 'now' nearer than 'when' one began, if one never began. And in case a person who never had begun to believe were to imitate this and say thoughtlessly, 'now is our salvation nearer than when we believed,' that is senseless.

Recite these words in order to test thine own life by means of them, so as to learn to know where thou 'now' art. If thou art to learn to know this, thou must accordingly make sure first that thou knowest with precision 'when' that time was when thou didst become a believer, or when occurred in thy life the decision to believe. Art thou well aware of this difficulty which attacks one as it were from behind? For the question is not whether thou hast gone backward since that time when thou didst become a believer, whether thou hast abandoned faith. For one might argue thus: It goes without saying that salvation is 'now' nearer than 'when' I believed; for the 'now' is a later instant than the 'when', so it is a matter of course—unless, as was said, thou hast since that time abandoned faith. But on the other hand nothing follows as a matter of course if it is not certain that thou didst once become a believer, that thou didst experience the instant when thou didst become a believer.

When didst thou become a believer? It is of immense importance to make this definite if thou art to be able to define where thou art 'now'. And in case the situation is of such a sort that it must contribute to leave gloaming in indefiniteness the question whether thou didst actually become a believer, in that case thou canst well perceive how near to thee is absurdity, how it encompasses thee as it were, how easy it would be to pass thy whole life in absurdity—and therefore how important it is for thee to tear thyself free from all illusion which would prevent thee from learning to know whether thou wast ever a believer, all illusion which would make it possible for thee even to hear a sermon on these words, 'now is salvation nearer than when we believed,' without discovering that these words were a mockery of thee, who didst remain nevertheless quite undisturbed in the absurd assurance that 'now' thou art nearer thy salvation than 'when' thou didst become a believer—thou who never didst become a believer. For perhaps the sermon prompted thee to test thy life as to whether thou hadst later renounced faith. In this respect, however, thou wast not conscious of any fault, thou didst search thy life and didst find that it was possible to say boldly that thou didst never deny the faith or publicly renounce it. So thou mightest 'now' be nearer to salvation than 'when' thou didst become a believer. Alas it was hid from thee that the misfortune precisely was that thou never didst become a believer—so that only in this sense is the affirmation quite correct that thou didst not later . . . renounce faith.

When didst thou become a believer; or, what is the same thing, art thou essentially conscious of having experienced this decision to become a believer? For the important thing is not that it was midday at 12 o'clock or the like. No, the whole thing is a spiritual affair and therefore has the true seriousness which is not inclined to ask about the hour or the stroke of the clock. But on the other hand it is perfectly evident that it would be a game like that called 'passing the house' if a man, being asked in his old age when he became a believer, were to reply, 'Well, it was a long time ago'; being asked if it was in his manhood, were to say, 'No, it was a longer time ago'; being asked if it was in his youth, were to say, 'It was even longer ago, in short, it was so long ago that I can't remember when.' It is evident that this would be a game, and that it is senseless for a man to say where he 'now' is in relation to salvation if the decision by which he became a believer recedes into the fabulous dimness of the nursery-tale.

When didst thou become a believer? Didst thou become a believer? It is not now as in those . . . difficult ages when a Jew or a pagan became a Christian in ripe years; for then surely he knew definitely *when* . . . and *that* he became a believer. We now live in more . . . favourable times, in Christendom; it is now far easier to become a Christian—in any case far easier to fool oneself into passing one's whole life in a vain conceit. Thou wast baptized as a child, instructed in the Christian religion, confirmed, everybody regards thee as a Christian, thou callest thyself such when there is any occasion to give thy name, thy position in life, and the religion thou dost profess. About whether thou art to be a merchant, a scholar, an artist, a soldier, etc., etc., about whether thou shalt marry this one or the other, where thou shalt dwell, in the town or in the country—all such questions thou hast had occasion at one time or another in thy life to propose and to answer, so thou wilt be able to say 'when', and also be able to determine in all these respects where thou 'now' art. But the question whether thou art a believer has perhaps never arisen for thee; as long back as thy memory extends it has been assumed that thou art a Christian, and at one time must have become such —God knows when.

And where art thou 'now'; art thou 'now' nearer thy salvation? Thou hast surely heard of that simple wise man of ancient times [1] who knew how to question so craftily. This question may easily sound like one of his, like a question which has the purpose of putting a man in embarrassment, of making evident the confusion on the part of the inquirer. Now I neither will nor can interrogate thee; but imagine that it is he, the simple wise man, who interrogates thee. Thou knowest that even in Christendom the catechetical art is modelled after him, but never has any catechist been capable of interrogating as he did. Think of this simple wise man, the determined hater of evasion and excuse and unclearness and misstatement, who moreover was cunning, sly, clever and bold in ferreting such things out; he who had no teaching which he would aloofly deliver to men in a lecture, but precisely in the rôle of a teacher pierced through men with his penetrating glance, so that the man who conversed with him seemed to be conversing with himself, so that his most inward thoughts were revealed to this teacher; he who not only fetched down wisdom from heaven, but knew how to penetrate with it 'the individual'. Think that it is this simple wise man that questions thee; think how he could persist in teasing a man with this question, whether he is 'now' nearer to his salvation; think how he could turn and twist this question in innumerable ways, but always banteringly, always with that smile upon his face which was so characteristic of him when he had a suspicion that he with whom he conversed did not

[1] Socrates.

know definitely for his part which was which, did not know whether he really understood or whether he did not understand, whether he had become a believer or whether he had not become a believer; think of his perseverance until he, the simple man, had got the questioner trapped and made it manifest that he had been under an illusion. 'Art thou "now" nearer to it (to salvation)?' 'Yes. But nearer than . . .?' This perhaps produces a pause, and when this pause occurs it has the power of transforming the whole discourse into confusion. So thou art now 'nearer'; this 'nearer' is comparative, but with what then dost thou compare? Can it properly be said that one man is bigger than another, if the other doesn't exist? There is something tempting, something persuasive in this 'more' of comparison, it allures one, as if in a way it were a matter of course, as if one ought not to be distrustful, for after all it is an advance. But if it is not certain that the beginning is given, all this allurement is only allurement into absurdity. No more than the man who is on board a ship ever gets farther than the ship, however many hours he may continue to travel on it, and however many miles he may journey—no more than that does he come in any sense nearer who never started upon the course which leads nearer and nearer. But the way to salvation is faith; and only then can there be any question of being 'now' nearer, when it is definitely settled that one became a believer.

Where art thou now; is thy salvation *now nearer?* Thy salvation! The question is about thy salvation, about coming nearer to thy salvation. And if this is what the question is about, the same question is about something else, about being lost. Thy perdition! Suppose thou hast made a mistake in life and become a merchant when really thou shouldest have been an artist. Well, good Lord, that may be pretty hard, but even that misfortune can be lived down. Suppose thou didst make a mistake in life and married the girl—but her sister would have suited thee better. Well, good Lord, one can put up with being out of luck. But if a man is out of luck with his salvation! Suppose that in the most vigorous moment of thy youth thou didst conceive the plan of a Herculean work which thou wouldst perform and which was to be thy life-work; but thou wast delayed on the way and hindered by various things, it was discovered that thou hadst not the strength for it, in short, at thy life's end thou wast not perceptibly nearer to it than at the beginning. Well, good Lord, there is consolation for this sorrow too. But if at thy life's end thou hast not come nearer to thy salvation! Is there anything more dreadful than to be far from one's salvation? And to be in this situation, far from one's salvation, means in fact to be receding farther and farther. Salvation is correlative to danger; one who is not in danger cannot be saved. So if thou art in danger, and thy salvation is not nearer, thou art sinking deeper and deeper into danger. Ah, like the shipwrecked man who has saved himself by a plank, and thus, tossed by the waves, hovering over the abyss, between life and death, gazes fixedly at the land—so should a man be concerned for his salvation. But can a man be farther away from his salvation than when he does not even know definitely whether he has begun to will to be saved?

Test thyself therefore by means of this saying. It is a blessed comfort to dare to know that one's salvation is nearer than when one became a believer—but surely it is true that one must be certain one has become a believer. This saying therefore may serve to comfort, but also it may as it were come upon one from behind. If it happen that thereby a man is prompted to take notice, it is indeed terrifying—oh, but even in this terror, in this salutary terror, there is some comfort. There is some comfort; for after all when a man has taken notice of the fact that he has not even begun, he is always somewhat nearer his salvation than he was so long as he was living on confidently in an illusion and a vain conceit.

One thing more, however: let us not forget that the expression used by the Apostle is different from the way we have interpreted this saying. He says, 'Now is our salvation nearer than when we became believers.' The words as we have used them concentrate the whole thought upon our own activity in the matter, and they are so used for the sake of making people take notice. The Apostolic words lay stress at the same time upon the fact that our salvation is from God. The Apostle does not say *that we come nearer to our salvation*, but *that salvation comes nearer to us*. And about this too it might be necessary to talk, so as to remind the *believer* that he is not to be in a hurry, not to think that he is to acquire what essentially is bestowed. It might well be necessary to talk about this—if only it always were clear where we are. But in order to become aware of this we must first know whether we have become believers.

VI

AFTER all, 'blessedness' is surely the highest good; so of this good that must be true which is true of the lesser goods. For if an orator or a poet were to describe the glory of some earthly good or another, he would surely make people desire it, so that they hardly would be able to keep still during the discourse, but would be impatient to be off and away in order to grasp it. And how much reason they would have to be angry with this orator for deluding them with this desirable prospect when the speech concluded with the warning that it is fortune which distributes these goods! If such were not the case, they must indeed feel that they never could sufficiently thank the orator who knew how to describe so invitingly and so fascinatingly the goods which every one could possess. But 'blessedness' is the highest good, and every man can get possession of this good. Accordingly it might be expected that people could hardly resolve to hear this discourse to the end for the impatience they must feel to acquire this good, the highest good, which nevertheless every man can acquire. It might be expected that they would feel concerned lest the moment employed in listening to this discourse might be a moment wasted, since it was not in the strictest sense employed in attaining.

And such a discourse on 'blessedness' we have from an age now long gone by. It was delivered upon a mountain which after it was called the Mount of the Beatitudes—for blessedness, in comparison with all earthly goods, stands fast and immovable like the mountain, and again, blessedness, in comparison with all earthly goods, is like a mountain lifted up above the low plains. This discourse was delivered by Him, the only one who at first hand could talk of blessedness, since this is associated with His name, the only one in whom is blessedness. In this discourse it is said: 'Blessed are they who have been persecuted for righteousness' sake, for theirs is the kingdom of heaven. Blessed are ye when men shall reproach you and persecute you and say all manner of evil against you falsely, for my sake. Rejoice and be

exceeding glad, for great is your reward in heaven; for so persecuted they the prophets which were before you.'

These words we shall lay at the foundation of the following
discourse on the theme:

IT IS BLESSED NEVERTHELESS . . . TO SUFFER DERISION
IN A GOOD CAUSE.

—in order that we for our edification may become aware of the
comfort, or rather of the joy which Christianity proclaims; for
these discourses are indeed 'for edification', in spite of the fact
that they 'wound from behind'.

But lest in any way this joy might be taken in vain, let us first
recite expressly the conditions upon which this experience can in
any sense be said to be blessed. It must be for a good cause one
is derided, or, as Christ says, 'for righteousness' sake'. And what
derision says must be false, for Christ says, 'when all men speak
all manner of evil against you falsely'. But given these factors,
everything else follows; yea, then it is blessed . . . to suffer
derision.

So then comfort thyself, thou derided man, or rather rejoice!—
What is the only thing that can deprive one of joy at having done
a good deed? It is to get a reward for it. But if thou art rewarded
by derision! Every other requital diminishes the good one has
done; the requital of derision increases it. It is blessed to suffer
derision in a good cause!—What is the only case in which a man
can have real merit? When he suffers because he does right. For
if he does right and is rewarded, he is an unprofitable servant. It
is blessed therefore to suffer derision in a good cause!—What is
required for mutual understanding? Only like understands like.
What is requisite for a covenant? Initiation: only the initiate is
in covenant with the initiates. That glorious One whom the race
cast out, mocked, derided, persecuted and slew—He exists indeed
for all men, many perhaps could give an account of His life and
describe it. But this understanding is that of the uninitiated, for
whom in a deeper sense He does not exist, since they are not
understood by Him any more than they understand Him. Only
he understood Him and was understood by Him, only he was
initiated into a covenant with Him, who himself suffered the like.
Blessed it is to be derided in a good cause!—What is it a man
inquires about who for a considerable time must change his

residence, moving from the town into the country, or from the country to town? He inquires about the society. But the man who suffers derision, when once he must change his residence and wander away, when he leaves the society in which he lived derided —then, precisely for the fact that he suffered derision, he has assured himself for an eternity of the society of that glorious One in daily confidential intercourse, in hearty understanding and in loving converse. It is blessed therefore to suffer derision in a good cause! [1]—What is the only distinction God makes? That between right and wrong. And what distinction does He make? That He is wrath and a curse upon him who does wrong. And in making this distinction He makes still another distinction: between him who does right and is rewarded for it, and him who does right and suffers for it. But the more distinction He makes, so much the nearer to Him is the man who is related to Him by this distinction. Blessed therefore is he who suffers derision in a good cause!—Why is it that God never leaves Himself without a witness? Because in being the Good He is *unchangeably* the same, the same unchanged God; when today all creatures, as a thousand years before, look up to Him and ask for food and clothing, He opens His bountiful hand and satisfies every living thing with blessing. But when he who suffers innocently for a good cause lifts up his glance prayerfully to God, this glance *moves* Him, this glance which is able to accomplish nothing, nothing whatever here on earth, *moves* God, it requires Him to give an even stronger witness. Blessed therefore is he who suffers derision in a good cause! What bond of communion between man and man is the most heartfelt? It is suffering. What is man's most blessed communion? That with God. It is blessed to suffer derision in a good cause!—Who possesses most? Is it he who possesses God and at the same time much else, or he who being deprived of all else possesses God alone? Surely it is the latter, for all else 'is loss'. But who is deprived of most? He who did not get his deserts but was rewarded with derision; for the only thing

---

[1] It becomes clearer and clearer that S. K. was moved to comfort the sufferer from derision by the comfort with which he himself was comforted of God for the derision he suffered from the *Corsair*, suffering, as he often said, 'in a good cause'. And surely he chose here to use the word 'derision', rather than a term which to us might seem more serious, like mocking, scorn, reviling, or persecution, because it was *only* derision he had suffered. Only! Hundreds of pages of the Journal reveal how keenly he suffered from the 'beastly grin', from being 'trampled to death by geese'.

a man essentially owns is his deserts, everything else he owns he owns only accidentally, so that it is not properly his possession. The derided man is deprived of everything; excluded from human society, he has only God—who is the richest of all. He has only God—ah, how blessed to be alone so as to have God; blessed be all the persecution, the scorn, the mockery which taught him, which constrained him, to be alone with God, to have God as his only possession. It is blessed to suffer derision in a good cause! —Where is Christ present? Wherever His name is called upon, though but two or three are gathered together in His name, He is present. Yea, and when one suffers innocently for righteousness sake and calls upon His name, there *is there*, besides the voice which calls upon Him, something which calls upon Him more mightily, and hence *there is* the communion of His suffering and the power of His resurrection. It is blessed to suffer derision in a good cause!—What is it a man desires as the highest reward? To have his name inscribed on the page of history. But think of it, that the man who is derided, precisely by suffering derision gets the highest reward, gets his name written in the Book of Life! For sure enough we are all immortal, even they who do wrong, also the most ungodly of all the ungodly. But to have one's name written in the Book of Life! Blessed it is to suffer derision in a good cause! Yea, blessed, blessed comfort, blessed joy!

But to whom does this discourse address itself? where is it? has it entirely forgotten itself? Perhaps in this distinguished assembly there is not a single man who suffers derision—but no, it is not 'perhaps', it is an impossibility that any derided man might venture into this distinguished assembly! One cannot at the same time be derided and also be here in a company where the honoured and esteemed are assembled. A derided man is like a leper, his place is appointed among the graves, he is shunned by everybody. 'Yes, but it is for a good cause he is derided.' By whom then is he derided? It cannot well be by those who themselves are derided, for that would put him among the persons highly regarded. Nor can the derided man be at once derided, and at the same time, by the very persons who deride him, be held in honour because he is derided in a good cause. Even in a comedy the same man could not be used at the same time in two places—to be derided, and also to be honoured because he was derided in a good cause.

A strange difficulty! And it is strange that this difficulty does not emerge at all when one contemplates history. Contemplate that witness for the truth; it is now several centuries since he lived, but when he lived he was derided and persecuted. In the service of the truth he had got far too long a start for limping justice to catch up with him as long as he lived, more especially because, without dawdling an instant to await limping justice, he made giant strides ahead. Then he died and lay still in the grave—then limping justice caught up with him: his name was honoured and extolled in history; we are now so accustomed to honour and extol him that finally some fall into the error of thinking that he was honoured and esteemed while he lived. For time exercises a fore-shortening spell. His name lives now honoured and extolled for three centuries—and as for him, well, he lived the usual human span of sixty or seventy years, so one can almost say that he has been constantly honoured and esteemed. Oh, yes, quite so, if one wants to talk nebulously—otherwise, no. He never lived honoured and esteemed—he lived despised, persecuted, mocked, as long as he lived. And at the time he lived it must have been the honoured and esteemed people that despised him—just as now it is the honoured and esteemed people that extol his name. But the witness for the truth triumphed, and as in other respects he altered the shape of the world, so too he altered the concept of honour: after his death he became the honoured one, and they who lived contemporary with him, the honoured and esteemed people, appear now in another light. So long as he lived this was not the case, for he had to comfort himself with the teaching of Christianity that it is blessed to suffer for righteousness sake. He both felt and understood these words. For whereas many, looking at history backwards, only get confusion out of it, Christianity, on the contrary, addresses itself undeviatingly to the living man and proclaims to him that it is blessed . . . to suffer derision in a good cause.

That is to say, Christianity has, generally speaking, a suspicion of the honour and esteem paid to man in his lifetime. Far from Christianity be the foolishness of saying that every one who was derided while he lived was therefore on the right path. It says merely: among those who while they lived were derided the true Christian is ordinarily to be found. For this is what Christianity thinks: the eternal, the true, cannot possibly win the applause of the instant, must necessarily win its disapprobation. By being among the honoured and esteemed, Christianity does not precisely mean being in the highest positions and offices—a remark which it is especially important to emphasize, and inexcusable to pass over in silence, in view of the claim of this age which contends obstinately against all government that this contentiousness is Christianity. It is also certain that such a life in high place and in power is often characterized by true renunciation of what is properly meant by being honoured and esteemed. No, Christianly understood, to be honoured and esteemed means: forgetful of the eternal, to serve idolatrously, to serve only, and to take sides with nothing else but what has power in the instant, to 'seek first' the instant, and thereby to reap its applause, that means, to be in the 'world' (and for the world Christianity has no liking), that is, to be on top, that is, as a certain sort of culture claims, 'to be abreast of the world,' in short, it is worldliness.[1] Christianity, on the other hand, requires self-denial with respect to honour and esteem even more definitely than in relation to money. For money is something purely external, but honour is a concept of the mind. Wherefore the Christian is required to ward off from him this sort of honour and esteem. For to be a Christian is a point of honour, and therefore every Christian, for the sake of his own honour and that of Christianity, is obliged to be on his guard to defend the true concept of honour, lest by accepting worldly honour and esteem he become an accomplice in the dissemination of the false concept.

But to whom does this discourse address itself? Does it not, instead of making due use of the place and of the moment, disap-

[1] Now that Christianity has appropriated the world to so large an extent, it is difficult to make out what the Scripture means by 'the world' which it so strongly denounces. In my youth I found it even more difficult to make any just discrimination between the world and 'the world', for a Protestantism which was still resolutely uneschatological could give me no reasonable clue. It was commonly explained that 'the world' meant cards and dancing. People are always ready to 'compound for sins they are inclined to by damning those they have no mind to'. At that time I grasped eagerly at the words of Leopardi, the melancholy Italian poet, which I then translated and am now about to quote here because they correspond strikingly with S. K.'s words. 'That adversary of everything intrinsically noble, that scoffer at every delicate sentiment, if he believes it to be genuine, that detractor of every high quality, unless he knows it to be feigned, that tyrant of the poor, adulator of the rich, the exploiter of mean things, the vulgarizer of everything noble, to whom Jesus gave a name which is still current in our day, "the world".'

point every reasonable expectation which might expect that *here* it should be made clear how great a good is honour and esteem, how glorious it is to be honoured and esteemed, and by what means one acquires a good so momentous; for, as the proverb says, 'He who loses honour cuts off his right hand,' so that he is not able to accomplish anything—as is to be seen in the example of the Apostles and the witnesses for the truth, for they were not able to accomplish anything. Yes, certainly, the discourse disappoints this expectation; but on the other hand it does not disappoint him who expected that it would preach Christianity.

'But is it not a great good to be honoured and esteemed?' About that the discourse knows nothing, it knows only that it is blessed to suffer derision in a good cause, and that this is Christianity. 'But did not this apply only in the first ages of Christianity when a man had to contend with Jews and pagans? Should the case be the same in Christendom, in the triumphant Church?' Well, yes, it goes without saying, that if a man were to imagine himself in a place where there lived only genuine Christians, it might then, as a matter of course, be taken as proof that a man was a genuine Christian if he had the applause of such people, was honoured and esteemed by those who themselves willed the true and had a true conception of it, were zealous for knowledge of the truth. But is so-called Christendom such a place? If so, then the consummation would have been reached—and then one might suppose that Christ was deeply absorbed in thought, had forgotten Himself, forgotten to come again; for His coming again corresponds to the consummation. But Christ has not yet come again—and if He were to come again, were to come 'to His own' in a still stricter sense than before, what would His reception be in Christendom? There is much which astonishes me, much which I find strange and inexplicable. When I hear a man say the correct thing—but it never occurs to him to make anything out of it . . . that astonishes me, I cannot understand him. But this is true of the exceedingly common witticism which I have so often heard and read, which is uttered by all sorts of people, but constantly given out as current coin which no one examines more closely, as one only does with rare, unknown, or foreign coins, since this is sufficiently well known as legal tender, which once a witty man uttered, and clever people seize upon and repeat: that if Christ were now to come again to the world, He would again be crucified . . . unless in that age the death-penalty had been abolished. And this a man says as carelessly as he would say 'Good day', only he utters it very impressively; and one finds it well said and strikingly apt—and it does not occur, not in the remotest way, to him who says it to ask himself if he is a Christian; and it does not occur to him who hears it to take notice of the blinding illusion of Christendom. Truly, to me this is incomprehensible. It has almost become a by-word in Christendom that if Christ were to come again He would encounter the same fate as before when He came to non-Christians—and yet Christendom is taken to be the triumphant Church, which, if things reached that point, is assumed to be ready to add to its triumphs the new one of crucifying Christ. Well, it's true enough, the 'triumphant Church' has outwardly triumphed over the world, that is to say, it can boast of a worldly triumph over the world (for only inwardly is a godly triumph over the world possible)— so, like all conquerors, it has only one triumph left, that of triumphing over oneself, of becoming a Christian. The concept of Christendom, so long as one does not take notice and scrutinize it, is of all illusions the most dangerous. In Christendom, in fact, Christianity is still militant. Just as little as one who has purchased and had elegantly bound the books he needs to use for his examination can truly be said to have taken his examination, just so little is Christendom in a Christian sense the triumphant Church. In Christendom there are perhaps not a few genuine Christians, but every such Christian is also militant.

'But is it really the intention of Christianity to extol the suffering of derision, however good the cause may be? It is quite another thing to have comfort in readiness for him who was unfortunate enough to come to grief in this way.' Yes, certainly, it is another thing; but this other is not the Christian alternative. There is no excuse for mistaking how this is to be understood. The words in Matthew read: 'Blessed are ye when all men revile you and persecute you and say all manner of evil against you falsely, for my sake; rejoice and be exceeding glad; for so persecuted they the prophets which were before you.' The corresponding passage in Luke (v. 26) reads: 'Woe unto you when all men shall speak well of you! For in the same manner did their fathers to the false prophets.' Woe unto you when all men speak well of you! Here the word 'falsely' is not added; presumably it was not needed, it is assumed that when all men speak well of one it is a lie, and that one's life is a lie. Woe unto you when all men speak well of you! For this is what Christianity means (and if this is not its meaning, there is no meaning in Christianity), that a man should live his life in such a decisive way, should so definitely and openly maintain what he wills, what he believes and hopes, that it is impossible all might speak well of him. It may be difficult enough to attain this aim, this dreadful aim of having all speak well of one; but, if one is to succeed, it can only be by a shrewd and cowardly effeminacy which Christianity abhors and condemns. If a man is to succeed, he must be like a reed before the wind, for even the least bush can put up at least a little bit of resistance; he must be without any deeper conviction, hollow within, so that, if one would liken time to the wind, he easily can be wafted by every breath of air, and, if one would liken time to a stream, he can as easily float upon the surface; he must be silent when he should speak, speak when he should be silent, say yes when he should say no, and no when he should say yes, answer evasively when he should answer decisively, answer decisively even though it were unto blood, sleep when he should be vigilant, yea, do his part to make others sleep, flee every danger in which forsaken truth can find a stay, and take part in every popular folly; he must entirely forget God and the seriousness of eternity and everything that is high and holy: thus perhaps he may succeed—woe unto him! This, as one sees in Christ's saying, is not only the most paltry inheritance of renown a man can leave behind him, that all men spoke well of him, but it is judgement: woe unto him that he succeeded! It must have been either a base inhuman man, or it must have been a false prophet.

It is blessed nevertheless . . . to suffer derision in a good cause: woe unto you when all men speak well of you. There is no excuse for mistaking how this saying is to be understood. It is blessed to suffer derision in a good cause, and this is Christianity.

Is this difficult to understand? By no means. Is it difficult to say? By no means—least of all when it is left quite indefinite to whom this is spoken. But is it possible for a discourse to produce a definite effect? No, the effect a discourse is to produce depends upon who the hearer is. The difficulty with Christianity emerges whenever it is to be *made present and actual*, whenever it is uttered as it is, and uttered now, at this instant, and to them, precisely to them who are now living. Hence it is that people are so eager to keep Christianity at some little distance. Either they will not express it exactly as it is (that is one way of keeping it at a distance), *or they will let it remain indefinite whether it is addressed quite to those who now are living*. So the orator fights the air and says, 'Thus it was, as bad as all that, eighteen hundred years ago, and seventeen hundred years ago, and a thousand years ago, and three hundred years ago, and a hundred years ago, and fifty years ago, and thirty-three years ago; but it is not so now.' Strange! And when one looks hard at the asseverating orator, to see if he is quite confident of what he says, he becomes a bit disquieted at this glance which comes so unexpectedly, and with a gesture of irresolution he forsakes for an instant his manuscript and adds extemporaneously: 'Well—I would not say that this world has become perfect, but yet it is not quite like that now, especially in the most recent times.' [1] Strange! For so much is certain, that when one goes backward in time a certain distance, it was formerly just as it is now: seventeen hundred years ago they said, 'So it was a hundred years ago; but it is not so now—well, at all events it is not quite so now, especially in the most recent times'; and three hundred years ago they said, 'So it was fifteen hundred years ago, and a thousand years ago, and three hundred years ago; but it is not so now—well, well, at all events, not in the most recent times.' There must be something lurking at the bottom of this expression, 'the most recent times.' Yes, undoubtedly. One comes as close as possible without actually speaking to the living —and in fact the living generation represents 'the most recent times'. If the address was made to a gathering of young people, one would doubtless say, 'the very most recent times', for then the old folks and elders would not be present, so one might well chastise them—but always preferably the dead, one chastises them at a convenient distance, unmindful of the fine rule of speaking only good of the dead.

So it stands then with respect to Christianity's teaching that it is blessed to suffer derision. If this is to be uttered at an instant of actuality, the discourse must be addressed to an assembly of persons who are honoured and esteemed in the instant. If to such an assembly the discourse is addressed, the blessed comfort and

[1] I have no doubt that S. K. heard these very words uttered by a preacher, and discomfited him by his glance, in just the way he describes.

joy of Christianity will sound like the profoundest mockery. This is not due to the discourse. But it would surely be difficult for a poet to invent a profounder mockery than this: Christianity's teaching on blessedness delivered before an assembly of . . . Christians who live their lives in categories entirely foreign to Christianity, and who therefore, in spite of the fact that they call themselves Christians, would prefer to decline with thanks this kind of comfort, and presumably would think it enough to drive one mad that this should be accounted a comfort which more than all else they shudder at. Imagine an assembly of worldly-minded, timorous people, whose highest law in everything was a servile regard for what others, what 'one', would think and judge, whose only concern was the unchristian concern that 'one' might everywhere 'speak well of them', whose loftiest aim was to be just like the others, whose only enthusiasm and only fear-inspiring idea was the majority, the crowd, its applause . . . its disapprobation —imagine such an assembly of the adorers and worshippers of the fear of man, hence an assembly of the honoured and esteemed (for how could such people not honour and esteem one another? To honour the other is in fact to flatter oneself)—and imagine that this assembly (yes, it's like a comedy), that this assembly is to be regarded as Christian. Before this assembly the sermon is preached on the words, 'It is blessed to suffer derision in a good cause!'

But it is blessed to suffer derision in a good cause!

VII

1 Tim. iii. 16. And without controversy great is the mystery of godliness: God was manifested in the flesh, justified in the spirit, seen of angels, preached among the nations, believed on in the world, received up in glory.

My hearer, without doubt thou dost know this passage in the Bible, hast known it from thy earliest childhood, knowest it by heart, thou hast often and often heard it recited, perhaps recited it thyself; when any one alludes to the beginning of this passage, thou art able from memory to supply the rest; if one were to begin with any single clause, thou dost at once recall the others. Thus for memory the passage has become a rounded whole, so that almost involuntarily one pieces together what properly belongs together. Thou canst begin backwards or forwards or in the middle, but wherever the beginning is made, thy memory will be able to collect all the parts and recite the passage as a whole.

However—but perhaps this has escaped thine *attention*, for it is not a matter of *memory*—there is a very notable difference between the several statements. Or rather there is one among them—in case thou dost cast an eye upon it, or it, as it were, casts an eye upon thee—one statement which alters everything, which in a curious way takes possession of thee, so that it does not occur to thy memory to want to add the rest, because this clause acquires over thee such dominance that it seems, for the moment at least, as though the rest were forgotten. For observe: 'God was manifested in the flesh,' this has no reference to thee, it refers to Him; 'He was justified in the spirit,' this has no reference to thee, it was He that was justified in the spirit, neither was it thou that wast 'seen of angels', it was He, and it was He that was 'preached among the nations', and He that was 'received up in glory'. But this: 'He was believed on in the world!'—this surely has reference to thee. Be careful at this point, give due heed—then it will be seen that it refers to thee alone, or is as if it referred to thee alone in the whole world.

It is of this we would speak:

He was believed on in the world.

So then, it looks as if the Apostle were saying something merely historical about Christ; and indeed he is saying something historical. But in the midst of this history he has introduced a little word which refers to thee. 'He was believed on in the world'—that is to say, Hast thou believed on Him? There is perhaps no way of asking a question which is so forcible, so impressive, as just this. If one would put to a man a question of conscience, but would do it precisely in such a way that it really becomes a question of conscience, in such a way therefore that there is not anything which obliges him to say yes or no in reply to the questioner (for by this the relationship to conscience is already somewhat disturbed), but in such a way that he is obliged to answer the question to himself, with the consequence that this question establishes itself in his inward man and suffers him no repose until before God he has answered it to himself— to accomplish this end one should do as follows. One recounts to him a history. This puts him entirely at his ease; for he understands very well that, since it is a history, it is not talking about him. In this history there is introduced a word which perhaps does not at first produce its effect, but some time later it transforms itself suddenly into the question of conscience. Thereby the thing becomes all the more heartfelt. Paul does not come to thee and ask thee pointedly whether thou hast believed, demanding to hear thy 'yes' or 'no'; but he says, 'He was believed on in the world'—and now it is left to thee, to thy conscience, to make answer to thyself. This one may call asking of one 'upon his conscience'; and of him upon whom it has such an effect one may say that he understands he is interrogated. Strangely enough, in the course of centuries there have been written innumerable interpretations of this passage, raising difficulties and removing difficulties, subjecting every phrase to a detailed and copious commentary—the only clause, so far as I know, which has not been made the subject of learned exposition (and that of course because one found it so easy to understand that every child can understand it) is just this: 'He was believed on in the world.' This indeed is very easy to understand; but take heed, this clause is the question addressed to 'thee'!

For, true enough, thou art living in the world. So when it is said, 'He was believed on in the world,' this brings as near as possible to thee the opportunity to question thyself, Have I then believed on Him? But who is it that asks? No one, nobody at all! But thou art well aware that the most dreadful, the most serious question is that of which it can be said that there is nobody who puts the question, and yet it is a question—and a question to thee *personally*. For when such is the case, it is conscience which questions. Also, thou hast surely heard speak of that crafty one [1] who thought it impossible for 'anybody' to outwit him with a question which he could not answer in such a way that the questioner would become the dupe; thou hast heard that the only thing he feared (convinced that he would be worsted) was that 'nobody' might put a question to him. Thou thyself hast surely been sensible of the solemnity when one is entirely alone in the stillness of the night, when everything is asleep; that is to say, when there is 'nobody'; as soon as there is 'somebody' the solemnity is less. Where there is 'nobody' who questions thee, and where nevertheless there is a personal question, *there* an invisible questioner is present, there thou hast in the deepest sense thyself to deal with, and this is the conscience-relationship. Hence this question has such a frightful power; for when somebody questions thee, thou canst manage to deceive him if it does not please thee to answer, or thou canst be wroth with him and ask him angrily who he is that he ventures to question thee, and what right he has to do it. But here—here there is . . . nobody!

He was believed on in the world. Yes, that is quite certain; thou knowest how many thousands have believed on Him, have lived in this faith, and died in this faith. And yet, no, this is not so. In case thou thyself dost not believe, thou canst not know whether any single soul has believed on Him; and in case thou thyself dost believe, thou knowest that He is believed on in the world, that there is one who has believed on Him. The one man cannot peer into the other man's heart where faith has its dwelling, or rather where one might descry whether faith is there or no; only the individual knows within himself before God and in his own case whether he believes in God or no. Every one else must be content with *protestations*. So then, thou canst not know that so and so many thousands have believed, thou knowest only (for what thou *canst not know* thou surely wilt not claim to know or make

[1] 'The Cyclops', in Homer's *Odyssey* ix. 366 ff.

pretence of knowing) that so and so many have asserted that they believed, that so and so many have died for this faith—but what am I saying! this thou knowest not, thou knowest only that they were put to death for this faith (by men who . . . could not know, however, that they had this faith), and that they asserted they died for this faith. More thou dost not know. This is not due to the special limitations of thy knowledge, but to the limitation of all human knowledge, to the fact that it is not the omniscience of the Searcher of Hearts. This is not due to the fact that thou art intimately acquainted with so few men; on the contrary, the more men thou dost think of, so much the less could there of course be any question of piercing into their inward hearts, and all the more necessary it is to rest content with assertions. But even if thou wert to single out an individual as the object of thy special attention—whether he is a believer thou canst not know, thou canst know only that he asserts it. In case thou thyself hast never been in love, thou dost not know whether any one has ever been loved in the world, thou knowest how many have asserted that they loved, asserted that they have sacrificed their lives for love. But whether they really have loved, thou canst not know; and if thou thyself hast loved, thou knowest that thou hast loved. The blind man cannot know the difference of colours, he must be content that others have assured him that it exists and that it is so and so.

Say not that this is stretching thought too taut, that it is too high strung. Oh, far from it, this is simply seriousness. For what is more serious than the question whether 'thou' hast believed or no? Note that for this cause it is essential to faith that it ward off all curiosity in order to concentrate the whole mind upon seriousness, it is essential to faith that it defend itself above all from this error, that a man can somehow have faith at second hand. And hence it is serviceable for thee to understand that thou really canst not know whether another man has believed, it is serviceable for thee in order that all the power of thy mind and attention (which in distraction might be squandered in busyness and curiousness about another man's faith) may be concentrated in the service of seriousness, so that thou, instead of running lightmindedly with the pack . . . and losing faith, mayest come to feel the whole weight of the fact that it is thou who art in question, that thou art referred to thyself alone, having nothing, absolutely nothing, to do with others, but all the more, or rather alone, to do with thyself, that really, so far as faith is concerned, thou canst know nothing about others. For it is a *historical* question how many have believed, that is the question history asks; but surely faith is not history. On the other hand, the question of faith is addressed to 'thee': Hast 'thou' believed? This question has to do with faith, the other with history. Faith is related to personality; but, personally understood, if 'I' have believed, it is a matter of in-difference how many and how many have believed; and if 'I' have not believed, it is a matter of indifference how many and how many have or have not believed.

It is a historical question how many have believed. 'And if so many and so many, such an innumerable number, have believed, there is no need of making much ado as to whether I have faith or no; I must surely have it after all, since so many have it. No, if faith were something one were alone with—well, then it would be rather different.' But that is just it, thou art alone with faith—in case thou hast it; in case thou art not alone with it, thou hast it not. Is this insane vanity, is it a proud madness which can only lead to the loss of one's reason? No, it is seriousness, it is the only thing which, if thou hast not faith, can lead thee to it. Is it also perhaps crazy vanity, is it also a proud madness, that thou, when death bereaves thee of thy beloved, wilt not understand, wilt not endure to hear, wilt only be disgusted as at an abomination, when they talk about this terrestrial globe being inhabited by several thousand millions of men, who die at the rate of many thousands every day, and every day there are presumably among the dead many lovers? I should rather think that it was madness, a proof of such a weakening of the mind that there could be no question of seriousness, if any one were to patter year in and year out this Biblical test, 'He was believed on in the world, He was believed on in the world,' without chancing to ask, Have 'I' believed on Him?

He was believed on in the world. So then he who understood Paul must understand that here there is a question. But now in case he who understood it were to answer, 'Yes, it is quite certain that He was believed on in the world, with every passing century one can say it with more and more reason; the believers become continually more and more numerous, Christianity has extended everywhere, especially since the discovery of America'—in this case would not Paul feel, alas, as one does when talking to a lunatic? For it is lunacy indeed for that chatty man [1] to talk continually about himself and his bit of a journey; but it is also lunacy when one is asked about faith and then talks about the whole world—except himself.

But he who understood the question and answered, 'I have believed on Him,' understood himself. And if he answered, 'I have not believed on him,' he too understood himself. Instead of the historical, 'He was believed on in the world,' we have the personal when the individual says, I have believed on Him.

'I have believed much in the world which trustworthy men related to me about things which I myself have neither heard nor seen, I have believed the testimony of history; in such manifold ways I have in daily life believed others. Among the things I have thus believed there is much that is unimportant and is forgotten the next day, much that has engaged my attention for a considerable time, much that I have transformed into my soul's possession and accepted as my necessary task—but yet, supposing that the whole sum of this were untrue, it is a loss I could put up with. But I have believed on Him—if in this too I am deceived, I am of all men most miserable, but then my life is nullified in its deepest root, so that nothing can either help or hurt me any more. For I have not held time at arm's length year after year, waiting for new and ever new security in order to dare to believe; no, by an eternal decision I have secured my life by believing on Him—if He is a delusion, my life is lost. But this is not so, for I *believe*. I have already encountered, therefore, and sustained the temptation involved in staking all upon uncertainty, which is what faith is.[2] But faith has conquered, I believe on Him. Will any one say to me, 'But *if*!', that is something I no longer understand. I understood it once at the instant of decision, now I understand it no more. Will any one be anxious and fearful on my account, that because of an 'if' or in spite of an 'if' I risked my life so far out—let him not bewail me but rather himself. I do not live by any 'if', I am stoutly against an 'if', in dread of this 'if'. I ventured out so far (that is what venturing properly means), now I believe. But that word 'if', which must be under-

---

[1] Geert Westphaler, in Holberg's comedy of that name.

[2] S. K. says in the *Postscript* (VII p. 189), 'Truth is objective uncertainty held fast by the most passionate appropriation of inwardness.' That is to say: faith is subjective certitude of the objectively uncertain.

stood in the first instance when one is grasping faith, is in turn the word and the thing which faith understands least of all.'

So might the individual speak.[1] And I allow him to speak on, so that he may interpret this clause in that Scriptural passage which otherwise is never interpreted. It is evidently no particular individual who is speaking here, neither thou nor I, so it is a *poetical* experiment. Only this would the discourse effect, it would make manifest how one talks as an individual.

'I have admired whatever of the noble and great and glorious has been produced among men. I do not mean that I am acquainted with it as a whole, but I know that in relation to what I am acquainted with my soul is not unacquainted with the pleasure of admiration, its blissful joy, a joy at once depressing and exalting, so I know what it is to admire. Perhaps it is only a little of the great I have been acquainted with, but that is of no consequence here; yea, if it were so, it would in this connexion (where it is not a question of the much one has admired, but of how much one has admired what one has admired) it would count rather for than against, if it were so that with entire devotion, gladly and enthusiastically, I have admired the little I was acquainted with. To take an example which, humanly speaking, stands absolutely alone, and which people are wont to bring into the closest connexion with Christianity, I have admired that noble, simple wise man of ancient times,[2] my heart too has beat violently as did that of the young man [3] when he conversed with him; the thought of him has been the enthusiasm of my youth and filled my soul to overflowing; I have longed for conversation with him as I never longed to talk with any man with whom I ever have talked; in the society of those who have comprehended everything and know how to talk about every possible subject I have many, many times sighed for his ignorance and to hear him who always said the same—'about the same things.' I have admired his wisdom, that he in wisdom remained simple! That he in wisdom remained simple so that he could catch the shrewd! That he in wisdom remained simple so that without having many thoughts or employing many words he could sacrifice his life in the service of the truth—oh, touching simplicity! That he with

[1] It is very clear here (in spite of the attempted evasion) that 'the individual' is S. K., making his personal profession of faith.

[2] Socrates.   [3] Alcibiades.

death before his eyes talked about himself, already condemned to die, just as simply as ever he talked in the market-place with a passer-by on the most commonplace topic; that he with the goblet of poison in his hand preserved the fine tone of festivity and talked as simply as ever he did at the banquet—oh, sublime simplicity! —But I have never believed on him, that never occurred to me. I count it also neither wise nor profound to institute a comparison between him, the simple wise man, and Him on whom I believe —that I count blasphemy. As soon as I reflect upon the matter of my salvation, then is he, the simple wise man, a person highly indifferent to me, an insignificance, a naught. I could not in any way, could not possibly get it into my head, or into my heart, or in any way across my lips, to make answer to the . . . blasphemous question, to which of these two I owe most: the simple wise man, or Him on whom I believe. But on the other hand I truly can make answer to the question, to whom I owe most—I surely should know to whom I owe most, most of all, most beyond all comparison. Him, namely, on whom I have believed, Him who staked His life for me also,[1] staked His life, not as one man can do that for another to *preserve* the other's life, no, to *give* me life. For without Him it is indifferent whether I live or die, it is an empty phrase to say that one has saved my life when this life he saved for me means after all to be dead. But He is the Life, life eternally understood I owe to Him, to Him on whom I believe.

'With the very feeling by which I am conscious by being myself I cling in filial devotion to the man to whom I owe life—but I crave to dispense from answering the question, to which of these I owe most, to him, my father, or to Him on whom I have believed. In case it were required of me, that is to say, in case He were to require it of me, I would not hesitate to wound myself more feelingly than any man could wound me, to let the son's love go—for love of Him on whom I believe. I love my wife as mine own self; if it were possible that she could be unfaithful to me, I would in this respect sorrow for her who had lost all that she had, for I could only love one; when death bereaves me of her I will affirm, and at the moment of mine own death I will again affirm what I have always said, that she was my only love. But if He on whom I believe, if it were possible that He might require

---

[1] 'Also for me' expresses one of the earliest religious thoughts registered in the Journal, II A 223.

it of me, this love I let go—for love of Him on whom I believe. I bear patiently mine own loss, and bear her wrath and misunderstanding, because she cannot understand me, until she shall understand me in eternity—that He will see to on whom I believe. I love my children, I would do for them everything that lies in a man's power, I should not know how to thank sufficiently him who by word and deed might truly have aided me in benefiting them, I am ready to lay down my life for them. But if He on whom I believe, if it were possible that He could require it of me, I am ready to let this love go—for love of Him on whom I believe. I take upon myself the pain of suffering and the burden of responsibility, bear patiently every harsh judgement upon me, even that of the loved ones, until in eternity they shall understand me—that He will see too on whom I believe.—And so likewise there is much that I love, in various ways, in various degrees; but if He on whom I believe require it of me, I let all this go—for love of Him on whom I believe.

'And if any one were to say to me, "That, however, would be an appalling 'if'. How is it possible to bear with life under such an 'if', which must kill all joy of living, with such an 'if' hovering over thy head in the spider-web of possibility? And is it not, moreover, a kind of faithlessness, to live in all these relationships of life, in the most tender relation to other people—and then to have to think of such an 'if'!" Then I would reply, Yes, certainly, this 'if' is appalling, fear-inspiring, this I have experienced at the moment of decision when I became a believer. In this terror consists the hazard of faith. But verily one can live under this 'if', and I do not feel it as a weight of anxiety but as a benediction upon me. For the fact that this 'if' has existed for me is a factor in my covenant with Him, and through it He blesses my relationship with whatever it is profitable for me to love. Without this 'if' it is impossible to be a believer, for the obedience of faith must go as far as this. But it does not follow that He requires this of me. And I believe that it is His will that the son shall love his father, the husband his wife, the father his children, and so on— I believe that this is His will, if there be not a difference of faith between them. So it is not faithlessness on my part that I recognize such an 'if'—it is faithlessness only towards them that do not know Him and will not know Him, faithlessness towards them that have not and will not have faith. Accordingly it is impossible that because of this 'if' (which is my soul's fear and trembling, but also my love, my only love, for in it I love Him in whom I believe) I should feel myself a stranger in the circle of those I love, with whom I have in common the same faith. But it is true that I feel myself a stranger in Christendom, in so far as the whole of Christendom is supposed to consist of nothing but believers; I am more of a stranger than if I lived amongst the heathen. For a man cannot feel so strange for the fact that a people who have another faith, another God, are indifferent to his faith, as he does for the fact that they who say they have the same faith are indifferent . . . to the same. It is one thing for a man to be indifferent to what I am engaged in when he is engaged in a different pursuit, and it is another thing when two men are engaged in the same pursuit, and the one is so indifferent, and the other so hearty in his pursuit . . . while it is the same pursuit they are both engaged in! I feel myself a stranger in Christendom, for the fact that what engages me early and late, people in Christendom think nobody can be so engaged in unless it is his livelihood, but that otherwise it would be queer and eccentric for any one to be so engaged in it. I draw from this no conclusion as to how many of all who live in Christendom are really Christians; with regard to other people's faith I know absolutely nothing. But this I know, 'He was believed on in the world,' and this I know quite simply for the fact that I have believed and do believe on Him.'

My hearer, this after all is a 'confession of faith', or at least the confession of one's faith. If a man is to be a Christian, it is doubtless requisite for him to believe something *definite*; but it is just as certainly requisite for him to be *quite definite* that 'he' believes. In the same degree that thou dost direct attention exclusively to the definite things a man must believe, in that same degree dost thou get away from faith. God does not let a particular species of fish inhabit a sea lacking the plant which is its nutriment. So one may argue in two ways: this plant grows here, *ergo* the fish is also to be found here; or, more securely, this fish is found here, *ergo* this plant grows here. But verily, as little as God lets a species of fish remain in a particular sea unless the plant also grows there which is its nutriment, just so little shall God leave in ignorance of what he must believe the man who was truly concerned. That is to say, the need brings with it the nutriment, the thing sought is in the seeking which seeks it; faith, in the concern at not having faith; love, in the concern at not loving. The need brings with it the nutriment, not *by itself*, as though it produced the nutriment, but by virtue of God's ordinance which joins together the need and nutriment, so that when one says that this is so, he must add, 'as certainly as God exists'; for if God did not exist, it would not be so. Be not deceived by appearance. The every-day speech between man and man contains many a delusion. So, for example, when one says, 'I had fully decided to venture this or that for one cause or another, but then there was one person and another who got me away from my resolution'—this sounds plausible. But one who knows the human heart sees very clearly the situation: the man has not in the deepest sense been resolved; for then he would not have applied to this person and that, but would have acted. He who is not made silent by being in love, is not in love, and so it is with true resolution. So likewise one who lives in Christendom says he is so eager to believe if only he could get it definitely established what he is to believe. That seems very plausible, and yet there is deceit in it; he is unwilling to venture out into the dangers and decisions where faith comes into existence, he would not be alone, alone in the danger of spiritual death, hence he talks of this in a different way. For in fact He who is the object of faith is considerably nearer to a man than the distance of eighteen hundred years suggests, mediated by the traditions which are like the precarious connexions of the diver, or, if there were the least doubt, through the obstacles and possible misunderstandings of eighteen hundred years. The nearest way is that of mortal danger; the most comfortable way (which, however, does not lead to faith) is being busy about the difficulty that one cannot get it historically established what one must believe. The most reliable intelligence is to be had in mortal danger, when one hears (what at bottom he knows) with a distinctness which only mortal danger supplies; for in mortal danger one becomes infinitely sharp of hearing, and what one must hear is infinitely near. Everybody living in Christendom has ordinarily (the Government sees to that) got more than enough information about Christianity; many have got much too much. What is lacking is surely something quite different, it is the inward transformation of the whole mind, whereby a man in danger of spiritual death comes to the point of believing at least something . . . of the much he knows. Everybody living in Christendom has absolutely enough information about Christianity to be able to invoke and supplicate, to be able to turn prayerfully to Christ. If he does that with a sense of inward need, in honesty of heart, he will yet become a believer. If only it is quite definite before God that this man feels the need of believing, he will in due time get to know quite definitely what he is to believe. The opposite case is: without need of believing, inquiringly, ponderingly, meditatively, more and more pettily willing to waste year after year of his life, and finally his blessedness, in order to get it quite, quite definite, even to the dot over a letter, what one is to believe. This opposite case is hollow sham, which merely makes itself more and more important, or it is a scientifically learned nature in the wrong place, and hence a scientifically learned un-nature, or it is a cowardly, unmanly, and so far forth also an ungodly fearfulness.

PART IV

FROM THE JOURNAL

The contrast between the third part and the fourth is as sharp as possible and as searching: the one is like a commemoration of the Cleansing of the Temple—and then the quiet and most heartfelt of all acts of worship: a communion on Fridays.

DISCOURSES AT THE COMMUNION ON FRIDAYS

CHRISTIAN DISCOURSES

by

S. KIERKEGAARD

Copenhagen
1848

CONTENTS

PREFACE

Among these discourses (which lack the essential requisite for being, and so are not called, sermons) there are two, the second and third, which were delivered in the Church of our Lady. Though he were not told it, the expert himself would know from the form and treatment that these two are 'delivered discourses', written to be delivered, or written as they were delivered.

S. K.

February 1848.

PRAYER

FATHER in heaven, well we know that it is Thou that givest both to will and to do, that also longing when it leads us to renew the fellowship with our Saviour and Redeemer is from Thee. But when longing lays hold of us, oh, that we might lay hold of the longing; when it would carry us away, that we also might give ourselves up; when Thou art near to summon us, that we also might keep near to Thee in supplication; when Thou in the longing dost offer us the highest good, that we might buy the opportune moment, might hold it fast, sanctify it in a quiet hour with serious thoughts, with pious resolutions, so that it might become the strong but also well-tested longing which is required of them that would worthily partake of the Holy Communion! Father in heaven, longing is Thy gift; no one can bestow it upon himself, when it is not given no one can buy it though he were willing to sell all—but when Thou givest it, then one can sell all to buy it. So we pray for them that are assembled here, that with hearty longing they may today approach the Lord's Table, and that when they go hence they may go with increased longing for Him, our Saviour and Redeemer.

Luke xxii. 15. I HAVE HEARTILY LONGED TO EAT THIS PASSOVER WITH YOU BEFORE I SUFFER.

The sacred words now read, which are Christ's own words, though they are not a part of the institution of the Lord's Supper, yet in the narrative they stand in the closest connexion with it. Immediately after these words follow the words of institution. It was in the night in which He was betrayed, or rather He already was betrayed, Judas was already bought to sell him, the betrayer was now merely seeking the 'opportune moment' to betray Him to the chief priests 'without making an uproar' (Luke xxii. 6). To do this, he chose the stillness of the night in which Christ, now for the last time, was assembled with His disciples. 'And when the hour was come, He sat down, and the Apostles with Him. And He said unto them, I have heartily longed to eat this passover with you before I suffer.'—That this was the last time

He did not learn after the event; He knew beforehand that it was the last time. Yet He was not disposed to initiate the Apostles completely into the knowledge that it was the last time, how near the danger is, that it is this very night, nor what the danger is, that it is the most ignominious death, nor how inevitable it is. He who alone bare the sin of the world, bears also here alone the terrible knowledge of what is to occur; He who strove alone in Gethsemane, alone because the disciples slept, is also alone here, although He sits at table with His only confidants. So what will come to pass that night, how it will come to pass, through whom it will come to pass, only one in that little circle knows, He who was betrayed—yes, and one more, the betrayer, who also was present. So Christ seats Himself at the table with the Apostles, and as He takes His seat He says, I have heartily longed for this supper.

Does it not seem to thee, my hearer, that in a deeper sense this belongs both inwardly and figuratively to the Lord's Supper, and not merely as belonging historically to the sacred text which reports it? For surely hearty longing is essentially in place at the Holy Supper. Would it not stand in the most strident contradiction to the sacred account of how heartily the Institutor longed for this supper, would it not be the most terrible contradiction if it were possible that any one out of habit, or because it was use and wont, or perhaps impelled by circumstances quite accidental, in short, if any one were to come to the Holy Communion without a hearty longing? So then, the sacred words which have been read are, if I may say so, the introduction to the institution of the Lord's Supper, and this again is for every individual the true and godly introduction or entrance: to come with a hearty longing.

Let us then employ the prescribed moment before the Communion in speaking of

THE HEARTY LONGING FOR THE HOLY SUPPER OF THE LORD.

It is nothing new we would teach thee, least of all, in leading thee forth into the presence of faith, would we lead thee into difficult investigations; we would strive only to explain what was moving within thee when thou didst become aware of the longing to go to the altar, the hearty longing with which art come hither today.

The wind bloweth where it listeth, thou art sensible of its sighing, but no man knoweth whence it cometh or whither it goeth. So also it is with longing, longing for God and eternity, longing for our Saviour and Redeemer. To grasp it is not in thy power, and that thou shalt not do, yea, thou shalt not even attempt it—but thou shalt employ the longing. Would a merchant be serious if he did not employ the opportune moment? would a seaman be serious if he did not employ the favourable wind?—and how much more the man who does not employ the opportunity of longing when it is presented! Oh, people talk piously about not wasting God's gifts; but what more properly and in a deeper sense can be called God's gifts than every prompting of the Spirit, every upward tug of the soul, every sincere motion of the heart, every holy feeling, every godly longing, which after all, in a much deeper sense than food and clothing, are God's gifts, because it is not merely that God gives them, but that God gives Himself in these gifts. And yet how often do men waste these gifts of God! Ah, if thou couldst peer into men's hearts, and peer right deeply into thine own, thou wouldst certainly discover with dismay how God, who never leaves Himself without a witness, doth lavish His best gifts upon every man, and, on the other hand, how man wastes these gifts, more or less, perhaps wastes them entirely. A dreadful responsibility, when one day, in eternity if not before, the memories arise in accusation against a man, memories of the many times and divers manners God spoke to him in his inward man, and spoke in vain. Memories, yea, for even if a man has long ago forgotten what he wasted, so that he does not remember it—God and eternity have not forgotten, it is recalled to him and becomes his remembrance in eternity. Such is the case with longing. A man can ignore his call, he can regard it as a momentary impulse, a whim, which vanishes the next moment without a trace, he can resist it, can prevent it from attaining within him a deeper hold, can let it die away like an unfruitful mood. But if thou dost receive it gratefully as a gift from God, it will become a blessing also unto thee. Never therefore let the holy longing depart in vain when it would visit thee. Even though it seems to thee that thou dost follow it in vain—do not believe that, it is not so, it is impossible that it might be so, it yet must become a blessing to thee.

So then longing awakened in thy soul. Even though it was

inexplicable, inasmuch as it comes indeed from God who by it draws thee; even though it was inexplicable, inasmuch as it is from Him who 'lifted up from the earth will draw all men unto Himself' (John xii. 32); even though it was inexplicable, inasmuch as it is the effect of the Spirit in thee—yet thou didst understand what was required of thee. For, verily, though God gives all, He also requires all, requires that a man shall do all in order rightly to employ what God gives. Ah, in the usual occupations of daily life how easy it is, spiritually understood, to slumber! In the habitual course of routine how difficult it is to find a place to break away! In this situation God helped thee by the longing which awakened in thy soul. Surely then thou didst promise thyself and God that now thou also wouldst thankfully employ it. Thou didst say to thyself, 'Since now the longing has wrenched me loose from that which so easily entangles a man in base enchantment, I will also for my part come to its assistance with serious thoughts, in order to wrench myself completely loose from that which still holds me back, and with holy resolutions I will hold fast to what the serious thoughts help me to understand; for resolutions serve to hold a man fast to what he has understood.

'How vain after all is the earthly and the temporal! And even if my life hitherto has been so fortunate, so completely care-free, so completely without knowledge through experience of the dreadful or even of the sad, yet I will summon serious thoughts, in alliance with the longing for eternity, and with the Holy Communion before my eyes, to which none may come without due preparation, I will not be afraid of being serious. For after all Christianity is not a melancholy thing, on the contrary it is so glad a thing that it is glad tidings to all melancholy men; only the frivolous and the defiant can it make gloomy.—Behold, everything, everything I see, so long as it exists, is subject to vanity and change, and in the end it is a prey to corruption. Therefore, like that pious man,[1] when the moon rises in its splendour, I will say to the star, I care not for thee, thou now art darkened; and when the sun rises in all its grandeur, I will say to the moon, I care not for thee, thou now art darkened; and when the sun goes down, I will say, I knew it full well, for all is vanity. And when I behold the bustle of the running water,

[1] Eccl. xii. 2, 8; cf. also i. 5–8.

I will say, Only keep on running, thou wilt never fill the sea; and to the wind I will say, yea, even if it were to tear up the trees by the roots, I will say to it, Blow on, in thee, however, there is neither meaning nor thought, thou symbol of inconstancy. And though the beauty of the field which captivates the eye by its enchantment, and though the melody of the birds' song which falls blissfully upon the ear, and though the peace of the forest which invitingly refreshes the heart, were to employ all their eloquence, I will not let myself be prevailed upon, will not let myself be infatuated, I will remind myself that it is all illusion. And though the stars for thousands of years have sat so securely without altering their position in the heavens, yet will I not let myself be deceived by this stability, I will remind myself that one day they are to fall.—Thus I will remind myself how uncertain everything is; that at birth a man is cast out into the world and from that moment lies with a depth beneath him of a thousand fathoms, and the future before him every instant, yea, every instant, is as the darkest night. I will remember that never has any one been so fortunate that he might not become unfortunate, nor ever any one so unfortunate that he might not become more unfortunate! That even were I to succeed in having all my wishes fulfilled, so that they resulted in one lofty structure—yet no one, no one will be able to vouch to me for it that the whole structure will not come toppling down about my ears. And if I were to succeed (in case this can be called success) in saving a wretched remnant of my former good fortune from this destruction, and if I admonished my soul to rest content with this—that yet no one, no one will be able to vouch to me for it that also this remainder will not be taken from me the next instant! And if there were one misfortune or another, one horror or another, whether a short-lasting or a long-drawn-out torture, which I especially dreaded, and if I had already become an old man—that no one, no one will be able to vouch that it might not yet overtake me at the last instant!—So I will remember that, as the uncertainty of every instant is like the dark night, so too the explanation of every individual occurrence or event is like a conundrum which no man has guessed. That no one who would speak truth in an eternal sense can tell me which is which, whether it would really be more advantageous to me that all my wishes were fulfilled, or that they were all denied me. And though I were to save myself upon a plank from certain death, and though friends gladly helped me to the shore, marvelling at my salvation—that nevertheless the wise man will be able to stand by and say, 'Perhaps, perhaps it would have been better for thee to perish in the waves', and that perhaps, perhaps he speaks exactly the truth! I will remind myself that the wisest man that ever lived, and the most shallow that ever lived, would get equally near to the truth when it is a question of vouching for the next instant, and when it is a question of explaining the least occurrence, get equally near to a perhaps, and that the more passionately a man raves against this perhaps, the nearer he comes only to losing his mind. For no mortal ever broke through, ever penetrated—yea, not even the prisoner confined within walls seven yards thick, bound hand and foot, and nailed to the floor, is so bound as every mortal is by these bonds constructed of nothing, by this perhaps. I will remind myself that even if I had in my soul one only wish, and were attached to it so desperately that I would be willing to throw away the blessedness of heaven to see this wish fulfilled—that yet no one can definitely tell me beforehand whether this wish, when it was fulfilled, might not seem to me empty and trivial. And what then would be the most miserable outcome? That the wish was not fulfilled, and I still retained the sorrow and pain conceived for the . . . good fortune I had missed? or that it was fulfilled, and I beheld it, embittered by the knowledge of how empty it was?—So I will reflect that death is the only certain thing, that death, mocking me and all the uncertainty of human life, which every instant is equally uncertain, is equally certain every instant; that death is not more certain for the old man than for the child born yesterday; that whether I abound in health or lie upon the sick-bed, death is every instant equally certain—a fact which only earthly dullness can contrive to ignore. I will recall that no covenant between man and man is entered into, not the tenderest, not the most heartfelt, without at the same time death entering into it, in the official capacity by virtue of which it has part in everything.—And I will remember that every man after all is solitary, solitary in the interminable world. True, in good days, when there is fair weather, when fortune smiles, it seems no doubt as if we were living in society with one another; but I will remind myself that no one can know when tidings might reach me, tidings of misfortune, misery, horror,

which along with the terror would also make me solitary, or reveal
how solitary I am, as every man is—would make me solitary,
forsaken by my nearest kin, misunderstood by my best friend,
an object of dread from which all flee. I will remember the
horrors which yet no scream of dread, no tears, no prayers
warded off, which have separated the lover from his beloved, the
friend from his friend, the parents from their children; and I will
remember how a little misunderstanding, when it so lucklessly
came between them, was sometimes enough to divide them
horribly. I will remember that, *humanly* speaking, there is no one,
absolutely no one to be relied on, not even God in heaven. For
in case I were to hold fast to Him so that I became His friend,
—oh, who has suffered more, who has been more tried in all
sufferings than the pious man who was God's friend?'

So didst thou talk with thyself; and the more thou didst
abandon thyself to these thoughts, so much the more did longing
for the eternal triumph in thee, a longing for fellowship with
God through thy Saviour, and thou didst say, 'Heartily I long
for this Supper. Oh, there is after all but one friend, one faithful
friend in heaven and on earth, Our Lord Jesus Christ. Ah, and
how many words a man employs, and how many times he will go
to get another man to do him a favour, and if this other does him
the favour with some little sacrifice to himself, he who has become
acquainted with man and knows how seldom favours are shown
to one who can make no return, oh, how tight does this man cling
to such a benefactor! But He who also for me (for that He did
the same for all others ought not to diminish my gratitude for
what in fact He did for me), He who for me entered into death—
should I not long for fellowship with Him? No friend ever was
able to do more than to be faithful *unto* death, but it was precisely
in death that He was faithful—His death was my salvation.
And at the very most, no friend can do more than *save* another's
life, but He *gave* me life by His death; it was I that was dead,
and His death gave me life.

'Yet, after all, the ruin of the nations and of every individual
man is *sin*; how then can I think seriously about life without duly
reflecting upon what Christianity teaches me, that the world
lieth in the evil? And even though my life has gone on hitherto
so quietly, so peacefully, so undisturbed by the attacks and per-
secutions of the evil world, and even though it seems to me that

the few people I am acquainted with are good and loving and benevolent—then I will reflect that this may well be due to the fact that neither they nor I have been led forth into such decisive situations of mortal spiritual danger in which the magnitude of the event reveals on an enormous scale what there is of good or evil in a man. So it well may be, and hence it may be necessary for revelation to teach what man himself cannot know—how deep humanity has sunk.

'Then I will recall what I have heard about all the abominable acts men have committed against men, enemies against their enemies, ah, and friend against friend, I will think about all the violence and murder and bloodthirstiness and beastly cruelty, about all the innocent blood which yet was so cruelly shed and crieth unto heaven, about guile and craft and deceit and faithlessness, about all those innocent ones, whose blood indeed was not shed, though they were horribly tortured and put to death. Above all I will remind myself how it fared with the Holy One when He wandered here upon earth, what opposition He suffered from sinners, how His whole life was nothing but suffering of soul on account of belonging to the fallen race which He would save and which would not be saved, that the living man who is cruelly chained to a corpse can suffer no more torture than He suffered in soul at being incorporated as man in the race! I will reflect how He was mocked, and how every man who invented a new mockery was hailed with applause, how there no longer was the least consideration of His innocence, not a thought even of His holiness, how the only extenuating word then uttered was the contemptuous pity of the saying, "Behold, what a man!"— Suppose I had lived as a contemporary of this dreadful scene, suppose I had been present among the "multitude" which mocked Him and spat upon Him! Suppose I had been present in this crowd—for I dare not presume that out of the whole race I might have been one of the Twelve—suppose I had been present! Well, but I cannot believe of myself that I might have been present *for the sake of* taking part in the scoffing. But suppose now that the people around me observed that I took no part—oh, already I see those fierce glances, I see the attack instantly turned against me, already I hear the cry, "He too is a Galilean, an adherent, put him to death, or let him take part in the mockery, in the people's cause!" Gracious God! After all, how many are there in any generation who have the courage to stand up for a conviction when they are in danger or mockery, when it is a question of life and death, and when moreover the challenge of danger unexpectedly overwhelms one so dreadfully! And I who was not a believer, not an adherent, how should I have the strength to venture, or how should it be possible that I in the instant of danger might become a believer, the challenge of decision helping me just as marvellously, though not quite in the same way, as it helped the thief on the cross; and in case I was not sincerely changed, how might I get the courage to venture this for one who to me was a stranger? Gracious God! Why then I would have taken part in the mocking . . . to save my life; yes, that is true, it was to save my own life! Yes, I know well that the parson talks in a different way; when he talks he describes the terrible blindness of these contemporaries—but we who are present to hear him are not men like that. Perhaps the parson has not the heart to talk severely to us—yea, and if I were the parson, I would not talk differently, I would not dare to say to any man that he would act thus; there are things one man cannot say to another. Oh, but to myself I dare say it, and unfortunately I must say it: with me it would have fared no better than with the multitude!'

Thus then didst thou talk with thyself. And the more thou didst abandon thyself to these thoughts, so much the more did the longing triumph in thee, longing for fellowship with Him the Holy One, and thou didst say to thyself, 'I heartily long for this Supper. I will away from this evil world where sin exercises dominion, and I will long for fellowship with Him! Away from it? That, however, is not so easy. Yet I can wish myself away from the vanity and corruption of the world, and even if the wish does not avail, the hearty longing for the eternal avails to carry me away; for in the longing itself the eternal *is*, just as God *is* in the sorrow which is sorrow *unto* God. But sin has a singular power of holding out, it has an outstanding debt to exact, a guilt it would have the sinner pay before he escapes. And sin knows how to stand up for its rights, verily it does not let itself be beguiled by vague words, even if men were to abolish entirely the word "sin" and put "weakness" in its place, even if in the strictest sense of the word it was only weakness of which a man was guilty. But for this reason I long the more heartily to renew my fellowship with Him who also has made satisfaction for my sin, made satisfaction for every least actual sin of mine, but also for that sin which perhaps lurks deepest in my soul without my being conscious of it, and which possibly might break out when I am led into terrible decisions. For were those Jews greater criminals than other men? Oh, no, but that they were contemporary with the Holy One made their crime infinitely more terrible.'

I heartily long for this Supper, for this Supper which is in remembrance of Him. But then when a man with hearty longing has partaken of the communion, is the longing quenched, shall the longing diminish as he goes away? If one dear to thee is dead, it will come to pass time after time that the longing to have him in remembrance will awaken in thee. So perhaps thou dost go to his grave, and as he lies now sunk in the bosom of the earth, so does thy soul sink deep in remembrance of him. Thereby thy longing is satisfied, as it were. Life again exercises its power over thee, and even if thou dost continue faithfully to remember the deceased and dost often long for him, yet this cannot mean that thou shouldst more and more be weaned from life and live in the grave with the dead one, so that longing would increase with every visit to the grave. Thou wilt surely admit that however much we might honour his faithfulness to the dead there is something morbid in such sorrow. No, thou dost understand that your paths are essentially divided, that it is to life thou dost belong, and to the demands life makes upon thee; thou dost understand that longing should not increase with the years so as to make thee more and more a companion of the grave. Oh, but longing for fellowship with thy Saviour and Redeemer, that precisely is the thing which should increase with every occasion of remembering Him. He is not dead but living, yea, thou shalt live thyself into and together with Him, He indeed is to be and to become thy life, so that thou dost not live thyself, no longer dost live thyself but Christ liveth in thee. And therefore as hearty longing belongs to a worthy remembrance of Him, so again it belongs to a hearty longing that it increases with remembrance, so that only he came worthily to the altar who went away with hearty longing, oh, went away with an even more hearty longing.

PRAYER

FATHER in heaven! As on other occasions the intercession of the congregation is that Thou wouldst comfort all them that are sick and sorrowful, so now at this hour its intercession is that to them that labour and are heavy laden Thou wouldst give rest for their souls. Oh, and yet this is hardly an intercession. Who might count himself so sound that he need only pray for others? Ah, no, every one prays on his own account that Thou wouldst give him rest for his soul. O God, to each one severally whom Thou beholdest labouring and heavy laden with the consciousness of sin, do Thou give rest for his soul.

Matt. xi. 28. COME UNTO ME, ALL YE THAT TRAVAIL AND ARE HEAVY LADEN,[1] AND I WILL GIVE YOU REST FOR YOUR SOULS.

'*Come hither, all ye that labour and are heavy laden.*' A strange invitation. For commonly when men assemble for joy or for united labour they say, it is true, to the strong and the joyful, 'Come hither, take part with us, unite your strength with ours.' But of the afflicted person they say, 'No, we will not have him with us, he only spoils the joy and retards the work.' Oh, yes, the afflicted man understands this well enough without need of hearing it told to him; and so perhaps many an afflicted person goes off by himself alone, will not take part with others lest he spoil their joy or retard their labour. But then this invitation, however, to *all* them that labour and are heavy laden must apply to him, since it applies to all the afflicted; how could any afflicted person say in this instance, 'No, this invitation does not apply to me'?

'*All they that labour and are heavy laden*', all of them, none is excepted, not one. Ah, what manifold diversities are suggested by these words. They that *labour*! For not only that man labours who in the sweat of his brow labours for his daily bread, nor he only who in lowly station bears the burden and heat of the day; ah, he also labours who struggles with sad thoughts, he too

[1] This is the text for the whole work entitled *Training in Christianity*.

269

labours who is concerned by the care of one or many, he too labours who contends with doubt, labouring in that sea as a swimmer is said to labour. They that are *heavy laden*! For not only is that man heavy laden who visibly bears the heavy burden, who is visibly situated in difficulties, but he too is heavy laden whose burden no one has seen, who perhaps even labours to hide it; and not only is he heavy laden before whom there lies a long life of trial saddened by recollection, but he too for whom, alas, there seems to be no future.

But how could this discourse ever reach an end if it were to enumerate all the diversities; and were it even to attempt to do so, the effort would perhaps guide astray instead of guiding aright, would distract attention to the diversities instead of concentrating the mind upon the one thing needful. For however many are the diversities, can it possibly be the meaning of the Gospel that there would be left over a little number of men or a great number who might be called fortunate as exempted from labour and care? Is it the meaning of the Gospel when it invites all them that labour and are heavy laden, that there are some, however, to whom this invitation does not apply because they are whole and have no need of a physician? So it is doubtless we do commonly talk. For if thou art watching a happy group of children, and to one child who is sick a kind man says, 'Come unto me, child, and we will play together', with that he does indeed imply that the child is sick, but at the same time he implies that the others are in sound health. Should then the Gospel talk in the same way, or should we talk so foolishly about the Gospel? For if this were so, then the Gospel does not apply to all, then it does not preach the equality of all men, but on the contrary it makes a distinction, excluding the joyful, just as the human invitation excludes the afflicted. We see then that the Gospel must be understood differently, it invites all, the Gospel is unwilling to be a by-path, offering comfort and consolation to certain persons in affliction; no, it addresses itself to all, and it *requires* that every man shall know what it is to labour and be heavy laden. Accordingly, even if thou wast the most fortunate of men, so fortunate, alas, that thou art envied by many, the Gospel addresses itself no less certainly to thee, requiring thee to labour and be heavy laden. Or if, without being the most fortunate man, a man especially favoured, thou art living in happy contentment, with thy dearest wishes fulfilled, and without want, the Gospel addresses itself no less certainly to thee with the requirement of the invitation. Or, on the contrary, if thou wast sitting in earthly want and need, this does not indicate thee as the one to whom the Gospel speaks. Yea, if thou wert so wretched that thou wert become a proverb, yet this does not indicate thee as the one to whom the Gospel speaks.

So the invitation is unwilling to be taken in vain, and hence it contains a requirement, it requires that the invited guest shall in a deeper sense labour and be heavy laden. For there is a sorrow unto God; it has to do with nothing earthly and temporal, not with thy outward circumstances, not with thy future, it is unto God. He who bears this sorrow quietly and humbly in his heart, he it is that labours. And there is a heavy burden; no worldly power can lay it upon thy shoulders, but neither can any man, any more than thou thyself, take it off. It is guilt and the consciousness of guilt, or still heavier, it is sin and the consciousness of sin. He who bears this burden, alas, he is laden, and heavy laden, but yet precisely so laden as the Gospel requires. And there is an affliction, a deep, an eternal affliction; it has not to do with thy outward circumstances, with thy lot in life, either past or to come, it has to do with thine actions, and, alas, it has to do precisely with those actions which a man would prefer to have forgotten, for it has to do with the actions whereby thou didst offend against God or against other men, whether they be hidden or manifest. This affliction is penitence. He who sighs penitently, yea, it is he that labours and is heavy laden. No one else labours so heavily, yet it is this precisely which the invitation of the Gospel requires.

But the invitation of the Gospel not only implies a demand, it also announces a promise: 'I will give you rest for your souls.' Rest! That is what the exhausted labourer and the weary wanderer desire; and the sailor tossed upon the sea seeks rest; and the old man tired out longs for rest; and the sick man who lies restlessly on the bed and finds no position of repose, he too craves rest; and the doubter who finds no secure footing on the sea of thought desires rest. Oh, but only the penitent thoroughly understands what it is to pray that he may have rest for his soul, that he may have rest in the only thought in which rest is to be found for a penitent, that there is forgiveness; rest in the only word that can reassure a penitent, that he is forgiven; rest on the only ground that can sustain a penitent, that satisfaction has been made.

But this is also what the Gospel promises, that he shall find rest for his soul. And it is in response to this invitation ye, my hearers, have come hither at this hour. And even if rest cannot be given in such a way that by this one time it is for ever decided, so that thou shouldst have no need of coming often to this holy place in search of rest—none the less is it peace for the soul. Thou art a wayfarer, and God's house is the baiting-place along the road where thou seekest rest for thy soul. But even though thou wilt need again to seek this rest, yet it is certain that this is the same rest in which one day when thy last hour is come thou wilt for the last time seek rest for thy soul. For whether it be as a youth thou art come today or in advanced years—oh, when the last time has arrived, and in the hour of death thou art lonesome and forsaken, thou wilt desire, as the very last thing in the world of which thou no longer art a part, thou wilt desire what today thou dost desire.

This was the promise of the invitation. But who then is the *inviter*? For it would be a terribly confusing thing if there were to be heard in the world the invitation, 'Come hither', but no indication was given whither one was to go. Therefore, if there were no inviter, or if forgetfulness and doubt had made away with the inviter, what then would it profit that the word of invitation continued to be heard, when it would be impossible to find the place? But thou, my hearer, dost know who the Inviter is, and thou hast followed the invitation in order to attach thyself more closely to Him. Behold, He spreads out His arms,[1] saying, 'Come hither, come hither to ME, all ye that labour and are heavy laden'; behold, He bares His breast, upon which all can lean in security, and all equally blessed, for it was only in our Saviour's earthly life that John lay closest to Him upon His breast. However it may be thou art come hither, in whatever sense it may be said of thee that thou art weary and heavy laden, whether thou hast offended in much or in little, whether the guilt be old and . . . I had almost said, forgotten; but no, it is not

---

[1] As this discourse was delivered in the Cathedral, S. K. had only to point to the famous statue by Torwaldsen which represents Christ spreading out His arms in welcome, corresponding with the inscription in bold letters on the base: COME UNTO ME.

forgotten, I would say rather, old and oft repented of—or it is fresh, and no soothing effect of distance has assuaged it—oh, with Him thou shalt find rest for thy soul. I know not what it is in particular that afflicts thee, my hearer; nor perhaps should I comprehend thy sorrow or be able to talk of it understandingly. Oh, but it is not to a man thou comest; after having made confession in secret, thou comest to Him, the merciful Inviter, to Him who is acquainted with all human sorrow, to Him who was tempted in all points, yet without sin. He too was acquainted with earthly need, He who was hungry in the wilderness, He who thirsted upon the cross; He too was acquainted with poverty, He who had not whereon to lay His head; His soul too was sorrowful unto death; yea, He has known all human sorrow more profoundly than any man, He who at the last was forsaken of God—when He bare all the sin of the world. And He indeed is not merely thy spiritual pastor, He is also thy Saviour; not only does He understand thy sorrow better than thou dost understand it thyself, ah, but he will take off from thee the burden and give thee peace for thy soul. It is hard—yes, that is true—it is hard not to be understood; but what would it help thee if there were one who could entirely understand thy sorrow, but could not take it from thee, could entirely understand thy strife, but could not give thee rest?

So then, there was an invitation: 'Come unto me, all ye that labour and are heavy laden'; and the invitation implies a demand: that the guests invited shall labour and be heavy laden with the consciousness of sin. And there is a reliable Inviter, He who here still stands by His word and invites all. God grant that he who seeks may also find; that he who seeks the right thing may also find the one thing needful; that he who comes hither seeking in the right place may also find rest for his soul. For, true enough, it is a restful position to kneel at the foot of the altar, but God grant that this in fact may be but a weak intimation that the soul finds rest in God through the consciousness of the forgiveness of sins.

PRAYER

FATHER in heaven, Thy grace and mercy change not with the changing times, they grow not older with the course of years, as if, like a man, Thou wert more gracious one day than another, more gracious at first than at the last; Thy grace remains unchanged, as Thou art unchangeable, it is ever the same, eternally young, new every day—for every day Thou sayest, 'yet today'. [1] Oh, but when one gives heed to this word, is impressed by it, and with a serious, holy resolution says to himself, 'yet today'—then for him this means that this very day he desires to be changed, desires that this very day might become important to him above all other days, important because of renewed confirmation in the good he once chose, or perhaps even because of his first choosing of the good. It is an expression of Thy grace and mercy that every day Thou dost say, 'yet today', but it would be to forfeit Thy grace and mercy and the season of grace if a man were to say unchangeably from day to day, 'yet today'; for it is Thou that bestowest the season of grace 'yet today', but it is man that must grasp the season of grace 'yet today'. Thus it is we talk with Thee, O God; between us there is a difference of language, and yet we strive to make ourselves understood of Thee, and Thou dost not blush to be called our God. That word which when Thou, O God, dost utter it is the eternal expression of Thy unchangeable grace, that same word when a man repeats it with due understanding is the strongest expression of the deepest change and decision—yea, as if all were lost if this change and decision did not come to pass 'yet today'. So do Thou grant to them that today are here assembled, to them

---

[1] 'Yet today' is a phrase which S. K. uses, not only here but in other places, with an emphasis which suggests profound significance. It is my guess that in Heb. iii. 13 he read: 'today while it is yet today'.

S. K. once remarked: 'In prayer my *forte* is thanksgiving.' Obviously, his *forte* was not the composition of *common* prayers. Lacking the criterion of a sound liturgical tradition, the prayers which introduce his 'discourses', though doubtless they are not too subtle for God to understand, are too complicated for a congregation to follow.

that without external prompting, and hence the more inwardly, have resolved 'yet today' to seek reconciliation with Thee by the confession of their sins, to them do Thou grant that this day may be truly blessed to them, that they may hear His voice whom Thou didst send to the world, the voice of the Good Shepherd, that He may know them, and that they may follow Him.

John x. 27. MY SHEEP SHALL HEAR MY VOICE, AND I KNOW THEM, AND THEY FOLLOW ME.

When the congregation assembles in the house of the Lord on a holy day, God Himself has ordained and commanded this. Today, however, is not a holy day, and yet a little group has assembled here in the sanctuary, not therefore because all are commanded to do so (since none is commanded), but because each single individual here present must severally have felt, though in different ways, a need to come here precisely today. For today is not a holiday, today every one else goes to his field, to his business, to his labour, and only this individual comes today to the house of the Lord.—So the individual departed from his house to come hither. On a holy day, when one who himself is going to church encounters a passer-by, he naturally assumes that the passer-by is also going to church; for on a holy day it is assumed—though not always rightly by any means— that the passer-by is a church-goer. But he who, impelled by an inward need, comes here today—who on meeting him as he went would chance to think that he was going to the house of God? Should therefore this visit to God's house be less solemn? To me it seems that this air of mystery must if possible make it even more inwardly solemn. Openly, before the eyes of all, and yet hidden, the individual came today to church—hidden, or by a hidden path. For no one knew his path except God, it occurred to no passer-by that thou wast on the way to God's house, which even thou dost not say, for thou sayest, 'I am going to the altar', as though this were a more inward and solemn thing than going to church. Thou didst not expect as on a holy day that the passers-by were going the same way or with the same thoughts, therefore thou didst walk hidden among the many, as a stranger. Thou didst not expect to see the same resolution expressed upon the faces of the passers-by, and therefore thou didst keep thine eyes to thyself, without greeting ceremoniously thine acquaintances as on holy days. No, for thee the passer-by did not exist: with downcast eyes thou didst flee hither, as it were, by stealth. Thine aim was not simply to make supplication, to offer praise, to give thanks unto God, as on a holy day, when accordingly thou couldst not desire to be alone; thine aim is to seek the forgiveness of sins—so that thou must desire to be alone. How quiet now and how solemn! On a holy day everything outside is quiet too; the customary labour gives place to repose; even he who does not visit God's house observes that it is a holy day. Today, however, is no holiday. The business of life outside barely penetrates to this vaulted hall, making the sacred quiet even more marked. For the quiet which the civil authority can exact by worldly ordinance is not the same as godly quiet, but this quiet while the bustle of the world continues is precisely the godly quiet.—So then, it was not thy duty to come hither today, it was a need within thee; there was no external prompting to determine thee, so thou must thyself have resolved upon it inwardly; no one could reproach thee for not coming, it was thine own free will to come; thou didst not do it because others did it, for today the others went every one to his own field, to his business, to his labour—but thou didst come to the house of God, to the altar of the Lord.

And thereby thou hast given precise expression to the fact that thou dost reckon thyself among those who would belong to Christ, who are described in the words just read, taken from the Gospel where Christ likens Himself to the good shepherd, and the true believers to the sheep. Of these a triple affirmation is made: they hear His voice; He knows them; they follow Him.

They hear His voice. And today it is especially, it is solely and alone, His voice that shall be heard. Everything else performed here is merely for the sake of concentrating attention upon the fact that it is His voice we are to hear. Today there is no preaching: a penitential address is not a sermon; it does not aim to instruct thee, nor to enforce upon thee the old and well-known doctrines, it would merely give thee pause on the way to the altar, in order that through the voice of the speaker thou mayest confess unto thyself before God in secret. Today there is no preaching. What we say here in the brief moment prescribed is not, as I have said, a sermon; and when we have said Amen, the divine service is not, as is usually the case, essentially finished, but at that point it essentially begins.[1] Our discourse therefore would merely give thee pause for an instant on the way to the altar; for today divine worship is not focused as usual upon the pulpit but upon the altar. And at the altar what counts above everything else is to hear *His* voice. It is true that a sermon should also bear witness to Him, proclaiming His word and His teaching, but for all that a sermon is not *His* voice. At the altar, on the other hand, it is *His* voice thou shalt hear. Though another man were to say to thee what is said at the altar, if all men were to unite in saying it to thee—in case thou dost not hear *His* voice, thou hast come in vain to the altar. When by the Lord's minister at the altar every word is said precisely as it was handed down from the fathers; when thou hearest precisely every word so that there does not escape thee the least thing, not a tittle—in case thou dost not hear *His* voice, thou hast come in vain to the altar; though thou art seriously resolved to take it to heart and to order thy life accordingly—in case thou dost not hear *His* voice, thou hast come in vain to the altar. It must be *His* voice thou hearest when He says, 'Come hither, all ye that labour and are heavy laden', hence His voice that invites thee; and it must be His voice thou hearest when He says, 'This is my body.' For at the altar there is no talk about Him; *there* He Himself is personally present, it is He that speaks—if not, then thou art not at the altar. Physically understood, one can point to the altar and say, 'There it is'; but, spiritually understood, it is only really *there*, if *there* thou dost hear *His* voice.

He knows them. That is as much as to say, those who do not hear His voice He does not know; and those He does not know are none of His. For with Him it is not as with a man, who well may have a friend or an adherent without being aware of it and without knowing him; but he whom Christ does not know is none of His, for Christ is omniscient.—He knows them, and He knows them each severally. The sacrifice He made was not made in a general sort of way, nor would He save man in a general sort of way—indeed in such a way it cannot be done. No, He sacrificed Himself to save each severally. Should He not

---

[1] A recognition of the incongruity of *concluding* common worship with the sermon, instead of employing the sermon as a preparation for worship, which it is assumed to be by the Book of Common Prayer, which prescribes the sermon only at the beginning of the Liturgy.

therefore know each severally? One surely should know the man for whom one lays down one's life!—When on feast days the congregation assembles in countless numbers, then too He knows them, and those whom He does not know are none of His. However, on such an occasion one may easily deceive oneself, as though the individual were hidden in the crowd. On the other hand, at the altar, however many are assembled there, yea, though all were assembled at the altar, there is no crowd. He Himself is personally present, and He knows them that are His. He knows thee, whoever thou art, whether known to many or as unknown to all, in case thou art His, He knows thee. Oh, the profound seriousness of eternity, to be known by Him! Oh, blessed comfort, to be known by Him. Yea, if thou wert to flee unto the uttermost parts of the earth, He knows thee; if thou wert to hide thyself in the abyss, He knows thee—but there is no cause to flee, no cause to seek a hiding-place, this very thing is blessedness, that He knows thee. Yet whether He knows thee, no third person can know, that thou must know for thyself alone, with Him—but if He knows thee not, thou art none of His.

Behold, the sun rises upon the earth every morning at the dawn of day, its beams everywhere penetrate to every point, no place is so remote that the sun does not penetrate it with its rays; however, it makes no distinction in this knowledge it possesses of the earth, it shines equally everywhere and knows every place. But He, the eternal Sun of mankind, with His knowledge of mankind penetrates also like the beams of light everywhere, to every man; but He makes a distinction. For there are also those He does not know, those to whom He will say, 'I know you not, I never knew you', those to whom He will say this in spite of the fact that they affirm that they know Him!—If thou wert to go up to the altar of the Lord and take part in the sacred function, though thou couldst prove ever so certainly that thou hadst been to the altar, though the minister of the Lord were to bear witness on thy behalf that to thee in particular, as to each of the others, he had handed the bread and the wine—in case He knows thee not, thou didst go in vain to the altar. For physically one can point to the altar and say, 'Behold, there it is', but, spiritually understood, the altar is *there* only if thou art known by Him.

They follow Him. For thou dost not remain at the altar, and thou art not to remain there. Thou wilt return again to thy business, to thy labour, to the joy which perhaps awaits thee, ah, or to sorrow—all such things today thou hast for a moment laid aside —but in case thou art His, thou dost follow Him. And when thou dost follow Him, thou dost leave the altar indeed when thou goest away from it, but it is as though the altar were following thee, for where He is, there is the altar. Ah, solemn seriousness of eternity, that wherever thou goest, whatever thou dost undertake, He follows thee! Oh, marvellous combination, that the solemn seriousness of eternity is also the most blessed comfort! The altar doubtless stays in the same place, therefore thou goest to the altar; but only then is it the altar if *He is there*—so where He is, there is the altar. He Himself says, 'When thou art offering thy gift at the altar, and there rememberest that thine enemy hath aught against thee, go hence, first be reconciled to thine enemy, and then come and offer thy gift'—ah, what sacrifice dost thou think is dearest to Him, the sacrifice thou offerest by being reconciled with thine enemy, that is, by sacrificing thy wrath to God—or the gift thou couldst offer upon the altar? But if the sacrifice of reconciliation is dearest to God and to Christ, the altar also is *there* where the acceptable sacrifice is offered. Abel sacrificed upon the altar, but Cain did not, for God had not respect unto the sacrifice of Cain—hence it was an altar, but unto Cain's sacrifice God had not respect. Oh, do not forget that where He is, there is the altar, that His altar is neither upon Mount Moria, nor upon Gerazim, nor at any visible *there*, but that it is there where He is. If this were not the case, thou mightest indeed remain at the altar, erect thy dwelling there, never budge from the spot; but such superstition is not Christianity. Today is not a holy day, divine service is held on a workday—oh, but in a Christian's life every day is worship! It is not as though therewith everything were settled by going on rare occasions to the altar; no, the appointed task is, on leaving the altar still to remain at the altar. Today, as we said, everything contributes to concentrate the attention of the mind upon the altar. But when thou dost leave it, remember that the cause is not completed; oh, no, it is just begun, the good cause, or, as the Scripture says, the good work, which God who began it will perfect unto the day of our Lord Jesus Christ. Today, if, as may God grant, it has for thee the right importance, thou mightest well call it the day of Jesus Christ; but after all there is only one day which properly is called the day of Jesus Christ. This 'today', on the other hand, will soon be past. God grant that when it is long past and forgotten, the blessing of this day, many, many times recalled, may still be a fresh memory to thee, so that the remembrance of the blessing may be a blessing within thee.

> Strive then, O day, which never more
> Mine eye shall here in time behold,
> Recede into the shade of night!
> Onward I strive to heaven's realm,
> To see my God eternally,
> On this it is my faith I build.[1]

[1] I have not attempted to reproduce the rhymes of these verses, which conclude the fifth of the 'Morning Sighs' by the Danish poet Kingo.

PRAYER

Remind me, Jesu, yet again
Of all Thine anguish and distress,
Remind me of Thy soul's deep pain.[1]

Ah, it is true, our Lord and Saviour, that not even in this respect dare we rely upon our own strength, as though we were able of ourselves to recall impressively enough and to retain steadily this remembrance of Thee, we who would so much rather dwell upon the joyful side than upon the sorrowful, we who all of us desire for ourselves good days and the peace and security of happy times, we who prefer to remain unaware in a profounder sense of the dreadful things, lest, as we foolishly think, they might make our happy life gloomy and serious, or indeed Thine unhappy life, as we are prone to regard it, all too gloomy and serious. Hence we pray Thee, since it is Thee we are now to remember, that Thou wouldst Thyself remind us of these things. Oh, it is a strange language a man talks when it is with Thee he has to talk; it is as though it had become unserviceable when it has to express our relationship to Thee or Thine to us. What is that for a remembrance when he who is to be remembered must himself remind the rememberer! Humanly, it is only the man highly exalted and mighty, with so many and such important things to think about, who says to the lowly man, 'You must yourself remind me to remember you.' Ah, and it is this very thing we say to Thee, Thou Saviour and Redeemer of the world! Ah, and this same thing when we say it to Thee is precisely the expression of our lowliness and nothingness in comparison with Thee who art with God exalted above all heavens! We pray that Thou Thyself wilt remind us of Thy suffering and death, wilt remind us again and again, in our labour, in our joy, and in our sorrow, of the night in which Thou wast betrayed. For this we

[1] Lines of a familiar Danish hymn. It should be remembered that from his childhood S. K. was absorbed with the thought of Christ's sufferings. To no other subject does he so often recur, and he talks with genuine feeling.

make supplication, and we give Thee thanks when Thou dost remind us, and now we thank Thee in behalf of them who are here assembled to approach Thine altar in order to renew their fellowship with Thee.

1 Cor. xi. 23. . . . THE LORD JESUS, IN THE NIGHT IN WHICH HE WAS BETRAYED.

In the night in which He was betrayed. Let it then become night around about thee, for this is in keeping with the sacred function. You who are here assembled to participate in the Supper which was instituted that night in remembrance of our Lord Jesus Christ have surely prayed that He would bring vividly before your eyes His suffering and death. Oh, there are those perhaps who pray that it might be granted them to see what kings and princes desired in vain to see, one of the days of His glory—do not regret your choice, for verily he has chosen the better part who prays first and foremost that the dreadful scene might stand out vividly before his eyes.—In the night in which He was betrayed. Humanly speaking, what a retrogression this was for Him! For Him who at one time the people would have acclaimed king, for Him upon whom at a later time the high priests dared not lay hands because all the people clung to Him; for Him who by His mighty words had gathered countless hosts about Him; for Him before whose authority as teacher all had bowed, the Pharisees defiantly but under compulsion, the people gladly and expectantly—He now is cast out of the world, He sits in a retired room with the Twelve. But the lot has been cast, His fate has been determined by the counsel of the Father and of the high priests. When He rises from the table to go out into the night, He goes also to meet His death. Then begins the spectacle of horror for which everything was in readiness, then He must live through the past once more in horror's rendering of it, more dreadfully in a certain sense than at the first: He is to be acclaimed king, but in scorn; He is actually to wear the purple, but in mockery; He is to gather the people about Him in even greater numbers; but the high priests would not any more be afraid to lay hands upon Him, rather would they be compelled to restrain the hands of the people, so that it might appear as if He were sentenced to death; so it was a judicial process, He was seized 'as a thief' and crucified 'as a transgressor'! Thus was His life retrogression instead of advancement, the opposite of what the human mind naturally thinks and desires. For in worldly advancement a man climbs up rung by rung in honour and prestige and power, there are constantly more and more who espouse his cause, until he who was always in the majority, at last, admired by all, stands upon the topmost rung. But He climbed rung by rung downward, and still He climbed. Yet the truth must suffer thus . . . or be singled out in the world, as surely as He was the Truth. At the first moment the truth seems to please all; but the more explicit it gradually became, the clearer and more definite, the more decisive it was, the more the trappings of illusion fell off, so much the more did the many also fall off—at last He stands alone. But not even there did He remain standing; He now climbs from rung to rung, through all the grades of humiliation, until at the end He is crucified. At the end—yet the conclusion was not far off, for from the instant when the spectacle of horror began in the night in which He was betrayed the decisive moment is at hand with sudden promptness, as when in an instant a tempest darkens heaven and earth. This night is the turning point—and then what a change! Yet in a sense everything is the same. The place is the same, the same high priests, the same governor, the people are the same—yes, and He also is the same: when once they would acclaim Him king, he fled, and when they come armed to seize Him, He advances to meet them, saying, 'Whom seek ye?' No doubt He once with a kiss hailed Judas as an Apostle, nor does He refuse the kiss of Judas who, as He knows, would betray Him. Is He not the same?

Ah, my hearer, as a man sometimes has a day or a night he might wish out of his life, so the race might wish this night out of its history! For if it was dark at the midnight hour when He was born, the night in which He was betrayed was still darker! The race might well wish this night out of its history; for this is not an occurrence long past and done with; Christ's suffering we should not and dare not remember as we remember those glorious ones who suffered death innocently, of whom we say, 'That is now long past.' His innocent sacrifice is not passed though the cup of suffering has been drained, it is not a passed event even though it is passed, not an event passed and done with though it was eighteen hundred years ago, it has not become that even if it was eighteen hundred years ago. He did not die a natural death, neither was it by accident He came to His end, nor was it any individual that fell upon Him and slew Him, nor was it that generation which crucified Him; it was the human race, and to that we surely belong if in fact we are men, and so we are present at that scene if in fact we are men. Moreover, we dare not wash our hands—at least we cannot do it, except as Pilate did; we are not spectators and beholders of a past event, we are in fact accomplices in a contemporary event. Hence we do not imagine presumptuously that in a poetical way what is required of us is sympathy—it is indeed His blood that is required of us also who belong to the race. And even the follower who resembled Him most closely, who did not, as super-stition requires, bear His wounds upon his body, but whose life was also retrogression instead of advancement, who also, in correspondence with the Christian order of rank, climbed from rung to rung, derided, mocked, persecuted, crucified—even such a follower, when he remembers that night and it is quite vivid in his thought, even he is present as an accomplice! And when the congregation, as often as these words are uttered, closes around Him, anxiously but heartily, as though to ward off the betrayal, as though to promise faithfulness to Him, even if all others were to forsake Him—yet none dare forget that he was that night involved as an accomplice, none dare forget that lamentable pattern, which yet in other respects he hardly resembles, the Apostle Peter. Oh, we men, even if we are of the truth and are on 'the truth's' side, if we were to follow shoulder to shoulder with the man who is 'the Truth', when truth is the standard of measurement—we are but children alongside of a giant, we still at the moment of decision are . . . accomplices.

In the night in which He was betrayed. What crime has more likeness to the night than a betrayal? And what crime is more unlike love than a betrayal? Most of all, alas, when it is accom-plished with a kiss! Judas indeed is the traitor, but at bottom all are traitors, only not like him for money. Judas betrays Him to the high priests, and the high priests betray Him to the people, and the people betray Him to Pilate, and Pilate for fear of the Emperor betrays Him to death, and for fear of man those disciples do the same who flee in the night, and Peter who denies Him in the court. This was the last betrayal. Oh, when the last spark is extinguished, how dark it all is! Of the whole race there is not one, not a single man, who will have anything to do with Him— and *He is the Truth*! And, oh, if thou art inclined to think that thou wouldst never have done this, never have laid thy hand upon Him, never have taken part in the mockery—but as for betraying Him, that thou hast done: thou didst flee, or didst shrewdly remain at home, keeping thyself out of it, letting thy servant report to thee what happened. Oh, but to betray! Thou canst deal love no blow so painful. There is no pain, not even the most torturing bodily pain, at which love winces so feelingly as betrayal; for the greatest felicity of love is faithfulness.

Oh, that this occurred is for me enough to insure that I never can be joyful, lightheartedly in a worldly sense, as the natural man is, as the youth is in his inexperience, as the child is in his innocence. I need see no more, if indeed anything more dreadful has occurred in the world, anything that can more appal the heart—there may be that which can more appal the senses. Nor is there need that anything dreadful should befall me—for me this is enough: I have seen 'Love' betrayed, and I have understood something about myself, that I also am a man, and that to be a man is to be a sinful man. Not for this have I become a hater of men, least of all a hater of other men; but I never forget this night, nor what I have understood about myself. He whom the race crucified was the Redeemer; just for this cause do I, as belonging to the race, feel the need of a redeemer—never was the need of a redeemer clearer than when the race crucified the Redeemer. From this moment I no longer trust myself, I will not let myself be deceived, as though I were better because I was not tried like those contemporaries. No, fearful of myself as I have become, I will seek refuge in Him the Crucified. To Him will I pray that He will deliver me from the evil, and deliver me from myself. Only as saved by Him and in His company, when He holds me fast, do I know that I shall not betray Him. The dread which would frighten me away from Him is precisely what shall bind me to Him. How should I not dare to hope this when that which would frighten me away is precisely what rivets me to Him? I will not do such a thing, and I cannot do it, for He moves me irresistibly, I will not shut myself up within myself with this dread of myself without having confidence in Him; I will not shut myself up within myself with this dread or with this consciousness of guilt in having also betrayed Him—rather as guilty I will belong to Him as my Saviour. Ah, when He wandered in Judea He moved many by His beneficent miracles; but nailed to the cross He did a still greater miracle, He did the miracle of love, that without *doing* anything but by suffering He moves every one who has a heart.

He was betrayed—but He was Love: *in the night in which He was betrayed* He instituted the supper of love! Always the same! For those that crucified Him He prayed; and in the night in which He was betrayed He utilised the opportunity (oh, infinite depth of love which finds precisely this moment opportune!), He utilised the opportunity to institute the supper of reconciliation. Verily, He came not into the world to receive service without making requital. A woman anoints His head, and for requital she is remembered through all the centuries! Yea, He made requital for what people did against Him! They crucified Him—in requital, this death of His upon the cross is the sacrifice of propitiation for the sin of the world, also for this of crucifying Him! They betray Him—in requital He institutes the supper of reconciliation for all! If Peter had not denied Him, there would have been one man who had not quite in the same way as every other individual of the race a need of reconciliation. But now they all betrayed Him, and so they all needed to participate in the supper of reconciliation!

Behold, everything is now ready; blessed is he who for his part also is ready! Behold, He is waiting here at His holy table—so therefore do this in remembrance of Him, and in expectation of blessing to yourselves.

PRAYER

O LORD JESUS CHRIST, who didst first love us, who until the end didst love them whom Thou didst love from the beginning, who unto the end of days dost continue to love him who would belong to Thee; Thy faithfulness cannot deny itself—oh, only when a man denies thee can he compel Thee as it were to deny him also, Thou loving One. So be this our comfort when we must accuse ourselves of the offences we have committed and of the things we have left undone, of our weakness in temptation, of our slow progress in the good, in short, of our unfaithfulness to Thee, to whom once in early youth and ofttimes again we promised faithfulness—this be our comfort, that even if we are unfaithful, Thou dost remain faithful, Thou canst not deny Thyself.

2 Tim. ii. 12, 13. IF WE SHALL DENY HIM, HE ALSO WILL DENY US; IF WE ARE FAITHLESS, HE REMAINS FAITHFUL, FOR HE CANNOT DENY HIMSELF.

It might seem as if the sacred words just read contained a contradiction, and if such were the case it not only would seem but would be a strange thing to draw your attention to these words in particular. This, however, is by no means the case. The contradiction might be supposed to lie in the fact that in the one clause it is said that if we shall deny Him, He will also deny us, and in the other clause, that He cannot deny Himself. But might there be no difference between denying Him and being unfaithful to Him? On the one hand it is clear enough that one who denies Him is also unfaithful to Him, for no one can deny Him in the stricter sense unless he had belonged to Him; but from this it does not follow that every one who is unfaithful to Him also denies Him. Hence there is no contradiction. The one is the stern word, the other is the gentle word; so here we have the Law and the Gospel; but both words are the truth. Neither is there any duplicity in the words, but it is one and the same word of truth which separates men, as the eternal truth separates them, both in time and in eternity, into the good and the evil. It is as when it is related in the sacred story, that only when the Pharisees had gone away did Christ begin to speak privately with His disciples—so it is that the first word relegates to a distance, points away, alas, to the left hand as it were, those who deny, whom He also shall deny; the latter word, the gentle word of comfort is spoken as to those on the right hand. For He who charged His disciples not to cast their pearls before swine—His love, though it would save all, is not a weakness which is whimperingly in want of those that might be saved, but it is compassion towards every one who wants to be saved.

But you who are assembled here to participate in the holy Supper have surely not denied Him, or at any rate you are assembled here to confess Him, or by the very fact of assembling here for this purpose you do confess Him. Though it may be profitable that the stern word be brought to remembrance, be heard along with the other, as it certainly belongs with it, though we ought not to separate what God hath joined together in Christ, add anything to it, or take anything from it, from gentleness take away severity which is in it, from the Gospel take away the Law which is in it, from salvation take away perdition which is in it; yet surely it is the latter word which is pre-eminently appropriate for us to dwell upon today. We allow the dreadful aspect to pass unnoticed, not as though it were irrelevant to us; oh, no, so long as he lives no man is saved in such a way that it would not be possible for him to be lost. As long as there is life there is hope—but as long as there is life there is also the possibility of danger, and so of fear; so long therefore shall there be fear and trembling. We let the dreadful aspect pass unnoticed; but we hope to God we dare let it pass us by while we comfort ourselves with the gentle word of the Gospel.

He abideth faithful. So in thy relationship with Him thou hast one concern the less, or rather one blessedness more than it is possible any man could ever have in his relationship with another man. In the relationship between two, every individual, humanly speaking, has constantly a double concern: he has it for himself, that he may now remain faithful; ah, but at the same time he is concerned lest the other may not remain faithful. But He, Jesus Christ, remains faithful. Hence in this relationship the peace and blessedness of eternity is complete, thou hast only one concern, the concern for thyself, that thou mayest remain faithful—

for He remains eternally faithful. Oh, surely there is no love completely fortunate except the love a man has for God, and no faithfulness completely blessed except the faithfulness with which a man attaches himself to Christ. Everything, absolutely everything God does is profitable to thee; thou hast no need to fear that anything might have escaped Him which might have been to thy profit, for only He knows what is profitable to thee; thou hast no need to fear lest thou mightest not be able to make thyself understood by Him, for He knows thee completely, far better than thou knowest thyself; thou hast only (oh, infinite felicity of love!), thou hast only to rejoice in His love—to be silent and give thanks! To be silent and give thanks; yes, for when thou art silent thou dost understand Him, and most of all when thou art completely silent; and when thou dost give thanks He understands thee, and most of all when thou art continually giving thanks. So fortunate is that love with which a man loves God. But so it is also with the faithfulness which attaches itself to Christ. Oh, in every man's soul there dwells a secret dread lest even he whom he trusted most might become unfaithful to him. No merely human love can completely drive out this dread, which may indeed remain hidden and unobserved in the security of a fortunate love-relationship, but which nevertheless may sometimes stir inexplicably, and which when the storms of life begin is suddenly present. There is only One whose faithfulness can drive away this dread; yea, though every other faithfulness were to fail, He still remains faithful every day of thy life, whatever may befall thee; He remains faithful to thee in death; He meets thee again in the world to come like a faithful friend. In thy relationship with Him thou hast no cause for concern about His faithfulness; thou never shouldst, nay, thou darest never be visited by this dread that when thou hast given thyself to Him, led thy whole life in Him, He might eventually become unfaithful to thee. No, strengthened by the certainty of eternity with regard to His faithfulness, thou hast (and this also is His gift) more abundant strength to employ all means in order to be faithful to Him. Thou art not as in other cases required to labour with anxious thoughts in two places at once; He by his faithfulness for which He eternally vouches will make thee unconcerned, will reassure thee, support thee, but then in turn by such faithfulness He will prompt thee to remain faithful to Him.

If we are faithless—He abideth faithful. So in thy relationship
with Him thou hast one concern the less, or rather one blessedness more than it is possible any man could ever have in relationship with another man. For in the relationship between two, in
case the one were to be faithless, but yet repented his unfaithfulness and turned back again—alas, his faithlessness might perhaps
have had the effect of so changing the other that he could not
make up his mind to forgive him. But He, our Lord Jesus
Christ, remains faithful to Himself. Indeed it would be presumptuous and blasphemous if any one were to suppose that by
his unfaithfulness he had power to change Him, power to make
Him less loving than He was, or rather than He is. But it would
also be ungodly if any one were to take His faithfulness in vain.
Thou shalt not take the name of the Lord thy God in vain; ah,
but beware also of taking His faithfulness in vain, so as to bring
it down as a punishment upon thyself. For as His unalterable
faithfulness means pardon to the penitent, does it not also imply
a curse upon him who hardens himself and impotently defies God?

Even if we are faithless, yet He remains faithful. When He
wandered here upon earth no sufferer came to Him without finding help, no troubled person went away from Him uncomforted,
not even did a sick person touch the border of His garment
without being healed (Mark vi. 56)—but if one had come the
seventieth time beseeching forgiveness for his unfaithfulness,
dost thou believe He would have become weary, or even if it had
been seven times seventy? No, sooner shall heaven be tired of
bearing the stars and shall cast them away. Oh, blessed thought
that there is after all one faithful, one trusty friend, and that (oh,
blessed thought, if indeed a man dare entertain such a thought
which is all the more blessed for its timerity) to the penitent, to
the unfaithful, He is the faithful friend! Alas, perfect faithfulness is never found in the world—assuming that one were justified in seeking it in others; but perfect faithfulness towards
unfaithfulness is found only with our heavenly Teacher and
Friend—and that we all have need to seek. Yea, if it were possible that Thou, our Teacher and Saviour, mightest some day
become weary of our continual protestations of faithfulness,
these protestations which doubtless are not hypocritical or
fictitious, but which to Thee must so often, or always, seem so
weak and childish, if Thou couldst have the heart for once to

put our faithfulness seriously to the test, if Thou wouldst throw
us out into the current, as teachers commonly do with their pupils,
and wert to say, 'Now I will give thee no help at all but merely
test thy faithfulness—with that we should instantly be lost! Oh,
this human language of ours is but a poor thing, capable only of
expressing half truth, when it is used to indicate our relationship
to the Deity. Even when we talk in the strongest terms about
God testing us, this talk is meaningless if the meaning is not
implied that essentially God is holding on to us. When we see a
mother playing the game with her child that the child is walking
alone, although the mother holds on to it behind—and then when
we behold the indescribable look on the child's face radiant with
joy, that look of contentment with itself and its manly bearing,
then we smile, for we see the whole situation. But when we ourselves talk about our relationship with God, this thing of walking
alone is taken with the utmost seriousness, and we talk in the
strongest terms of God laying His hand heavily upon us, as if He
were actually employing His hand for no other purpose, or as if
He had not two hands, so that, even at such a moment, with the
one hand He is holding on to us. Therefore verily we do not
presume to require of Thee, our Teacher and Saviour, that Thou
shouldst put to the test our faithfulness to Thee; for we know
well that at the moment of testing, Thou Thyself must hold on
to us, that is, we know that at bottom we are unfaithful, and that
every instant it is Thou *at bottom* that holdest us.

My hearers, you are today assembled here to renew your vows
of faithfulness. But what path have you taken to reach your
destination. It passes through confession. Is not this a detour?
Why dost thou not go straight to the altar? Oh, even if it were
not prescribed by sacred custom, wouldst thou not feel the need
of taking that path to the altar? The shrift will not impose upon
thee the guilty burden of unfaithfulness, on the contrary it will
help thee through confession to lay aside the burden. Shrift
would not compel thee to make confession, on the contrary it
would ease thee through confession; in the confessional there is
no one to accuse thee in case thou dost not accuse thyself. My
hearer, what the priest said in the confessional was heard by you
all; but what thou didst say to thyself no one knew but thou who
didst say it and God who heard it. After all, it is not the priest
that is to go to the altar, but it is thou; neither was it the priest

that confessed, he did not even confess thee, but it was thou that didst make confession before God in secret.[1] This God has heard, but what God has heard, that has been heard also by Him whom thou goest to meet at the altar. Hast thou forgotten something, or hast thou deceitfully forgotten something, ah, that God knows, and that He too knows whom thou goest to meet at the altar? For far be it from us even to essay with this discourse to rehearse as it were all the disloyalties with which a man may have to reproach himself, which moreover are so exceedingly various. No, according to the sacred custom of our Church this is left to thy honesty towards God. But yet reflect that even if the time which has elapsed since last thou didst renew thy fellowship was what men might humbly call a better season—ah, how much unfaithfulness there was place for in thy relationship with Him to whom thou didst not promise faithfulness in one single matter, neither in this nor in that, but absolutely in everything! Ah, who knows himself! Is it not precisely to this that all serious and honest self-examination leads as to the last and surest result, to this humble confession, 'Who can understand his errors: cleanse Thou me from secret faults' (Ps. xix. 12)? And when a man examines his relationship to Christ, who is it then that entirely understands his unfaithfulness? Who is the man that would dare to maintain that again in self-examination there might not be unfaithfulness? In this way therefore thou dost find no repose. Repose then, seek rest for thy soul in the blessed comfort that even though we are faithless, He still is faithful.

He cannot deny Himself. No, He with His love cannot shut Himself up within Himself, He who out of love gave Himself up for the world. But he who shuts himself up within himself and will have nothing to do with others does in fact deny himself. He denies himself to visitors, and if thou wert to make him a visit and wert to succeed in seeing him, thou wilt in vain seek to grasp his hand, for he withdraws it, he denies himself, thou wilt in vain seek an expression of sympathy in his attitude, for he withdraws himself and denies himself. But He, our Lord Jesus Christ, does not deny Himself, He cannot deny Himself. Behold, therefore, He spreads out His arms here at the altar, He bares His breast for all; thou dost behold it in His attitude,

---

[1] The Lutheran confession is not auricular confession—not confession into the ear of the priest.

He does not deny Himself. He does not deny Himself, neither does He deny what thou prayest Him for when thou art renewing thy loyalty to Him. He is the same: He was faithful to thee, and He abideth faithful.

PRAYER

GREAT art Thou, O God; though it is in a dark saying we know Thee and as in a mirror, yet we adore Thy greatness with wonder—how much more must we one day extol it when we learn to know it more fully! When I stand under the dome of heaven, surrounded by the marvels of creation, I extol Thy greatness with a heart deeply stirred to adoration for Thee who dost easily support the stars in infinite space and with fatherly care dost concern Thyself with the sparrow. But when we are assembled here in Thy holy house we are everywhere surrounded with that which in a deeper sense reminds us of Thy greatness. For great art Thou, the Creator and Sustainer of the world; but when Thou, O God, didst forgive the sin of the world and didst reconcile Thyself with the fallen race, ah, then Thou wast still greater in Thine inconceivable compassion! How could we then but with faith render unto Thee praise and thanksgiving and adoration in Thy holy house where everything reminds us of this, and reminds especially those who today are assembled to receive the forgiveness of sins [1] and to appropriate to themselves anew the reconciliation with Thee in Jesus Christ?

I John iii. 20. . . . THOUGH OUR HEART CONDEMN US, GOD IS GREATER THAN OUR HEART.

Even though our heart condemn us. When the Pharisees and scribes had brought into the Temple a woman who was apprehended openly in sin in order to accuse her before Christ, and when they, put to shame by His reply, had all gone away, Christ said unto her, 'Did no one condemn thee?' but she said, 'No one, Lord.' So there was no one that condemned her. So it is also in this sanctuary, there is no one that condemns thee; whether thy heart condemns thee, thou alone must know. No other man dare know it; for this other man also is concerned today with his own heart, whether it condemns him. Whether thy heart condemns

---

[1] In these discourses it is often evident that in the Lutheran view the Holy Communion was regarded predominantly as an experience of forgiveness.

thee is something which concerns no other man; for this other man also has only to do with his own heart, with its condemning or acquitting thoughts. How thou dost feel at hearing these words read, 'though our heart condemn us', is no business of any other man; for this other man also devoutly refers everything to himself, thinks only of how he felt, whether the words took him by surprise as a sudden thought, or he heard, alas, what he had said to himself, or he heard what he thought had no application to him. For it may be that a heart accuses itself, but from this it does not follow that it condemns itself; and we are not inculcating melancholy exaggeration, any more than we are inculcating frivolous absolution and indulgence. But when one has to speak upon the words which have just been read, where might one find better hearers than on such a day as this, and among such as have come hither today, not from the distractions of the world, but from the spiritual collectedness of the confessional where each one severally has made an accounting with God, where each one severally has let his heart be the accuser, which it well may be, for it is an accessory, and as it had better be in good time, lest one day it might become an accuser against a man's will. There is a difference between guilt and guilt,[1] there is a difference between owing five hundred shillings and fifty; one man may have far more to reproach himself with than another, there may be one who says to himself that his heart condemns him; perhaps there may be such a man here present, or perhaps there is no one of the sort here present—but comfort we all of us need. And it cannot well be discomforting for any one that the word of comfort is so rich in compassion that it includes every one, this cannot surely be discomforting to any one, even though his heart does not condemn him. After all, it is essentially the same comfort we all have need of: God's greatness, that He is greater than our heart.

God's greatness lies in forgiving, in showing mercy, and in this greatness He is greater than the heart which condemns itself. Behold, this is that greatness of God which we have to speak of especially within the sanctuary; for here we know God differently, more closely—from the other side, if one may say so—than out there, where doubtless He is revealed, is to be known in His works, whereas here He is to be known as He has revealed Himself, as He would be known by Christians. The tokens by which God's

---

[1] In Danish the same word serves for 'guilt' and 'debt'.

greatness can be known in nature every one can behold with
wonder, or rather there is no special token, for the works themselves are the tokens; thus every one can see the rainbow and
must wonder when he sees it. But the token of God's greatness
in showing mercy exists only *for faith*; this token is in fact the
Sacrament. God's greatness in nature is *manifest*, but God's
greatness in showing mercy is a *secret* which has to be believed.
Precisely because it is not directly manifest to every one it is
called and is *revelation*. God's greatness in nature awakens at once
amazement, and then *adoration*; God's greatness in showing mercy
is first a stumbling-block, and then it is *for faith*. When God had
created all things, He saw, and, lo, 'it was very good'; and along
with every work of His there stands inscribed as it were: *Extol,
praise, adore the Creator*. But along with His greatness in showing mercy stands: *Blessed is he who is not offended*.

All our talk about God is of course human talk. However
much we may strive to prevent misunderstanding by withdrawing again what we have asserted—if we would not be completely
silent, we must after all employ the human measuring-rod when
we as men talk about God. What then is the true greatness of
man? Surely it is greatness of heart, we do not rightly say that a
man is great who has much power and dominion; yea, if there
were living or had lived a king whose sovereignty extended over
the whole earth—however hasty amazement may be to call him
at once great, the deeper man will not let himself be misled by
external circumstance. And on the other hand, though it were
the lowliest man that ever lived—when thou art a witness of his
actions at a decisive moment, seeing that in truth he acts nobly,
forgives his enemies magnanimously with his whole heart, makes
the utmost sacrifice self-denyingly, or when thou art a witness of
the inward forbearance with which he lovingly endures evil from
year to year, then thou dost say, 'For all that, he is great, he is
truly great.' So greatness of heart is the true human greatness;
but greatness of heart is precisely this, to overcome oneself in love.

So then, if we, being men, would form a conception of God's
greatness, we must think of the true human greatness, that is, of
love, and of the love which forgives and shows mercy. But what
does this signify? Might the meaning be that we would compare
God with man, even with the noblest man, the purest, the most
compassionate, the most loving man that ever lived? Far from it.

Neither does the Apostle speak in this sense. He does not say that God is greater than the most loving man, but that He is greater than the heart which condemns itself. So then God and man resemble one another only inversely. It is not by the steps of direct resemblance—great, greater, greatest—thou dost attain the possibility of comparison, it is possible to attain it only conversely; neither is it by lifting up his head more and more that a man approaches closer and closer to God, but conversely, by throwing himself down more and more deeply in adoration. The contrite heart which condemns itself cannot get, seeks in vain to find, a term strong enough to express its guilt, its wretchedness, its defilement—still greater is God in showing mercy! Strange comparison! All human purity, all human mercy, is unfit for comparison; but the penitent heart which condemns itself—it is with this the Apostle compares God's greatness in showing mercy, only that it is greater. Deeply as the heart can abase itself, and yet never deeply enough to satisfy it, just in that measure is God's greatness infinitely exalted, or infinitely more exalted, in showing mercy. Lo, language as it were bursts and cracks under the strain of expressing God's greatness in showing mercy; thought was seeking in vain for a comparison, then finally it discovered it in what humanly speaking is no comparison, the contrition of a penitent heart—still greater is God's compassion. A penitent heart, when in contrition it condemns itself—yea, this heart allowed itself no rest, not for a single instant, it found no hiding-place where it might flee from itself, it found no excuse possible, rather it found it to be a new and the most terrible fault to seek an excuse, it found no assuagement, even the most compassionate word which the most heartfelt of all compassion was able to invent sounded, to this heart which dared not wish to be comforted, like a new condemnation upon it—so infinite is God's greatness in showing mercy, or it is still greater. This holds good, this comparison—it is the comparison a man always makes after he has striven with God. It is far-fetched, this comparison—without doubt, for it was found and fetched from afar after rejecting with godly fear all human comparison. If man dare not make unto himself any image of God, then he certainly cannot imagine that the human might furnish a direct comparison. Let no one be hasty in seeking, no one be precipitate in willing to find a comparison for God's greatness in showing mercy; every mouth shall be stopped, and every man shall smite upon his breast—for there is only one comparison which is in any way adequate: a fearful heart which condemns itself.

But God is greater than this heart! So then be comforted. Perhaps thou hast had occasion earlier to learn from experience how hard a thing it is with such a heart to be brought before the judgement of Pharisees and scribes, or to encounter the misunderstanding which knows only how to bruise it more and more, or the narrow-mindedness which constricts the heart still more straitly, O thou who in so high a degree didst stand in need of one who was great. God in heaven is greater; He is not greater than the Pharisees and scribes, not greater than misunderstanding and narrow-mindedness, not greater than the man who yet knew how to speak an assuaging word to thee, with whom thou didst find some solace, because he was not narrow-minded, would not depress thee even more, but would raise thee up—God is not greater than he (comfortless comparison!), no, God is greater than thine own heart! Oh, whether it was a sickness of the soul which every night so darkened thy mind that at last with deathly anguish, brought near to madness by the apprehension of God's holiness, thou didst feel that thou must condemn thyself, whatever the dreadful thing was which so weighed upon thy conscience that thy heart condemned thee—God is greater! Wilt thou not believe, dost thou not dare to believe without seeing signs? Well, they are presented. He who came to earth to die, died also for thee. He did not die for men in a general sort of way; oh, exactly the contrary, He died for some one in particular, not for the ninety and nine—and, alas, thou art too wretched to be reckoned vaguely in the round number, upon thee falls the emphasis of wretchedness and guilt so dreadfully that thou art counted apart. And He who died for thee when thou wast a stranger, might He forsake His own? If God so loved the world that He gave His only begotten Son that no one might be lost, how should He not preserve them that were bought with a price? Oh, torture not thyself; if they are the fears of melancholy that ensnare thee, God knows all, and He is great! And if it is the heavy weight of guilt which rests upon thee like a ton, He who (as it never entered into the heart of man to believe) had compassion upon the world—He is great! Do not torment thyself, remember that woman, that there was no one to condemn her, and reflect that the same thing can also be expressed in another way: Christ was present. Just because He was present, there was therefore no one who condemned her. He delivered her from the condemnation of the Pharisees and the scribes; they went away ashamed, for Christ was present: there was no one that condemned her. So Christ alone remained with her—but there was no one that condemned her. Just the fact that He alone remained with her signifies in a far deeper sense that there is no one that condemns her. It would have helped her but little that the Pharisees and the scribes went away, they might indeed have come again with their condemnation. But the Saviour remained alone with her: therefore there was no one that condemned her. Ah, there is only one guilt God cannot forgive, that is, not being willing to believe in His greatness!

For He is greater than the heart which condemns itself. But on the other hand, nothing is stated about His being greater than the worldly, frivolous, trifling heart which foolishly counts upon God's fancied greatness in forgiving. No, God can be just as precise in reckoning as He is great and can be great in showing mercy. Thus it is that God's nature always unites contrary aspects, just as in that miracle of the five small loaves. The people had nothing to eat—by a miracle abundance is provided; but, lo, Christ thereupon bids them gather up every scrap that was left over. How divine! For one man may squander, and another be thrifty; but in case there were a man who by a miracle could every instant . . . provide abundance, dost thou not believe that he . . . humanly would have despised the scraps, dost thou believe that he . . . divinely would have gathered up the scraps? So it is also with God's greatness in showing mercy, a man has hardly a bare notion how precise God can be. Let us not deceive ourselves, not lie to ourselves, and, what is the same thing, diminish God's greatness, by wanting to make ourselves out better than we are, less guilty, or by calling our sins by a more frivolous name, for thereby we diminish God's greatness in forgiving. But neither let us be mad enough to sin still more so as to make forgiveness even greater; for God is equally great in being precise in His reckoning.

And so let us here in Thy holy house praise Thy greatness, O God, who incomprehensibly didst show mercy and didst reconcile the world unto Thyself. Behold, outside the stars proclaim Thy majesty, the perfection of all proclaims Thy greatness; but here within it is the imperfect, the sinner, that extols Thy still greater greatness!—The supper of remembrance is again ready, so here within be Thou remembered and be praised for Thy greatness in showing mercy.

PRAYER

Thou who didst come down from heaven to bring a blessing to the fallen race; Thou who didst wander here upon earth, unappreciated, betrayed, mocked, condemned—but blessing; Thou who in the act of blessing wast parted from Thine own as Thou didst ascend again into heaven, Thou our Saviour and Redeemer, bless also to them that today are here assembled their participation in the holy Supper in remembrance of Thee. Oh, if at every meal something is wanting in case the blessing is lacking, what then might be this holy meal of grace without Thy blessing? It would not even exist, for it is indeed the supper of blessing!

Luke xxiv. 51. And it came to pass, while He blessed them, He parted from them.

'While He blessed them, He parted from them.' These words give an account of His ascension, He parted from them 'and was carried up into heaven' (Luke xxiv. 51), 'a cloud received Him out of their sight' (Acts i. 9), but the blessing remained behind; they beheld Him no more, but they were sensible of the blessing; 'they looked stedfastly towards heaven' (Acts i. 10), for He parted from them *with a blessing*. But so it is He always parts from His own, with a blessing; ah, and so it is He always comes to His own, with a blessing; and so abiding with His own He is always blessing. In no other way does He part from any one, unless this man himself bears the dreadful responsibility for it. As that forefather of the Jewish people said when he strove with God, 'I will not let Thee go unless Thou bless me'—so likewise says He, 'I will not leave thee without blessing thee; and every time thou dost visit me again I will not part from thee without blessing thee.' When they who are assembled here to meet with Him return home from this meeting, they are greeted with the wish that it may be for their blessing, for they are convinced that when they parted from Him, or He parted from them, He blessed them.

My hearers, whatever a man is about to undertake, whether the work be great and important, or lowly and unimportant, he is able to accomplish nothing if God give not His blessing. The builder labours but in vain if God give not His blessing, in vain does the wise man ponder if God give not His blessing, in vain does the rich man gather abundance if God give not His blessing; for it is true either way you take it, that when one has abundance it is the blessing which satisfies with contentment, and it is the blessing which transforms poverty into abundance. But is it true then that no labour succeeds and prospers unless God blesses it? Ah, how often one may see an undertaking succeed, even in an extraordinary degree, although God certainly did not bless it! Yes, thus it is, and hence we must say that he who would . . . have the aid of God's blessing merely in order that, humanly speaking, his undertaking may succeed, does not pray worthily, he does not clearly comprehend what he prays for, or he may even presume to will that God should serve him instead of himself serving God. No, the blessing is the Good in itself, is the one thing needful, is infinitely more glorious and blessed than all success. What then is the blessing? The blessing is God's consent that the undertaking which one prays God to bless may be undertaken. And what does it signify that a man prays for the blessing? It signifies that he consecrates himself and the undertaking to God's service—regardless of whether it succeeds and prospers or no. Hence we must say that every godly undertaking is in vain if God does not bless it, for only when God blesses it is it a godly undertaking.

Doubtless every undertaking may be and ought to be a godly undertaking; but the more decisively it is a godly undertaking in the stricter sense, and the more clearly a man is conscious that it is a godly undertaking he has in hand, with all the greater clearness also, and all the more deeply, does he feel that he needs the blessing, that the undertaking is in vain if God does not bless it. Accordingly, it is a godly undertaking to engage in prayer; but is not this then the thought that comes first to the prayerful man, not that God will grant his petition, but that He will bless his prayer, so that it may be or become the right prayer? What does a man pray for? For the blessing—but first and foremost this means the blessing of prayer or a blessing upon the prayer. It is a godly undertaking to go up to the house of the Lord; but is not this also the thought that comes first of all, that it may be a blessing? What is it a man seeks in the house of God? A blessing—

but first and foremost this means that God will 'bless thine in-coming', as the pious phrase has it. The clearer it becomes that it is a godly action thou hast in hand, in that same degree does the need of the blessing become clear to thee; for the more thou art concerned with God, the clearer it becomes how much less thou thyself art able to do. If with all thy mind and with all thy strength thou art concerned with Him, then it becomes entirely clear that thou thyself art not able to do anything whatever, and it becomes clear that thou art entirely in need of the blessing.

But to go to the altar is surely a holy action in the strictest sense, a godly undertaking. Thou art going to the altar—it is for this holy action ye are today assembled here. Thou art going to the altar to meet Him for whom thou dost long more ardently every time thou art parted from Him. But if thou, as a man, art nothing before God and therefore needy—at the altar, as a sinner in relation to the Redeemer, thou art less than nothing, and so all the more deeply dost thou feel the need of the blessing. At the altar thou art able to do nothing. And yet precisely at the altar it is a question of satisfaction to be made for guilt and sin, for thy guilt and thy sin. All the more necessary it is that thou shouldst be able to do something; and the more this necessity is made clear, whilst thou art able to do nothing, all the clearer it becomes then, and all the more clearly dost thou understand it, that thou art able to do less than nothing—but all the clearer also is the need of the blessing, or that the blessing is everything. At the altar thou art able to do nothing whatever.[1] Satisfaction is made . . . but by another, the sacrifice is offered . . . but by another, the redemption is accomplished . . . but by the Redeemer!—all the clearer it is that the blessing is everything and does all. At the altar thou art able to do less than nothing. At the altar it is thou that art sin's insolvent debtor, thou that by sin art separated from God, thou that art so infinitely far off, thou that hast for-

---

[1] It needs to be said somewhere that all this insistence upon human impotence is prompted not merely by the fact that it is a distinctive feature of Lutheran doctrine, but by the undue stress the Danish parsons were accustomed to lay upon this dogma 'on Sundays'. Here S. K. deals seriously with man's impotence; but in the *Postscript*, in a long passage which he describes as 'an edifying diversion' (§ 2 under Section ii. of Chapter 4, in Part Second of Division II.—pp. 458 ff. of the 2nd Danish edition) he deals humorously with the extravagant assertion of the parson and the hypocritical acceptance of the people, 'on Sunday', of the dictum that 'a man can do nothing at all'.

feited all, thou that darest not stand boldly forth—it is another that paid the debt, another that made reconciliation, another that brought thee near to God, another that suffered and died to restore everything, another that stands forth in thy behalf. If at the altar thou wert able to do the least thing, even were it merely to stand boldly forth, thou wouldst derange everything, prevent reconciliation, make impossible the satisfaction. At the altar it is in place to say, as was said to that ungodly man who in a storm called upon heaven for help,[1] 'Hush! Don't let God know you are present!' All depends upon the presence of another, upon whom God looks, instead of looking upon thee, another upon whom thou dost reckon because thou art only a subtraction. At the altar therefore He is present with a blessing, He who parted from His own with a blessing, He to whom thou art in the same relation as the tender infant whom He took up in His arms and blessed, He who is thy Saviour and Redeemer. Him thou canst not meet before the altar as a fellow-worker, as in thy work thou canst meet God as a fellow-worker. The fellow-worker with Christ in relation to the atonement thou canst not be, not in the remotest way. Thou art wholly in debt, He wholly makes satisfaction. So much the clearer it is that the blessing is everything. For what is the blessing? The blessing is what God does; everything that God does is the blessing. The share of the work with reference to which thou callest thyself a fellow-worker is the share God does, that is the blessing. But at the altar Christ is the blessing. The divine work of reconciliation is Christ's work, and in relation to that man can do only less than nothing—so then the blessing is everything. But if the work is Christ's, then Christ is the blessing.

At the altar thou art able to do nothing whatever, not even to hold fast the thought of thine unworthiness, and by that to make thyself susceptive of the blessing. Or wouldst thou dare, even though it were at the last instant as thou art stepping up to the altar, wouldst thou dare, even though it only had to do with the thought which recognizes its own unworthiness, wouldst thou dare to vouch to thyself for it that thou wouldst be able to ward off every disturbing reflection, every anxious thought of recollection which, alas, wounds from behind, every suddenly awakened distrust which turns against thee as though thou wert not yet

[1] Said by the wise Bias in Diogenes Laertius, I. 5.

completely prepared, every fleeting conceit of self-assurance? Oh, no, thou art able to do nothing whatever, not even to keep thy soul alert to the consciousness that thou art completely in need of grace and blessing. As another supported Moses when he prayed, so must thou at the altar be supported by the blessing when thou art to receive the blessing, it must support thee in its embrace while it is imparted to thee. The priest who is present at the altar is not able to impart to thee the blessing, nor to support thee; only He is able to do it who is personally present, He who not merely imparts but is the blessing. He Himself is present, He blesses the bread when it is broken, it is His blessing in the chalice which is handed to thee. But it is not merely the gifts that are blest, but thou, in partaking of the bread and the wine, dost partake of the blessing, and properly this is the Supper. Only He who instituted this Supper can prepare it—for at the altar He is the blessing.

Behold, therefore, He spreads out His arms yonder at the altar, He inclines His head towards thee . . . in blessing! Thus it is He is present at the altar. Then thou dost part from Him again, or He again departs from thee . . . but with a blessing. God grant that the good wish may be verified, and that to thee it may be a blessing.

THE LILIES OF THE FIELD AND THE BIRDS OF THE AIR

THREE GODLY DISCOURSES

by
S. KIERKEGAARD

Copenhagen
1849

PREFACE

This little book (which in view of the circumstances [1] under which it is issued reminds me of my first, and more especially of the first to my first, the Preface to the *Two Edifying Discourses* of 1843,[2] which came out immediately after *Either/Or*) will, as I hope, recall this to 'that single individual whom I with joy and gratitude call *my* reader': 'it desires to remain in retirement, as it was in concealment it had its origin—a little flower in the cover of a great forest.' Of this he will be reminded by the circumstances; and I hope moreover that it will remind him, as it does me, of the Preface to the *Two Edifying Discourses* of 1844: 'it is offered with the right hand'—in contrast to the pseudonyms, which were handed out and are still handed out with the left.

5th of May 1849.   S. K.

---

[1] These *Three Godly Discourses* were issued to 'accompany' the second edition of *Either/Or*.

[2] The Preface to the *Two Edifying Discourses* of 1843 is translated in my *Kierkegaard*, pp. 272 f.

It bears the date of May 5, S. K's birthday. Note that again, six years later, he dated the preface on his birthday—just ninety years before the date on which I finished the translation of this volume and signed my preface to it, on May 5, 1939.

PRAYER

Father in heaven! What one in society with men, especially there in the human swarm, with so much difficulty learns to know, and what, in case one has elsewhere learned to know it, is so easily forgotten in society with men, namely, what it is to be man, and what in a godly understanding of it is the requirement for being man—oh, that we might learn this, or, if it is forgotten, that we again might learn it from the lilies and the birds; that we might learn it, if not all at once and all in all, yet at least something of it, and little by little; that at this time we might from the lilies and the birds learn silence, obedience, joy!

No man can serve two masters: for either he will hate the one and love the other; or else he will hold to the one, and despise the other. Ye cannot serve God and mammon. Therefore I say unto you, Be not anxious for your life, what ye shall eat, or what ye shall drink; nor yet for your body, what ye shall put on. Is not the life more than food, and the body than raiment? Behold the birds of the heaven, that they sow not, neither do they reap, nor gather into barns; and your heavenly Father feedeth them. Are not ye of much more value than they? And which of you by being anxious can add one cubit unto the measure of his life? And why are ye anxious concerning raiment? Consider the lilies of the field, how they grow; they toil not, neither do they spin: yet I say unto you, that even Solomon in all his glory was not arrayed like one of these. But if God doth so clothe the grass of the field, which today is, and tomorrow is cast into the oven, shall he not much more clothe you, O ye of little faith? Be not therefore anxious, saying, What shall we eat? or What shall we drink? or Wherewithal shall we be clothed? For after all these things do the Gentiles seek; for your heavenly Father knoweth that ye have need of all these things. But seek ye first his kingdom and his righteousness; and all these things shall be added unto you. Be not therefore anxious for the morrow; for the morrow will be anxious for itself. Sufficient unto the day is the evil thereof.

I

'BEHOLD THE BIRDS OF THE AIR; CONSIDER THE LILIES OF THE
FIELD'

BUT thou wilt say perhaps with the 'poet', and thou art
immensely pleased when the poet talks thus: 'Oh, would
I were a bird, or would I were like a bird, like a free bird
which gratifies its *Wanderlust* by flying far, far away over sea and
land, so near to heaven, unto distant climes—ah, poor me, who
feel only too much bound to the spot, bound and nailed there,
where I am the mark of daily cares and sufferings and adversities,
compelled to dwell there, and for the whole duration of my life!
Oh, would I were a bird, or would I were like a bird, which rises
into the air lighter than the air itself, oh, would I were like the
airy bird which when it lacks a footing can build its nest upon the
surface of the sea—while I, alas, with every slightest movement,
even when I merely turn upon my bed, feel how gravity weighs
me down! Oh, would I were a bird, or would I were like a bird,
free from all concern, like the little song-bird that sings so
humbly, notwithstanding no one listens, or which sings . . . so
proudly, notwithstanding no one listens—while I, alas, have not
an instant to myself but am distracted by a thousand concerns!
Oh, would I were a flower, or would I were like the flower of the
field, happily in love with myself, and with that enough said—
alas for me, who feel in my own heart also the all-too-human-
hearted discord, neither to be able in self-love to break with all
else, not to be able in love to sacrifice all.'

Thus the poet. Cursorily hearing this, it sounds almost as if he
said what the Gospel says, when he employs the strongest expressions to extol the happiness of birds and lilies. But hear him
farther. 'Therefore it comes near to being a cruelty on the part of
the Gospel to extol the lilies and the birds and say, Thou shalt
be such as these—alas for me in whom this wish is so real, so real,
so real—oh, would I were like a bird of the air or like a lily of the
field. But that I might become such a thing is indeed an impossibility; just for this reason is the wish so hearty in me, so tenderly
sad and so ardent. How cruel then of the Gospel to talk to me

thus, it is as though it would compel me to lose my senses by saying that I *must* be what I am not and cannot be. I cannot understand the Gospel; between us there is a difference of language
which would kill me if I could understand it.'

And so it always is with the poet in relation to the Gospel; it is
the same likewise with regard to the saying of the Gospel about
being a child. 'Oh, would I were a child,' says the poet, 'or would
I were like a child; ah, a child, innocent and happy; alas for me,
who only become old and guilty and sorrowful!'

This is strange, for one says indeed rightly that the poet is a
child. And yet the poet cannot come to an understanding with
the Gospel. For at bottom the poet's life is despair of being able
to become the thing he wishes; and this despair begets 'the wish'.
But the wish is the invention of disconsolateness. For it is true
that the wish consoles for an instant, but upon closer inspection
it is nevertheless evident that it does not console; and hence we
say that the wish is the consolation which disconsolateness invents. Strange self-contradiction! Yes, but the poet himself is
this same contradiction. The poet is the child of pain, whom the
father calls son of joy. It is in pain that the wish arises in the poet;
and this wish, this ardent wish, gladdens man's heart more than
wine cheers it, more than the first star, which one who is weary of
the day gladly hails in longing for the night, more than the last
star in the heavens, of which one takes leave as the day dawns.
The poet is the child of eternity, but he lacks the seriousness of
eternity. When he thinks of the birds and the lilies he weeps, and
in spite of weeping he finds in weeping relief, the wish comes into
being, and with it the eloquence of the wish: 'Oh, would I were
a bird, the bird I read of as a child in the picture-book; oh, would
I were a flower of the field, the flower that stood in my mother's
garden.' But if one were to say to him in accordance with the
Gospel, 'This is seriousness, precisely this is seriousness, that the
bird seriously is a teacher,' then the poet might laugh—and he
makes jest of the birds and the lilies, so wittily that he makes us
all laugh, even the most serious man that ever lived would have
to laugh; but he does not affect the Gospel in this way. So serious
is the Gospel that all the poet's sadness does not change it, as even
the most serious man is changed by it, so that for an instant he
yields, enters into the poet's thought, sighs with him and says,
'My dear fellow, if that really is an impossibility for thee, well

then, I dare not say to thee, "Thou shalt." ' But the Gospel dares to command the poet that he *shall* be as the birds. And so serious is the Gospel that the poet's most irresistible invention does not avail to make it smile.

Thou shalt become a child again, and therefore, or to this end, thou shalt begin by being able and willing to understand the word which is as though coined for the child, and which every child understands, this word thou shalt understand as the child understands it: the word, 'Thou *shalt*.' The child never asks for reasons, this the child dare not do, nor has it any need to ask for reasons; it is reason enough for the child that it shall; yea, all the reasons united would not to the same extent be reason enough for the child. And the child never says, 'I cannot.' This the child dare not say, nor is it true—the one thing corresponds perfectly with the other: for just because the child dare not say, I cannot,' therefore it is not at all true that it cannot, and hence it appears that the truth is that it can, for it is impossible not to be able to do a thing when one dare not do otherwise, nothing is more certain—it only depends upon whether it is certain that one cannot do otherwise.[1] And the child never seeks evasions or excuses; for the child understands with frightful realism that for it there is no evasion or excuse, that there is no hiding-place, either in heaven or on earth, either in the parlour or in the garden, where it could hide from the 'Thou shalt'. And when one is quite certain that there is no such hiding-place, then there is no attempt at evasion or excuse. And when one knows with frightful realism that there is no evasion or excuse—then, well then one naturally forgoes finding it, for what does not exist is not to be found—but one also forgoes the seeking of it; and so one does what one 'shall'. And the child never requires long deliberation; for when it 'shall', and perhaps at once, there is no opportunity for deliberation; and even if this opportunity were not lacking, when nevertheless it 'shall'—yea, even if one were to give it an eternity for deliberation, the child would have no need of it, the child would say, 'What is the use of all this time, if nevertheless I have to do it?' And if the child were to take time, it would employ the time in another way, in play, in pleasure, and so forth; for what the

---

[1] Whether this is sound logic or not, it expresses a feeling very characteristic of S. K., who affirmed that it had never entered his head that anything might be impossible to him—except escape from his melancholy.

child shall do is a thing that stands fast and has nothing whatever
to do with deliberation.[1]

So in accordance with the directions of the Gospel let us consider seriously the lilies and the birds as teachers. Seriously, for
the Gospel is not so spiritually exalted that it can have no use for
the lilies and the birds; but neither is it so earthly that it can
consider the lilies and the birds only with a sad face or with a
smile.

From the lilies and the birds as teachers let us learn

SILENCE, or learn TO BE SILENT.

For no doubt it is speech which distinguishes man above the
beasts, and hence, if one so will, very far above the lilies. But
because it is an advantage to be able to speak, it does not follow
that to be able to keep silent is no art, or that it is a humble art.
On the contrary, just because a man is able to speak, it is an art
to be able to keep silent; and just because this advantage of man
is so easily a temptation to him, it is a great art to be able to keep
silent. But this we may learn from the silent teachers, the lilies
and the birds.

'SEEK YE FIRST GOD'S KINGDOM AND HIS RIGHTEOUSNESS.'

But what does this mean, what have I to do, or what sort of
effort is it that can be said to seek or pursue the kingdom of God?
Shall I try to get a job suitable to my talents and powers in order
thereby to exert an influence? No, thou shalt *first* seek God's
kingdom. Shall I then give all my fortune to the poor? No, thou
shalt *first* seek God's kingdom. Shall I then go out to proclaim
this teaching to the world? No, thou shalt *first* seek God's kingdom. But then in a certain sense it is nothing I shall do.
Yes, certainly, in a certain sense it is nothing; thou shalt in
the deepest sense make thyself nothing, become nothing before
God, learn to keep silent; in this silence is the beginning, which
is, *first* to seek God's kingdom.

In this wise, a godly wise, one gets to the beginning by going,
in a sense, backwards. The beginning is not that with which one
begins, but at which one arrives, and one arrives at the beginning
backwards. The beginning is this art of *becoming* silent; for to be

[1] In affirming of the child that it 'never . . .' S. K. surely means 'hardly ever'—
or rather he would describe what is characteristic of the child.

silent, as nature is, is not an art. And to become thus silent in the deepest sense, silent directly before God, is the beginning of godly fear, for as the fear of God is the beginning of wisdom, so is silence the beginning of godly fear. And as the fear of God is more than the beginning of wisdom, or rather is wisdom, so is silence more than the beginning of godly fear, it is godly fear. In this silence the many thoughts of wish and desire are rendered mute by godly fear, in this silence the prolix eloquence of thanksgiving is rendered mute by godly fear.

It is man's superiority over the beast to be able to speak; but in relation to God it can easily become the ruin of man who is able to speak that he is too willing to speak. God is in heaven, man upon earth—therefore they cannot well talk together. What man knows is idle chatter, therefore they cannot well talk together. God is love, man is (as one says to a child) a silly little thing, even so far as his own wellbeing is concerned. Only in much fear and trembling can a man talk with God; in much fear and trembling. But to talk in much fear and trembling is difficult for a further reason; for as a sense of dread causes the bodily voice to fail, so also does much fear and trembling render the voice mute in silence. This the true man of prayer knows well, and he who was not the true man of prayer learned perhaps precisely this by praying. There was something which lay so close to his heart, a matter of so much consequence to him, it was so important that he should make God understand him, he was afraid that in his prayer he might forget something; ah, and if he had forgotten it, he was afraid that God might not Himself remember it—therefore he would collect himself to pray right earnestly. And what happened then?—in case he did indeed pray right earnestly. The surprising happened to him. In proportion as he became more and more earnest in prayer, he had less and less to say, and in the end he became quite silent. He became silent—indeed, what is if possible still more expressly the opposite of speaking, he became a hearer. He had supposed that to pray is to speak; he learnt that to pray is not merely to be silent but to hear. And so it is; to pray is not to hear oneself speak, but it is to be silent, and to remain silent, to wait, until the man who prays hears God.

Hence it is that the word of the Gospel, 'Seek *first* God's kingdom,' as though by way of education seals man's mouth by replying to every single question he asks as to whether it is 'this' he is to do, with a 'No, thou shalt seek *first* God's kingdom.' And hence it is that one can paraphrase this word of the Gospel thus: Thou shalt begin by praying. Not as though prayer always began with silence (which we have seen is not the case), but when prayer has really become prayer it has become silence. Seek first God's kingdom—that means, Pray! In case thou dost ask—yea, though in asking thou wert to traverse every single possibility, inquiring if it is 'this' that I shall do, and if I do it, is this then to seek God's kingdom?—the answer must be, No, thou shalt first seek God's kingdom. But to pray, that is, to pray aright, is to become silent, and that is to seek first God's kingdom.

This silence thou canst learn from the lilies and the birds. That is to say, their silence is no art, but when thou becomest silent like the lilies and the birds, thou art at the beginning, which is *first* to seek God's kingdom.

How solemn it is out there under God's heaven with the lilies and the birds. And why? Ask the poet. He replies, 'Because there is silence.' And he longs for this solemn silence, far away from worldliness in the human world where there is so much talk, far away from all the worldly human life, which only in a sorry way gives proof that man by speech distinguishes himself above the beasts. 'For,' as the poet will say, 'is this indeed to distinguish oneself? No, I much prefer the silence out there; I prefer it, indeed it distinguishes itself infinitely above men who are able to talk.' In this silence of nature the poet believes he is able to apprehend God's voice, but not at all to apprehend that man has kinship with God. The poet says, 'Speech is man's advantage over the beasts—yes, true enough . . . in case he is able to keep silent.'

But to be able to keep silent is something thou canst learn out there with the lilies and the birds, where there is silence, and where there is something divine in this silence. And there there is silence; and that not only when everything holds its peace in the silent night, but also when day is vibrating with a thousand notes and all is like a sea of sound, there still is silence out there; each one in particular does its part so well that no one of them breaks the solemn silence, and not all of them together. The forest is silent; even when it whispers it still is silent; for the trees, even when they are most closely crowded together, hold to one another, as men so seldom do, in spite of plighted promises— this being said between ourselves. The sea is silent; even when it rages noisily, it yet is silent. In the first instant thou hearest perhaps amiss, and thou hearest it make a noise. In case thou art in haste to carry this report, thou dost do the sea an injustice. On the other hand, if thou wilt give thyself time and listen more attentively, thou dost hear—how amazing!—thou dost hear silence; for after all uniformity also is silence. In the evening, when silence broods over the countryside and thou from the meadow dost hear the distant lowing, or far from the farmer's house dost hear the dog's domestic voice—one cannot say that this lowing or this voice disturbs the silence; no, this belongs to silence, is in mysterious but again in silent accord with silence.

And let us now consider more closely the lilies and the birds from whom we are to learn. The bird is *silent* and *waits*: it knows, or rather it firmly believes, that everything occurs in its season, hence the bird waits; but it knows that it is not for it to know the time or the day, hence it keeps silent. It will yet occur in due time, says the bird—yet no, the bird does not say this, it keeps silent, but its silence is eloquent, and this silence says that it believes this, and because it believes this it keeps silent and waits.[1] Then when the instant is come, the silent bird understands that it is the instant, it employs it, and it never is put to shame. So likewise with the lily, it keeps silent and waits. It does not ask impatiently, 'When is spring coming?' For it knows that it comes in due time, it knows that for itself it would be far from serviceable if it were allowed to determine the season of the year. It does not say, 'When are we going to have rain?' or 'When are we going to have sunshine?' or 'Now we've got too much rain', or 'Now the heat is too great'; it does not ask beforehand what sort of a summer it will be this year, how long or how short; it keeps silent and waits—so simpleminded it is, but yet it is never deceived, that being a thing which can happen only to shrewdness, not to simplicity, which neither deceives nor is deceived. Then comes the instant, and then the silent lily understands that now is the instant, and employs it. O ye profound teachers of simplicity! But might it not also be possible when one speaks to hit upon 'the instant'? No, only by keeping silent does one hit upon the instant; while one is talking, though one says only a word, one

[1] *Tier og bier* is the Danish, and it is awkward to have to translate these two short words by 'Keeps silent and waits'.

misses the instant. And hence it so seldom happens that man succeeds in understanding when it is the instant, and in rightly employing the instant, because he cannot keep silent. He cannot keep silent and wait, and perhaps this explains why for him the instant never arrives; he cannot keep silence and wait, and perhaps this explains why he did not notice the instant when it came for him. For the instant, although it is pregnant with rich significance, sends no messenger before it to announce its arrival, it comes too suddenly for that, when it comes there is not an instant's time before its coming; nor, however significant the instant is in itself, does it come with noise and outcry; no, it comes quietly, with lighter step than any creature's lightest tread, for it comes with the light step of the sudden, it comes stealing upon one, therefore one must be quite silent if one is to sense that 'now it is there'; and the next instant it is gone, therefore one must have been quite silent if one is to succeed in employing it. But yet everything depends upon the instant. And this doubtless is the misfortune in the lives of the great majority of men, that they never sense the instant, that in their lives the eternal and the temporal are merely separate things.[1] And why? Because they could not keep silent.

The bird is *silent* and *suffers*. However much heartache it has, it keeps silent. Even the melancholy elegiac bird of the desert and of loneliness is silent: it sighs thrice, and thereupon falls silent, it sighs again thrice; but essentially it is silent. For what it is that ails it, it does not say, it does not complain of anything, it does not reproach any one, it sighs in order to be silent again. It is as if silence would burst it, hence it must sigh for the sake of being able to keep silent. The bird is by no means exempted from suffering; but the silent bird exempts itself from that which makes suffering harder, the misapprehending sympathy of others, from that which makes suffering more protracted, the much talk about suffering, from that which makes suffering more than suffering, the sin of impatience and acidia. For do not suppose that it is merely a piece of duplicity on the part of the bird that it is silent when it suffers, that in its inmost parts, however silent it is with others, it does not keep silent, that it bewails its fate,

[1] S. K. said of 'the instant' that 'it is not an atom of time, but an atom of eternity', i.e. it is eternity tangential to time, time and eternity for an instant united—not 'separate'.

complains of God and man, and lets 'the heart sin in sorrow'.[1]
No, the bird keeps silent and waits. Alas, man does not do that.
But how comes it that human suffering, as compared with that of
the birds, is so frightful? Is it not for the reason that man is able
to talk? No, not for this reason, for this is indeed an advantage,
but for the reason that man is not able to keep silent. For it is not
as the impatient man is inclined to understand it, and still more
vehemently the man in despair, when he says or shrieks (and this
already is an abuse of speech and voice), 'Would that I had a voice
like that of the tempest, that I might give utterance to all my
sufferings as I feel them!' Ah, that would be but a foolish remedy,
for in that very degree he would feel them the more. No, but if
thou wert able to keep silent, if thou hadst the silence of the bird,
the sufferings would surely be less.

And like the bird, the lily also keeps silent. Though it suffers
when it fades, it keeps silent; the innocent child is unable to
dissemble (nor is this required of it, and it is its good fortune that
it cannot, for verily the art of being able to dissemble is dearly
bought),[2] it cannot dissemble, it cannot help changing colour and
thereby betraying that it suffers, as one can detect by the pallid
change of colour; but still it keeps silent. It would fain hold itself
erect to conceal the fact that it suffers, but its strength is not equal
to this, it has not so much mastery over itself, its head sinks and
is languidly bowed down, and the passer-by (if he has so much
sympathy that he observes it) understands what this signifies, it
is eloquent enough; but the lily keeps silent. But how comes it
that human suffering, as compared with that of the lily, seems so
frightful? Is it not for the reason that the lily is unable to talk?
And if (like man, alas!) it had not learnt the art of silence, would
not then its sufferings also be frightful? Suffering for the lily is
simply suffering, neither more nor less. But precisely when
suffering is neither more nor less than suffering, is suffering as
far as possible narrowed down and simplified and made as small
as possible. Less than this, suffering cannot become, for it nevertheless is, and is what it is. But on the other hand, suffering can
become endlessly greater when it is not exactly neither more nor
less than it is. When suffering is neither more nor less, that is,

---

[1] Quoted from a Danish hymn.

[2] Even as a child S. K. was skilled in the art of dissimulation, and for him it was
an art 'dearly bought'.

when it is merely that definite thing which it is, then, even though it were the greatest suffering, it is the least that it can be. But when it becomes indefinite, however great the suffering really is, this indefiniteness increases the suffering endlessly. And this indefiniteness emerges precisely with man's ambiguous advantage of being able to talk. On the other hand, the definiteness of suffering, the experience that it is neither more nor less than it is, is attained only by being able to keep silent; and this silence thou canst learn from the birds and the lilies.

Out there with the lilies and the birds there is silence. But what does this silence express? It expresses reverence before God, that it is He who disposes, and He alone, to whom belongeth wisdom and understanding. And just because this silence is reverence before God, it is (so far as it can be in nature) worship. Just for this reason is the silence so solemn. And because this silence is so solemn, therefore it is that one senses God in nature —what wonder indeed when everything keeps silent in reverence before Him! Even if *He* does not speak, the fact that everything keeps silent in reverence before Him affects one as if He were speaking.

That which thou, however, without the aid of any poet canst learn from the silence out there in company with the lilies and the birds, that which only the Gospel can teach thee, is that this is seriousness, that it must be taken seriously, that the birds and the lilies *shall* be thy teachers, that thou shalt imitate them, learn of them, quite seriously, that thou shalt be silent like the lilies and the birds. And already this is seriousness (when it is rightly understood, and not as the dreaming poet understands it, who lets nature dream around him), this fact, that out there with the lilies and the birds thou dost sense that *thou art before God*, a fact which is generally so entirely forgotten in speech and conversation with other men. For when there are two of us only that talk together, not to say ten or more, it is so easily forgotten that thou and I, we two, or we ten, are before God. But the lily who is the teacher is profound. It does not enter into conversation with thee, it keeps silent, and by keeping silent it would signify to thee that thou art before God, that thou shouldst remember that thou art before God—that thou also in seriousness and truth mightest become silent before God.

And silent before God like the lily and the bird thou *shalt* become. Thou shalt not say, 'Of course the birds and the lilies keep silent, they are unable indeed to talk.' This thou shalt not say, thou shalt in fact say absolutely nothing, not make even the least attempt to render impossible the instruction in silence by foolishly and senselessly (instead of being serious about keeping silence) mixing up silence with speech, perhaps as the subject of speech, so that there is no trace of silence, but on the contrary a speech comes into existence . . . about being silent. Thou shalt before God not be more self-important than a lily or a bird—yet indeed if there is truth and seriousness in the experience that thou art before God, the latter will follow from the former. And although what thou wouldst accomplish in the world were the most astonishing achievement—thou shalt recognize the lilies and the birds as thy teachers, and shalt not become before God more self-important than the lilies and the birds. And although the whole world were not big enough to contain thy plans when thou wouldst unfold them—from the lilies and the birds as teachers thou shalt learn before God to be able to fold up all thy plans together very simply in what requires less room than a point and makes less fuss than the most insignificant trifle—in silence. And although what thou didst suffer in this world were more agonizing than has ever been experienced—thou shalt recognize the lilies and the birds as thy teachers and not become more self-important than are the lilies and the birds in their little sorrows.

So it is when the Gospel takes seriously the thought that the birds and the lilies are to be teachers. It is otherwise with the poet, or with the man who, just for lack of seriousness, in the silence amongst the lilies and the birds does not become perfectly silent . . . but becomes a poet. For it is true that poet-speech is different exceedingly from common human speech, is so solemn that in comparison with common human speech it is almost like silence, but nevertheless it is not silence. Nor does the silence of the poet seek to be dumb, but on the contrary it seeks to express itself in speech . . . as a poet speaks. In the silence out there the poet dreams of achievement which however he never carries out (for the poet is not a hero); and he becomes eloquent (perhaps he becomes eloquent precisely because he is the unfortunate lover of achievement, whereas the hero is the fortunate lover, that is, because the regret makes him eloquent, as it is regret which essentially makes the poet), he becomes eloquent; this eloquence of his is the poem. Out there in the silence he devises great plans to transform the world and render it blissful, great plans which never are realized—no, they become in fact the poem. And there in the silence he broods over his pain, lets everything (yes, even the teachers, birds and lilies, must serve him instead of teaching him), he lets everything echo his pain; and the echo of this pain is the poem; for a mere scream is not a poem, but the endless echo of the scream within itself, that is the poem.

So the poet is never silent in the silence with the lilies and the birds—and why not? Just because he inverts the relationship, thinks himself the more essential thing in comparison with the lilies and the birds, imagines that he has, as the phrase goes, rendered a service to the birds and the lilies by lending them words and speech, whereas his task was to learn silence from the lilies and the birds.

Ah, if only the Gospel might succeed with the aid of the lilies and the birds in teaching thee, my hearer, seriousness, and me too, in making thee perfectly silent before God! That thou in silence mightest forget thyself, what thy name is, thine own name, the renowned name, the pitiful name, the insignificant name, for the sake of praying in silence to God, 'Hallowed be *Thy* name!' That thou in silence mightest forget thyself, thy plans, the great, the all-comprehensive plans, or the petty plans regarding thy life and its future, for the sake of praying in silence to God, '*Thy* kingdom come!' That thou in silence mightest forget thy will, thy self-will, for the sake of praying in silence to God, '*Thy* will be done!' Yea, if thou couldst learn from the lilies and the birds to become perfectly silent before God, what might not the Gospel help thee to accomplish, then nothing would be impossible for thee! But if only the Gospel with the aid of the lilies and the birds has taught thee silence, how much has it already helped thee to accomplish! For, as has been said, the fear of God is the beginning of wisdom, and so is silence the beginning of godly fear. Go to the ant and be wise, says Solomon; go to the birds and the lilies and learn silence, says the Gospel.

'Seek ye *first* the kingdom of God and his righteousness.' But the expression for the fact that one seeks first God's kingdom is precisely silence like that of the lilies and the birds. The lilies and the birds seek God's kingdom and nothing else whatsoever, all the rest will be added unto them. But then are they seeking

God's kingdom *first* when they seek nothing else whatsoever? How comes it then that the Gospel says, 'Seek *first* God's kingdom,' and thereby seems to mean that there was something else to seek subsequently, in spite of the fact that it evidently is the meaning of the Gospel that God's kingdom is the only thing that is to be sought? This surely is due to the fact that God's kingdom only can be sought when it is sought first; he who does not seek God's kingdom first does not seek it at all. It is due moreover to the fact that being able to seek implies the possibility of being able to seek something else; and hence the Gospel, which for the time being is extraneous to man, who thus can seek something else, must say, 'God's kingdom thou shalt seek first.' And finally it is due to the fact that the Gospel gently and lovingly condescends to man, talks to him so mildly in order to entice him to choose the good. If the Gospel were to say at once, 'Thou shalt solely and only seek God's kingdom,' this would surely seem to man to be requiring too much, half impatiently and half fearfully he would draw back. But now the Gospel accommodates itself to him a little. There stands man with the many things before his eyes which he would seek—then the Gospel addresses him and says, 'Seek first God's kingdom.' Then man thinks, 'All right, if afterwards I am permitted to seek something else, I may as well begin by seeking God's kingdom.' If then he really begins with this, the Gospel knows very well what the consequence will be, namely, that he will become so content and satisfied with this seeking that he entirely forgets to seek anything else—so that it now becomes true that he seeks solely and only God's kingdom. So does the Gospel behave, and so indeed do the parents speak to a child. Imagine a child who is very hungry; when the mother sets the food on the table, and the child catches a sight of what is placed there, then the child is on the point of tears and says, 'What does that little bit amount to? When I have eaten that I shall be just as hungry as ever.' Perhaps the child becomes so impatient that it will not even begin to eat, 'because that little bit can't be worth while.' But the mother, knowing very well that this is all a misunderstanding, says, 'Well, well, my little friend, first eat this now, and then we can always manage to get a little more.' So the child sets to work—and what happens? The child is sated before the half is eaten. If the mother had rebuked the child and said, 'It is really more than enough,' she would not have been in the wrong, but she would not by her behaviour have given example of the wisdom which is characteristic of good child-training, as in fact she now did. So it is with the Gospel. The most important thing with the Gospel is not to scold and rebuke, what is most important with the Gospel is to get men to follow it. Hence it says 'Seek first'. Thereby it stops the mouth, so to speak, of all man's objections, brings him to silence, and gets him actually to begin with this seeking; and then this seeking so satisfies man that it becomes true that he seeks solely and only God's kingdom.

Seek first God's kingdom, that is, become like the lilies and the birds, that is, become perfectly silent—then shall the rest be added unto you.

II

'No man can serve two masters; for either he will love the one and hate the other, or else he will hold to the one and despise the other'

My hearer. Thou knowest that in the world there is often talk about an either/or; and this either/or awakens a great sensation, engages the attention of various persons in the most various ways, in hope, in fear, in busy activity, in tense inactivity, etc. Thou knowest also that in the same world there is heard talk about there being no either/or, and the assertion that this wisdom[1] has made just as much sensation as the most significant either/or. But out there in the silence with the lilies and the birds, could it be doubtful whether there is an either/or, or could it there be doubtful what this either/or is, or could it there be doubtful whether this either/or is not in the deepest sense the only either/or?

No, here in this solemn silence, not only under God's heaven, but in the solemn silence before God, there can be no doubt about it. There is an either/or: either God/or . . . the rest is indifferent. Whatsoever a man chooses, when he does not choose God, he has missed either/or, or he is in perdition with his either/or. So then: either *God/*. Thou seest that no stress falls upon the second term, except by reason of opposition to God, whereby the stress is laid infinitely upon God, so that properly it is God who, as Himself the object of the choice, makes the decision tense, so that the choice becomes truly an either/or. If in lightmindedness or melancholy a man could think that where God is involved as one of the choices there are nevertheless three things to choose amongst—he is lost, or he has lost God, and therefore for him there really is no either/or at all; for along with God, when the idea of God vanishes or is jumbled, the either/or also vanishes. But how could this happen to any one in the silence with the lilies and the birds?

So then, either/or: either God—and that in the way the Gospel explains it, either to love God/*or* to hate Him. Oh, yes, when

---

[1] Hegelianism.

there is noise all around thee, or when thou art in a mood of distraction, this seems to be almost an exaggeration, there seems to be too great a distance between loving and hating to justify one in approaching them so near to one another, in one breath, in a single thought, in two words, without intervening clauses, without a word being interjected to effect a closer agreement, the one following upon the other immediately without the slightest sign of separation. But just as in a vacuum a body falls with infinite velocity, so does the silence, the silence out there with the lilies and the birds, the solemn silence before God, bring it about that these two contraries touch and repel one another in one and the same instant, yea, they come into existence in the same instant: either love/or hate. Just as little as there is in the vacuum a third factor which retards the falling body, just so little is there in this solemn silence before God a third factor which could hold hating and loving at a distance which retards their approach.—Either God/—and that as the Gospel explains it: either hold to Him or despise Him. In the society of men, in common dealings, in intercourse with the many, there seems to lie a great distance between holding to a man and despising him. 'I do not need to have intercourse with that person,' some one says, 'but from this it does not by any means follow that I despise him.' And so it is also in the case of intercourse with the many with whom one has to do 'socially', without essential cordiality, and with more or less indifference. But the smaller the number is, so much the less social, in the conventional sense, does this intercourse become; that is to say, the more cordial the intercourse becomes, so much the more does either/or begin to be the law for the relationship; and intercourse with God is in the deepest sense and absolutely nonsocial. Take merely the case of two lovers, a relationship which also is non-social just because it is so cordial—for them and for their relationship the rule holds good: either we hold to one another/or despise one another. And now, in the solemn silence before God with the lilies and the birds, where accordingly there is nobody at all present, where accordingly there is no other intercourse for thee but with God—there indeed the rule holds good: either hold to Him/or despise Him. There is no excuse, for no one else is present, in any case no one is present in such a wise that thou canst hold to him without despising God; for precisely there in the silence it is clear how close God is to thee. The two

lovers are so close to one another that the one, so long as the other
lives, cannot hold to any one else without *despising* the other.
Herein consists whatever there may be of either/or in this relationship. For the question whether there exists this either/or
(either hold to/or despise) depends upon how close the two are to
one another. But God who never dies is still closer to thee,
infinitely closer, than two lovers are to one another, He who is
thy Creator and thy supporter, He in whom thou dost live and
move and have thy being, He by whose grace thou dost receive
everything. So there is no exaggeration in this notion of either
holding to God/or despising Him; it is not as when a person
introduces either/or for a trivial reason, a person of whom it can
therefore be justly said that he is captious. It is not so here. For
in the first place, God after all is God. And in the second place,
He does not introduce this with reference to things indifferent—
either a rose/or a tulip. But He introduces it with reference to
Himself and says, Either me—either thou holdest to me, and that
unconditionally and in every case/or thou dost . . . despise me.
Surely God could not speak otherwise about Himself. If God
were to speak or could speak of Himself as if He were not absolutely No. 1, as if He were not the only one, absolutely everything, but merely another something or another, one who in-
dulged the hope that he also might perhaps be taken into account
along with other things—in such a case God would have lost
Himself, lost the notion of what He is, and He would not be
God.

So then, in the silence with the lilies and the birds there is an
either/or, either God/—and one which is to be thus understood:
either hold to Him/or . . . despise Him.

What then does this either/or signify? what does God demand?
For either/or is a demand—as indeed the lovers demand love
when one says to the other, Either/or. But God is not related to
thee as a lover, neither art thou related to Him as a lover. The
relationship is a different one: that of the creature to the Creator.
What then does He demand by this either/or? He demands
obedience, unconditional obedience. If thou art not obedient in
everything unconditionally, then thou lovest Him not, and if
thou lovest Him not—then thou dost hate Him; if thou art not
obedient in everything unconditionally, then thou holdest not to
Him, or if thou holdest not to Him in everything unconditionally,

then thou holdest not to Him then . . . thou dost despise Him.

This unconditional obedience (corresponding to the formula that if a man does not love God, he hates Him, and if he does not hold to him unconditionally and in all respects, he despises Him), this unconditional obedience thou canst learn from the teachers which the Gospel indicates, from the lilies and the birds. By learning to obey, one learns to rule, it is said; but still more certain it is that by being oneself obedient one can learn obedience from oneself. So it is with the lilies and the birds. They have no power to compel the learner, they have only their own obedience as the compulsive force. Lilies and birds are 'the obedient teachers'. Is not this a strange expression? 'Obedient' is the word one ordinarily employs for the pupil, of whom it is required that he must be obedient; but here it is the teacher himself that must be obedient! And in what subject does he give instruction? In obedience. And by what means does he impart this instruction? By obedience. If thou couldst become as obedient as the lilies and the birds, thou wouldst also by obedience be able to learn obedience from thyself. But since thou surely art not so obedient, nor I, let us from the lilies and the birds learn:

OBEDIENCE.

Out there with the lilies and the birds there is silence, we said. But this silence, or to be silent, as we sought to learn from it, is the first prerequisite for being able truly to obey. When all around thee is solemn silence, as out there, and when there is silence within thee, then thou dost apprehend, and apprehend with the emphasis of inwardness, the truth of the saying, 'Thou shalt love the Lord thy God, and him only shalt thou serve,' and thou dost apprehend that it is 'thou', thou who shalt love God, thou, thou alone in the whole world, thou who art alone in the environment of the solemn silence, so alone that every doubt, and every objection, and every excuse, and every evasion, and every question, in short, every voice, is reduced to silence in thine own inward man, every voice, that is to say, every other voice but God's, which about thee and within thee talks to thee by means of the silence. If there never were such silence about thee and within thee, thou never didst learn or dost learn obedience.

Give heed then to nature around thee. In nature all is obedience, unconditional obedience. Here 'God's will is done, as in heaven, so on earth', or, if some one translates the sacred words in another fashion, they are just as applicable: here in nature 'God's will is done, on earth as it is in heaven'. In nature all is unconditional obedience; here it is not merely (as also it is in the human world) that because God is the Almighty, therefore nothing comes to pass, not the least thing even, without His will; no, here it is at the same time because all is unconditional obedience. But this surely is an infinite difference; for it is one thing that not the most cowardly and not the most defiant human disobedience, that not the disobedience of the individual, nor that of the whole race, can do even the least thing against the will of Him who is the Almighty—and it is another thing that His will is done because everything obeys Him unconditionally, because there is no other will but His in heaven or on earth; and this is the case in nature. In nature it is true, as the Scripture says, that 'not one sparrow falls to the ground without His will', and that not merely because He is almighty, but because all is unconditional obedience, His will the only will: there is not even the least protest, not a word, not a sigh is heard; the absolutely obedient sparrow falls absolutely obedient to the ground because it is His will. In nature all is unconditional obedience. The soughing of the wind, the echo of the forest, the purling of the brook, the humming of summer, the whispering of the leaves, the whistle of the grass, every sound, every sound thou hearest is all assent,[1] unconditional obedience, so that in it thou canst hear God, as thou canst hear Him in the music which is the movement of the heavenly bodies in obedience. And the mettlesome force of the rushing wind, and the easy pliancy of the cloud, and the liquid fluidity of the sea and its consistency, and the swiftness of light, and the still greater swiftness of lightning—it is all obedience. And the sun's rising on the stroke of the clock, and its setting on the stroke of the clock, and the shifting of the weather as upon a signal, and the alteration of the rising and the ebbing tide at definite times, and the correspondence of the seasons in their precise changes—all, all of it, and altogether, is obedience. Yea, if there were a star in heaven which would have its own will, or a grain of dust upon the earth—in that same instant they are both

---

[1] Here there is a play on words which cannot be rendered. In Danish, *Lyd* is sound, *Adlyden* is assent, *Lydighed* is obedience.

brought to naught, and with the same ease. For nature so understood is all of it naught, it is nothing else but unconditionally God's will; the very instant it is not unconditionally God's will it has ceased to exist.

So let us consider more closely, and humanly, the lilies and the birds, in order to learn obedience. The lilies and the birds are unconditionally obedient to God. Herein they are masters. They understand, as beseemeth schoolmasters, masterfully to hit the unconditional—which, alas, most men miss and fail to hit. For there is one thing the lilies and the birds absolutely do not understand, namely, half-measures—which, alas, most men understand best. That a little disobedience, that this might not be absolute disobedience, is something the lilies and the birds cannot and will not understand. That the least, the very least disobedience, might in truth have any other name than . . . contempt of God—that the lilies and the birds cannot and will not understand. That there might be something else, or some one else, which one with divided heart *also* might serve besides God, and that this might not . . . also be to despise God—that the lilies and the birds cannot and will not understand. Marvellous sureness in hitting the mark and in having one's life in the unconditional! And yet—O ye profound teachers!—might it indeed be possible that in any other place security were to be found but in the unconditional, since the conditional in fact is in itself insecurity? So I ought rather to speak differently, I ought not to admire the sureness with which they hit the unconditional, but say rather that it is the unconditional which gives them the marvellous sureness which makes them teachers in obedience. For the lilies and the birds are unconditionally obedient to God, in obedience they are so simple or so exalted *that they believe that all which comes to pass is unconditionally God's will, and that they have nothing else in the world to do but unconditionally to do God's will, or with unconditional obedience to submit to God's will.*

Though the place allotted the lily is as disadvantageous as possible, so that it easily can be foreseen that it will be entirely superfluous all its life long, not be noticed by any one who might rejoice in it; though the place and the environment is (why, here I have forgotten that it is the lily I am talking about!)—is so 'desperately' disadvantageous that not only is it not sought out but is avoided, nevertheless the obedient lily puts up obediently with its circumstances and shoots up in all its beauty. We men, or a man in the situation of the lily, would surely say, 'It is hard, it is not to be endured, when one is a lily and beautiful as a lily, then to be allotted a place in such a situation, to bloom there in an environment which is as unfavourable as possible, as though expressly calculated to annihilate the impression of one's beauty; no, that is not to be put up with, that is indeed a self-contradiction on the part of the Creator!' So it is we men would likely think and talk, if we were in the situation of the lily, and thereupon we would wither with grief. But the lily thinks differently, it thinks thus: 'I myself have not been able to determine the situation and the circumstances, and so it is not in the remotest way my affair; that I stand where I stand is God's will.' So thinks the lily, and it actually is God's will as it thinks; one can perceive this in it, for it is beautiful—not even Solomon in all his glory was so arrayed. And if there were as between lily and lily a difference in beauty, this lily must be accorded the prize—it has one beauty the more; for to be beautiful when one is a lily is really no art, but in such conditions to be beautiful, in such an environment which does everything to hinder it, in such an environment to be completely oneself and to preserve one's identity, to deride the power of the environment—no, not to deride, that the lily does not do, but to be perfectly care-free in all its beauty! For the lily is, in spite of the environment, itself, because it is absolutely obedient to God; and because it is absolutely obedient to God, therefore it is absolutely care-free, as only the absolutely obedient (especially under such conditions) can be. And because it is fully and completely itself, and absolutely care-free (two things which correspond to one another directly and inversely), therefore it is beautiful. Only by absolute obedience can one with absolute accuracy hit upon the 'spot' where one is to stand, and when one hits upon it absolutely one understands that it is absolutely indifferent whether the spot be a dunghill.—Though it happens as unfortunately as possible for the lily that precisely the instant when it is on the point of shooting up is so unfavourable that (as with approach to certainty it can discern beforehand) at that very instant it will be broken, so that its coming into being becomes its destruction, indeed it seems as if it came into existence and became beautiful only to be destroyed—yet the obedient lily obediently submits to this, it knows that such is God's will, and it shoots up—if thou wert to see it at that instant, there would not be the least thing to suggest that this unfolding was also its destruction, so fully developed, so rich and beauteous, did it shoot up, so rich and beauteous did it advance obediently to its destruction—for in fact it all occurred in an instant. A man, or we men, in the situation of the lily would be in despair at the thought that coming into existence and destruction was one thing, and thereupon would prevent ourselves by despair from becoming what we might have become, though it were but for an instant. With the lily it is otherwise. It was absolutely obedient, hence it became itself in its beauty, it became actually its whole possibility, undisturbed, absolutely undisturbed by the thought that the same instant was its death. Oh, if as between lily and lily there were a difference in beauty, this lily must be accorded the prize; it had one beauty the more, that of being so beautiful in spite of the certainty of destruction at the same instant. And, verily, with destruction before its eyes, to have courage and faith to come into being in all its beauty—that only absolute obedience is capable of. The certainty of destruction would, as was said, so disturb a man that he did not become his possibility, notwithstanding this was granted him, although but the briefest term of existence was meted out to him. 'To what purpose?' he would say, or 'Why?' he would say, or 'What is the use?' he would say—and so he did not unfold his whole possibility, but had his deserts, in that stunted and ill-formed he sank beforehand under the instant. Only absolute obedience can with absolute precision hit 'the instant'; only absolute obedience can embrace the instant, absolutely undisturbed by the next instant.

Although for the bird, when the instant arrives for it to make its journey, it is as certain as can be, according to the bird's way of thinking, that it is well enough off where it is, so that it is letting go the certain to grasp the uncertain, nevertheless the obedient bird sets out instantly upon the journey; in its simplicity, by the aid of absolute obedience, it understands only one thing, but this it understands absolutely, that now is the absolute instant. —When the bird is painfully impressed by the harshness of life, when it is tried by hardships and adversity, when every morning for several days it finds its nest disturbed, the obedient bird begins its work over again from the very start every day, with the same eagerness and solicitude as at the first; in its simplicity, by the aid of absolute obedience, it understands one thing, but this it understands absolutely, that this is its work, that it has only to do its task.—When the bird must experience this world's wickedness, when the little song-bird which sings in God's honour must endure that a naughty child finds entertainment in mimicking it, to disturb thereby if possible the solemn silence; or when the solitary bird has found an environment which it loves, a beloved bough upon which it especially loves to sit, perhaps additionally dear to it for the fondest memories—and then there is a man who takes pleasure in chasing it away from this spot, by throwing stones or in some other way, a man, alas, who is as indefatigable in evil as the bird, though expelled and frightened away, is indefatigable in returning to its love and to the old position; nevertheless the obedient bird puts up absolutely with everything, in its simplicity, by the aid of absolute obedience, it understands one thing, but this it understands absolutely, that everything which thus befalls it does not properly concern it, that is, it concerns it only improperly, or rather that what properly concerns it, but that absolutely, is with absolute obedience to God to submit to it.

So it is with the lilies and the birds from whom we should learn. Therefore thou shalt not say, 'The lilies and the birds, of course, can be obedient, in fact there is nothing else they can be, or they cannot be otherwise; to be in that way a paragon of obedience is to make a virtue of necessity.' This thou shalt not say, thou shalt in fact say nothing, thou shalt be silent and obey, so that, if indeed it is true that the lily and the bird make a virtue of necessity, thou mightest also succeed in making a virtue of necessity. Thou too art subjected to necessity; God's will is done nevertheless, so strive to make a virtue of necessity by submitting with absolute obedience to God's will, so absolutely obedient that thou mightest be able to say of thyself in relation to doing God's will or submitting to it, 'I can do nothing else, I can do no otherwise.'[1]

For this thou shouldst strive, and thou shouldst consider that, however it may be with the lilies and the birds, whether it really is more difficult for a man to be absolutely obedient, there is also for man an additional danger, which, if I dare say so, might make this easier for him, namely, the danger of wearing out God's patience. For if thou hast ever quite seriously considered thine

---

[1] Recalling Luther's reply at the Diet of Worms.

own life, or considered the lives of men, the human world which is so different from nature where all is absolute obedience, if thou hast ever reflected upon this, hardly without a shudder couldst thou apprehend with how much truth it is God calls Himself 'the God of patience', apprehend that He is the God who says either/ or, and that in the sense of either love me/or hate me, either hold to me/or despise me—and that He has the patience to bear with thee and with me and with us all! If God were a man, what then? How long, long, long ago must He then (to take myself as an instance) have become tired and weary of me and of having to deal with me, and said, but with far better reason than human parents have for saying it, 'The child is both ugly and ailing, and stupid and intractable, and if for all that there was something good about it, but with all that it is so very bad that no man can put up with it.' No, there is no man who can put up with it, only the God of patience can.

And then think of the innumerable multitudes of men now living! We men speak of its being a work of patience to be a school-teacher for little children; and then think of God, who must be the school-teacher for this innumerable multitude! What patience! And then what makes the tax upon patience infinitely greater is that where God is school-teacher all the children suffer more or less from the delusion that they are big grown-up men, a delusion from which the lilies and the birds are quite free—and surely just for this reason, that absolute obedience comes so easy to them. 'If on top of everything else,' a human school-teacher might say, 'if on top of everything else the children got the notion that they were grown-up men, one must lose all patience and must despair; for that would be something no man could endure.' No, surely no man could endure it, only the God of patience can. Hence it is that God calls Himself the God of patience. And he knows well what He says. It was not in a transient mood it occurred to Him to call Himself by this name; no, He does not vary in mood, that indeed would be impatience. He knows it from all eternity, and He knows it from the daily experience of thousands and thousands of years, He knows from all eternity that so long as the temporal lasts, and the human race within it, He must be the God of patience, for otherwise human disobedience could not be endured. In relation to the lilies and the birds God is the fatherly Creator and Sustainer, only in relation to man is He the God of patience. True enough there is a comfort, a very necessary and indescribable comfort, wherefore the Scripture says also that God is the God of patience . . . and comfort—but at the same time this is a terribly serious thing, that man might take God's patience in vain. Man discovered an attribute of God which the lilies and the birds, which are absolutely obedient, did not know, or God was so loving towards man as to let it be revealed to him that He has this attribute, that He is patience. But also (oh, frightful responsibility!) there is in a sense a correspondence between man's disobedience and God's patience. That is the comfort—but under a terrible responsibility. Man dares to know that even though all men were to give him up, yea, even though he were near to giving up himself, God is nevertheless the God of patience. This is inestimable riches. Oh, but use it rightly, remember that it is a savings-account; for the sake of God in heaven use it rightly, otherwise it precipitates thee into still greater misery, it transforms itself into its opposite, it is no longer comfort, but becomes the most frightful of all indictments against thee. For if it seem to thee too hard a saying (though it is not harder than the truth) that this thing of not holding to God absolutely and in all things, that this is 'straightway' . . . to despise Him—yet it cannot be too hard a saying that this thing of taking His patience in vain is to despise God!

Be attentive therefore, according to the instruction of the Gospel, to learn obedience from the lily and the bird. Be not affrighted, do not despair, when thou comparest thy life with these teachers. There is nothing to despair about, for indeed thou *shalt* learn from them; and the Gospel first comforts thee by telling thee that God is the God of patience, but then it adds: Thou shalt learn from the lilies and the birds, learn to be absolutely obedient like the lilies and the birds, learn not to serve two masters; for no man can serve two masters, he must either . . . or.

But if thou canst become absolutely obedient like the lilies and the birds, then thou hast learnt what thou hast to learn, and then thou hast learnt from the lilies and the birds (and if thou hast fully learnt it, thou hast then become more perfect than they, so that the lilies and the birds instead of being teachers become a symbol), thou hast learnt only to serve one master, to love Him alone, and to hold to Him absolutely in all things. Then should also the prayer (which indeed is fulfilled nevertheless) be fulfilled also in thee when thou prayest to God, 'Lead us not into temptation,' for if thou art absolutely obedient to God, then there is no ambiguity in thee, and if there is no ambiguity in thee, then art thou mere simplicity before God. But one thing there is which all Satan's cunning and all the snares of temptation cannot take by surprise, and that is simplicity. What Satan spies with keenness of sight as his prey (but what never is found in the lilies and the birds), what all temptation aims at, certain of its prey (but what never is found in the lilies and the birds)—is the ambiguous. Where the ambiguous is, there is temptation, and there it proves only too easily the stronger. But where the ambiguous is, there also, in one way or another, is disobedience down at the bottom; and just for this reason there is no ambiguity in the lilies and the birds, because absolute obedience is deepest and everywhere at the bottom; and just for this reason it is impossible to lead the lilies and the birds into temptation. Where there is no ambiguity, Satan is powerless, where there is no ambiguity, temptation is as powerless as a bird-catcher with his trap when there is no bird to be discovered—but with the merest glimpse of the ambiguous Satan is strong and temptation is enticing; and keen-sighted is the evil one whose trap is called temptation and whose prey is called the human soul. It is not really from him temptation comes, but no ambiguity, absolutely none, can hide itself from him, and if he discovers it, temptation is then at hand. But the man who with absolute obedience hides himself in God is absolutely safe; from his safe hiding-place he can see the devil, but the devil cannot see him. From his safe hiding-place—for keen-sighted as the devil is with respect to ambiguity, just so blind is he when he looks upon simplicity, he becomes blind, or is stricken with blindness. But it is not without a shudder the absolutely obedient man regards him; this glittering glance which looks as if it could penetrate earth and ocean and the heart's most hidden secret, as indeed it can—and then, that with such a glance he is . . . blind! But if he who spreads the traps of temptation is blind with respect to him who by absolute obedience is hid in God, then for this man there is no temptation, for 'God tempteth no man'. And so his prayer is heard, 'Lead us not into temptation'; that is to say, Let me never at any time by disobedience venture outside my hiding-place, and in so far as I nevertheless am guilty of a disobedience, do not immediately drive me from my hiding-place, outside of which I am instantly led into temptation. And if with absolute obedience he remains in his hiding-place, then is he also 'delivered from the evil'.

No man can serve two masters, he must either love the one and hate the other, or hold to the one and despise the other, ye cannot serve God and mammon, nor God and the world, good and evil; and the reason why a man only can serve one master is surely this, that these two powers, though the one is infinitely stronger than the other, are in mortal strife one with another. This tremendous danger in which man finds himself by being man (a danger which the lilies and the birds are spared in their absolute obedience, which is happy innocence, for it is not over them that God and the world are at strife, or good and evil), the tremendous danger which consists in the fact that man is placed between these tremendous powers and the choice left to him, this tremendous danger brings it about that man must either love or hate, that not to love is to hate; for so hostile are these two powers that the slightest inclination towards the one side becomes absolute opposite as seen from the other side. When man forgets this tremendous danger in which he is (and a danger, be it noted, of a sort that to forget it is verily not an efficient way of meeting it), when man forgets that he is in this tremendous danger, when he even says, 'Peace and no danger'—then the saying of the Gospel must seem to him a foolish exaggeration. Ah, but that is just because he is so deeply sunken, so lost in perdition, that he neither has a conception of the love with which God loves him, along with the fact that it is precisely out of love that God requires absolute obedience, nor a conception of the power and craftiness of evil, along with a conception of his own weakness. And from the very first, man is too childish to understand the Gospel, its talk about either/or seems to him a false exaggeration—that the danger should be so great, that absolute obedience should be necessary, that the requirement of absolute obedience should be grounded in love—that is something man cannot get into his head.

What then does the Gospel do? The Gospel, which is the wisdom of child-training, does not enter into strife with man about thoughts and words, in order to *prove* to him that this is so; the Gospel knows full well that it is not thus the thing is accomplished, that it is not as though a man first understands that it is so as it is said to be, and thereupon resolves unconditionally to obey, but conversely, that by obeying unconditionally a man first comes to understand that it is so as the Gospel says. Therefore the Gospel asserts authority and says, *Thou shalt*. But at the same instant this is softened so that it might be capable of moving the hardest heart; it takes thee as it were by the hand—and does as a loving father does with his child—and says, 'Come, let us go out among the lilies and the birds.' And there it continues thus: 'Consider the lilies and the birds, abandon thyself to them, lose thyself in them. Does not this sight move thee?' Then when the solemn silence among the lilies and the birds moves thee profoundly, the Gospel explains farther and says, 'But why is this silence so solemn? Because it expresses the unconditional obedience with which everything only serves one master, turns in serviceable obedience only to one, united in perfect unity, in a solemn divine service—so let thyself be affected by this great thought, for it is all only one thought, and learn from the lilies and the birds.' But do not forget, thou *shalt* learn from the lilies and the birds, thou shalt become absolutely obedient like the lilies and the birds. Reflect that it was man's sin which (by not willing to serve one master, or by willing to serve another master, or by willing to serve two, yea, many masters) disturbed all the beauty of the world, where hitherto everything was so very good, his sin which created a discord in a world of harmony; and reflect that every sin is disobedience, and every disobedience sin.

III

'BEHOLD THE BIRDS OF THE AIR: THEY SOW NOT, NEITHER DO THEY REAP, NOR GATHER INTO BARNS'——*UNCONCERNED FOR THE MORROW.* 'CONSIDER THE GRASS OF THE FIELD——*WHICH TODAY IS.*'

DO THIS AND LEARN JOYFULNESS

So let us then consider the lilies and the birds, these joyous schoolmasters. 'These joyous schoolmasters,' yes, for thou knowest that joy is infectious, and therefore no one is more capable of giving instruction on the subject of joy than he who himself is joyous. The teacher of joy has really nothing else to do but to be himself joyful, or to be joy; however he may exert himself to communicate joy—if he is not himself joyful, the instruction is incomplete. So there is no subject in which it is easier to give instruction than joy—ah, one only needs to be truly joyful oneself. But this 'ah' signifies, alas, that after all it is not so easy, that is to say, not so easy to be truly joyful oneself—for that it is easy enough to give instruction in joy when one is joyful oneself . . . is as certain as can be.

But out there with the lilies and the birds, or out there where the lilies and the birds give instruction in joy, there always is joy. And never do the lilies and the birds get into embarrassment, as sometimes a human teacher does who has the subject-matter of his teaching inscribed upon paper or kept in his library, that is, in another place and not always with him; no, *there* where the lilies and the birds give instruction in joy, there always is joy—in fact it is in the lilies and the birds. What joy when the day dawns and the birds awaken early to the joy of the day; what joy, although tuned to another key, when the evening draws near and the birds hasten joyously home to their nests; and what joy all the long summer day! What joy when the bird—who does not merely sing at his work like a joyous labourer, but whose essential work it is to sing—joyfully begins its song; what new joy when there-upon its neighbour begins, and then its opposite neighbour; and when then the whole chorus joins in, what joy; and when at last it is like a sea of tones to which forest and vale, heaven and earth, respond, a sea of tones in which he who struck the first note now tumbles head over heels with joy—what joy, what joy! And so it is throughout the bird's whole life; everywhere and always it finds something, or rather it finds enough to rejoice over; it wastes not a single instant, but it would account every single instant wasted in which it was not joyful.—What joy when the dew falls and refreshes the lily, which now that it is cooled is ready for repose; what joy when the lily after its bath dries itself luxuriously in the first rays of the sun; and what joy all the long summer day! Oh then, consider it—consider the lily, and consider the bird, and behold them both together! What joy when the bird hides itself by the lily, where it has its nest and where it finds itself so indescribably cosy, while for pastime it jests with the lily and hears its banter! What joy when from the bough high up, or even higher up, from the sky, the bird keeps its eye upon the nest, and upon the lily which smilingly turns its eye up to it! Happy and blissful existence, so rich in joy! Or is perhaps its joy the less because, narrow-mindedly understood, it is a little thing which makes it so joyful? No, this narrow-minded understanding is surely a misunderstanding, ah, a very sorry and dismal misunderstanding; for precisely the fact that it is a little thing which makes it so joyful is proof that the bird is itself joy or is joy itself. For this is surely true, is it not, that in case the thing one rejoices over is nothing at all, and yet one were to be indescribably joyful, it would be the very best proof that the man himself is joy or is joy itself—just as the lilies and the birds are, the joyous teachers of joy, who just because they are *unconditionally joyful* are joy itself. For he whose joy is dependent upon certain conditions is not joy itself, his joy is in fact dependent upon conditions and is conditioned by them. But he who is joy itself is unconditionally joyful, just as, to state the converse proposition, he who is unconditionally joyful is joy itself. Ah, the conditions for becoming joyful put us men to much pains and anxious thought—and perhaps even if we were to attain all of these conditions, we nevertheless might not become unconditionally joyful. Yet is it not true, O ye profound teachers of joy, that it cannot be otherwise? For by the help of conditions, even if it were of all conditions, it is impossible indeed to be more than or otherwise than conditionally joyful. Conditions and the conditional correspond in fact to one another.

No, he only becomes unconditionally joyful who is joy itself, and only by being unconditionally joyful does one become joy itself.

But might it not be possible to state quite briefly how it is that joy is the content of this instruction of the lilies and the birds, or what is the content of this instruction of theirs on the subject of joy, that is to say, might it not be possible to define very briefly the thought-content of this instruction of theirs? Yes indeed, that is easy to do; for simple as the lilies and the birds are, they certainly are not scatter-brained. So then this is easily done; and let us not forget that in this direction a very great abridgement is already accomplished by the fact that the lilies and the birds are themselves what they give instruction in, do themselves express that wherein as teachers they give instruction. This (in contrast to the direct and primitive originality which consists in the fact that the lilies and the birds possess in the strictest sense at first hand the matter in which they give instruction)—this is acquired originality. And again this acquired originality in the lilies and the birds is simplicity; for the simplicity of instruction does not so much depend upon whether one employs simple and everyday expressions or grandiloquent and learned expressions; no, simplicity consists in the fact that the teacher himself is that wherein he imparts instruction. And such is the case with the lilies and the birds. But their instruction in joy (which their lives in turn express) is quite simply as follows. There is a today. Upon the word '*is*' there falls an infinite emphasis. There is a today—and again, there is no concern at all for the morrow or for the day after. This is not frivolity on the part of the lilies and the birds, but it is the joy of silence and obedience. For when thou dost hold thy peace in the solemn silence which prevails in nature, the morrow is non-existent; and when thou dost obey as the creatures obey, the morrow is non-existent—that baleful day which is the invention of chattering and disobedience. But when by reason of silence and obedience the morrow is non-existent, today is, it *is*—and then there is joy, as there is in the lilies and the birds.[1]

What is joy? or what is it to be joyful? It is to be present to oneself; but to be truly present to oneself is this thing of 'today', that is, this thing of *being* today, of truly *being today*. And in the

[1] Cf. what is said about the lilies and the birds in the *Christian Discourses*.

same degree that it is more true that *thou* art today, in the same degree that thou art quite present to thyself in being today, in that very same degree is the baleful tomorrow non-existent for thee. Joy is the present tense, with the whole emphasis upon the *present*. Therefore it is that God is blessed, who eternally says, Today. And therefore it is that the lilies and the birds are joy, because with silence and unconditional obedience they are entirely present to themselves in being today.

'But', thou wilt say, 'the lilies and the birds, of course they can.' The answer is: It is not with a 'but' thou must respond, but thou must learn of the lilies and the birds to be as entirely present to thyself in being today, and then thou too art joy. But, as I have said, let there by no 'but'; for it is seriousness that thou *shalt* learn of the lilies and the birds. And still less shouldst thou become self-important, so that because the lilies and the birds are simple, and perhaps because thou wouldst feel thy superiority as a man, thou wouldst become witty and wouldst say in view of a particular tomorrow, 'The lilies and the birds, of course they can, since they do not even have tomorrow to worry about, whereas man has not only to be anxious for the morrow what he shall eat, but also for yesterday, in view of what he has eaten . . . and not paid for!' [1] No, let there be no witticism which naughtily disturbs the instruction. But learn, begin at least to learn of the lilies and the birds. For surely nobody can seriously think that what the lilies and the birds rejoice over, and the like of that, is nothing to be glad about! As this: that thou didst come into existence, that thou art in existence, that 'today' thou hast what is needful for existing; that thou didst come into being, that thou didst become a man; that thou canst see—only think, that thou canst see!—that thou canst hear, thou canst smell, thou canst taste, thou canst feel; that the sun shines upon thee . . . and for thy sake, that when the sun is weary the moon then begins, then the stars are lit; that it becomes winter, that the whole of nature dons a white robe, pretends to be a stranger . . . to delight thee; that it becomes spring, that the birds arrive in numerous flocks . . . and all this for thy delight;

---

[1] This pathetic observation would hardly have occurred to S. K. in his comparative opulence, but he was ready to appreciate both the seriousness of it and the wit, when he read it in a letter addressed to him by a pastor who presumably was far from opulent, F. L. B. Zeuthen. He not only jotted it down in his Journal, but quoted it thrice in his works.

that the green leaves burgeon, that the forest becomes beautiful as a bride . . . and this to delight thee; that it becomes autumn, that the birds depart on their journeys . . . not because they would make themselves more precious, ah, no, but lest thou shouldst grow tired of them; that the forest keeps its finery in hiding for the next time, in order, in fact, that the next time it may delight thee—and this, they say, is nothing to be glad of! Oh, if I might venture to scold! But this, out of reverence for the lilies and the birds, I dare not do; and therefore, instead of saying that this is nothing to be glad of, I will say, If this is nothing to be glad of, then there is nothing to be glad of. Consider that the lilies and the birds are joy and yet, even so considered, have in fact much less to rejoice over than thou, who hast also the lilies and the birds to rejoice over. Therefore learn of the lilies, and learn of the birds, who are teachers—teachers that exist, *are today*, and are joy. If thou canst not behold with joy the lilies and the birds, which indeed are joy itself, if thou canst not behold them with joy so that thou dost become willing to learn of them—then it is with thee as when the teacher says of the child, 'Lack of ability it is not, and the subject anyway is so easy that it could not be lack of ability; so it must be something else, perhaps only that he is out of sorts, which is not a thing to be dealt with sternly and treated as unwillingness or maybe as refractoriness.'

Thus it is that the lilies and the birds are teachers of joy. And yet in fact the lilies and the birds also have sorrow, as the whole of nature has sorrow. Does not the whole creation groan under the corruption to which it was subjected against its will? It is all of it subjected to corruption! The stars, firmly as they are fixed in heaven, yea, even that which is fixed most firmly, shall none the less change place by falling, and that which never changed its place shall nevertheless one day change its place by toppling into the abyss; and all this world with all that is within it shall be changed as one changes a garment when it is put off, a prey to corruption! And the lily, even if it escapes the fate of being at once cast into the oven, must nevertheless fade, after already having suffered this and that. And the bird, even if it is allowed to die of old age, must one day die nevertheless, and be separated from its beloved, after already having suffered this and that. Ah, it is all corruption, and all shall one day become what it is, a prey to corruption! This is the *groan*—for to be subjected to corruption is what a groan signifies: to be in confinement, in bondage, in prison. And the content of the groan is: Corruption, corruption!

And yet the lilies and the birds are unconditionally joyful; and it is here most properly thou mayest perceive how true it is when the Gospel says, Thou *shalt* learn joyfulness from the lilies and the birds. A better teacher thou couldst not possibly require than one who, though he himself carries such an infinitely deep sorrow, is yet unconditionally joyful and is joy itself.

How do the lilies and the birds behave in a case like this which seems almost like a miracle: in the deepest sorrow to be unconditionally joyful, when there is such a dreadful tomorrow, nevertheless *to be*—that is, to be unconditionally joyful today—how do they comport themselves? They behave quite simply and with simplicity (as the lilies and the birds always do), and they get this tomorrow out of the way as if it were non-existent. There is a saying of the Apostle Peter which the lilies and the birds have laid to heart, and, simple as they are, they take it quite literally—ah, and just this fact, that they take it quite literally, just this it is that helps them. There is an immense force in this saying when it is taken quite literally; when it is not taken literally, exactly according to the letter, it is more or less powerless, and at last only an unmeaning phrase; but it absolutely requires simplicity to take it absolutely with perfect literalness. 'Cast *all* your care upon God.' Behold, this is what the lilies and the birds do absolutely. By the help of absolute silence and absolute obedience they cast it—yea, as the most powerful catapult casts something from it, with such passion as that with which one casts from oneself what one most abhors—they cast all care away, and cast it—with such sureness as the surest gun can shoot, and with a trust and confidence of hitting the mark such as only the most practised marksman has—they cast it upon God. In a trice (and this trice is counted from the very first instant, is today, is contemporaneous with the first instant of existence), in a trice they are absolutely joyful. Marvellous dexterity! To be able thus to get hold of all one's care all at once, and then to be able to cast it so dexterously from it, and to hit so surely the mark! Yet this is what the lilies and the birds do, and therefore in that same trice they are absolutely joyful. And indeed this is quite natural, for God the Almighty supports the whole world and all the world's care (including that of the lilies and the birds) with infinite ease. What indescribable joy!—joy over God the Almighty.

So learn then of the lilies and the birds, learn of them this marvellous dexterity of theirs. True enough, it is a marvellous trick, but just for this cause thou shalt pay closer attention to the lilies and the birds. It is a marvellous trick, and like 'the trick of meekness' it contains a contradiction, or it is a trick which resolves a contradiction. The word 'cast' suggests an expenditure of force, as if one had to collect all one's forces and with an immense expenditure of force . . . cast care away by sheer strength; and yet 'strength' is exactly the thing which is not to be employed. What is to be employed is . . . 'compliance'—and yet one is to cast care away. And one is to cast 'all' care away; if one does not cast all care away, one thus retains much of it, something of it, a little, and does not become absolutely joyful. And if one does not cast it absolutely *upon God*, but in some other direction, one is not absolutely rid of it, in one way or another it returns again, most likely in the form of a still greater and more bitter sorrow. For to cast care away, but not . . . upon God—that is 'distraction'. But distraction is a doubtful and ambiguous remedy for care and sorrow. But on the other hand, to cast all care absolutely . . . upon God is 'collectedness', and yet—yea, marvellous is this trick of contradiction!—it is a *collection* by which thou dost *become rid* absolutely of care.

Learn then of the lilies and the birds. Cast all thy care upon God! But joy thou shalt not cast away, that on the contrary thou shalt hold fast, with all thy might, with all thy vital power. If thou wilt do this, it is easy to reckon that thou wilt always retain some joy; for if thou dost cast all care away, thou dost still retain whatever thou hast of joyfulness. This, however, avails but little. Learn therefore furthermore from the lilies and the birds: cast all thy care upon God, entirely, absolutely, as the lilies and the birds do—then thou dost become absolutely joyful like the lilies and the birds. For this is the absolute joy, to adore the almighty power with which God the Almighty bears all thy care and sorrow as easily as nothing. And this also is the absolute joy, the next one, which in fact the Apostle subjoins, adoringly to dare to believe that 'God careth for thee.' The absolute joy is precisely joy over God, over whom and in whom thou canst always rejoice. If in this relationship thou art not absolutely joyful, the fault lies absolutely in thee, in thy lack of dexterity in casting thy care upon Him, in thine unwillingness to do it, in thy self-conceit, in short, it lies in the fact that thou art not like the lilies and the birds. There is but one sorrow with respect to which the lilies and the birds cannot be our teachers, about which sorrow we therefore do not speak here, namely, sorrow for sin. With respect to all other care and sorrow it holds good that, if thou dost not become absolutely joyful, the fault is thine, that thou wilt not learn of the lilies and the birds with absolute silence and obedience to become absolutely joyful over God.

Still one thing more. Perhaps thou art inclined to say with the 'poet', 'Yes, if one could build a nest and live alongside of the bird, where the bird and its mate make a pair, but where apart from this there is no society, or if one could live along with the lily in the peace of the field, where each lily shifts for itself and there is no society; then indeed one could cast all one's care upon God and be or become absolutely joyful. For it is "society", precisely this it is which is the misfortune, the fact that man is the only being which torments itself with the unhappy delusion about society and the happiness of being in society, and this all the more in the precise degree that society, to his destruction and its own, becomes greater.' Thus, however, thou must not talk. No, consider the case more closely and confess to thy shame that it is the ineffable forest-joy, in spite of sorrow, by reason of which the birds, him and her, are a pair, and the self-contented joy of single blessedness, in spite of sorrow, by reason of which the lily is solitary—that properly it is this joy which ensures that society does not disturb them; for after all there is in fact society. Consider it still more closely, and admit with shame that it is really the absolute silence and the absolute obedience by reason of which the lilies and the birds are absolutely joyful over God—that it really is this which explains how it is that the lilies and the birds are just as joyful, and just as absolutely joyful, in solitude and in society. So learn then of the lilies and the birds.

And if thou couldst learn to be entirely like the lilies and the birds—ah, and if I could learn it—then would also the prayer of truth be true in thee and in me, the last prayer in 'the Prayer' which (a model of all true prayer, which indeed prays itself joyful, and more joyful, and absolutely joyful) at last has nothing, nothing whatever more to pray for or to desire, but with absolute joyfulness concludes with prayer and worship, the prayer: 'For thine is the kingdom and the power and the glory.' Yes, *His* is the kingdom; and therefore thou art to be absolutely silent, lest thou mightest make it disturbingly noticeable that thou dost exist, but that with absolute silence thou mayest express the fact that the kingdom is His. And *His* is the power; and therefore thou art to be absolutely obedient and art with absolute obedience to bear with everything, for His is the power. And *His* is the glory; therefore in all that thou doest and in all that thou endurest, thou hast absolutely one thing more to do; to give Him the glory, for the glory is His.

Oh, absolute joy, that His is the kingdom and the power and the glory—for ever and ever, for eternity! 'For eternity'—behold, this day, the day of eternity, never comes to an end. Only hold fast therefore to this, that His is the kingdom and the power and the glory in eternity, and thus for thee there is a day which never comes to an end, a day in which thou canst remain eternally present to thyself. Then let the heavens fall and the stars change their place in the overturning of all things, let the bird die and the lily fade—yet thy joy in worship outlives, and thou in thy joy dost outlive, even now *today*, every destruction. Consider what applies to thee, if not as a man, at least as a Christian, that even the danger of death is for thee so unimportant that it is said, 'Even now today art thou in Paradise,' and thus the transition from time to eternity (the greatest possible transition) is so swift—and though it were to occur in the midst of universal destruction, it is yet so swift that thou even now today art in Paradise, for the fact that thou dost Christianly *remain* in God. For if thou dost remain in God, then whether thou dost live or die, and whether it goes well with thee or ill whilst thou livest, whether thou diest today or only after seventy years, or whether thou findest thy death at the bottom of the sea where it is deepest, or thou art scattered in the air—thou dost not find thyself outside of God, thou *remainest*, and so thou remainest present to thyself in God, and art therefore at the day of thy death even now today in Paradise. The bird and the lily live only one day, and that day a very short one, and yet they are joy because (as was shown) they properly are TODAY, are *present to themselves* in this today. And thou to whom the longest day is granted—to live today . . . and even now today to be in Paradise —shouldest not thou be absolutely joyful, thou who art even in duty bound, as indeed thou art able, to outdo by far the birds in joyfulness? Of which thou art reminded as often as thou dost make this prayer, and dost approximate it as often as thou dost sincerely make this prayer of joy: 'Thine is the kingdom and the power and the glory, for ever and ever. Amen.'

'THE HIGH PRIEST'—'THE PUBLICAN'—
'THE WOMAN THAT WAS A SINNER'

THREE DISCOURSES
AT THE COMMUNION ON FRIDAYS

by
S. KIERKEGAARD

Copenhagen
1849

May 'that single individual whom I with joy and gratitude call *my* reader' receive this gift. Truly it is more blessed to give than to receive; but if this be so, then the giver is in a sense the needy one, in need of the blessedness of giving; and if this be so, then the greater beneficence is that of him who receives—and so after all it is more blessed to receive than to give.

May he receive it! That which in imagination I saw when I first sent forth the little book (cf. the Preface to the *Two Edifying Discourses* of 1843) which I compared, and which indeed can best be compared, with 'an insignificant little flower hid in the covert of a great forest', that which then in imagination I saw, that I see again, 'how a little bird which I call *my* reader suddenly cast an eye upon it, swooped down in its flight, plucked it and carried it off'; or, on the other hand, and employing a different figure, I see again what I then saw, how the little book 'made its way along solitary paths, or went solitary along the highways . . . until finally it encountered that individual whom I call *my* reader, that individual whom it seeks, towards whom as it were it stretches out its arms'—that is, I saw and see that the little book is received by that single individual whom it seeks and who seeks it.

S. K.

September 1, *1849.*

PRAYER

WHITHER should we turn, if not to Thee, Lord Jesus Christ? Where might the sufferer find consolation, if not in Thee? Ah, and where the penitent, if not with Thee, Lord Jesus Christ?

Heb. iv. 15. FOR WE HAVE NOT A HIGH PRIEST WHO IS UNABLE TO FEEL COMPASSION WITH OUR INFIRMITIES, BUT ONE WHO IN ALL POINTS WAS TRIED IN LIKE MANNER, YET WITHOUT SIN.

My hearer, whether it be that thou thyself hast been a sufferer, as is only too possible, or whether thou hast learnt to know sufferers, perhaps with the fine purpose of wanting to give consolation, this doubtless thou hast often heard this which is the universal complaint of sufferers: 'Thou dost not understand me, oh, thou dost not understand, thou dost not put thyself in my place, or if thou couldst put thyself in my place, if thou couldst put thyself entirely in my place, and so understand me entirely, thou wouldst talk differently.' 'Thou wouldst talk differently'— by this the sufferer means to say, 'Thou also wouldst perceive that there is no consolation.'

So this is the complaint; almost always the sufferer complains that he who would console him does not put himself in his place. Doubtless the sufferer has generally some justification; for no man experiences quite the same thing as another man, and even if such a thing were possible, it is definitely the universal and reciprocal limit of every man in particular, that he cannot entirely put himself in another man's place, that even with the best will he cannot entirely perceive, feel, think, like another man. But in another respect the sufferer is in the wrong, inasmuch as he would signify by this that there is no consolation for the sufferer; for this might signify as well that every sufferer is to seek comfort in himself, that is, from God. It was surely not in any way God's will that the one man should be able to find complete consolation in the other man; on the contrary it is God's good pleasure that every sufferer should seek it from God, that when the consolations which others offer become insipid to him, he then should seek after God, in conformity with the saying of the Scriptures: 'Have salt in yourselves, and have peace one with another.' O thou sufferer, and, O thou who perhaps honestly and well-meaningly dost desire to console—strive not with one another in this useless strife! Thou the compassionate one, show true compassion by not requiring that thou be able to put thyself entirely in the other's place; and thou the sufferer, show true gratitude by not requiring of another the impossible—there is indeed One who is able to put Himself entirely in thy place and in the place of every sufferer: the Lord Jesus Christ.

Of this consolation speaks the sacred text which has been read. 'We have not a high priest who is unable to feel compassion with our infirmities'—that is, we have one who is able to feel compassion with our infirmities; and further, 'we have one who in all points was tried in like manner.' This actually is the condition for *being able* to have true compassion—for the compassion of the inexperienced and the untried is misunderstanding, most commonly it is for the sufferer a more or less grievous and painful misunderstanding—this is the condition; to be tried in like manner. When such is the case, one can entirely put oneself in the sufferer's place; and when in all points one is tried in like manner, one can put oneself entirely in the place of every sufferer. Such a High Priest we have, who *can* be compassionate; and that He *must* be compassionate thou canst perceive in the fact that it was out of compassion He was in all points tried in like manner —it was indeed this which determined Him to come to the world, and again it was compassion, it was in order that He might truly be compassionate, that by His own free resolution He was in all points tried in like manner, He who entirely can put Himself, and can put Himself entirely, in thy place, in mine, in yours.

About this we would speak in the brief moment prescribed.

Christ put Himself entirely in thy place. He was God and became man—thus it was He put Himself in thy place. This indeed is what true compassion is so fain to do, it so fain would put itself in the sufferer's place, in order to be able to give effectual consolation. But this at the same time is what human compassion is unable to do; only divine compassion is able—and God became man. He became man; and He became the man who of all men, absolutely all, suffered the most; never was there born,

never shall there or can there be born a man who shall suffer as
He did. Oh, what security for His compassion! Oh, what compassion to give such security! Compassion impels Him to throw
open His arms for all sufferers. 'Come unto me', saith He, 'all
ye that suffer and are heavy laden'; 'Come unto me,' saith He;
and He vouches for what He says, for (and this is the second call
of the invitation) He was absolutely the greatest sufferer. Already
it is something great if human compassion ventures to suffer
almost as much as the sufferer—but out of compassion, for the
sake of making the comfort sure, to suffer infinitely more than
the sufferer . . . how great is that compassion! Human compassion, however, shrinks back with a shudder, it would rather
remain sympathetically upon the secure seashore; or, if it ventures
out, it is not willing to go by any means so far out as where the
sufferer is—but what compassion, to go still farther out! Thou
sufferer, what is it thou dost require? Thou requirest that the
compassionate man shall put himself in thy place—and He, Compassion itself, not only put Himself entirely in thy place, but He
had to suffer infinitely more than thou! Ah, sometimes it seems
perhaps to the sufferer in his despondency as if compassion were
almost treacherously holding back a little—but here is compassion gone beyond thee in the suffering which is infinitely great!

*He put Himself, He can put Himself, entirely in thy place, thou
sufferer, whosoever thou art.*—Is it a question of temporal and
earthly care, of poverty, anxiety about one's livelihood and all that
this implies?—He also suffered hunger and thirst, and that just at
the most difficult moments of His life, when at the same time he
was contending spiritually in the desert and on the cross; and for
everyday use He had no more possessions than have the lilies of
the field and the birds of the air—so much as this, however, even
the poorest man surely must possess! And He who was born in
a stable, swaddled in rags, laid in a manger, had throughout His
life nothing whereon He could lay His head—as much homely
shelter as this however even the homeless surely possess! Would
He not then be entirely able to put Himself in thy place and
understand thee?—Or is it sorrow of heart?—He also once had
friends, or rather He thought once that He had them; but then
when the decisive moment came they all forsook Him, yet no, not
all, two remained behind, the one betrayed Him, the other denied
Him! So then He once had friends, or thought once that He had

them, they attached themselves to Him so closely, they even contended which should occupy the place at His right hand, and which at His left hand, until the decisive moment came and He, instead of being raised to the throne was lifted up upon the cross —then were two robbers compelled against their will to occupy the empty place at His right hand and the empty place at His left hand! Dost thou not think that He can entirely put Himself in thy place?—Or is it sorrow over the evil of the world, over the opposition which thou and the Good must suffer, assuming as quite certain that it is thou that willest the Good and the True?— oh, in this respect, thou, a man, surely wouldst not venture to compare thyself with Him, thou, a sinner, surely wouldst not venture to compare thyself with Him, the holy One, who first experienced these sufferings (so that at the utmost thou canst suffer in His likeness), and sanctified these sufferings (thy sufferings also, if so be that thou dost suffer in likeness to Him)—Him who was despised, persecuted, reviled, mocked, spat upon, scourged, evil entreated, tortured, crucified, forsaken by God, crucified amidst universal jubilation—whatsoever thou hast suffered, and whosoever thou art, dost thou not think that He can entirely put Himself in thy place?—Or is it sorrow for the world's sin and ungodliness, sorrow that the world lieth in the evil one, sorrow at how deep man has fallen, sorrow for the fact that gold is virtue, that might is right, that the crowd is the truth, that only lies prosper, that only evil triumphs, that only self-love is loved, that only mediocrity is blest, that only shrewdness is esteemed, that only half-measures are praised, and only paltriness succeeds?—oh, in this respect, thou, a man, surely wouldst not venture to compare thy sorrow with that sorrow which was in the Saviour of the world, as though He were not entirely able to put Himself in thy place!—And so it is with respect to every suffering.

And therefore, thou sufferer, shut not thyself up despairingly with thy sufferings, as though no one, not even He, could understand thee; neither appeal impatiently to thy sufferings as though they were so frightful that not even He were able entirely to put Himself in thy place—presume not to utter this falsehood, bear in mind that He, absolutely, and absolutely beyond comparison, was of all sufferers the greatest sufferer. For if thou wouldst know who the greatest sufferer is, very well, I will tell thee. It is not the silent suppressed shriek of despair, and not that which strikes terror into others, the loudness of the shriek, which decides the matter; no, precisely the opposite. He is absolutely the greatest sufferer of whom in truth it is true (owing to the fact that he does it) that he has absolutely no other consolation than that . . . of consoling others; for this and this only is Truth's expression for the fact that in truth no one can put oneself in His place, along with the fact that this is truth in Him. And thus it was with Him, the Lord Jesus Christ; He was not a sufferer who sought consolation from others, still less one who found it in others, still less one who complained of not finding it in others; no, He was *the* sufferer whose only, absolutely His only consolation was to console others. Behold, here thou art come to suffering's utmost possibility, but also to suffering's limit, where everything is inverted; for He, none other than He, is 'the Comforter'. Thou complainest that no one can put himself in thy place; preoccupied day and night with this thought, it perhaps never occurs to thee, I can fancy, that thou shouldst comfort others—and He, 'the Comforter,' He the only one of whom it truly holds good that no one can put himself in His place—how true it would have been if He had made such complaint!—He, 'the Comforter,' in whose place no one can put himself, can entirely put Himself in thy place and in the place of every sufferer. If it were true that no one can put himself in thy place, all right, then give proof of it; one thing only is left for thee: become thyself the one who comforts others. This is the only proof that can be adduced for the assertion that it is truth that no one can put himself in thy place. So long as thou wilt continue to talk about no one being able to put himself in thy place, just so long art thou not absolutely clear in thine own mind about it, otherwise thou wouldst at least hold thy peace. But even if thou wert to keep silent, so long as this does not have the effect that thou undertakest to comfort others, just so long art thou not absolutely clear in thine own mind about no one being able to put himself in thy place, thou sittest brooding in sheer despair, again and again engaged with the thought that no one is able to put himself in thy place; that is, thou must make this thought secure every moment; that is, it is not secure, thou art not clear in thine own mind about it; that is, this is not entirely truth in thee. Truth, however, it cannot possibly be in any man, that no one, absolutely no one, can put himself in his place; for precisely He, Jesus Christ, in whose place no one, either entirely or in any measure, can put himself, precisely He can put Himself entirely in thy place.

He put Himself entirely in thy place, whosoever thou art who art assaulted by temptations and trial,[1] *He put Himself entirely in thy place,* 'being tried in all points in like manner.'

As it is with the sufferer, so it is with the man who is tempted and tried, he too is inclined to complain that the person who would comfort or counsel or admonish him does not understand him, cannot entirely put himself in his place. 'If thou wert in my place,' says he, 'or if thou wert able to put thyself in my place, thou couldst understand with what dreadful power temptation besets me, thou couldst understand how frightfully every effort of mine is mocked by trials of constancy—then thou wouldst pronounce a different judgment. But having thyself no experience of this, thou canst of course talk calmly about it, and of course take advantage of the opportunity to feel thyself a better man because thou hast not fallen into temptation nor succumbed to trial, that is to say, because thou wast not assaulted either by the one or the other. If thou wert in my place!'

Oh, my friend, do not contend in a useless strife which only embitters the more thy life and that of another—there is after all One who entirely can put Himself in thy place, the Lord Jesus Christ, who 'for the fact that He Himself suffered temptation is able to succour them that are tempted' (Heb. ii. 18); He it is who can entirely put Himself in thy place, Jesus Christ, who learned to know truly every temptation by withstanding every temptation.—Is it a question of concern about food, and quite literally concern about food in the strictest sense, so that death from starvation threatens thee—He too was tempted thus. Is it rash daring which tempts—He too was tempted thus. Is it to fall away from God thou art tempted—He too was tempted thus; He can entirely put Himself in thy place, whosoever thou art. Art thou tempted in solitude—so was He whom the evil spirit led out into the solitude in order to tempt Him. Art thou tempted in the confusion of the world—so was He whose good spirit prevented Him from deserting the world before He had completed His work of love. Art thou tempted in the great moment of decision when it is a question of renouncing everything—so was He. Or

---

[1] It is notorious that the distinction between *Fristelse* and *Anfægtelse* cannot be rendered in English.

is it at the next instant when thou art tempted to regret that thou didst sacrifice all—He too. Sinking under the possibility, art thou tempted to wish that the reality of danger were present—He too. In languishing weakness art thou tempted to desire thy death—so was He. Is the temptation that of being forsaken by men—He too was tempted. Is it that . . . but no, this trial surely no man has experienced, the trial of being deserted by God; but He was tempted thus. And so it is in every way.

Oh, thou therefore who art tempted, be not mute in despair, as though the temptation were superhuman and no one could understand it; neither depict impatiently the magnitude of thy temptation, as though even He could not entirely put Himself in thy place! For wilt thou know what is requisite in order truly to be able to judge how great a temptation truly is, very well then, I will tell thee. It is requisite . . . that thou hast withstood the temptation. Only then dost thou get to know truly how great the temptation was; so long as thou hast not withstood the temptation thou knowest only falsehood, only what temptation, precisely for the sake of tempting, makes thee believe about how frightful it is. To require from temptation the truth is asking too much; temptation is a deceiver and a liar which takes good care not to utter the truth, for its power is simply falsehood. If thou wouldst get the truth out of it as to how great it really is, thou must take pains to be the stronger, take pains to withstand temptation—then thou dost get to know the truth, or thou dost get the truth out of it. And hence there is but One who truly knows with perfect accuracy the magnitude of every temptation and can entirely put Himself in the place of every one who is tempted—He who was tried in all points in like manner, was tempted, but withstood every temptation. Beware therefore of describing the magnitude of the temptation or of complaining of it more and more passionately—with every step thou takest along that path thou dost merely accuse thyself more and more, it is not possible along these lines to conduct thy defence for succumbing to temptation, by describing with more and more exaggeration the magnitude of the temptation; for everything of the sort that thou sayest is falsehood, since thou couldst get to know the truth only by withstanding temptation. Perhaps another man could help thee, if thou wouldst let thyself be helped—another man who was tempted in the same way but withstood temptation; for he knows the truth. But even if there is no other man who can tell thee the truth—there is however One who entirely can put Himself in thy place, He who was tried in all points in like manner, was tried and withstood temptation. From Him thou wilt be able to get to know the truth, yet only on the condition that He perceives it is thine honest intention to will to withstand temptation. And then when thou hast withstood temptation, thou dost not complain that no one can entirely put himself in thy place—for in case thou hast withstood temptation, it would be a matter of indifference to thee, certainly nothing to complain of, if it were true that no one could put himself in thy place. This complaint is the invention of the falsehood which belongs to temptation, and the purport of this falsehood is, that if any one were to understand thee entirely, it must be one who also succumbed to temptation, so that the two of you understood one another . . . in falsehood. Is this to 'understand' one another? No, here is the limit where everything is inverted: there is only One who truly can put Himself in thy place who art tempted—and that He can do just because He alone withstood every temptation. But at the same time—oh, do not forget this!—He can entirely put Himself in thy place.

He put Himself entirely in thy place, was tried in all points in like manner—YET WITHOUT SIN. So then, in this respect He did not put Himself in thy place—how could that be possible for Him, the holy One? If the difference is infinite between God who is in heaven and thee who art on earth, the difference is infinitely greater between the holy One and the sinner.

Oh, and yet even in this respect, though in another way, He put Himself entirely in thy place. For when He, when the suffering and death of the Atoner is the satisfaction for thy sin and guilt—being a satisfaction it assumes in fact thy place, or He, the Substitute, steps into thy place, suffering in thy place the punishment for sin, that thou mightest be saved, in thy place suffering death for thee, that thou mightest live—did He not put Himself entirely in thy place? Here indeed it is more literally true that He entirely puts Himself in thy place than it was when we talked of this in the foregoing, where it merely denoted that He could understand thee entirely, whereas thou remainest still in thy place and He in His place. But the satisfaction of the atonement signifies that thou dost step aside and that He assumes thy place—does He not then put Himself entirely in thy place?

For what else is the Atoner than a substitute (*Stedfortraeder*) who entirely puts Himself in thy place? And what is the comfort of it but this, that the Substitute puts Himself entirely in my place and thine? So when retributive justice, either here on earth or hereafter at the Day of Judgement, seeks the place where I a sinner stand with all my guilt—it does not find me, I no longer stand in that place, I have left it, Another stands in my place, Another who entirely puts Himself in my place. For this I thank Thee, Lord Jesus Christ.

My hearer, such a High Priest have we—whosoever thou art, and howsoever thou dost suffer, He can entirely put Himself in thy place; whosoever thou art, O sinner, as all of us are, He puts Himself entirely in thy place! Thou art now going up to the altar, bread is handed thee and wine, His sacred body and blood, again presented as an eternal pledge that He by His suffering and death put Himself entirely in thy place, that thou, saved by standing behind Him, when the Judgement is over mayest enter into life, where again He hath prepared a place for thee.

PRAYER

LORD JESUS CHRIST, let Thy Holy Spirit enlighten our minds and convince us thoroughly of our sin, so that, humbled and with downcast eyes, we may recognize that we stand far, far off and with a sigh, 'God be merciful to me a sinner'; but then let it befall us by Thy grace as it befell that publican who went up to the Temple to pray and went down to his house justified.

LUKE xviii. 13. AND THE PUBLICAN STOOD AFAR OFF AND WOULD NOT EVEN LIFT UP HIS EYES UNTO HEAVEN, BUT SMOTE UPON HIS BREAST, SAYING, GOD BE MERCIFUL TO ME A SINNER.

My hearer, the sacred text just read belongs, as thou knowest, to the Gospel story of the Pharisee and the publican. The Pharisee represents the hypocrite who deceives himself and would deceive God, whereas the publican represents the sincere man whom God justifies. But there is also another sort of hypocrisy, there are hypocrites who, according to the Bible's description of the Pharisee, 'trust in themselves that they are righteous and despise others,' whereas they conform their appearance nevertheless to that of the publican, with mock piety stand afar off, unlike the Pharisee who proudly thanked God that he was righteous; with mock piety they cast their eyes to the ground, unlike the Pharisee who proudly directed his glance towards heaven; with mock piety they sigh, 'God be merciful to me a sinner,' unlike the Pharisee who proudly thanked God that he was righteous—hypocrites who like the Pharisee that impiously said in his prayer, 'I thank Thee, O God, that I am not like this publican,' say with mock piety, 'I thank Thee, O God, that I am not like this Pharisee.' Yes, alas, it indubitably is so; Christianity came into the world and taught humility, but not all learned humility from Christianity, hypocrisy learned to change its mask and remained the same, or rather became even worse. Christianity came into the world and taught that thou shalt not in pride and vainglory seek out the highest seats at table, but sit in the lowest—and soon pride and vainglory were sitting vainly in the lowest seats at table, the same pride and vainglory . . . oh, no, not the same but still

BB*

worse. So one might perhaps think it necessary to invert this passage and nearly all the Gospel passages, in consideration of the fact that hypocrisy and pride and vainglory and the worldly mind may want to invert the situation. But how would that be of any avail? It surely can only be the notion of morbid acumen and vain shrewdness to want to be so shrewd that by shrewdness misuse can be prevented. No, there is only one thing which overcomes, which more than overcomes, from the very beginning has endlessly overcome, all cunning, and that is the simplicity of the Gospel, which in its simplicity lets itself be deceived as it were, and yet in simplicity continues to be the simple. And this too is the edifying feature of the Gospel's simplicity, that the Evil could not prevail over it to the point of making it wish to be shrewd. Verily the Evil has won a victory, and a very serious victory, when it has prompted simplicity to wish to be shrewd . . . for the sake of making itself secure. For simplicity is made secure, eternally secure, only by letting itself in its simplicity be deceived, however clearly it sees through the deceit.

Let us then, in the brief moment prescribed, consider with all simplicity the publican. Throughout all ages he has been represented as the model of a sincere and Godfearing church-goer. And yet it seems to me that he is still more closely related to the act of going to the Holy Communion, this man who said, 'God be merciful to me a sinner'—is not this as though he were going up to the altar? this man of whom it is said, 'he went down to his house justified'—is it not as though now he were going home from the altar?

The publican *stood afar off*. What does this mean? It means to stand by himself, alone with himself and God—thus thou art far off, far from men, and far from God, with whom nevertheless thou art alone; for in relation to a man it is true that when thou art alone with him thou art closest to him, when there are others present thou art farther away; but in relation to God it is true that when there are several persons present it seems to thee as though thou wert closer, and only when thou art literally alone with Him thou dost discover how far off thou art. Oh, even though thou be not such a sinner as the publican, whom civil justice also accounts guilty—in case thou art alone with thyself before God, thou also standest afar off. So soon as there is somebody between God and thee, thou art easily deceived, as though thou wert not so far off;

yea, even if it were the case that he or they who before thee stand between God and thee were in thine opinion better and more perfect than thou—thou art still not so far off as when thou art alone before God. So soon as any one comes between God and thee (regardless of whether it is one whom thou dost consider more perfect than thou or one whom thou dost consider more imperfect) thou dost get a deceitful standard of measurement, the standard of human comparison. It is as though thou couldst measure out how far thou art away, and so thou art not far away.

But the Pharisee who, in fact, according to the saying of the Scripture, 'stood by himself,' was he not standing afar off? Yes, if in truth he had stood by himself. The Gospel says that he stood by himself and thanked God 'that he was not like other men'. And where one has the other men with one, one does not stand by oneself. The Pharisee's pride consisted just in this, that he proudly used the other men to measure his distance from them, that before God he would not let go the thought of the other men, but would hold this thought fast, in order thus to stand proudly by himself . . . in contrast with other men; but this indeed is not to stand by oneself, least of all to stand by oneself before God.

The publican stood afar off. Being conscious of his guilt and crime, it was perhaps easier for him not to be tempted by the thought of the other men, who, as he must in fact admit, were better than he. About this, however, we will not presume to decide; but it is certain that he had forgotten all the others. He was alone, alone with the consciousness of his guilt and crime, he had entirely forgotten that there were in fact many other publicans beside him, it was as if he were the only one. He was not alone with his guilt in the face of a righteous man, he was alone before God—ah, that is to be afar off. For what is farther from guilt and sin than God's holiness?—and so, for one who is himself a sinner to be alone with this, is it not to be endlessly far off?

He would not even lift up his eyes unto heaven; so then, he cast them down. Yes, and what wonder! Oh, even physically there is something in endless space which overwhelms a man for the fact that the eye has nothing to fix itself upon, this effect is called dizziness—so that one has to shut one's eyes. And he who, alone with his guilt and sin, knows that were he to cast his eyes up he would behold God's holiness and nothing else, he surely learns to cast his eyes down; or perhaps he looked up and beheld God's holiness—and cast down his eyes. He looked down, beheld his wretchedness; and heavier than sleep upon tired eyelids, heavier than weighs the sleep of death, the conception of God's holiness weighed down his eyes; like a man exhausted, yea, like a dying man, so he was unable to lift up his eyes.

He would not even lift up his eyes unto heaven; but he with his eyes cast down, turned *in*ward, had only *in*sight for his own wretchedness, *nor did he look to one side*, like the Pharisee who saw the publican; for we read in fact that he thanked God he was not like this publican. 'This publican,' yes, it is precisely this publican of whom we are talking; there were in fact two men who went up to the Temple to pray. The Scripture does not say that two men went up together to the Temple to pray—indeed it hardly would have been fit company for a Pharisee had he gone up to the Temple in company with a publican; and in the Temple they seem to have been as far as possible from being in company, the Pharisee stands by himself, the publican stands afar off—and yet, and yet, the Pharisee saw the publican, this publican, but the publican (ah, well dost thou deserve to be called in a distinguishing sense 'this publican')—the publican did not see the Pharisee; when the Pharisee came home he knew very well that this publican had been in church, but this publican knew nothing of this Pharisee's having been in church. Proudly the Pharisee found satisfaction in seeing the publican; humbly the publican saw no one, saw not the Pharisee; with eyes cast down and turned inward he was in truth . . . before God.

And he smote upon his breast and said, God be merciful to me a sinner. Oh, my hearer, when in the solitude of the desert a man is attacked by a ferocious beast, the cry verily issues of itself; and when in an unfrequented path thou dost fall amongst robbers, fright itself invents the cry. So it is also in the case of that which is infinitely more dreadful. When thou art alone, alone in the place which is more lonesome than the desert—for even in the loneliest desert it would still be possible that another man might come there; alone in the place which is more lonesome than the most unfrequented path, where it still would be possible that another might come along; alone in individuality, or as a single individual, and face to face with God's holiness—then the cry issues of itself. And if thou, alone before God's holiness, hast learnt that it avails thee nothing though thy cry would call upon some one else to help, that *there* where thou art as the single individual there is literally no one else but thee, that it is the most impossible of all things that *there* there might be or come any one else but thee—then terror discovers, as need discovered prayer, it discovers this cry, 'God be merciful to me a sinner.' And the cry, the sigh, is so sincere in thee—yea, how could it but be that! What hypocrisy could there be in the fact that a man cries out when the abyss opens in peril at sea? Even though he knows that the storm mocks his weak voice, and that the birds out there listen to him with indifference, he cries out nevertheless, to such a degree is the cry true and the truth. So it is also in the case of that which in quite a different way is infinitely more terrible, the conception of God's holiness, when one, himself a sinner, is alone before it—what hypocrisy could there well be in this cry: 'God be merciful to me a sinner'? If only the danger and the terror are real, this cry is always sincere, yet withal, God be praised, it is never in vain.

The Pharisee on the contrary was not in danger, he stood proudly and securely self-satisfied, from him no cry was heard. What is the meaning of this? It means also something quite different—it means that he was not before God.

And now for the conclusion. *The publican went down to his house justified.*

He went home to his house justified. For to this publican applies what the Scripture says of all publicans and sinners, that they drew *near* to Christ—just by standing afar off he drew near to Him, whereas the Pharisee with presumptuous insolence (*Naergaaenhed*) stood far, far off. Thus the picture is inverted. It begins with the Pharisee standing near, the publican afar off; it ends with the Pharisee standing afar off, the publican near.— He went to his house justified. For he cast down his eyes; but the averted eye *sees* God, and the eye cast down signifies the lifting up of the heart. No glance is so sharp-sighted as that of faith, and yet, humanly speaking, faith is blind; for reason, understanding, is, humanly speaking, the faculty of seeing, but faith is against the understanding. So the cast down eye is the seeing eye, and the humility indicated by the downcast glance is exaltation. Again the picture is inverted when the two go home from the Temple. He who was exalted was the publican, therewith it ended; but to the Pharisee who began by proudly lifting up his eyes to heaven God is opposed, and God's opposition is annihilating abasement. In ancient times it was not as now when the astronomer erects upon an eminence the building from which he would observe the stars, in ancient times he dug down in the earth to find a place from whence to observe the stars—in relation to God no change has taken place: to be exalted to God is possible only by descending. As little as water changes its nature so as to run up hill, so little can a man succeed in lifting himself up to God . . . by pride.—He went to his house justified. For self-accusation is the possibility of *justification*. And the publican accused himself. There was no one that accused him; it was not civil justice which grabbed him by the throat and said, 'Thou art a criminal'—but he smote upon his breast and said, 'God be merciful to me a sinner'; it was not the men whom perhaps he had swindled who smote him on the breast and said, 'Thou art a swindler'—but he smote himself on his breast and said, 'God be merciful to me a sinner'; he accused himself as a sinner before God. The picture is again inverted. The Pharisee—who, far from accusing himself, proudly praises himself—as he goes away is accused by God; he does not know it, but as he goes away he accuses himself before God: the publican began by accusing himself. The Pharisee goes home with a new sin, in the strictest sense a revolting [literally, to-heaven-crying] sin, with one more sin in addition to the earlier sins which he retained: the publican went home justified. Before God 'to wish to justify oneself', that precisely is to denounce oneself as guilty; but before God to smite oneself upon the breast, saying, 'God be merciful to me a sinner,' that precisely is to justify oneself, or rather it is the condition for God's pronouncing thee justified.

Thus it was with the publican. But now as for thee, my hearer! The similarity so readily suggests itself. From confession thou goest up to the altar. But to make confession is precisely *to stand afar off*; the more sincere thy confession is, the farther off thou dost stand—and all the more true is this for the fact that thou kneelest at the altar, since to kneel is a symbol of standing afar off, far from Him who is in heaven, from whom accordingly the distance is the greatest possible when thou dost sink to the ground upon thy knees—and yet it is at the altar thou art nearest to God. —To make confession is precisely *to cast down the eyes*, not to wish to look up unto heaven, not to wish to see any one else; the more sincere thy confession is, all the more wilt thou cast down thine eyes, all the less wilt thou see any one else—and all the more true is this for the fact that thou dost kneel there at the altar, since to kneel down is even a stronger expression for what is implied by casting down the eyes, for he who merely casts down his eyes stands nevertheless comparatively erect—and yet it is at the altar the heart is lifted up to God.—To make confession is precisely *to smite oneself upon the breast*, and, without being too much disturbed by the thought of the individual sins, to gather them most briefly and truly into one expression, 'God be merciful to me a sinner.' The more hearty thy confession, all the more surely will thy confession end with this silent expression of smiting thyself upon the breast, and in the sigh, 'God be merciful to me a sinner'—and all the more true is this for the fact that thou dost kneel there at the altar, a kneeler who by this expresses that he, condemning himself, only prays for grace—and yet at the altar there is justification.

He went home to his house justified. And thou, my hearer, when thou from the altar dost return home to thy house, pious sympathy greets thee with the wish, 'Good luck and blessing,' well assured that at the altar thou didst find justification, that the visit brought thee good luck and blessing. Now, before thou goest up to the altar, the same wish: that it may bring thee good luck and blessing. Ah, the natural man finds most satisfaction in standing erect: he who truly has learnt to know God, and by learning to know God has learnt to know himself, finds blessedness only in falling upon his knees, in adoration when he thinks of God, in penitence when he thinks of himself. Offer this man what thou wilt, he craves only one thing, like that woman who chose—not the best part, oh, no, how could there here be any question of comparison!—no, she who, according to the word of the Scripture, chose the good part when she sat at the Saviour's feet—she craved only one thing: to kneel at His altar.

PRAYER

LORD JESUS CHRIST, that we may be able rightly to pray Thee for all things, we pray first for one: help us to love Thee much, increase love and inflame it. Oh, this is a prayer Thou wilt surely hear, Thou who indeed art not love of such a sort—so cruel a sort—that Thou art only the object, indifferent to whether any one loves Thee or not; Thou indeed art not love of such a sort—in wrath—that Thou art only judgement, jealous of who loves Thee and who does not. Oh, no, such Thou art not; Thou wouldst thus only inspire fear and dread, it would then be terrible 'to come to Thee', frightful 'to abide with Thee', and Thou wouldst not be the perfect love which casteth out fear. No, compassionate, or loving, or in love, Thou art love of such a sort that Thou Thyself dost woo forth the love which loves Thee, dost foster it to love Thee much.

Luke vii. 47. WHEREFORE I SAY UNTO THEE, HER MANY SINS ARE FORGIVEN HER; FOR SHE LOVED MUCH.

My hearer, thou knowest of whom the text speaks, that it is of that woman whose name is, 'a woman that was a sinner.' 'When she knew that Christ sat at meat in the Pharisee's house, she brought an alabaster cruse of ointment, and stood at His feet behind Him weeping, and began to wash His feet with tears, and did wipe them with the hairs of her head, and kissed His feet, and anointed them with the ointment.'

Yea, she loved much. For there are two opposites which are opposed to one another in a life and death struggle, or at least for one of the opposites it is the most frightful annihilation to approach the other. Thus it is when one is a sinner—to approach the holy One, to be revealed before His face in the illumination of holiness. Oh, the night does not flee with greater terror from the face of the day which is to annihilate it, and, if there be ghosts, a spectre does not collapse in greater dread when it begins to dawn, than a sinner shrinks from holiness which like the day brings everything to light. So long as he can the sinner flees, avoids so long as he can the march to death, this encounter with

379

light, inventing every shirking excuse and evasion and deceit and palliation. But she loved much. And what is the strongest expression for loving much? It is to hate oneself—*she entered in where the holy One was*. She, a sinful woman! Ah, a woman! And yet the power of shame is strongest in a woman, stronger than life, she would rather give up life than give up the sense of shame. True enough, this sense of shame ought indeed to have withheld her from sinning and prevented her; but yet again it is also true that when a woman comes to herself again the sense of shame is all the stronger, crushing, annihilating. Perhaps it was this that made for her the way to annihilation easier, the fact that she was already annihilated. And yet, humanly speaking, there might still be a question of lenience. Oh, even a sinner who has truly acknowledged to herself, or at least knows within herself, that she is annihilated, would perhaps be inclined to spare herself, if face to face she should become revealed before the holy One; she might have been fain to spare herself—that is to say, she still loved herself so much. But as for her—is there then no lenience towards herself, none whatever? No, there is no lenience!—she hated herself: she loved much.—She went in to the holy One *in the Pharisee's house*, where many Pharisees were assembled who would condemn her, reproaching her also for the vanity, a vanity peculiarly disgusting in a woman, of putting herself forward with her sin, a woman who ought to hide herself from the eyes of all men in a remote corner of the world. She might have wandered the world around and been certain of finding in no place so stern a condemnation as that which awaited her in the Pharisee's house from the proud Pharisees; and on the other hand there is perhaps no suffering so calculated to torture a woman in particular as the cruelty of mockery which awaited her in the Pharisee's house from the proud Pharisees. But as for her—is there no compassion which spares her this cruelty. No, there is no compassion!—she hated herself: she loved much.—She went in to the Holy One in the Pharisee's house, *to the banquet*. To a banquet! Thou dost shudder, thou dost shrink from following her; thou canst easily convince thyself how shuddering a thought it is, for thou art constantly inclined to the temptation to forget that the whole thing is enacted at a banquet, that it is not a 'house of mourning' but a 'house of mirth'.

To a banquet there comes a woman, she brings with her an

alabaster cruse containing ointment—well, that is appropriate to the banquet; she sits at the feet of one of the guests and weeps— that is not appropriate to the banquet. In truth the banquet is disturbed by this woman! Yes, but she was not disturbed, this sinful woman, she who certainly not without a shudder, not without shrinking, went straight ahead to the banquet . . . and to confession; she hated herself: she loved much. Oh, heavily as nothing else weighs upon a man weighs sin's heavy secret; there is only one thing heavier—to have to go to confession. Oh, frightful as no other secret is, is the secret of sin; there is only one thing more frightful—the admission of it. For this reason human compassion has sympathetically invented what may alleviate and assist this difficult delivery. In the holy edifice where all is quiet and grave solemnity, and in a more hidden enclosure within it, where all is silent as the tomb, and there is such lenience as that which passes judgement upon the departed—there the sinner is given opportunity to confess his sin. And human compassion invented an alleviation in the provision that he who received the confession was hidden, so that the sight of him might not make it too hard for him, yes, too hard for the sinner to lighten his conscience. Finally human compassion discovered that there was no necessity even of such a confession or of such a hidden hearer; discovered that in secret before God, who nevertheless knows all, confession should be made and might then remain hidden in one's inmost soul. But at a banquet—and a woman! A banquet! That is very far from being a hidden, retired spot, nor is the mood like that among the tombs, and the hearer is neither hidden nor unseen. No, if concealment and subdued light and a retired spot and everything which is in harmony with this is an alleviation in the confession of one's sin—a banquet was surely the cruelest invention. Who is the cruel inventor, that we by our prayers might appease him and persuade him to spare her. No invention of a cruel man was so cruel as this, it was she only, the sinful woman, who invented such a thing. Ah, commonly the cruel man is one, and the tortured person is another—she herself invented this torture, was herself the cruel one, she hated herself: she loved much.

Yea, she loved much. 'She sat at the feet of Christ, wet them with tears, dried them with the hairs of her head'—by this she expressed: I am able to do literally nothing; He is able to do absolutely everything. But this indeed is to love much. When one thinks that one is able of oneself to do something, one may love in a way, but one does not love much; and just in the degree that one thinks that of oneself one can do more, in the same degree one loves less. She on the contrary loved much. She utters not a word, least of all does she 'protest'—ah, how all too often is this a deceitful word which so easily makes a new protest necessary, the protest that it really is as one protests. She does not protest, she acts: she weeps, she kisses His feet. She is not careful to stifle her tears; no, to weep is her proper work. She weeps, it is not her eyes that weep, but it is with the hairs of her head she wipes his feet: she is able to do literally nothing, He everything —she loved much. Oh, eternal truth, that He is able to do absolutely everything! Oh, indescribable truth in this woman! Oh, indescribable power of truth in this woman who powerfully expressed the impotence of being able to do literally nothing! She loved much.

Yea, she loved much. She sits weeping at His feet: she has altogether forgotten herself, forgotten every disturbing thought in her own inward world, is perfectly quiet, or is quieted like a sick babe at the mother's breast, where it weeps itself out and forgets itself; for one does not succeed in forgetting such thoughts while yet remembering oneself—therefore she weeps, and whilst she weeps she forgets herself. Ah, blessed tears; ah, that in weeping there is also this blessing—forgetfulness! She has entirely forgotten herself, forgotten the environment with all that is disturbing in it; for it is impossible to forget such an environment if one does not forget oneself, it was indeed an environment calculated to remind her frightfully and anguishingly of herself: but she weeps, and whilst she weeps she forgets herself. Ah, blessed tears of self-forgetfulness, when the fact that she weeps, when not even this reminds her any longer of what she weeps over: thus it was she entirely forgot herself. But the true expression for loving much is precisely this: to forget oneself entirely. When one remembers oneself, one can love in a way, but one does not love much; and just in the degree that one remembers oneself the more, in the same degree one loves the less. She, however, had entirely forgotten herself. But the stronger the impulse is at a given moment to remember or to think of oneself—if one nevertheless forgets oneself and thinks of the other, so much the more does one love. Such is the case in fact in the relation of man to man, and though this relationship does not correspond precisely with what we are talking about, it may nevertheless illuminate it. He who at the moment when he himself is most occupied, the moment which to him is the most precious, forgets himself and thinks of the other, he it is who loves much; he who being hungry himself forgets himself and gives to the other the meagre provision which is sufficient only for one, he it is who loves much; he who in mortal danger forgets himself and leaves to the other the only plank of safety on the waves, he it is who loves much. So also he who at the moment when everything within him and everything about him not only reminds him of himself but would compel him against his will to remember himself—when nevertheless he forgets himself, he loves much, as she did. 'She sits at his feet, anoints them with ointment, dries them with the hairs of her head, kisses them—and weeps.' She says nothing, she is not therefore what she says, but she is what she does not say, or, what she does not say, that she is, she *is* a characterization, like a picture—she has forgotten speech and language and the restlessness of thoughts and (what is even more restless) this self, has forgotten herself, she, the lost woman, who now is lost in her Saviour and as lost in Him rests at His feet—like a picture. And it is almost as if the Saviour for a moment regarded her and the situation thus, as though she were not a real person but a picture. It is certain that in order to make the application to the persons present more impressive, He does not speak *to* her, He does not say, 'Thy sins are forgiven thee,' He speaks *about* her, He says, 'Her many sins are forgiven because she loved much'; notwithstanding she is present, it is almost as if she were absent, it is almost as if He transformed her into a picture, a parable, almost as if He said, 'Simon, I have somewhat to say unto thee. Once upon a time there was a woman, she was a sinner. When one day the Son of Man sat at table in the house of a Pharisee, she too came in. The Pharisees scoffed at her and condemned her as a sinner. But she sat at his feet, anointed them with ointment, wiped them with the hairs of her head, kissed them and wept—Simon, I would say somewhat unto thee: Her many sins were forgiven her because she loved much.' It is almost like a story, a sacred story, a parable—and yet that very thing was occurring in reality at that same moment.

But 'her many sins are forgiven her'—and how could this be more strongly expressed than by the fact that everything is forgotten, that she, the great sinner, is transformed into a picture! When it is said, 'Thy sins are forgiven thee,' ah, how readily does the remembrance of herself return to her, if she were not fortified by this boundless forgetfulness: 'Her many sins are forgiven her.' She loved much, hence she forgot herself entirely; she forgot herself entirely, 'hence her many sins were forgiven'—forgotten,[1] yea, they were drowned with her as it were in forgetfulness, she herself, being transformed into a picture, became a recollection, yet not as though it recalled her to herself; no, as she forgot the recollection by forgetting herself, the recollection also (not gradually but at once) forgot her name—her name is 'a woman that was a sinner', neither more nor less.

And suppose some one were to say, 'There was nevertheless some self-love in this woman's love. The Pharisees censored her indeed also for the fact that she drew near to Christ, and from this inferred something disparaging to Him, that He was no prophet—so that it was she who exposed Him to this, she with her love, that is, with her self-love.' Would any one say that there was an element of self-love in this woman's love, that in her need it was essentially herself she loved—if any one were to speak thus, I would reply: 'Naturally', and thereupon I would add, 'God be gracious to us, but there simply is no other way'—and then add, 'God forbid that I might ever presume to love my God or my Saviour in any other way; for if there were in my love nothing of self-love in that significance of the word, I would only be imagining that I could love Him without having need of Him—and from this presumption God preserve me!'

My hearer, this woman was a sinner. The Pharisees condemned her, they even condemned Christ for being willing to consort with her, they judged—and for this reason precisely—that He was no prophet, not to say the Saviour of the world, and yet it was precisely by this He showed Himself to be the Saviour of the world. This woman was a sinner—yet she became and is a pattern; blessed is he who resembles her in loving much! The forgiveness of sins which Christ offered while He lived on earth,

---

[1] To recognize the personal pathos in this passage one must know that S. K. had recently been transformed by the sudden experience that his sins were not only forgiven by God but 'forgotten'.

continues to be, from generation to generation, offered to all in Christ. It is said to all, and to each one severally, 'Thy sins are forgiven thee'; they all, and each one severally, receive at the altar the pledge that their sins are forgiven—blessed is he who resembles that woman in loving much! For though it is said to all, it is nevertheless only true when it is said to him who like that woman loved much! It is true, thy sins are forgiven thee in Christ; but this truth (which also for this reason is declared to each one severally) is nevertheless in another sense not true, it must be made true by each one severally. Thus is this woman an eternal picture; by her great love she made herself, if I dare say so, indispensable to the Saviour. For that it was the forgiveness of sins she gained, she made to be truth, she who loved much.[1] Thou canst therefore turn it in whatever way thou wilt and still be saying the same thing. Thou canst extol her as blessed because her many sins were forgiven her, or thou canst extol her as blessed because she loved much. Substantially thou art saying the same thing—if only thou dost note well that He whom she loved much was Christ, and if at the same time thou dost not forget that Christ is grace and the giver of grace. For what sort of a test is it in which her love is tried? In consideration of what it is she loves much, what is it she loves less? Is this the test: to love Christ more dearly than mother and father, than gold and goods, than honour and reputation? No, the test by which this woman was tried is: to love her Saviour more than her sin. Ah, there was perhaps one who loved Christ more than father and mother and gold and goods and honour and reputation, and yet loved his sin more than his Saviour, loved it, not in the sense of willing to remain in it, to continue to sin, but in the sense of not being quite willing to confess it. Frightful this is in a sense, but it is true, and every one who has merely some little knowledge of the human heart can verify it: there is nothing to which a man holds so desperately fast as to his sin. And hence a complete, honest, deep, utterly true, entirely unvarnished confession of sin

---

[1] In a large volume of discourses entitled *The Works of Love* (1847), S. K. had already contravened sharply the fundamental distinction of Protestant doctrine, 'salvation by faith alone.' His way of stating the case was persuasive and incontrovertible (at all events it has never been controverted); for if 'faith without works' is not palpably absurd, love without works is a contradiction in terms—and surely love is a part of faith. On the other hand, this woman knew that 'she was able literally to do nothing'.

is the perfect love, to make such a confession of sin is to love much.[1]

Now the discourse is ended. But surely it is true that, though the Pharisees accounted that this woman pressed in upon the banquet very inopportunely—yet today she has not come to the wrong place, between the confessional and the altar! Oh, forget the orator who has been speaking, forget his art, if so be he has displayed any, forget his defects, which perhaps were many, forget the discourse about her—but forget her not; along this road she is a guide, she who loved much, and to whom therefore her many sins were forgiven. She is far from being a deterrent picture; on the contrary, she is more of an incentive than the incentives of all orators, when it is a question of following that invitation which leads to the altar: 'Come hither, all ye that labour and are heavy laden'; for there she marches in the van, she who loved much, she who therefore found rest for her soul in loving much, yea, or in the fact that her many sins were forgiven her, yea, or let us say, she who, because she loved much, found rest in the fact that her many sins were forgiven her.

[1] This I understand as a sigh. S. K. never made *such* a confession. He recalls with evident sympathy that his father sighed for 'a good old father confessor', which as a Protestant he did not have. And above he has described with rare sympathy the Catholic 'invention' of the confessional box—which as a Protestant he could not avail himself of. For a long while he felt impelled to make a *public* confession of the sin which most tormented him—but he did not do it, and in the end he no longer felt the need. It may be said indeed that the whole literature he produced was a confession—but it was an anonymous confession, and as such it was, as he himself perceived, a species of daimonia.

INDEX

Abundance, 27–38.
Abyss, 52 f., 60, 279.
Admiration, 135 ff.
Afar off, 372 ff.
Affliction, 111–18.
Altar, 276 f., 307 f., 376, 386.
Ambiguity, 344.
Anxiety, 17–93.
Asceticism, 195.
Atonement, 368 f.
Authority, 214.

Banquet, 380 f.
Became a believer, 221–7.
Becoming something, 44.
Before God, 43 f., 46, 175, 328.
Beginning, 41 f.
Being oneself, 42 ff.
Being today, 349 f.
Being what one is, 46 f., 48.
'Believed on', 239–50.
Believing (see Faith).
Betrayed, 284 ff.

Cast your care, 352 ff.
Certitude, 203.
Christendom, 13 f., 221 f., 224 f., 235, 249 f.
Christian, the, 13–38.
Christianity, 221 f., 234 ff.
Christians, 13 ff.
Christ's blessing, 305–9.
'Communication', 121 ff.
Comparison, 48.
Concern, 198 f.
Confession, 117, 294, 376, 381, 385 f.
Confession of faith, 248 f.
Contemporary with oneself, 77.
Contentment, 24.
Conversion, 156 f.
Covetousness, 24.
Credulity, 70 f.

Cross-ways, 23.
'Cure for Heretics', 78.

Daily bread, 17 ff., 25.
Defence of Christianity, 168.
Defiance, 136 f.
Denial, 289–95.
Derision, 228–38.
Disconsolateness, 83–93.
Dismaying, the, 101 f.
Doubt, 199.
Draught, a, 80 f.
Dreams of youth, 112 ff.
Duty, 214.

Easy to understand, 151, 236, 240.
Edification, 101 ff., 179, 229.
Either God, 333 ff.
Either/or, 333 ff., 345.
Enough, 27 ff.
Envy, 136.
Equality, 122.
Eternal, the, 139–48, 156 ff., 174, 216.

Faith, 151 f., 182.
Faithfulness, 289 ff.
Father in heaven, 19, 35.
Felix, 213.
Fickleness, 83–93.
Following Christ, 186, 279 f.
Forsaking all, 186–96.
Freedom of man, 132 ff.

Gain, 139–48.
Gain all, 149–53.
Goal, 155 ff.
God and man, 66 ff., 202 f.
God's greatness, 297–303.
God's patience, 341 ff.
God's will, 338 f.
Good fortune, 154–63.
Goods of the spirit, 121 ff.